Ethics of 21st Century Military Conflict

Ethics of 21st Century Military Conflict

E. L. Gaston & Patti Tamara Lenard, editors

International Debate Education Association

New York, London & Amsterdam

Published by
International Debate Education Association
105 East 22nd Street
New York, NY 10010

This book is published with the generous support of the Open Society
Foundations.

The editors would like to thank Paul Simon for his excellent research
assistance and Paul Robinson for his advice and guidance in the early stages of
the project.

Library of Congress Cataloging-in-Publication Data

Ethics of 21st century military conflict / Patti Tamara Lenard & E.L. Gaston,
editors.
     p. cm.
  ISBN 978-1-61770-041-5
  1. War--Moral and ethical aspects. 2. War (Philosophy) I. Lenard, Patti
Tamara, 1975- II. Gaston, E. L. III. Title: Ethics of twenty-first century military
conflict.
  U22.E85 2012
  172'.42--dc23
                              2012012706

 IDEBATE Press
Typeset by Richard Johnson
Printed in the USA

This volume is dedicated to John Lavinsky and Sarah Stewart Johnson on the occasion of their second wedding anniversary.

Contents

Introduction

To many, the concept of an ethics of war is paradoxical. Ethics is a branch of philosophy that emphasizes the *right* thing to do, whereas war necessarily involves extreme violence and harm toward others. To suggest that some of these acts might be justified, if not moral, seems to confer legitimacy on the violence and ugliness that war inevitably produces.

Yet it is an unfortunate fact of human history that states have been prone to launch and fight wars. Historically, moreover, it seems clear that too many wars were launched for bad reasons, for example, to acquire more territory, to convert others to the "right" religion, to eradicate entire cultures or ethnic groups, and so on. Yet, for every bad reason to launch a war, it seems logical that there might also be a good reason—to prevent the eradication of a religious group or to protect the sovereignty of an invaded state. To put it crudely, and in ways that will be questioned in the contributions to follow, whereas we can condemn aggressive wars as unethical, defensive wars—wars that defend some good that we believe as a human community is valuable—may be justifiable and thus ethical.

For those who remain unconvinced of the value of ethical thinking in war—in particular, pacifists who reject all reasons to launch war—the harms caused by actions in warfare are so severe that whatever benefit can be said to come from war will inevitably be outweighed by the far more severe harms that *all* forms of warfare produce. In this view, while some may concede the plausibility of identifying good reasons to launch war, the actions taken by combatants are so harmful—i.e., unethical—that they will supersede any allegedly "good" reasons. As a result, war must be categorically rejected.

Again, however, in the view of most of the contributors to this book, discomfort with the overall fact of war should not prevent us from considering whether certain actions should be banned from war and whether others can be defended. The killing and destruction indicative of warfare may be condemnable, but are all acts in war morally indistinguishable? Can we say that the deprivations of liberty and the discomfort that form the experience of any prisoner of war are comparable to the concrete evidence of abuse, torture, and personal humiliation of detainees in Abu Ghraib during the U.S.-led intervention in Iraq? A Canadian soldier killed an unarmed and seriously injured Afghan soldier on the battlefield—did his actions constitute a moral wrong or were they justifiable as a "mercy killing"?[1] Or, to take a historical example, when the Allies in World War II carpet-bombed Dresden in order to hasten the defeat of Nazi Germany, we asked (and we continue to ask) whether the actions taken, and in particular the killing of thousands of innocent civilians and the destruction of the city, were proportional to the expected gain.[2] These examples at least *suggest* that we can have a discussion about the genuinely ethical questions that emerge *during* warfare, and not simply about the launching of war itself.

This book therefore asks readers to consider seriously whether space exists for ethical thinking in war and in particular to consider the good and bad reasons to launch war, alongside the justified and unjustified actions that combatants take once war is launched.

BACKGROUND ON MORAL THEORY

There are two broad moral frameworks running through the selections in this book. These frameworks can help us think through the difficult moral questions that arise in our lives in general and in military conflict in particular. They are *consequentialism*, or more specifically utilitarianism, and *absolutism*, sometimes called deontology. As the name suggests, consequentalists evaluate moral actions from the perspective of the consequences that these actions produce. Consider a doctor, with limited time and resources, faced with two patients, one of whom is a known murderer and one of whom is a renowned cardiologist. Only one can be saved. A consequentialist might argue that the best way to determine who the doctor should save is by evaluating the consequences of possible actions. In this case, consequentialist moral theorizing leads the doctor to save the cardiologist, knowing that additional lives will be saved (rather than lost, as might be the case if the murderer were to be saved).

Utilitarian thinking is a specific kind of consequentialism: to be utilitarian is to be concerned not simply with consequences of actions, but with consequences of a particular kind, namely, consequences that produce the greatest happiness or pleasure for the greatest number of people.[3] Thus, when a utilitarian considers her options, she is guided to choose actions that will maximize the happiness—sometimes this is translated into "minimizing suffering" or "minimizing harm"—of others. To take an example familiar to philosophers, consider a train barreling toward five people who are very likely to be killed by its impact. In front of you is a very fat man who, although innocent of wrongdoing, would be able to stop the train if he were pushed in front of it. In this case, a utilitarian will guide you to push the fat man, to his certain death, in front of the train and thereby stop it from barreling into the five people. Five lives will be saved and only one lost: the greatest happiness, and the least suffering, will be produced by your decision to push the fat man in front of the train, and the decision to do so is therefore ethical by utilitarian standards.

Many of those who consider this example are uncomfortable with the suggestion that killing an innocent person is the ethical thing to do, even when the result of doing so is saving the lives of five others. The discomfort stems from the common belief that killing others is *wrong*, even when the consequences of doing so may be overall better according to some measure. The moral view that accounts for this belief is called absolutism or deontological, and it is the view that some actions are wrong, *absolutely*, and they are wrong because they violate the fundamental rights of individuals. The difficulty for this view stems from the challenges of identifying which actions are subject to an absolute ban. But where this challenge is resolved, we have a list of actions that can never, ethically, be performed. Since the right to life is fundamental, the deliberate killing of others is typically on the list of actions that are absolutely prohibited. Thus, if we revisit the utilitarian demand that you push the fat man to his certain death to save five others, an absolutist recommends against this action because killing another is *absolutely* wrong. For an absolutist some moral rules can never be broken.

Over the course of this book, we shall see what happens as these two moral frameworks are translated to situations of military conflict. But the conflict between the recommendations each of these two views will offer should already be coming into focus. A utilitarian may be willing to countenance the killing of innocents in an effort to save a greater number of innocents (the dropping of atomic bombs on Japan is often justified in utilitarian terms on the grounds that it brought the overall war to a close sooner), while an absolutist would not abide such killing. An absolutist may argue that certain actions—torture, for example—can never be justified, on the grounds that we have an absolute requirement to respect the bodily integrity of others, whereas a utilitarian may be comfortable recommending torture when there is persuasive evidence that it will save the lives of others. More than likely, readers will find that a combination of both moral frameworks is necessary to understand what constitutes ethical action in times of military conflict.

Introduction to the Parts

To begin, the selections in Part 1: Theories of War present the three main ethical approaches to war. In the first piece included in this collection, Thomas

Nagel argues that even in war some absolute constraints—particularly the right to life—may never be violated.[4] In the second, Richard Norman defends the pacifist position, according to which the unavoidable fact that war will result in the killing of innocents—it is simply impossible to imagine a war that does not have, as an effect, the murder of civilians—renders all war unethical. George F. Kennan defends the realist position, according to which ethical thinking has no place in military conflict. The international system is composed of sovereign states and sovereign states possess the right to wage war; the decision to wage war is made primarily for reasons of national self-interest. Finally, a fourth perspective—and the one taken by most of the contributors to the book—acknowledges that ethical thinking must play a role in war but does not categorically reject all wars or all actions in war. This view can broadly be termed "just war theory," as described by Michael Walzer. In this view, we can think seriously about both the good and the bad reasons presented to justify the launching of war—or about the justice and injustice of launching a particular war—as well as about the actions that can legitimately be defended over the course of war. This selection therefore outlines the perspective that informs nearly all the subsequent readings.

Typically, just war theory divides war into three parts, signified by Latin terms: *jus ad bellum*, translated as "just cause for war," *jus in bello*, translated as "justice in war," and *jus post bellum*, translated as "justice after war." The next two chapters offer selections that engage in the first two of these: Part 2 offers selections that focus on the morality of going to war and Part 3 offers selections that focus on the morality of actions taken in war.

Part 2: Going to War: *Jus ad Bellum* considers the reasons for which states may justifiably resort to war, what is often termed *jus ad bellum*. Brian Orend lays out six principles, or conditions, that should be met before a state might consider resorting to war. For example, it must be for just cause, it must be a last resort, and it must have a chance of success, among other considerations. Michael Walzer outlines the most defensible reason to declare war: defense against an act of aggression by another state. Neta C. Crawford questions how far a self-defense rationale might be stretched. She observes that we see justifications for war—as in the case of the American-led intervention in Iraq—made in terms of "pre-emptive" self-defense, where states justify their right to invade another state by claiming defense against a threat of war (or extreme danger) that has not yet materialized. Meanwhile, Michael Ignatieff argues in defense of "humanitarian intervention"—using armed force to stop massive human rights violations—not only on moral grounds but also on pragmatic, self-interested ones. Given the increasing interconnectedness of the world and the global nature of threats, states may be motivated to use humanitarian intervention not only out of interest for the innocent lives saved but also for fear that the situation of instability would spill over onto their interests or borders.

One significant reason to be reluctant to launch military interventions of any kind, as observed above, is because of the necessarily harmful effect they will have on innocent civilians, who are merely bystanders in the conflict. Here we enter the terrain of *jus in bello*, whether actions can be considered just or unjust during warfare. Part 3: Who Merits Protection in Warfare? *Jus in Bello* considers who should rightly be considered innocent in wartime and how the inevitable harm that will come to civilians should be balanced against the imperatives of war. G. E. M. Anscombe's letter "Mr. Truman's Degree" is heavily critical of the intentional harming of civilians as a tactic in war, particularly in the cases of the nuclear bombing of Nagasaki and Hiroshima in World War II. Alex J. Bellamy concurs, arguing that "supreme emergency" justifications for wartime actions that result in the massacre of civilians are often ways to justify profoundly unethical actions by claiming they are "exceptional" in some way. Distinguishing between "innocent" civilians and "guilty" soldiers may be a difficult task, however; often civilians are vitally important to the war effort, perhaps in ways that, if they were prevented from contributing, would bring a war to an end. James M. Dubik expresses skepticism of the easy prioritizing of the lives of civilians, however, arguing that combatants—even though they are soldiering—are equally imbued with the right to life. We should be careful, he argues, before we agree that soldiers have given up this right simply by virtue of participating in war, and therefore that protecting innocents must absolutely be prioritized. Even more complicated are the cases, outlined by Emanuel Gross, in which enemy combatants have deliberately placed innocent civilians in harm's way, and therefore where our military action will deliberately and knowingly harm innocents.

Part 4: Who Makes Up the Fighting Forces? considers the composition of the fighting combatants. Which is more defensible, an all-volunteer force or a conscripted military force? Is soldiering a job like any other, albeit one that carries substantial risk, or a duty from which no one is excluded? For William A. Galston, citizenship status not only confers a package of rights, it equally imposes a set of duties on citizens, one of which is contribution to the nation's defense. From this perspective, the deployment of mercenaries—private companies or non-citizens who are motivated by economic incentives to participate in a nation's military—is objectionable, since it confuses the reasons for which one should participate in one's national military. For Cécile Fabre, however, mercenaries are perfectly defensible members of a nation's military.

The basic question—who should form the nation's military—underpins some of the questions we now face in more contemporary warfare, namely, what should be the proper role of "unmanned" or "autonomous" weapons systems? These are weapons that can be deployed in conflict zones by soldiers sitting safely in their home country—imagine American soldiers launching drones into Pakistan or Yemen from the safety of their offices in Nevada. For some, including Paul W. Kahn, among the considerations that make actions in war *just* is the presence of *risk*. That soldiers are willing and able to put themselves at risk in pursuit of victory is essential to justifying the actions they take in the first place. We should therefore be wary of the trend toward deploying unmanned weapons during war. Yet, one common defense of the use of unmanned, or robotic, warfare, as Peter M. Asaro points out, derives from its capacity to protect soldiers from dangerous environments. Surely it is a good thing, and indeed among the objectives of a responsible state, to do what it can to protect its soldiers from harm. According to Asaro, however, unmanned weapons may be problematic from another perspective: it is not clear that they can distinguish between civilians and combatants as well as soldiers can. So long as we lack confidence that robots can make this distinction in practice, we should be wary of over-relying on them on the battlefield.

Finally, Part 5: Absolute Prohibitions: Terrorism and Torture considers whether the conditions of 21st century conflict change our ethical view of some of these *jus in bello* dilemmas. Terrorist tactics—more prominent in the last decade—often rely on the deliberate targeting of unarmed civilians. Should such tactics have a real place in war? Virginia Held argues that if war can be just, so too can terrorism, in at least some of its permutations. For Samuel Scheffler, terrorism is indefensible for its commitment to inflicting "terror" on innocent civilians, and additionally for its reliance on unconventional methods of fighting.

An equally salient dilemma is whether the use of such tactics by terrorists or other non-state actors justifies more aggressive, arguably more morally suspect, tactics by state parties trying to prevent them from harming civilians, including the use of torture. For Alan M. Dershowitz, torture can be justified morally in narrow circumstances where it prevents the killing of significant numbers of civilians. Aryeh Neier counters that torture is beyond the pale: there are no conditions under which the human right to bodily integrity can be sacrificed in pursuit of some good, however valuable that good may be.

How to Use This Book

The articles collected in this book engage readers in the ethical questions that surround conflict. They consider, in the first place, whether ethical thinking has a place in war and how we should deploy ethical principles in evaluating whether to go to war and the actions taken over the course of war by the multiple actors involved.

In some cases, the selections or introductions to a part refer to international legal documents, like the United Nations Charter or the Geneva Conventions, which contain the core of international law protections during warfare. Just war thinking—which has been around for far longer than the modern international law framework—has shaped many of these international law instruments. Nonetheless, as the debates in this book illustrate, no consensus exists about what ethical rules should guide the use of armed force. International legal instruments often represent a codification of one view, but they could be mistaken. Certainly many just war theorists, as well as state parties, human rights groups, and all manner of other public figures vehemently dispute and debate provisions of international law. Where you see these international law references, think about whether you agree that the given position should be the status quo.

The debates that occupy the authors in this collection are debates with which everyone can and should be engaging. The 21st century, though only just past its first decade, has already been ripe with military conflict; from the wars in Iraq and Afghanistan, to the multiple conflicts and genocide in Sudan, to the violent resistance—in some cases rising to civil war—engulfing multiple Arab countries as part of the "Arab Spring." Whether troops should be withdrawn from the former conflicts, and what role additional troops should play in the latter conflicts, are matters of present-day ethical discussion. We may perhaps look forward to a future that is warless, but a realistic and sober evaluation of human history tells us that this future is unlikely. It is therefore incumbent on us, as responsible democratic citizens, to understand the conditions under which war can be waged justly.

Notes

1. Peter Bradley, "Is Battlefield Mercy Killing Morally Justifiable?," *Canadian Military Journal* 11, no. 1 (2011). http://www.journal.forces.gc.ca/vol11/no1/04-bradley-eng.asp (accessed March 22, 2012).

2. Michael Walzer, *Just and Unjust Wars: A Moral Argument with Historical Illustrations* (New York: Basic Books, 1977), 255–262.

3. John Stuart Mill, "Utilitarianism," 1863, in *On Liberty and Other Essays*, ed. John Gray (Oxford: Oxford University Press, 1991), 130–203.

4. Thomas Nagel, "War and Massacre," *Philosophy and Public Affairs* 1, no. 2 (1972): 123–144.

Part 1: Theories of War

For those who haven't given it much thought, considering the role of ethics in military conflict may seem counter-intuitive. We have all heard it said that "military ethics" is an oxymoron: a concept that is inherently paradoxical. After all, war necessarily involves the killing of others, many of whom will inevitably be innocent bystanders, and it is hard to imagine that actions that allow for the killing of others, especially innocents, can properly be described as ethical. The selections in this section consider whether there is a genuine role for ethical thinking in military conflict. What ethical frameworks do we have for thinking about actions in general and military actions in particular? Is war simply a matter of states pursuing their own interests in an international environment that is fundamentally amoral? Is the only ethical perspective on war one that abandons it altogether? Given the seeming inevitability of war, should we take seriously the possibility that there are better or worse actions to be pursued by those involved in military conflict, and perhaps others that are ruled out absolutely even in the extreme conditions of war?

The general introduction outlined two significant moral frameworks that will guide you in reading the selections in this book: utilitarianism and absolutism, or deontology. Utilitarians believe actions are ethical if and only if they produce the best outcome for the greatest number of people. The danger, as the introduction observed, is that a focus on the *outcome* can sometimes blind us to the rights—in the case of war, the right to life in particular—that can be violated in pursuit of an outcome that seems to be best overall. Absolutists believe, on the contrary, that there are certain rights—again the right to life is most prominent here—that can never be violated, regardless of whether doing so would produce outcomes that appear better overall. In the opening selection, Thomas Nagel considers which of these views is generally more appropriate for evaluating the ethics of military action and concludes that while utilitarian thinking is often most appropriate when weighing possible options in the course of military conflict, absolutism is required in order to constrain certain actions that might otherwise appear to be justifiable. Nagel writes: "It is particularly important not to lose confidence in our absolutist intuitions, for they are often the only barrier before the abyss of utilitarian apologetics for widespread murder."[1]

THE PACIFIST: WAR IS WRONG

When considering possible ethical responses one might have to military conflict, the pacifist offers the clearest example of an absolutist view. It is possible to adopt a pacifist view for consequentialist reasons, of course: some pacifists might argue that there are simply *never* situations in which war will produce the greatest happiness for the greatest number, and therefore that we will never be guided to pursue military action against others. However, most pacifists are absolutist, or deontological, pacifists, who argue that there are no morally acceptable reasons to resort to war, which, inevitably, requires the killing of others. As Richard Norman explains in "The Case for Pacifism," for the pacifist "war is morally unacceptable because it is the unjustified taking of human life."[2] It is from a respect for human life that a pacifist concludes that war can never be justified. This position is often justified by reference to religious doctrine—many religious communities, the Quakers perhaps most prominently, object to war on religious grounds.

The pacifist is commonly accused of rejecting all forms of violence, and even all forms of killing, and therefore adhering to an impracticable standard. For example, some argue that pacifism must be abandoned because it disallows as morally unacceptable the killing of others in self-defense. Surely, they say, if a man is pointing a gun at you, it is morally acceptable to kill him in order to save your life. But pacifists typically object not to violence per se, or even all forms of killing. Rather they object to war specifically because it necessarily implies the killing of others for (merely) political reasons. Thus, for the pacifist, it is not the untenable position that killing others can never be justified. Rather, the position is that the injunction against killing is a fundamental principle that "can in principle be overridden, but only in special cases."[3]

THE REALIST: ETHICS HAVE NO PLACE IN THINKING ABOUT WAR

Another extreme position is that of the "realist," according to which ethics has no role whatsoever to play in international relations. For the realist, the international environment is simply composed of individual nation-states that are required to provide for their citizens. As George Kennan explains, a government must focus on: "military security, the integrity of its political life and the well-being of its people. These needs have no moral quality."[4] In providing and protecting these goods for their citizens, governments may be required to go to war. In fact, claim most realists, an honest interpretation of history tells us that war has been, and will continue to be, an inevitable part of global interaction.

Since global interaction is not governed by moral principle, states are legitimately entitled to launch wars when doing so is in their national interest, and they are equally entitled to do what they must in order to win wars once they have begun.

To be a realist thus demands a particular interpretation of the world environment as characterized by anarchy and an absence of order. It also demands our thinking that states are not capable of simultaneously acting in the interests of their citizens and of acting morally in the global environment. In the face of this impossibility, realism argues that the former prevails.

But, say some critics, positing an inevitable conflict between moral interaction in the global environment and the state's obligation to protect the interests of citizens is a mistake. States after all do seem responsive to moral concerns. Consider, for example, the language surrounding whether outside states should intervene in the civil war in Libya. In early 2011, civil war broke out in Libya, between rebel Libyans protesting Muammar Gaddafi's brutal 40-year reign and Gaddafi supporters. Those in the international community in favor of outside state intervention to support the rebels argued that military intervention was justified because Libyans were being brutally repressed by a self-serving dictator. The United Nations Security Council passed a resolution early in the conflict permitting multistate military operations in support of the rebels; in particular, these operations enforced a no-fly zone over Libya and launched air strikes targeted at Gaddafi's forces. In justifying the commitment of American military resources to the joint effort, President Barack Obama said:

> Gaddafi declared that he would show "no mercy" to his own people. He compared them to rats, and threatened to go door to door to inflict punishment. In the past, we have seen him hang civilians in the streets, and kill over a thousand people in a single day. We knew that if we waited one more day Benghazi . . . could suffer a massacre that would have reverberated across the region and stained the conscience of the world.[5]

Obama emphasized that our *conscience* required us to act in defense of Libyan civilians. Although reasons of national self-interest may have guided intervening states to action, the public justification was stated clearly in moral terms. In October 2011, the war was declared over and won by the National Transitional Council, the body representing those who fought to oust Gaddafi and who took control following Gaddafi's fall from power.

That states feel obligated to justify their resort to war, as well as the actions undertaken in the course of war, on moral terms suggests that realism's commitment to the irrelevance of morality in international relations in general, and in war in particular, is inadequate. Yet, we need to be careful in understanding the claim that realists reject the value of moral thinking in international relations. As Kennan observes, there may be good reasons to abide by what appear to be "moral" rules in international relations—states may have a desire to follow agreed "moral" codes in war and elsewhere simply to preserve their reputation or to protect the institutional structure that governs international relations more generally. What defines the realist position, in other words, is not a commitment to acting immorally; rather, the position is defined by what might be described as a utilitarian commitment to moral behavior in international relations. According to the realist, states behave morally only to the extent that it suits their national interests. When abandoning moral action is more likely to serve national interests, however, states will do so easily. In this view, realists might argue Americans had reasons of national security to offer support to the rebels, in addition to the publicly stated moral reasons.

THE MIDDLE WAY: JUST WAR THEORY

Between the extreme views of realism and pacifism—the view that ethics has no role to play in military conflict and the view that military conflict can never be justified—is a middle way. Just war theory recognizes the likelihood of war and therefore the need to think carefully about when war should be launched. It rejects the pacifist view for being an impracticable standard for contemporary political life and the realist view that morality has no role to play in international relations, and specifically in warfare. Instead, just war theorists recognize that even when war is underway, and even given the violence and destruction that inevitably accompanies war, certain actions are absolutely, morally, unacceptable, even in the most extreme circumstances.

Though just war theory has a long historical pedigree, its relative dominance as a framework for thinking through military conflict is recent. As early as St. Augustine in the mid-300s, Christian scholars were arguing for the justice of at least some wars, in particular those fought in pursuit of peace or, indeed, in pursuit of protecting space for the practice of Christianity. Attempts to justify military force in pursuit of religious objectives, however, were equally rejected by many early just war theorists. In the early 1500s, Spanish theologian Francisco de Vitoria, for example, emphasized that military action was justified only when harm had already been inflicted on innocents and certainly not in pursuit of religious objectives.

In his recounting of just war theory's history, Michael Walzer notes in this section's selection that "the rulers of this world embraced the theory, and did not fight a single war without describing it, or hiring intellectuals to describe it, as a war for peace and justice."[6] Yet, as Walzer notes, these rulers were fundamentally realists, and the proclamations of the need for war in terms of protecting peace or justice were more often than not "hypocritical." The modern shift away from realism, and the "mainstreaming" of just war theory, can be traced to the protests against the Vietnam War, in which Americans were forced to confront what Walzer termed the "systematic exposure of Vietnamese civilians to the violence of American war-making."[7] Since then, Walzer argues, moral theory has become an active constraint on war-making, not just for Americans but broadly among Western nations. "[J]ustice has become, in all Western countries, one of the tests that any proposed military strategy or tactic has to meet—only one of the tests and not the most important one, but this still gives just war theory a place and standing that it never had before."[8]

Whether just war theory is as widely embraced as Walzer suggests or lives up to its promise of bringing justice to the business of war, at a minimum, just war theory provides critical tools we need to evaluate and criticize war-launching and war-making. Thus, the authors in the subsequent parts of this book largely engage within the context of just war theory. While certain authors or arguments may reflect realist or pacifist strains of thought, the premise underlying the selection of readings is that just war theory has much to offer thinking about military conflict.

As readers will see, there is much dispute concerning what justifies the decision to go to war and which actions can legitimately be taken in war. That said, it seems possible to accept Nagel's general conclusion that engaging in the process of determining what is acceptable and what isn't acceptable, absolutely, seems an essential part of avoiding the conclusions that a strict utilitarian position might countenance. A strict utilitarian approach to war may allow us to justify some horrific actions on the grounds that the greatest happiness will be produced. Yet, this seems wrong. Rather, as Nagel noted, absolute moral principles constrain the possible actions we may take, by delimiting a threshold beyond which we may not go.

As you read the excerpts in this section, consider some of the following questions:
- If you agree that war is inevitable, does that mean that pacifism is irrelevant?
- Should states take ethical concerns seriously when determining whether to go to war? Why or why not?
- Should states that go to war for self-interested reasons be subject to international condemnation? Why or why not?

- Do you think that states that appear to behave morally in the international environment are doing so for reasons of self-interest or because they are committed to moral principles?
- Do you believe that religious principles can be utilized in support of military conflict or that they should be used only to reject military conflict?
- Is just war theory merely an attempt to balance the insights of realism and pacifism, or does it have an independent moral status?
- Is the claim that the "ethics of military conflict" is paradoxical in fact paradoxical? Does just war theory serve to erase the apparent paradox? Why or why not?

Notes

1. Thomas Nagel, "War and Massacre," *Philosophy and Public Affairs* 1, no. 2 (1972): 126.

2. Richard Norman, "The Case for Pacifism," *Journal of Applied Philosophy* 5 (1988): 198.

3. Ibid., 202.

4. George F. Kennan, "Morality and Foreign Policy," *Foreign Affairs* 64, no. 2 (1985): 206.

5. Speech by Barack Obama, President of the United States, Remarks by the President in Address to the Nation on Libya, National Defense University, Washington, DC, March 28, 2011, http://www.whitehouse.gov/the-press-office/2011/03/28/remarks-president-address-nation-libya.

6. Michael Walzer, "The Triumph of Just War Theory—And the Dangers of Success," *Social Research* (Winter, 2002): 1.

7. Ibid., 7.

8. Ibid., 12.

War and Massacre

by Thomas Nagel*

From the apathetic reaction to atrocities committed in Vietnam by the United States and its allies, one may conclude that moral restrictions on the conduct of war command almost as little sympathy among the general public as they do among those charged with the formation of U.S. military policy. Even when restrictions on the conduct of warfare are defended, it is usually on legal grounds alone: their moral basis is often poorly understood. I wish to argue that certain restrictions are neither arbitrary nor merely conventional, and that their validity does not depend simply on their usefulness. There is, in other words, a moral basis for the rules of war, even though the conventions now officially in force are far from giving it perfect expression.[1]

I

No elaborate moral theory is required to account for what is wrong in cases like the Mylai massacre, since it did not serve, and was not intended to serve, any strategic purpose. Moreover, if the participation of the United States in the Indo-Chinese war is entirely wrong to begin with, then that engagement is incapable of providing a justification for *any* measures taken in its pursuit—not only for the measures which are atrocities in every war, however just its aims.

But this war has revealed attitudes of a more general kind, that influenced the conduct of earlier wars as well. After it has ended, we shall still be faced with the problem of how warfare may be conducted, and the attitudes that have resulted in the specific conduct of this war will not have disappeared. Moreover, similar problems can arise in wars or rebellions fought for very different reasons, and against very different opponents. It is not easy to keep a firm grip on the idea of what is not permissible in warfare, because while some military actions are obvious atrocities, other cases are more difficult to assess, and the general principles underlying these judgments remain obscure. Such obscurity can lead to the abandonment of sound intuitions in favor of criteria whose rationale may be more obvious. If such a tendency is to be resisted, it will require a better understanding of the restrictions than we now have.

I propose to discuss the most general moral problem raised by the conduct of warfare: the problem of means and ends. In one view, there are limits on what may be done even in the service of an end worth pursuing-and even when adherence to the restriction may be very costly. A person who acknowledges the force of such restrictions can find himself in acute moral dilemmas. He may believe, for example, that by torturing a prisoner he can obtain information necessary to prevent a disaster, or that by obliterating one village with bombs he can halt a campaign of terrorism. If he believes that the gains from a certain measure will clearly outweigh its costs, yet still suspects that he ought not to adopt it, then he is in a dilemma produced by the conflict between two disparate categories of moral reason: categories that may be called *utilitarian* and *absolutist*.

Utilitarianism gives primacy to a concern with what will *happen*. Absolutism gives primacy to a concern with what one is *doing*. The conflict between them arises because the alternatives we face are rarely just choices between *total outcomes*: they are also choices between alternative pathways or measures to be taken. When one of the choices is to do terrible things to another person, the problem is altered fundamentally; it is no longer merely a question of which outcome would be worse.

Few of us are completely immune to either of these types of moral intuition, though in some people, either naturally or for doctrinal reasons, one type will be dominant and the other suppressed or weak. But it is perfectly possible to feel the force of both types of reason very strongly; in that case the moral dilemma in certain situations of crisis will be acute, and it may appear that every possible course of action or inaction is unacceptable for one reason or another.

II

Although it is this dilemma that I propose to explore, most of the discussion will be devoted to its absolutist component. The utilitarian component is straightforward by comparison, and has a natural appeal to anyone who is not a complete skeptic about ethics. Utilitarianism says that one should try, either individually or through institutions, to maximize good and minimize evil (the definition of these categories need not enter into the schematic formulation of the view), and that if faced with the possibility of preventing a great evil by producing a lesser, one should choose the lesser evil. There are certainly problems about the formulation of utilitarianism, and much has been written about it, but its intent is morally transparent. Nevertheless, despite the addition of various refinements, it continues to leave large portions of ethics unaccounted for. I do not suggest that some form of absolutism can account for them all, only that an examination of absolutism will lead us to see the complexity, and perhaps the incoherence, of our moral ideas.

Utilitarianism certainly justifies *some* restrictions on the conduct of warfare. There are strong utilitarian reasons for adhering to any limitation which seems natural to most people—particularly if the limitation is widely accepted already. An exceptional measure which seems to be justified by its results in a particular conflict may create a precedent with disastrous long-term effects.[2] It may even be argued that war involves violence on such a scale that it is never justified on utilitarian grounds—the consequences of refusing to go to war will never be as bad as the war itself would be, even if atrocities were not committed. Or in a more sophisticated vein it might be claimed that a uniform policy of never resorting to military force would do less harm in the long run, if followed consistently, than a policy of deciding each case on utilitarian grounds (even though on occasion particular applications of the pacifist policy might have worse results than a specific utilitarian decision). But I shall not consider these arguments, for my concern is with reasons of a different kind, which may remain when reasons of utility and interest fail.[3]

In the final analysis, I believe that the dilemma cannot always be resolved. While not every conflict between absolutism and utilitarianism creates an insoluble dilemma, and while it is certainly right to adhere to absolutist restrictions unless the utilitarian considerations favoring violation are overpoweringly weighty and extremely certain—nevertheless, when that special condition is met, it may become impossible to adhere to an absolutist position. What I shall offer, therefore, is a somewhat qualified defense of absolutism. I believe it underlies a valid and fundamental type of moral judgment—which cannot be reduced to or overridden by other principles. And while there may be other principles just as fundamental, it is particularly important not to lose confidence in our absolutist intuitions, for they are often the only barrier before the abyss of utilitarian apologetics for large-scale murder.

III

One absolutist position that creates no problems of interpretation is pacifism: the view that one may not kill another person under any circumstances, no matter what good would be achieved or evil averted thereby. The type of absolutist position that I am going to discuss is different. Pacifism draws the conflict with utilitarian considerations very starkly. But there are other views according to which violence may be undertaken, even on a large scale, in a clearly just cause, so long as certain absolute restrictions on the character and direction of that violence are observed. The line is drawn somewhat closer to the bone, but it exists.

The philosopher who has done most to advance contemporary philosophical discussion of such a view, and to explain it to those unfamiliar with its extensive treatment in Roman Catholic moral theology, is G.E.M. Anscombe. In 1958 Miss Anscombe published a pamphlet entitled *Mr. Truman's Degree*,[4] on the occasion of the award by Oxford University of an honorary doctorate to Harry Truman. The pamphlet explained why she had opposed the decision to award that degree, recounted the story of her unsuccessful opposition, and offered some reflections on the history of Truman's decision to drop atom bombs on Hiroshima and Nagasaki, and on the difference between murder and allowable killing in warfare. She pointed out that the policy of deliberately killing large numbers of civilians either as a means or as an end in itself did not originate with Truman, and was common practice among all parties during World War II for some time before Hiroshima. The Allied area bombings of German cities by conventional explosives included raids which killed more civilians than did the atomic attacks; the same is true of certain fire-bomb raids on Japan.

The policy of attacking the civilian population in order to induce an enemy to surrender, or to damage his morale, seems to have been widely accepted in the civilized world, and seems to be accepted still, at least if the stakes are high enough. It gives evidence of a moral conviction that the deliberate killing of noncombatants-women, children, old people—is permissible if enough can be gained by it. This follows from the more general position that any means can in principle be justified if it leads to a sufficiently worthy end. Such an attitude is evident not only in the more spectacular current weapons systems but also in the day-to-day conduct of the nonglobal war in Indochina; the indiscriminate destructiveness of antipersonnel weapons, napalm, and aerial bombardment; cruelty to prisoners; massive relocation of civilians; destruction of crops; and so forth. An absolutist position opposes to this the view that certain acts cannot be justified no matter what the consequences. Among those acts is murder— the deliberate killing of the harmless: civilians, prisoners of war, and medical personnel.

In the present war such measures are sometimes said to be regrettable, but they are generally defended by reference to military necessity and the impor-tance of the long-term consequences of success or failure in the war. I shall pass over the inadequacy of this consequentialist defense in its own terms. (That is the dominant form of moral criticism of the war, for it is part of what people mean when they ask, "Is it worth it?") I am concerned rather to account for the inappropriateness of offering any defense of that kind for such actions.

Many people feel, without being able to say much more about it, that something has gone seriously wrong when certain measures are admitted into consideration in the first place. The fundamental mistake is made there, rather than at the point where the overall benefit of some monstrous measure is judged to outweigh its disadvantages, and it is adopted. An account of absolutism might help us to understand this. If it is not allowable to *do* certain things, such as killing unarmed prisoners or civilians, then no argument about what will happen if one doesn't do them can show that doing them would be all right.

Absolutism does not, of course, require one to ignore the consequences of one's acts. It operates as a limitation on utilitarian reasoning, not as a substitute for it. An absolutist can be expected to try to maximize good and minimize evil, so long as this does not require him to transgress an absolute prohibition like that against murder. But when such a conflict occurs, the prohibition takes complete precedence over any consideration of consequences. Some of the results of this view are clear enough. It requires us to forgo certain potentially useful military measures, such as the slaughter of hostages and prisoners or indiscriminate attempts to reduce the enemy civilian population by starvation, epidemic infectious diseases like anthrax and bubonic plague, or mass incineration. It means that we cannot deliberate on whether such measures are justified by the fact that they will avert still greater evils, for as intentional measures they cannot be justified in terms of any consequences whatever.

Someone unfamiliar with the events of this century might imagine that utilitarian arguments, or arguments of national interest, would suffice to deter measures of this sort. But it has become evident that such considerations are insufficient to prevent the adoption and employment of enormous antipopulation weapons once their use is considered a serious moral possibility. The same is true of the piecemeal wiping out of rural civilian populations in airborne antiguerrilla warfare. Once the door is opened to calculations of utility and national interest, the usual speculations about the future of freedom, peace, and economic prosperity can be brought to bear to ease the consciences of those responsible for a certain number of charred babies.

For this reason alone it is important to decide what is wrong with the frame of mind which allows such arguments to begin. But it is also important to understand absolutism in the cases where it genuinely conflicts with utility. Despite its appeal, it is a paradoxical position, for it can require that one refrain from choosing the lesser of two evils when that is the only choice one has. And it is additionally paradoxical because, unlike pacifism, it permits one to do horrible things to people in some circumstances but not in others.

IV

Before going on to say what, if anything, lies behind the position, there remain a few relatively technical matters which are best discussed at this point.

First, it is important to specify as clearly as possible the kind of thing to which absolutist prohibitions can apply. We must take seriously the proviso that they concern what we deliberately do to people. There could not, for example, without incoherence, be an absolute prohibition against *bringing about* the death of an innocent person. For one may find oneself in a situation in which, no matter what one does, some innocent people will die as a result. I do not mean just that there are cases in which someone will die no matter what one does, because one is not in a position to affect the outcome one way or the other. That, it is to be hoped, is one's relation to the deaths of most innocent people. I have in mind, rather, a case in which someone is bound to die, but who it is will depend on what one does. Sometimes these situations have natural causes, as when too few resources (medicine, lifeboats) are available to rescue everyone threatened with a certain catastrophe. Sometimes the situations are manmade, as when the only way to control a campaign of terrorism is to employ terrorist tactics against the community from which it has arisen. Whatever one does in cases such as these, some innocent people will die as a result. If the absolutist prohibition forbade doing what would result in the deaths of innocent people, it would have the consequence that in such cases nothing one could do would be morally permissible.

This problem is avoided, however, because what absolutism forbids is *doing* certain things to people, rather than bringing about certain *results*. Not everything that happens to others as a result of what one does is something that one has *done* to them. Catholic moral theology seeks to make this distinction precise in a doctrine known as the law of double effect, which asserts that there is a morally relevant distinction between bringing about the death of an innocent person deliberately, either as an end in itself or as a means, and bringing it about as a side effect of something else one does deliberately. In the latter case, even if the outcome is foreseen, it is not murder, and does not fall under the absolute prohibition, though of course it may still be wrong for other reasons (reasons of utility, for example). Briefly, the principle states that one is sometimes permitted knowingly to bring about as a side effect of one's actions something which it would be absolutely impermissible to bring about deliberately as an end or as a means. In application to war or revolution, the law of double effect permits a certain amount of civilian carnage as a side effect of bombing munitions plants or attacking enemy soldiers. And even this is permissible only if the cost is not too great to be justified by one's objectives.

However, despite its importance and its usefulness in accounting for certain plausible moral judgments, I do not believe that the law of double effect is a generally applicable test for the consequences of an absolutist position. Its own application is not always clear, so that it introduces uncertainty where there need not be uncertainty.

In Indochina, for example, there is a great deal of aerial bombardment, strafing, spraying of napalm, and employment of pellet- or needle-spraying antipersonnel weapons against rural villages in which guerrillas are suspected to be hiding, or from which small-arms fire has been received. The majority of those killed and wounded in these aerial attacks are reported to be women and children, even when some combatants are caught as well. However, the government regards these civilian casualties as a regrettable side effect of what is a legitimate attack against an armed enemy.

It might be thought easy to dismiss this as sophistry: if one bombs, burns, or strafes a village containing a hundred people, twenty of whom one believes to be guerrillas, so that by killing most of them one will be statistically likely to kill most of the guerrillas, then isn't one's attack on the group of one hundred a *means* of destroying the guerrillas, pure and simple? If one makes no attempt to discriminate between guerrillas and civilians, as is impossible in an aerial attack on a small village, then one cannot regard as a mere side effect the deaths of those in the group that one would not have bothered to kill if more selective means had been available.

The difficulty is that this argument depends on one particular description of the act, and the reply might be that the means used against the guerrillas is not killing everybody in the village, but rather obliteration bombing of the *area* in which the twenty guerrillas are known to be located. If there are civilians in the area as well, they will be killed as a side effect of such action.[5]

Because of casuistical problems like this, I prefer to stay with the original, unanalyzed distinction between what one does to people and what merely happens to them as a result of what one does. The law of double effect provides an approximation to that distinction in many cases, and perhaps it can be sharpened to the point where it does better than that. Certainly the original distinction itself needs clarification, particularly since some of the things we do to people involve things happening to them as a result of other things we do. In a case like the one discussed, however, it is clear that by bombing the village one slaughters and maims the civilians in it. Whereas by giving the only available medicine to one of two sufferers from a disease, one does not kill the other, even if he dies as a result.

The second technical point to take up concerns a possible misinterpretation of this feature of the position. The absolutist focus on actions rather than out-comes does not merely introduce a new, outstanding item into the catalogue of evils. That is, it does not say that the worst thing in the world is the deliberate murder of an innocent person. For if that were all, then one could presumably justify one such murder on the ground that it would prevent several others, or ten thousand on the ground that they would prevent a hundred thousand more. That is a familiar argument. But if this is allowable, then there is no absolute prohibition against murder after all. Absolutism requires that we *avoid* murder at all costs, not that we *prevent* it at all costs.[6] Finally, let me remark on a frequent criticism of absolutism that depends on a misunderstanding. It is sometimes sug-gested that such prohibitions depend on a kind of moral self-interest, a primary obligation to preserve one's own moral purity, to keep one's hands clean no matter what happens to the rest of the world. If this were the position, it might be exposed to the charge of self-indulgence. After all, what gives one man a right to put the purity of his soul or the cleanness of his hands above the lives or welfare of large numbers of other people? It might be argued that a public ser-vant like Truman has no right to put himself first in that way; therefore if he is convinced that the alternatives would be worse, he must give the order to drop the bombs, and take the burden of those deaths on himself, as he must do other distasteful things for the general good.

But there are two confusions behind the view that moral self-interest under-lies moral absolutism. First, it is a confusion to suggest that the need to preserve one's moral purity might be the *source* of an obligation. For if by committing murder one sacrifices one's moral purity or integrity, that can only be because there is *already* something wrong with murder. The general reason against com-mitting murder cannot therefore be merely that it makes one an immoral per-son. Secondly, the notion that one might sacrifice one's moral integrity justifi-ably, in the service of a sufficiently worthy end, is an incoherent notion. For if one were justified in making such a sacrifice (or even morally required to make it), then one would not be sacrificing one's moral integrity by adopting that course: one would be preserving it.

Moral absolutism is not unique among moral theories in requiring each per-son to do what will preserve his own moral purity in all circumstances. This is equally true of utilitarianism, or of any other theory which distinguishes be-tween right and wrong. Any theory which defines the right course of action in various circumstances and asserts that one should adopt that course, ipso facto asserts that one should do what will preserve one's moral purity, simply be-cause the right course of action *is* what will preserve one's moral purity in those circumstances. Of course utilitarianism does not assert that this is *why* one should adopt that course, but we have seen that the same is true of absolutism.

V

It is easier to dispose of false explanations of absolutism than to produce a true one. A positive account of the matter must begin with the observation that war, conflict, and aggression are relations between persons. The view that it can be wrong to consider merely the overall effect of one's actions on the general welfare comes into prominence when those actions involve relations with others. A man's acts usually affect more people than he deals with directly, and those effects must naturally be considered in his decisions. But if there are special principles governing the manner in which he should *treat* people, that will require special attention to the particular persons toward whom the act is directed, rather than just to its total effect.

Absolutist restrictions in warfare appear to be of two types: restrictions on the class of persons at whom aggression or violence may be directed and restrictions on the manner of attack, given that the object falls within that class. These can be combined, however, under the principle that hostile treatment of any person must be justified in terms of something *about that person* which makes the treatment appropriate. Hostility is a personal relation, and it must be suited to its target. One consequence of this condition will be that certain persons may not be subjected to hostile treatment in war at all, since nothing about them justifies such treatment. Others will be proper objects of hostility only in certain circumstances, or when they are engaged in certain pursuits. And the appropriate manner and extent of hostile treatment will depend on what is justified by the particular case.

A coherent view of this type will hold that extremely hostile behavior toward another is compatible with treating him as a person—even perhaps as an end in himself. This is possible only if one has not automatically stopped treating him as a person as soon as one starts to fight with him. If hostile, aggressive, or combative treatment of others always violated the condition that they be treated as human beings, it would be difficult to make further distinctions on that score *within* the class of hostile actions. That point of view, on the level of international relations, leads to the position that if complete pacifism is not accepted, no holds need be barred at all, and we may slaughter and massacre to our hearts' content, if it seems advisable. Such a position is often expressed in discussions of war crimes.

But the fact is that ordinary people do not believe this about conflicts, physical or otherwise, between individuals, and there is no more reason why it should be true of conflicts between nations. There seems to be a perfectly natural conception of the distinction between fighting clean and fighting dirty. To fight dirty is to direct one's hostility or aggression not at its proper object, but at a peripheral target which may be more vulnerable, and through which the proper object can be attacked indirectly. This applies in a fist fight, an election campaign, a duel, or a philosophical argument. If the concept is general enough to apply to all these matters, it should apply to war—both to the conduct of individual soldiers and to the conduct of nations.

Suppose that you are a candidate for public office, convinced that the election of your opponent would be a disaster, that he is an unscrupulous demagogue who will serve a narrow range of interests and seriously infringe the rights of those who disagree with him; and suppose you are convinced that you cannot defeat him by conventional means. Now imagine that various unconventional means present themselves as possibilities: you possess information about his sex life which would scandalize the electorate if made public; or you learn that his wife is an alcoholic or that in his youth he was associated for a brief period with a proscribed political party, and you believe that this information could be used to blackmail him into withdrawing his candidacy; or you can have a team of your supporters flatten the tires of a crucial subset of his supporters on election day; or you are in a position to stuff the ballot boxes; or, more simply, you can have him assassinated. What is wrong with these methods, given that they will achieve an overwhelmingly desirable result?

There are, of course, many things wrong with them: some are against the law; some infringe the procedures of an electoral process to which you are presumably committed by taking part in it; very importantly, some may backfire, and it is in the interest of all political candidates to adhere to an unspoken agreement not to allow certain personal matters to intrude into a campaign. But that is not all. We have in addition the feeling that these measures, these methods of attack are *irrelevant* to the issue between you and your opponent, that in taking them up you would not be directing yourself to that which makes him an object of your opposition. You would be directing your attack not at the true target of your hostility, but at peripheral targets that happen to be vulnerable.

The same is true of a fight or argument outside the framework of any system of regulations or law. In an altercation with a taxi driver over an excessive fare, it is inappropriate to taunt him about his accent, flatten one of his tires, or smear chewing gum on his windshield; and it remains inappropriate even if he casts aspersions on your race, politics, or religion, or dumps the contents of your suitcase into the street.[7]

The importance of such restrictions may vary with the seriousness of the case; and what is unjustifiable in one case may be justified in a more extreme one. But they all derive from a single principle: that hostility or aggression should be directed at its true object. This means both that it should be directed at the person or persons who provoke it and that it should aim more specifically at what is provocative about them. The second condition will determine what form the hostility may appropriately take.

It is evident that some idea of the relation in which one should stand to other people underlies this principle, but the idea is difficult to state. I believe it is roughly this: whatever one does to another person intentionally must be aimed at him as a subject, with the intention that he receive it as a subject. It should manifest an attitude to *him* rather than just to the situation, and he should be able to recognize it and identify himself as its object. The procedures by which such an attitude is manifested need not be addressed to the person directly. Surgery, for example, is not a form of personal confrontation but part of a medical treatment that can be offered to a patient face to face and received by him as a response to his needs and the natural outcome of an attitude toward *him*.

Hostile treatment, unlike surgery, is already addressed *to* a person, and does not take its interpersonal meaning from a wider context. But hostile acts can serve as the expression or implementation of only a limited range of attitudes to the person who is attacked. Those attitudes in turn have as objects certain real or presumed characteristics or activities of the person which are thought to justify them. When this background is absent, hostile or aggressive behavior can no longer be intended for the reception of the victim as a subject. Instead it takes on the character of a purely bureaucratic operation. This occurs when one attacks someone who is not the true object of one's hostility—the true object may be someone else, who can be attacked through the victim; or one may not be manifesting a hostile attitude toward anyone, but merely using the easiest available path to some desired goal. One finds oneself not facing or addressing the victim at all, but operating on him—without the larger context of personal interaction that surrounds a surgical operation.

If absolutism is to defend its claim to priority over considerations of utility, it must hold that the maintenance of a direct interpersonal response to the people one deals with is a requirement which no advantages can justify one in abandoning. The requirement is absolute only if it rules out any calculation of what would justify its violation. I have said earlier that there may be circumstances so extreme that they render an absolutist position untenable. One may find then that one has no choice but to do something terrible. Nevertheless, even in such cases absolutism retains its force in that one cannot claim *justification* for the violation. It does not become *all right*.

As a tentative effort to explain this, let me try to connect absolutist limitations with the possibility of justifying *to the victim* what is being done to him. If one abandons a person in the course of rescuing several others from a fire or a sinking ship, one *could* say to him, "You understand, I have to leave you to save the others." Similarly, if one subjects an unwilling child to a painful surgical procedure, one can say to him, "If you could understand, you would realize that I am doing this to help you." One could *even* say, as one bayonets an enemy soldier, "It's either you or me." But one cannot really say while torturing a prisoner, "You understand, I have to pull out your fingernails because it is absolutely essential that we have the names of your confederates"; nor can one say to the victims of Hiroshima, "You understand, we have to incinerate you to provide the Japanese government with an incentive to surrender."

This does not take us very far, of course, since a utilitarian would presumably be willing to offer justifications of the latter sort to his victims, in cases where he thought they were sufficient. They are really justifications to the world at large, which the victim, as a reasonable man, would be expected to appreciate. However, there seems to me something wrong with this view, for it ignores the possibility that to treat someone else horribly puts you in a special relation to him, which may have to be defended in terms of other features of your relation to him. The suggestion needs much more development; but it may help us to understand how there may be requirements which are absolute in the sense that there can be no justification for violating them. If the justification for what one did to another person had to be such that it could be offered to him specifically, rather than just to the world at large, that would be a significant source of restraint.

If the account is to be deepened, I would hope for some results along the following lines. Absolutism is associated with a view of oneself as a small being interacting with others in a large world. The justifications it requires are primarily interpersonal. Utilitarianism is associated with a view of oneself as a benevolent bureaucrat distributing such benefits as one can control to countless other beings, with whom one may have various relations or none. The justifications it requires are primarily administrative. The argument between the two moral attitudes may depend on the relative priority of these two conceptions.[8]

VI

Some of the restrictions on methods of warfare which have been adhered to from time to time are to be explained by the mutual interests of the involved parties: restrictions on weaponry, treatment of prisoners, etc. But that is not all there is to it. The conditions of directness and relevance which I have argued apply to relations of conflict and aggression apply to war as well. I have said that there are two types of absolutist restrictions on the conduct of war: those that limit the legitimate targets of hostility and those that limit its character, even when the target is acceptable. I shall say something about each of these. As will become clear, the principle I have sketched does not yield an unambiguous answer in every case.

First let us see how it implies that attacks on some people are allowed, but not attacks on others. It may seem paradoxical to assert that to fire a machine gun at someone who is throwing hand grenades at your emplacement is to treat him as a human being. Yet the relation with him is direct and straightforward.[9] The attack is aimed specifically against the threat presented by a dangerous adversary, and not against a peripheral target through which he happens to be vulnerable but which has nothing to do with that threat. For example, you might stop him by machine-gunning his wife and children, who are standing nearby, thus distracting him from his aim of blowing you up and enabling you to capture him. But if his wife and children are not threatening your life, that would be to treat them as means with a vengeance.

This, however, is just Hiroshima on a smaller scale. One objection to weapons of mass annihilation—nuclear, thermonuclear, biological, or chemical—is that their indiscriminateness disqualifies them as direct instruments for the expression of hostile relations. In attacking the civilian population, one treats neither the military enemy nor the civilians with that minimal respect which is owed to them as human beings. This is clearly true of the direct attack on people who present no threat at all. But it is also true of the character of the attack on those who *are* threatening you, viz., the government and military forces of the enemy. Your aggression is directed against an area of vulnerability quite distinct from any threat presented by them which you may be justified in meeting. You are taking aim at them through the mundane life and survival of their countrymen, instead of aiming at the destruction of their military capacity. And of course it does not require hydrogen bombs to commit such crimes.

This way of looking at the matter also helps us to understand the importance of the distinction between combatants and noncombatants, and the irrelevance of much of the criticism offered against its intelligibility and moral significance. According to an absolutist position, deliberate killing of the innocent is murder, and in warfare the role of the innocent is filled by noncombatants. This has been thought to raise two sorts of problems: first, the widely imagined difficulty of making a division, in modern warfare, between combatants and noncombatants; second, problems deriving from the connotation of the word "innocence."

Let me take up the latter question first.[10] In the absolutist position, the operative notion of innocence is not moral innocence, and it is not opposed to moral guilt. If it were, then we would be justified in killing a wicked but noncombatant hairdresser in an enemy city who supported the evil policies of his government, and unjustified in killing a morally pure conscript who was driving a tank toward us with the profoundest regrets and nothing but love in his heart. But moral innocence has very little to do with it, for in the definition of murder "innocent" means "currently harmless," and it is opposed not to "guilty" but to "doing harm." It should be noted that such an analysis has the consequence that in war we may often be justified in killing people who do not deserve to die, and unjustified in killing people who do deserve to die, if anyone does.

So we must distinguish combatants from noncombatants on the basis of their immediate threat or harmfulness. I do not claim that the line is a sharp one, but it is not so difficult as is often supposed to place individuals on one side of it or the other. Children are not combatants even though they may join the armed forces if they are allowed to grow up. Women are not combatants just because they bear children or offer comfort to the soldiers. More problematic are the supporting personnel, whether in or out of uniform, from drivers of munitions trucks and army cooks to civilian munitions workers and farmers. I believe they can be plausibly classified by applying the condition that the prosecution of conflict must direct itself to the cause of danger, and not to what is peripheral. The threat presented by an army and its members does not consist merely in the fact that they are men, but in the fact that they are armed and are using their arms in the pursuit of certain objectives. Contributions to their arms and logistics are contributions to this threat; contributions to their mere existence as men are not. It is therefore wrong to direct an attack against those who merely serve the combatants' needs as human beings, such as farmers and food suppliers, even though survival as a human being is a necessary condition of efficient functioning as a soldier.

This brings us to the second group of restrictions: those that limit what may be done even to combatants. These limits are harder to explain clearly. Some of them may be arbitrary or conventional, and some may have to be derived from other sources; but I believe that the condition of directness and relevance in hostile relations accounts for them to a considerable extent.

Consider first a case which involves both a protected class of noncombatants and a restriction on the measures that may be used against combatants. One provision of the rules of war which is universally recognized, though it seems to be turning into a dead letter in Vietnam, is the special status of medical personnel and the wounded in warfare. It might be more efficient to shoot medical officers on sight and to let the enemy wounded die rather than be patched up to fight another day. But someone with medical insignia is supposed to be left alone and permitted to tend and retrieve the wounded. I believe this is because medical attention is a species of attention to completely general human needs, not specifically the needs of a combat soldier, and our conflict with the soldier is not with his existence as a human being.

By extending the application of this idea, one can justify prohibitions against certain particularly cruel weapons: starvation, poisoning, infectious diseases (supposing they could be inflicted on combatants only), weapons designed to maim or disfigure or torture the opponent rather than merely to stop him. It is not, I think, mere casuistry to claim that such weapons attack the men, not the soldiers. The effect of dum-dum bullets, for example, is much more extended than necessary to cope with the combat situation in which they are used. They abandon any attempt to discriminate in their effects between the combatant and the human being. For this reason the use of flamethrowers and napalm is an atrocity in all circumstances that I can imagine, whoever the target may be. Burns are both extremely painful and extremely disfiguring—far more than any other category of wound. That this well-known fact plays no (inhibiting) part in the determination of U.S. weapons policy suggests that moral sensitivity among public officials has not increased markedly since the Spanish Inquisition.[11]

Finally, the same condition of appropriateness to the true object of hostility should limit the scope of attacks on an enemy country: its economy, agriculture, transportation system, and so forth. Even if the parties to a military conflict are considered to be not armies or governments but entire nations (which is usually a grave error), that does not justify one nation in warring against every aspect or element of another nation. That is not justified in a conflict between individuals, and nations are even more complex than individuals, so the same reasons apply. Like a human being, a nation is engaged in countless other pursuits while waging war, and it is not in those respects that it is an enemy.

The burden of the argument has been that absolutism about murder has a foundation in principles governing all one's relations to other persons, whether aggressive or amiable, and that these principles, and that absolutism, apply to warfare as well, with the result that certain measures are impermissible no matter what the consequences.[12] I do not mean to romanticize war. It is sufficiently utopian to suggest that when nations conflict they might rise to the level of limited barbarity that typically characterizes violent conflict between individuals, rather than wallowing in the moral pit where they appear to have settled, surrounded by enormous arsenals.

VII

Having described the elements of the absolutist position, we must now return to the conflict between it and utilitarianism. Even if certain types of dirty tactics become acceptable when the stakes are high enough, the most serious of the prohibited acts, like murder and torture, are not just supposed to require unusually strong justification. They are supposed *never* to be done, because no quantity of resulting benefit is thought capable of *justifying* such treatment of a person.

The fact remains that when an absolutist knows or believes that the utilitarian cost of refusing to adopt a prohibited course will be very high, he may hold to his refusal to adopt it, but he will find it difficult to feel that a moral dilemma has been satisfactorily resolved. The same may be true of someone who rejects an absolutist requirement and adopts instead the course yielding the most acceptable consequences. In either case, it is possible to feel that one has acted for reasons insufficient to justify violation of the opposing principle. In situations of deadly conflict, particularly where a weaker party is threatened with annihilation or enslavement by a stronger one, the argument for resorting to atrocities can be powerful, and the dilemma acute.

There may exist principles, not yet codified, which would enable us to resolve such dilemmas. But then again there may not. We must face the pessimistic alternative that these two forms of moral intuition are not capable of being brought together into a single, coherent moral system, and that the world can present us with situations in which there is no honorable or moral course for a man to take, no course free of guilt and responsibility for evil.

The idea of a moral blind alley is a perfectly intelligible one. It is possible to get into such a situation by one's own fault, and people do it all the time. If, for example, one makes two incompatible promises or commitments—becomes engaged to two people, for example—then there is no course one can take which is not wrong, for one must break one's promise to at least one of them. Making a clean breast of the whole thing will not be enough to remove one's reprehensibility. The existence of such cases is not morally disturbing, however, because we feel that the situation was not unavoidable: one had to do something wrong in the first place to get into it. But what if the world itself, or someone else's actions, could face a previously innocent person with a choice between morally abominable courses of action, and leave him no way to escape with his honor? Our intuitions rebel at the idea, for we feel that the constructibility of such a case must show a contradiction in our moral views. But it is not in itself a contradiction to say that someone can do X or not do X, and that for him to take either course would be wrong. It merely contradicts the supposition that *ought* implies *can*—since presumably one ought to refrain from what is wrong, and in such a case it is impossible to do so.[13] Given the limitations on human action, it is naive to suppose that there is a solution to every moral problem with which the world can face us. We have always known that the world is a bad place. It appears that it may be an evil place as well.

NOTES

1. This paper grew out of discussions at the Society for Ethical and Legal Philosophy, and I am indebted to my fellow members for their help.

2. Straightforward considerations of national interest often tend in the same direction: the inadvisability of using nuclear weapons seems to be overdetermined in this way.

3. These reasons, moreover, have special importance in that they are available even to one who denies the appropriateness of utilitarian considerations in international matters. He may acknowledge limitations on what may be done to the soldiers and civilians of other countries in pursuit of his nation's military objectives, while denying that one country should in general consider the interests of nationals of other countries in determining its policies.

4. (Privately printed.) See also her essay "War and Murder," in *Nuclear Weapons and Christian Conscience*, ed. Walter Stein (London, 1963). The present paper is much indebted to these two essays throughout. These and related subjects are extensively treated by Paul Ramsey in *The Just War* (New York, 1968). Among recent writings that bear on the moral problem are Jonathan Bennett, "Whatever the Consequences," *Analysis* 26, no. 3 (1966): 83–102; and Philippa Foot, "The Problem of Abortion and the Doctrine of the Double Effect," *The Oxford Review* 5 (1967): 5–15. Miss Anscombe's replies are "A Note on Mr. Bennett," *Analysis* 26, no. 3 (1966): 208, and "Who is Wronged?" *The Oxford Review* 5 (1967): 16–17.

5. This counterargument was suggested by Rogers Albritton.

6. Someone might of course acknowledge the *moral relevance* of the distinction between deliberate and nondeliberate killing, without being an absolutist. That is, he might believe simply that it was *worse* to bring about a death deliberately than as a secondary effect. But that would be merely a special assignment of value, and not an absolute prohibition.

7. Why, on the other hand, does it seem appropriate, rather than irrelevant, to punch someone in the mouth if he insults you? The answer is that in our culture it is an insult to punch someone

in the mouth, and not just an injury. This reveals, by the way, a perfectly unobjectionable sense in which convention may play a part in determining exactly what falls under an absolutist restriction and what does not. I am indebted to Robert Fogelin for this point.

8. Finally, I should mention a different possibility, suggested by Robert Nozick: that there is a strong general presumption against benefiting from the calamity of another, whether or not it has been deliberately inflicted for that or any other reason. This broader principle may well lend its force to the absolutist position.

9. It has been remarked that according to my view, shooting at someone establishes an I-thou relationship.

10. What I say on this subject derives from Anscombe.

11. Beyond this I feel uncertain. Ordinary bullets, after all, can cause death, and nothing is more permanent than that. I am not at all sure why we are justified in trying to kill those who are trying to kill us (rather than merely in trying to stop them with force which may also result in their deaths). It is often argued that incapacitating gases are a relatively humane weapon (when not used, as in Vietnam, merely to make people easier to shoot). Perhaps the legitimacy of restrictions against them must depend on the dangers of escalation, and the great utility of maintaining any conventional category of restriction so long as nations are willing to adhere to it.

Let me make clear that I do not regard my argument as a defense of the moral immutability of the Hague and Geneva Conventions. Rather, I believe that they rest partly on a moral foundation, and that modifications of them should also be assessed on moral grounds.

But even this connection with the actual laws of war is not essential to my claims about what is permissible and what is not. Since completing this paper I have read an essay by Richard Wasserstrom entitled "The Laws of War" (forthcoming in *The Monist*), which argues that the existing laws and conventions do not even attempt to embody a decent moral position, that their provisions have been determined by other interests, that they are in fact immoral in substance, and that it is a grave mistake to refer to them as standards in forming moral judgments about warfare. This possibility deserves serious consideration, and I am not sure what to say about it, but it does not affect my view of the moral issues.

12. It is possible to draw a more radical conclusion, which I shall not pursue here. Perhaps the technology and organization of modern war are such as to make it impossible to wage as an acceptable form of interpersonal or even international hostility. Perhaps it is too impersonal and large-scale for that. If so, then absolutism would in practice imply pacifism, given the present state of things. On the other hand, I am skeptical about the unstated assumption that a technology dictates its own use.

13. This was first pointed out to me by Christopher Boorse.

***Thomas Nagel** is university professor of philosophy and law at New York University.

Thomas Nagel, "War and Massacre," *Philosophy and Public Affairs* 1, no. 2 (1972): 123–144.
Copyright © 1972, Princeton University Press.

The Case for Pacifism

by Richard Norman*

ABSTRACT *I present the case for pacifism by formulating what I take to be the most plausible version of the idea of respect for human life. This generates a very strong, though not necessarily absolute, moral presumption against killing, in war or any other situation. I then show how difficult it is for this presumption to be overridden, either by the considerations invoked in 'just war' theory, or by consequentialist claims about what can be achieved through war.*

Despite the strength of the moral case against war, people sometimes say that they have no choice but to fight. In the concluding section of the paper I attempt to identify the relevant sense in which this could be said, and I discuss briefly how this affects the case for pacifism.

The conclusion of this paper will not be an unqualified endorsement of pacifism. I nevertheless want to present the case for pacifism as strongly as I can, for I do not think that the plausibility of that case has been adequately recognised in the philosophical literature. An unconditional rejection of, say, abortion, or euthanasia, or the death penalty, or even the killing of animals, has been treated as a standard position in philosophical discussions, and as an appropriate point of reference for other, more nuanced positions. When it comes to the morality of war, however, pacifism—the unconditional rejection of war—has typically been treated as an eccentric or marginal position, with the implication that the important issues and arguments are to be found elsewhere[1]. I want to maintain, on the contrary, that pacifism is central to the arguments, and that other positions ought to define themselves primarily in relation to pacifism. To describe the position which eventually emerges in this paper I am inclined to adopt a recent suggestion and call it 'pacificist' rather than 'pacifist'[2]. I believe that the case for pacifism is very strong indeed, and I shall set out that case, but I shall also suggest that there are situations where people can properly say that, in a sense which I shall try to explain, they have no choice but to resort to war. I am inclined to think that, at least at the theoretical level, there is no way of resolving the ethical dilemma posed by war and pacifism. Nevertheless, en route to that rather unsatisfactory conclusion, I shall argue that the case for pacifism is stronger, and the standard justifications for war are weaker, then they are generally taken to be.

I define 'pacifism' as the view that it is always wrong to go to war. As such it is addressed to governments, and to political movements, especially those which aspire to be governments, since these are the bodies which, by definition, are capable of waging wars and therefore have to decide whether or not to do so. Violence or killing engaged in by individuals solely as individuals would not be war, whatever else it might be. However, as individuals we can, to a greater or lesser extent, influence governments, and we can either support or oppose the decisions of governments and political movements to resort to war. Pacifism, therefore, would require us as individuals to oppose any resort to war. There remains the question what the individual should do if his or her government has in fact embarked on a war. Pacifism has normally been taken to require that even if one is unable to prevent one's own country going to war, one should still refuse to participate; this however raises further questions about the nature of political allegiance, which I shall not discuss. I shall focus on the initial, and logically primary, claim that it can never be right for governments or would-be governments to resort to war.

The absolutist formulation of that claim is crucial. The horrors of war are obvious, they increase with every advance in men's technical capacity to inflict death and destruction, and, reviewing the historical record, one might doubt whether any war could achieve sufficient good to counterbalance those horrors. One might then arrive at the position which Anne Seller has called 'unprincipled pacifism'. That phrase, however, is deliberately paradoxical. One thinks of pacifism as, par excellence, a principled position, not just a rule-of-thumb about probable consequences. The principle which underlies it is, I suggest, that of the wrongness of killing: war is morally unacceptable because it is the unjustified taking of human life. I am aware that pacifism is not always formulated in such terms. In particular, it is sometimes formulated as the view that it is always wrong to employ force, or to employ violence. These various formulations, in terms of force, or violence, or killing, will have importantly different implications, which I cannot explore here. I can only state dogmatically that the most plausible of the three versions seems to me to be that which is formulated in terms of the wrongness of killing. This does not mean that I want to dispense with the vocabulary of 'violence' and 'non-violence'. The phrase 'non-violent resistance' is well-entrenched as a way of referring to alternatives to war; it is the most convenient way of identifying an important tradition of thought and action, and in due course I shall myself use it in that way. Nevertheless I want to put the main weight of the ethical case for pacifism on the concept of 'killing' rather than the concept of 'violence'.

I do not want to maintain that the pacifist, as an absolutist about killing in war, needs to be an absolutist about the wrongness of killing in general, nor about the killing of human beings generally. That again would make pacifism less plausible than it needs to be. What I shall do is to offer an account of the wrongness of killing which is grounded in the attitude of respect for human life as such. I shall try to show how deeply rooted that attitude is in our moral thinking, and hence how difficult it is for the presumption against killing to be overridden. Although there are possible circumstances in which an exception could justifiably be made to the principle of not taking human life, the standard justifications for overriding that principle in war are, I shall suggest, inadequate; hence the strength of the case for pacifism.

RESPECT FOR HUMAN LIFE

What is wrong with taking human life? Two obvious answers are that to kill someone against their will is to override their autonomy, and the utilitarian answer that to kill someone normally causes great suffering and deprives the victim of possible happiness. An account composed exclusively of these two elements, however, seems to rule out the attitude of respect for human life as such, and hence the idea that killing is wrong just because it is the taking of life. There are familiar difficulties with that idea. Respect for human life as such seems to attribute value to the mere fact of being alive, even if in an irreversible coma. And if we respect human life, are we not being arbitrarily 'speciesist' unless we extend the same respect to all life, including the bacteria which are killed by medicines, the weeds which are killed by any gardener, and the crops which are harvested for food?

To meet these difficulties, I want to defend the suggestion which has been made by James Rachels[3], that we should interpret the idea of respect for life as referring not to the merely biological condition of 'being alive', but to that of 'having a life'. We should think of human life as something which is *lived*, something in which a human being is actively engaged. Of course, in a weak sense any living thing 'lives' its own life, but I have in mind something stronger—the ability of a normal human being to give a distinctive shape to his or her life as a whole. We typically think of a human life as following a distinctive pattern, developing from birth, through childhood, youth and maturity to old age. These are the characteristic contours of human life. Within this framework, each person will live his or her own life in his or her own way, giving it a particular content and making something meaningful out of it. People do this in innumerable different ways: they may pursue a career, or devote themselves to a cause or a movement or a set of beliefs; their lives may revolve around a close relationship

with another person, or around family relationships, around the process of growing up within a family and then raising the next generation. These possibilities
are of course neither exclusive nor exhaustive, but I list them as typical ways
in which people live their lives, shaping them and making something of them.
They all illustrate what I mean when I speak of a human life as something which
is actively lived.

I do not want to suggest that, to count as living his or her own life, a person
must consciously think about his or her life as a whole in this sort of way. That
would be an absurdly intellectualist understanding of what it is to live one's own
life. Nevertheless my account does presuppose certain minimal abilities, those
which are required if one is to be capable of acting in the sorts of ways which
do, as a matter of fact, give a shape to a person's life. This means being able, at
least to some extent, to reflect on one's past experiences, to feel satisfaction or
regret concerning them and to act in the light of such reflections. Similarly it
means being able to entertain hopes and aspirations for one's life which extend
beyond the immediate future. These conditions remain exceedingly vague, and
much more would need to be said about them. Nevertheless they serve to distinguish, for example, the muddled, the lazy, the unambitious, the bedridden, the
neurotic or the psychotic, all of whom can (though their capacity for effective
action is curtailed) uncontroversially be said to live their own lives, from the
anencephalic or the permanently comatose, who cannot.

More worryingly, these conditions may seem to exclude infants. Here I want
to say that the new-born child, though as yet it lacks a sense of its own past and
future, has embarked on the process of learning, of interacting with its environment and forming relationships with others, and has thus taken its first steps in
making a life. Again the idea of the shape of a life as a whole is important. A
being whose activity remained always at the level of the new-born baby could
not be said to live its own life in the sense I am proposing. The picture changes
when we see those infant activities as the beginning of a process of development, as leading naturally into the more sophisticated activities which I have
taken to be distinctive of 'living a life'. In a sense, then, I am employing a notion
of 'potentiality'—but in a strong sense; I am referring not just to the baby's future capacities, but to what it is already doing, because 'what it is already doing'
is the beginning of a continuing process, and it is in the light of the later stages
in the process that we can see these initial stages also as 'the living of a life'.

This way of thinking about a human life leads us to a proper understanding of
the act of killing. We should think of killing, correspondingly, not just as the destruction of a biological condition but as depriving someone of the opportunity

actively to live his or her own life. Understanding the wrongness of killing in this way then enables us to see why it is ethically fundamental. In particular—and this will be important for later stages of my argument—it enables us to see why respect for human life is more fundamental than the value of freedom or autonomy, and more fundamental than a utilitarian evaluation of consequences. Take first the point about autonomy. It will be apparent that my interpretation of respect for human life brings it close to the Kantian notion of 'respect for persons'. This latter has, in turn, been assimilated by many recent philosophers to the idea of respect for people's autonomy. The problem is then that the capacity for autonomy, in the full sense of the ability to make conscious choices and decisions about one's own life, is a capacity which is not fully realised at birth but develops only slowly and gradually. Nevertheless, as I have indicated, even the new-born baby has embarked on the process of living its life, and as such is entitled to respect. Respect for persons, then, I take to mean respect for the uniqueness of each individual life and for the person who lives it. It will mean also respect for the conscious choices which the person makes in directing and shaping his or her own life, but this is derivative from the more general notion of respect for the life itself.

The same can be said of the relation between respect for life and utilitarian ethics. One of the notorious problems at the heart of utilitarianism is: why should we be concerned to promote the general happiness at all? Why does it matter? Utilitarians sometimes seem to suggest that this question can be answered by saying that happiness, in some abstract sense, 'has value' and therefore the more of it we create, the better. I must confess that I find this notion of happiness as some kind of free-floating 'value' quite unintelligible. Surely the reason why we are concerned to promote happiness is that we are concerned for the people who may be happy or unhappy. Many utilitarians talk as though what is logically prior is the requirement to maximise happiness, and as though we then need to make people happy because we need them to be the vehicles for this maximised happiness. The truth of the matter, however, is surely that happiness matters because people matter, not vice versa. And what I have been claiming about happiness goes also for all values, or at any rate for all human goods. If we value anything at all in people's lives, it must be because we respect those lives as such, and that is why our sense of the wrongness of destroying human lives is morally fundamental.

Can we go further and say that the wrongness of killing is an absolute principle—that is, that the taking of human life can never be justified? I do not think that this follows, but the preceding considerations do serve to establish how difficult it is to defend the idea of sacrificing a human life for the sake of some supposed greater good. I have alluded briefly to the idea of the *uniqueness* of each individual human life. That idea is important, but the connection between 'uniqueness' and 'value' needs clarifying. The point is not that, being qualitatively unique, each individual life has a kind of scarcity value, like a signed artistic masterpiece—as though the lives of identical twins thereby became less valuable because there were two of them. Rather, it is connected with my previous point about human lives as the bearer or the focus of value. Things have value because of the part they play in people's lives. Therefore, if one person's life is destroyed, this cannot be compensated for by the promotion of values in other people's lives. It cannot be compensated for, just because the values promoted for others will not compensate the person who has been killed. We could speak of the one person's loss being cancelled out by the other people's gains only if values could be computed in some impersonal way, apart from the context of separate human lives; but this is just what I am denying. There is no group consciousness, no supra-individual being which can experience both the losses and the gains and accept the former as an acceptable price to pay for the latter.

Nevertheless the fact also remains that people's lives do, inescapably, conflict. There just *are* cases where one person's life can be preserved only by sacrificing someone else's life. Consider the classic example where A is threatening B, and B's life can be saved only by killing A. If one kills A, the loss is, in the sense I have tried to indicate, a total loss. It is the extinction of one individual life, one consciousness for which things have value and within which goods are experienced. No preservation of values within B's life can cancel out that loss. On the other hand, exactly the same is true if one fails to save B's life. That loss, too, is total. A choice therefore has to be made, not because of some spurious computation of an overall impersonal good, but simply because, either way, someone will be killed. The only way to maintain an absolute prohibition against killing in such cases would be to invoke a distinction between 'killing' and 'failing to save someone's life', or to invoke the doctrine of 'double effect'. One could then say that it is always and absolutely wrong intentionally to kill any human being, and that therefore it would be wrong to kill A in this example; though B would then die, this would be describable as a failure to save his life rather than an act of killing him, or as a foreseen but unintended consequence of the refusal to kill A, and so would not be a violation of an absolute prohibition against intentional killing. Since however I do not want to say either of these things or invoke either of these distinctions, I have to say that in the light of such examples the principle of not taking human life cannot be maintained as an absolute principle.

I want to make two other points about the example. Given that a choice has to be made between two lives, how is it to be made? Again, not on utilitarian grounds. It would not be a matter of deciding which of the two is likely to have the happier life and/or to do more good in the world and, on those grounds, opting for the death of the other. (Similarly, to change the example, it would not be right to kill C in order to provide a liver transplant for D and thereby save D's life on the grounds that it could do more good than C's.) The relevant consideration is surely that A is threatening B's life, and that therefore if the choice has to be made it is A's life that must be taken, since it is he who is responsible for the fact that one or the other life must be sacrificed. The second point to be stressed is that all of this would remain true if it were B himself who had to make the choice. If B's life were threatened by A, and B could preserve himself only by killing A, he would be justified in doing so. Again, however, he would not be entitled to do so merely on utilitarian grounds. I stress these two points because between them they spell out the idea of justified killing in self-defence, to which we shall return in due course.

So far I have allowed that the principle of not taking human life cannot be an absolute principle because there are cases where a choice has to be made between two lives. Having made that concession, I think it also has to be conceded that the wrongness of killing could in principle be overridden by other considerations. I have argued that respect for human life is more fundamental than the value of freedom and than utilitarian values, and, as such, carries greater weight. That, however, is not enough to show that, in order to prevent oppression or suffering on a very great scale, it might not be necessary to take human lives. Once again the judgement cannot be a purely utilitarian one, nor can it be simply a matter of calculating alternative levels of freedom and oppression. The wrongness of killing carries an independent weight, and it weighs very heavily in the balance, but we cannot rule out the possibility that it might be outweighed by a sufficiently great prospect of the alleviation of oppression or suffering. Nor should we rule out the possibility that, in cases other than that of 'self-defence' in the narrow sense (as the defence of one's own life), it might be permissible to kill someone who has, through the wickedness of his own action, brought it upon himself. (An example might be killing in self-defence by a rape victim[4].) If anything is a candidate for being an absolute principle, then the principle of not taking human life is; but the trouble with any absolutism is that we simply cannot rule out, in advance, the possibility that considerations of one kind might come into conflict with considerations of any other kind and might, in some cases, be outweighed by them.

In summary, what I want to say about the principle of not taking human life is this. It is not an absolute principle, but it is a fundamental one and it carries very great weight. It can in principle be overridden, but only in special cases, and it cannot be overridden on the basis of a purely utilitarian calculation. This may look like a regrettably untidy and vague position. It is, however, a position of a recognisable kind in ethics. It is, for example, what many philosophers have wanted to say about the concept of basic moral rights. I am myself unenthusiastic about the concept of moral rights, finding it more confusing than helpful. Those who are more attached to the concept might nevertheless like to reformulate my discussion as a defence of a very strong right to life which, although it is not inviolable and although it can perhaps be forfeited in special cases, is more basic than any other moral right and more basic than utilitarian considerations.

To conclude this section I want to comment briefly on the relation between the *principle* of the wrongness of killing and the *attitude* of respect for human life. Pacifism, I have said, is a principled position, and the relevant principle to which it appeals is the principle of not taking human life. That, however, is not just an abstract principle whose validity is self-evident. The principle matters because it articulates the moral implications of the underlying basic response of a human being confronted with another human life. That is why the case for pacifism is made most powerfully not by rational arguments such as I am presenting in this paper, but by the portrayal of that basic response in works of imaginative literature. In war poems and novels and autobiographies one experience stands out: that of the soldier who kills an enemy and then confronts the fact that the person whom he has killed is not just an enemy but another human being like himself[5]. Through the direct personal encounter with the dying man—perhaps talking to him as he dies, perhaps looking through his personal documents—the killer comes face to face with the uniqueness of the individual human life which he has destroyed, with the enormity of what he has done, and with the fact that this is what war requires people to do. And this sense of the inviolability of another human life is what I refer to as the attitude of respect.

It may be said that a rational moral position cannot be founded on the emotional responses which people may or may not happen to feel on this or that occasion. I am not suggesting, however, that our moral commitments are the direct expression of felt emotional responses. The picture which I would offer is a more complex one. Our most fundamental, shared responses are embodied and expressed in the concepts of our shared moral vocabulary. It is in terms of this common vocabulary that we attempt to make sense of our moral world and to formulate the settled moral beliefs and principles with which we assess our actions. Ultimately, however, those beliefs and principles derive their force from the natural human responses on which they rest; and one example of this is the relation between the principle of the wrongness of killing and the underlying attitude of respect.

This, then, is the basis on which I shall build the case for pacifism. Respect for human life establishes a very strong presumption against killing, in war or in any other circumstances. What I now want to do is to show how difficult it is for this presumption to be overridden by the sorts of considerations which are normally thought to justify killing in war. I want to look at two kinds of justification which are standardly offered: first, those which feature in the tradition of 'just war' theory, and secondly, justifications couched in consequentialist terms.

'JUST WAR' AND AGGRESSION

'Just war' theory is a complex body of doctrine, in an evolving tradition. I want to focus on the two points which have become central in recent discussions, and which are the twin pillars of the most recent extended defence of 'just war' theory, Michael Walzer's book *Just and Unjust Wars*. Walzer adopts the traditional distinction between *jus ad bellum* and *jus in bello*; the former provides the account of what justifies resort to war, the latter provides the account of what are just and unjust ways of fighting a war. According to Walzer the central principles of each are, respectively, that going to war is justified when it is the defence of a political community against aggression, and that a war is fought justly only if the immunity of non-combatants is respected.

Consider first, then, the suggestion that war can be justified as a response to aggression. Walzer defends this idea by reference to a morality of *rights*. "Individual rights (to life and liberty)", he says, "underlie the most important judgements that we make about war. . . . States' rights are simply their collective form"[6]. The comparison between individual rights and states' rights is then spelled out as follows.

> Over a long period of time, shared experiences and cooperative activity
> of many different kinds shape a common life. "Contract" is a metaphor
> for a process of association and mutuality, the on-going character of
> which the state claims to protect against external encroachment. The
> protection extends not only to the lives and liberties of individuals, but
> also to their shared life and liberty, the independent community they
> have made, for which individuals are sometimes sacrificed. . . . Given a
> genuine "contract," it makes sense to say that territorial integrity and

political sovereignty can be defended in exactly the same way as individual life and liberty[7].

Walzer's case depends, then, on this analogy between a state's rights to territorial integrity and political sovereignty on the one hand and an individual's right to life and liberty on the other. Certainly there is something in this analogy. One can see a resemblance between the death of an individual and the destruction of the life of a political community when it is invaded and conquered; and between the oppression of an individual and the oppression of a community when its sovereign independence is violated. I want to say, however, that this analogy cannot do what is required of it for the argument. It is at best an imperfect analogy. And it is no more than an analogy; it does not show that the territorial integrity of a community has the *same* fundamental ethical status as the lives of human beings.

First, then, it is an imperfect analogy. Foreign conquest and domination may, in a loose sense, be construed as 'the death of a nation', but it rarely amounts to the complete destruction of a community. The shared way of life usually continues, in an attenuated form. Overall political control may be in the hands of the conqueror, but many other institutions, cultural and economic and religious, are likely to continue, and to embody at least some of the 'shared experiences and cooperative activity' which, as Walzer says, 'shape a common life'. Even in the minority of cases where the conquering power does aim at eliminating entirely the indigenous culture, it may well find it difficult to do so. The communal life may go underground, traditions may be preserved in secret, or in exile. I do not say that this is a happy state of affairs, but it is not the death of a community in the full sense which would make it entirely analogous to the death of an individual human being.

Suppose, however, that the analogy is complete, and that a whole way of life really is wiped out for ever. Then indeed a great wrong has been done, but it is still not a wrong of the same order as the taking of human lives. It may be analogous, but it is *only* analogous, it is not ethically equivalent. Even if their community has completely disintegrated, individuals live on. They may perhaps eventually create a new identity for themselves within the conquering society, or as refugees they may find a place in the life of some other community. Where this is not so, where the individual lives do not continue, we are no longer talking about the crime of aggression, we are talking about genocide, and we have then gone beyond Walzer's analogy altogether.

It may be objected that my position undervalues the importance which shared experiences and a common life have for individuals. Indeed, that objection might be held to carry particular weight since it seems to be supported by other features of my argument. My account of respect for life invoked a richer notion of a human life as more than a mere biological existence; but the relevant capacity to make sense of and give significance to their lives is something which individuals can acquire only through their participation in shared traditions and ways of life. Subtract from a human life everything which derives from the community and one is indeed left with a purely biological existence. Doesn't it follow, then, that the common way of life will be as valuable as life itself, and won't the principle of self-defence then have to embrace the defence of the community as well as the defence of the individual lives?

The starting-point of this objection is one which I would certainly accept. The capacity to live a meaningful life is a capacity derived from one's participation in a human community. However, I also want to reiterate that that capacity, once acquired, can survive the destruction of a particular community. Why is this? First, because there are many kinds and levels of community. A war of defence against aggression is normally thought of as a war in defence of one kind of community, a nation-state, identified by its territorial boundaries. The destruction of the nation-state, however, can leave intact many other overlapping communities, smaller and larger. There remain families and localities and networks of friendship. There remain intellectual, moral, religious, political or artistic movements and traditions, and though some of these may have been defining features of a particular nation, they are not necessarily destroyed when the nation loses its independence.

The second reason is the simple fact that the human capacities derived from participation in a community can be realised only in individual lives. This takes us, I think, to the element of truth in individualism. The philosophical conflict between individualism and communitarianism cannot be resolved by the simple vindication of one side. The truth of communitarianism is that distinctively human activities are made possible by participation in a community. The truth of individualism is the uniqueness and irreplaceability of each individual consciousness. If a community is destroyed, individuals retain the ability to speak the language and engage in the practices which they learned in that community, and they may be able, even under conditions of extreme hardship and persecution, to exercise that ability. When a human being dies, the value of that individual life is gone for good; in the sense I have tried to indicate, the life is irreplaceable and the loss is total. Tragic though the destruction of a community may be, the destruction of individual human lives is of a different order again.

I submit, then, that the analogy between individuals' rights and states' rights fails to establish that the need to resist aggression is a sufficient justification for resort to war. Given that there is a very strong presumption against the whole-sale taking of life which war involves, the analogy is too weak to show that military resistance to aggression has sufficient ethical weight to override the presumption. There remains the possibility that resistance to genocide might be sufficient to justify waging war, and we shall have to return to that.

'JUST WAR' AND NON-COMBATANT IMMUNITY

The second principle of 'just war' theory which I want to consider is the principle of non-combatant immunity. This principle might at first be thought irrelevant to our present concerns, since its purpose is not to identify a possible justification for waging war, but to impose a further moral constraint which must limit the actions even of those who are justified in waging war. Neverthe-less the principle does constitute an important point of disagreement with paci-fism, and we can see this if we remind ourselves that the 'just war' theorist says about the killing of non-combatants what the pacifist says about all killing in war: that it must not be done, even as a means of resistance against aggression. This implies that, for the 'just war' theorist, there is something about the status of combatants which makes it permissible to kill them in resistance to aggres-sion; and that is what the pacifist denies[8].

What are we to make of this suggestion? Why should there be an ethically significant distinction between combatants and non-combatants which makes it permissible to kill the one but not the other? The standard explanation is that the killing of non-combatants is wrong even in a justified war because it would be a case of killing the innocent. What contrast is implied here? If non-combat-ants are innocent, what are combatants? 'Guilty' is the contrast one would ex-pect, but this immediately takes us to the heart of the problem, for it is difficult to find any convincing sense in which the ordinary combatant in war is guilty. In what sense, then, can non-combatants be called 'innocent', and what is the nature of the contrast with combatants?

One of the best discussions of this problem is Jeffrie Murphy's paper 'The Killing of the Innocent', and I shall consider that paper as an example of the attempt to make ethical sense of the 'combatant'/'non-combatant' distinction[9]. Murphy first points out that the 'innocence' of non-combatants can hardly be taken to mean moral innocence in a general sense. Military action against civil-ians, such as the bombing of a city, may kill all sorts of disreputable characters. Nor can 'innocence' mean moral innocence *of the war*. "Consider", says Mur-phy, "the octogenarian civilian in Dresden who is an avid supporter of Hitler's war effort . . . and contrast his case with that of the poor, frightened, pacifist frontline soldier who is only where he is because of duress. . . ."[10]. The former is uncontroversially more responsible for the war than the latter. The relevant distinction, according to Murphy, is this: combatants are "all those of whom it is reasonable to believe that they are engaged in an attempt at your destruction"[11]. This includes not only soldiers but their military and political leaders, and others who contribute directly to the war effort such as, perhaps, workers in munitions factories. Because they are engaged in an attempt to destroy you, it is permissible to kill them. Non-combatants are not directly engaged in such an attempt, and in that sense they are 'innocent'.

The problem now shifts. Such a contrast can indeed be drawn, but why should it carry this ethical significance? If 'innocence' does not mean 'moral innocence', why should it determine who may be killed and who may not? There are two main elements in Murphy's answer. In general terms he appeals to a theory of rights. Normally, he says, to kill someone is to violate his right against interference. However, "when a person uses his freedom to invade the rights of others, he forfeits certain of his own rights and renders interference by others legitimate"[12]. This is why, when combatants are engaged in an attempt to destroy you, they forfeit their right not to be killed by you. However, if Murphy is going to talk about 'forfeiting one's rights', he surely needs to employ precisely those notions of moral guilt and innocence which he has shown to be unavailable in this context. One does not forfeit one's rights merely because one is, objectively, a danger to others. It must be the case that one is *morally guilty* of attempting to destroy others. We are then back with the fact that vast numbers of combatants, even if they are fighting an aggressive war, are not themselves morally responsible for the aggression, or at any rate are much less responsible than their leaders. Therefore they have not forfeited their rights, and killing them cannot be justified by claiming that they have done so.

Murphy also appeals more specifically to the idea of 'self-defence' to fill out his theory of rights. He says: "If one believes (as I do) that the only even remotely plausible justification for war is self-defence, then one must in waging war confine one's hostility to those against whom one is defending oneself. . . ."[13] And those against whom one is defending oneself are, he says, the combatants who are engaged in an attempt to destroy you and have thereby forfeited their rights.

Here we need to recall the problems with the idea of 'resistance to aggression'. A war of 'self-defence' is typically taken to mean a war to defend a nation's territorial integrity against an aggressive invader. I have argued that this justification for war is unconvincing. Murphy has his own doubts about it. He says:

> . . . with respect to nations, the whole idea of self-defence is strongly in need of analysis. What, for example, is it for a state to die or be threatened with death?

> . . . I am sceptical that the "self" to be legitimately defended must always be the nation or state. It is at least worth considering the possibility that the only moral problems arising in war are the oldest and most common and most important—namely, are human beings being hurt and killed, who are they, and why are they?[14]

And when he goes on to link the idea of self-defence with that of rights, he takes as his example the case of individual self-defence[15].

There are, of course, plenty of situations in war where the question of individual self-defence does arise. The combatant who is actually engaged in fighting is likely to find himself in situations where, unless he kills the person who is about to fire on him, he will himself be killed. But if that is the only killing which the 'combatant'/'non-combatant' distinction can justify, it is a great deal less than the theory is intended to justify. The theory is supposed to justify combatants killing enemy combatants in order to win; in fact it will only justify killing combatants in order to survive.

At this point we are, I think, forced back to the conclusion that the most that 'just war' theory can justify is a war against genocide. I suggested earlier that the first component of the theory, the principle of resistance to aggression, is plausible only if it goes beyond a mere analogy between 'territorial integrity' and 'the right to life'; it will justify resistance to aggression only if the aggression is *literally* an attempt to destroy the lives of the members of the community. Similarly the 'combatant'/'non-combatant' distinction, if it amounts to no more than a principle of self-defence, will justify a community only in fighting to defend the lives of its members. And note that even a principle of self-defence will still have to employ notions of moral responsibility, of moral guilt and innocence. I may not kill just anyone whose death would help to preserve my life or the life of another, but only someone who is morally responsible for the threat to that life. (Recall my earlier example of killing someone because you need a liver transplant.) So even if a community is justified in killing to defend itself against genocide, its resistance must be directed against those who are responsible for the threat of genocide. And if, as is likely, that means not the enemy combatants but their political leaders, then what will be justified will be something rather different from war—a campaign of assassination, perhaps.

Consequentialist Justifications

I turn now from 'just war' theory to consequentialist considerations, that is, to the suggestion that wars can be justified by what they achieve. As I have said, something more is needed here than simply a utilitarian calculation. The fact that a war involves the taking of vast numbers of human lives must itself carry a very great independent weight, quite apart from the obvious disutilities of war such as the human grief and suffering, the massive destruction of resources and the dislocation of civil life. A consequentialist justification of war would have to show, in any particular case, that all of this can be outweighed by the good that waging war can achieve, or rather, by the even greater evils which it can prevent or eliminate. Can this be done?

There are strong reasons for doubting it. We might first look at the historical record. What is striking here is the way in which each war, in its outcome, sows the seeds of a future military conflict. Take the case of the Second World War. If ever any war has been justified by its aims and its results, then surely this war was. Of course it achieved its results at an immense cost, involving millions of deaths and appalling suffering, but by such means it brought about the overthrow of Nazism. At this point, however, we should remember that the purpose for which Britain declared war on Germany was not the defeat of Nazism as a political system, and that most of those who fought against it did so in complete ignorance of the concentration camps and the other distinctive features of Nazism. The occasion for Britain's entry into the war was the commitment to the independence of Poland, and it is at least debatable whether in 1945 this had been fully achieved. This should remind us that what the war did produce, as its direct consequence, was the division of Europe into two military power blocs, posing the danger of an even more destructive war, a nuclear war which would destroy European civilisation and perhaps even eliminate the human race altogether. If we then consider the possibility that Nazism could have been overthrown in other ways, without war, as Spanish fascism was eventually overcome, we may seriously wonder whether the achievements of the Second World War were as positive as they are usually thought to have been. And just as our present perilous situation is the outcome of that war, so also the ground for that war was laid by the Treaty of Versailles at the end of the First World War; the First World War was in turn a product, in part, of the settlement at the end of the Franco-Prussian War of 1870–1; and so on.

That then is an example of the historical record, and of the way in which the outcome of one war becomes the cause for the next war. Nor should this surprise us. The settlement reached at the end of any war is, almost by definition, imposed by the military force of the victors, and as such it is bound to breed resentment and a smouldering desire for revenge. Pacifists would say that this illustrates a basic truth of human psychology: that violence breeds violence. It may be somewhat hazardous to infer from the facts of interpersonal behaviour to a conclusion about the political behaviour of states, but the inference does seem to be backed by historical experience. Of course causal claims about historical events are themselves notoriously conjectural. We can but guess at what might have happened if Nazism had not been resisted by military means, and at whether it could eventually have been overthrown without recourse to war. But this scepticism about predicting the consequences of waging or not waging war can itself be turned to account by pacifism. It is very difficult to tell whether fighting a war will achieve anything positive, and what its long-term consequences will be. We do know however, with very much greater certainty, that it will involve immense suffering and great loss of life. Therefore, weighing the certainty of suffering and death against the mere possibility of long-term good consequences, we may well conclude that war is never worth the risk.

Now scepticism about the positive achievements of war does not by itself entail pacifism. Nor does scepticism about 'just war' theory. Nor does respect for human life. What I have been claiming is that respect for human life sets up a very strong presumption against the justifiability of killing in war. Doubts about 'just war' theory, and doubts about the positive achievements of war, make it very difficult to see how that presumption could be overridden. That is the case for pacifism, and it is a very strong case.

HAVING NO CHOICE

'And yet . . .' Those words of hesitation are inevitable, I think. Though I recognise the strength of the case, I still hesitate to accept it, and many people feel the same. Why is this? How is it that, though pacifism seems to be ethically compelling, doubts arise as soon as we start to think about actually applying it?

Those doubts are typically articulated by saying that, however ethically appalling it may be to contemplate fighting a war, there are situations in which people have no choice. I suggest that if we can pin down the sense of the statement 'We have no choice', we may be in a position to understand why pacifism remains difficult to accept.

Now of course it will never be the case literally and without qualification that one has no choice. One can always refuse to fight. But when people say that one sometimes has no choice, what they mean, I think, is that by refusing to fight, say, against aggression, or indeed against internal oppression, one is acquiescing in a very great evil, and by acquiescing in it one is tacitly endorsing it. Morally speaking, faced with that evil, we have no choice but to resist it, and if the only way to resist it is to fight, then we have no choice but to fight.

Now this reading of the situation might be challenged. Suppose that this country had been overrun by a Nazi invasion in 1940, and suppose that one had refused to fight against it. One might say: "I have not acquiesced in Nazism. I refuse to engage in military resistance to it, because that too would be ethically indefensible, but that does not mean that I accept Nazism. I reject it whole-heartedly, I will give no support to it, and if the Nazis order me to cooperate with their crimes I shall disobey even though I may be shot." One might say all this, and one might act accordingly.

Nevertheless, even if many people had thought and acted thus, it could re-main true that, in an important sense, Nazism had not been resisted. This is be-cause resistance to a social phenomenon such as aggression or oppression must, if it is really to count as resistance, take a socially identifiable form. It is here that the communitarian perspective may properly come into play. 'Aggression' or 'oppression' are constituted as such by the overall social meaning of innu-merable individual human actions. Therefore one cannot resist them simply in virtue of one's own interpretation of one's own action—not because one will not be effective but because action does not count as 'resistance' unless it is so-cially understood as such. What forms of resistance are available will therefore depend upon the institutions and traditions of the community; and if the only recognised and organisable form of resistance is military resistance, then not fighting will mean not resisting. This, I think, is the significant sense in which people could say 'We have no choice but to fight'.

What also follows, however, is that what forms of resistance are socially available is itself something that can be changed, over time, by social action. In particular, institutional procedures for settling disputes without recourse to war, and traditions of non-violent resistance to invasion and oppression, can be gradually built up. And if they *can* be, they *should* be; for the stronger such tradi-tions become, the less likely it is that people will find themselves in a situation where they have to say 'We have no choice but to fight'.

At the theoretical level, I find insoluble the dilemma posed by pacifism: that fighting in war is ethically indefensible, but is also sometimes the only thing that people can do. The interplay between individualist and communitarian perspectives, which has been a thread running through this paper, may perhaps help us to explain why the dilemma seems irresolvable. I have said that the truth of individualism is the irreplaceability of individual human lives. When we think in those terms the overwhelming fact of war is the loss of vast numbers of individual lives, and it is difficult to see how anything else can have a countervailing moral weight. But when we think in communitarian terms, we see war as a conflict between different social institutions or movements, and if the only socially recognised form of resistance to evil social practices is military resistance, then war may seem morally inescapable. The best conclusion I can offer, therefore, is this possibility of a solution at the practical level: that by building up a tradition of non-violent resistance to aggression and oppression, we can bring it about that people do have a choice and are not faced with an impossible ethical dilemma. It might then be possible to be unhesitatingly a pacifist[16].

NOTES

1. A notable exception is JENNY TEICHMAN (1986) *Pacifism and the Just War* (Oxford, Blackwell) and her earlier article 'Pacifism' in *Philosophical Investigations*, 5 (1982).

2. MARTIN CEADEL (1987) *Thinking About Peace and War* (Oxford, Oxford University Press). Ceadel's typology of positions in the war-and-peace debate follows the sequence from 'militarism', through 'crusading', 'defencism', and 'pacific-ism', to 'pacifism'. He derives from A. J. P. Taylor the distinction between 'pacific-ism' and 'pacifism'.

3. JAMES RACHELS (1986) *The End of Life* (Oxford, Oxford University Press), especially Chapter 2.

4. Note, however, that such cases are controversial and that, even if it is accepted that they involve a right to kill, it is severely limited. Consider the recent legal case where a woman was acquitted of murder after killing a man who had raped her. "Judge Hazan warned that his ruling was not to be regarded in any way as a charter for victims of serious crimes—even rape—to kill their attackers. 'Revenge killings are unlawful and, depending on the circumstances, amount to murder or manslaughter,' he said. 'It is only killing in lawful self-defence that is justified'." (*The Guardian*, 1.10.87.) Note also that the woman had told the police: "I didn't mean to kill him, I only meant to get him off me—I was so frightened".

5. Classic examples are Wilfred Owen's poem 'Strange Meeting', and chapter IX of Erich Maria Remarque's *All Quiet on the Western Front*.

6. MICHAEL WALZER (1980) *Just and Unjust Wars* (London, Penguin), p. 54.

7. Ibid.

8. This conflict between pacifism and 'just war' theory is exemplified in G. E. M. ANSCOMBE (1961) War and murder. Anscombe suggests that "pacifism teaches people to make no distinction between the shedding of innocent blood and the shedding of any human blood. And in this way pacifism has corrupted enormous numbers of people who will not act according to its tenets". The paper first appeared in: WALTER STEIN (Ed.) *Nuclear Weapons: a Catholic response* (London, Merlin Press), and has been reprinted in various places including Anscombe's (1981) *Collected Papers*, III (Oxford, Blackwell).

9. JEFFRIE MURPHY (1973) The killing of the innocent, *The Monist*, 57.

10. Ibid., p. 531.

11. Ibid., p. 536.

12. Ibid., pp. 546–7. Cf. Walzer's linking of non-combatant immunity and rights, op. cit., p. 135.

13. Ibid., p. 538.

14. Ibid., p. 539.

15. Ibid., p. 547.

16. Many thanks for helpful comments from Tony Skillen, Karen Jones, Anne Seller, the *Journal of Applied Philosophy* referee, and philosophers at the University of Bristol and the Open University.

***Richard Norman** is emeritus professor of moral philosophy at the University of Kent. He is the author of *The Moral Philosophers*; *Ethics, Killing and War*; and *On Humanism*.

NORMAN, RICHARD. (1988), The Case for Pacifism. Journal of Applied Philosophy 5, 197–210. doi: 10.111/j.1468-5930.1988.tb00242.x.

Morality and Foreign Policy

*by George F. Kennan**

In a small volume of lectures published nearly thirty-five years ago,[1] I had the temerity to suggest that the American statesmen of the turn of the twentieth century were unduly legalistic and moralistic in their judgment of the actions of other governments. This seemed to be an approach that carried them away from the sterner requirements of political realism and caused their statements and actions, however impressive to the domestic political audience, to lose effectiveness in the international arena.

These observations were doubtless brought forward too cryptically and thus invited a wide variety of interpretations, not excluding the thesis that I had advocated an amoral, or even immoral, foreign policy for this country. There have since been demands, particularly from the younger generation, that I should make clearer my views on the relationship of moral considerations to American foreign policy. The challenge is a fair one and deserves a response.

II

Certain distinctions should be made before one wanders farther into this thicket of problems.

First of all, the conduct of diplomacy is the responsibility of governments. For purely practical reasons, this is unavoidable and inalterable. This responsibility is not diminished by the fact that government, in formulating foreign policy, may choose to be influenced by private opinion. What we are talking about, therefore, when we attempt to relate moral considerations to foreign policy, is the behavior of governments, not of individuals or entire peoples.

Second, let us recognize that the functions, commitments and moral obligations of governments are not the same as those of the individual. Government is an agent, not a principal. Its primary obligation is to the *interests* of the national society it represents, not to the moral impulses that individual elements of that society may experience. No more than the attorney vis-à-vis the client, nor the doctor vis-à-vis the patient, can government attempt to insert itself into the consciences of those whose interests it represents.

Let me explain. The interests of the national society for which government has to concern itself are basically those of its military security, the integrity of its political life and the well-being of its people. These needs have no moral quality. They arise from the very existence of the national state in question and from the status of national sovereignty it enjoys. They are the unavoidable necessities of a national existence and therefore not subject to classification as either "good" or "bad." They may be questioned from a detached philosophic point of view. But the government of the sovereign state cannot make such judgments. When it accepts the responsibilities of governing, implicit in that acceptance is the assumption that it is right that the state should be sovereign, that the integrity of its political life should be assured, that its people should enjoy the blessings of military security, material prosperity and a reasonable opportunity for, as the Declaration of Independence put it, the pursuit of happiness. For these assumptions the government needs no moral justification, nor need it accept any moral reproach for acting on the basis of them.

This assertion assumes, however, that the concept of national security taken as the basis for governmental concern is one reasonably, not extravagantly, conceived. In an age of nuclear striking power, national security can never be more than relative; and to the extent that it can be assured at all, it must find its sanction in the intentions of rival powers as well as in their capabilities. A concept of national security that ignores this reality and, above all, one that fails to concede the same legitimacy to the security needs of others that it claims for its own, lays itself open to the same moral reproach from which, in normal circumstances, it would be immune.

Whoever looks thoughtfully at the present situation of the United States in particular will have to agree that to assure these blessings to the American people is a task of such dimensions that the government attempting to meet it successfully will have very little, if any, energy and attention left to devote to other undertakings, including those suggested by the moral impulses of these or those of its citizens.

Finally, let us note that there are no internationally accepted standards of morality to which the U.S. government could appeal if it wished to act in the name of moral principles. It is true that there are certain words and phrases sufficiently high-sounding the world over so that most governments, when asked to declare themselves for or against, will cheerfully subscribe to them, considering that such is their vagueness that the mere act of subscribing to them carries with it no danger of having one's freedom of action significantly impaired. To this category of pronouncements belong such documents as the Kellogg-Briand Pact, the Atlantic Charter, the Yalta Declaration on Liberated Europe, and the prologues of innumerable other international agreements.

Ever since Secretary of State John Hay staged a political coup in 1899 by summoning the supposedly wicked European powers to sign up to the lofty principles of his Open Door notes (principles which neither they nor we had any awkward intention of observing), American statesmen have had a fondness for hurling just such semantic challenges at their foreign counterparts, thereby placing themselves in a graceful posture before domestic American opinion and reaping whatever political fruits are to be derived from the somewhat grudging and embarrassed responses these challenges evoke.

To say these things, I know, is to invite the question: how about the Helsinki accords of 1975? These, of course, were numerous and varied. There is no disposition here to question the value of many of them as refinements of the norms of international intercourse. But there were some, particularly those related to human rights, which it is hard to relegate to any category other than that of the high-minded but innocuous professions just referred to. These accords were declaratory in nature, not contractual. The very general terms in which they were drawn up, involving the use of words and phrases that had different meanings for different people, deprived them of the character of specific obligations to which signatory governments could usefully be held. The Western statesmen who pressed for Soviet adherence to these pronouncements must have been aware that some of them could not be implemented on the Soviet side, within the meanings we would normally attach to their workings, without fundamental changes in the Soviet system of power—changes we had no reason to expect would, or could, be introduced by the men then in power. Whether it is morally commendable to induce others to sign up to declarations, however high-minded in resonance, which one knows will not and cannot be implemented, is a reasonable question. The Western negotiators, in any case, had no reason to plead naïveté as their excuse for doing so.

When we talk about the application of moral standards to foreign policy, therefore, we are not talking about compliance with some clear and generally accepted international code of behavior. If the policies and actions of the U.S. government are to be made to conform to moral standards, those standards are going to have to be America's own, founded on traditional American principles of justice and propriety. When others fail to conform to those principles, and when their failure to conform has an adverse effect on American *interests*, as distinct from political tastes, we have every right to complain and, if necessary, to take retaliatory action. What we cannot do is to assume that our moral standards are theirs as well, and to appeal to those standards as the source of our grievances.

III

So much for basic principles. Let us now consider some categories of action that the U.S. government is frequently asked to take, and sometimes does take, in the name of moral principle.

These actions fall into two broad general categories: those that relate to the behavior of other governments that we find morally unacceptable, and those that relate to the behavior of our own government. Let us take them in that order.

There have been many instances, particularly in recent years, when the U.S. government has taken umbrage at the behavior of other governments on grounds that at least implied moral criteria for judgment, and in some of these instances the verbal protests have been reinforced by more tangible means of pressure. These various interventions have marched, so to speak, under a number of banners: democracy, human rights, majority rule, fidelity to treaties, fidelity to the U.N. Charter, and so on. Their targets have sometimes been the external policies and actions of the offending states, more often the internal practices. The interventions have served, in the eyes of their American inspirers, as demonstrations not only of the moral deficiencies of others but of the positive morality of ourselves; for it was seen as our moral duty to detect these lapses on the part of others, to denounce them before the world, and to assure—as far as we could with measures short of military action—that they were corrected.

Those who have inspired or initiated efforts of this nature would certainly have claimed to be acting in the name of moral principle, and in many instances they would no doubt have been sincere in doing so. But whether the results of this inspiration, like those of so many other good intentions, would justify this claim is questionable from a number of standpoints.

Let us take first those of our interventions that relate to internal practices of the offending governments. Let us reflect for a moment on how these interventions appear in the eyes of the governments in question and of many outsiders.

The situations that arouse our discontent are ones existing, as a rule, far from our own shores. Few of us can profess to be perfect judges of their rights and their wrongs. These are, for the governments in question, matters of internal affairs. It is customary for governments to resent interference by outside powers in affairs of this nature, and if our diplomatic history is any indication, we ourselves are not above resenting and resisting it when we find ourselves its object.

Interventions of this nature can be formally defensible only if the practices against which they are directed are seriously injurious to our interests, rather than just our sensibilities. There will, of course, be those readers who will argue that the encouragement and promotion of democracy elsewhere is always in the interests of the security, political integrity and prosperity of the United States. If this can be demonstrated in a given instance, well and good. But it is not invariably the case. Democracy is a loose term. Many varieties of folly and injustice contrive to masquerade under this designation. The mere fact that a country acquires the trappings of self-government does not automatically mean that the interests of the United States are thereby furthered. There are forms of plebiscitary "democracy" that may well prove less favorable to American interests than a wise and benevolent authoritarianism. There can be tyrannies of a majority as well as tyrannies of a minority, with the one hardly less odious than the other. Hitler came into power (albeit under highly unusual circumstances) with an electoral mandate, and there is scarcely a dictatorship of this age that would not claim the legitimacy of mass support.

There are parts of the world where the main requirement of American security is not an unnatural imitation of the American model but sheer stability, and this last is not always assured by a government of what appears to be popular acclaim. In approaching this question, Americans must overcome their tendency toward generalization and learn to examine each case on its own merits. The best measure of these merits is not the attractiveness of certain general semantic symbols but the effect of the given situation on the tangible and demonstrable interests of the United States.

Furthermore, while we are quick to allege that this or that practice in a foreign country is bad and deserves correction, seldom if ever do we seem to occupy ourselves seriously or realistically with the conceivable alternatives. It seems seldom to occur to us that even if a given situation is bad, the alternatives to it might be worse—even though history provides plenty of examples of just this phenomenon. In the eyes of many Americans it is enough for us to indicate the changes that ought, as we see it, to be made. We assume, of course, that the consequences will be benign and happy ones. But this is not always assured. It is, in any case, not we who are going to have to live with those consequences: it is the offending government and its people. We are demanding, in effect, a species of veto power over those of their practices that we dislike, while denying responsibility for whatever may flow from the acceptance of our demands.

Finally, we might note that our government, in raising such demands, is frequently responding not to its own moral impulses or to any wide general movements of American opinion but rather to pressures generated by politically influential minority elements among us that have some special interest—

ethnic, racial, religious, ideological or several of these together—in the foreign situation in question. Sometimes it is the sympathies of these minorities that are most prominently aroused, sometimes their antipathies. But in view of this diversity of motive, the U.S. government, in responding to such pressures and making itself their spokesman, seldom acts consistently. Practices or policies that arouse our official displeasure in one country are cheerfully condoned or ignored in another. What is bad in the behavior of our opponents is good, or at least acceptable, in the case of our friends. What is unobjectionable to us at one period of our history is seen as offensive in another.

This is unfortunate, for a lack of consistency implies a lack of principle in the eyes of much of the world; whereas morality, if not principled, is not really morality. Foreigners, observing these anomalies, may be forgiven for suspecting that what passes as the product of moral inspiration in the rhetoric of our government is more likely to be a fair reflection of the mosaic of residual ethnic loyalties and passions that make themselves felt in the rough and tumble of our political life.

Similar things could be said when it is not the internal practices of the offending government but its actions on the international scene that are at issue. There is, here, the same reluctance to occupy one's self with the conceivable alternatives to the procedures one complains about or with the consequences likely to flow from the acceptance of one's demands. And there is frequently the same lack of consistency in the reaction. The Soviet action in Afghanistan, for example, is condemned, resented and responded to by sanctions. One recalls little of such reaction in the case of the somewhat similar, and apparently no less drastic, action taken by China in Tibet some years ago. The question inevitably arises: is it principle that determines our reaction? Or are there other motives?

Where measures taken by foreign governments affect adversely American interests rather than just American moral sensibilities, protests and retaliation are obviously in order; but then they should be carried forward frankly for what they are, and not allowed to masquerade under the mantle of moral principle.

There will be a tendency, I know, on the part of some readers to see in these observations an apology for the various situations, both domestic and international, against which we have protested and acted in the past. They are not meant to have any such connotations. These words are being written—for whatever this is worth—by one who regards the action in Afghanistan as a grievous and reprehensible mistake of Soviet policy, a mistake that could and should certainly have been avoided. Certain of the procedures of the South African police have been no less odious to me than to many others.

What is being said here does not relate to the reactions of individual Americans, of private organizations in this country, or of the media, to the situations in question. All these may think and say what they like. It relates to the reactions of the U.S. government, as a government among governments, and to the motivation cited for those reactions. Democracy, as Americans understand it, is not necessarily the future of all mankind, nor is it the duty of the U.S. government to assure that it becomes that. Despite frequent assertions to the contrary, not everyone in this world is responsible, after all, for the actions of everyone else, everywhere. Without the power to compel change, there is no responsibility for its absence. In the case of governments it is important for purely practical reasons that the lines of responsibility be kept straight, and that there be, in particular, a clear association of the power to act with the consequences of action or inaction.

IV

If, then, the criticism and reproof of perceived moral lapses in the conduct of others are at best a dubious way of expressing our moral commitment, how about our own policies and actions? Here, at least, the connection between power and responsibility—between the sowing and the reaping—is integral. Can it be true that here, too, there is no room for the application of moral principle and that all must be left to the workings of expediency, national egoism and cynicism?

The answer, of course, is no, but the possibilities that exist are only too often ones that run against the grain of powerful tendencies and reflexes in our political establishment.

In a less than perfect world, where the ideal so obviously lies beyond human reach, it is natural that the avoidance of the worst should often be a more practical undertaking than the achievement of the best, and that some of the strongest imperatives of moral conduct should be ones of a negative rather than a positive nature. The strictures of the Ten Commandments are perhaps the best illustration of this state of affairs. This being the case, it is not surprising that some of the most significant possibilities for the observance of moral considerations in American foreign policy relate to the avoidance of actions that have a negative moral significance, rather than to those from which positive results are to be expected.

Many of these possibilities lie in the intuitive qualities of diplomacy—such things as the methodology, manners, style, restraint and elevation of diplomatic discourse—and they can be illustrated only on the basis of a multitude of minor practical examples, for which this article is not the place. There are, however, two negative considerations that deserve mention here.

The first of these relates to the avoidance of what might be called the histrionics of moralism at the expense of its substance. By that is meant the projection of attitudes, poses and rhetoric that cause us to appear noble and altruistic in the mirror of our own vanity but lack substance when related to the realities of international life. It is a sad feature of the human predicament, in personal as in public life, that whenever one has the agreeable sensation of being impressively moral, one probably is not. What one does without self-consciousness or self-admiration, as a matter of duty or common decency, is apt to be closer to the real thing.

The second of these negative considerations pertains to something commonly called secret operations—a branch of governmental activity closely connected with, but not to be confused with, secret intelligence.

Earlier in this century the great secular despotisms headed by Hitler and Stalin introduced into the pattern of their interaction with other governments' clandestine methods of operation that can only be described as ones of unbridled cynicism, audacity and brutality. These were expressed not only by a total lack of scruple on their own part but also by a boundless contempt for the countries against which these efforts were directed (and, one feels, a certain contempt for themselves as well). This was in essence not new, of course; the relations among the nation-states of earlier centuries abounded in examples of clandestine iniquities of every conceivable variety. But these were usually moderated in practice by a greater underlying sense of humanity and a greater respect for at least the outward decencies of national power. Seldom was their intent so cynically destructive, and never was their scale remotely so great, as some of the efforts we have witnessed in this century.

In recent years these undertakings have been supplemented, in their effects on the Western public, by a wholly different phenomenon arising in a wholly different quarter: namely, the unrestrained personal terrorism that has been employed by certain governments or political movements on the fringes of Europe as well as by radical-criminal elements within Western society itself. These phenomena have represented, at different times, serious challenges to the security of nearly all Western countries. It is not surprising, therefore, that among the reactions evoked has been a demand that fire should be fought with fire, that the countries threatened by efforts of this nature should respond with similar efforts.

No one will deny that resistance to these attacks requires secret intelligence of a superior quality and a severe ruthlessness of punishment wherever they fall afoul of the judicial systems of the countries against which they are directed. It is not intended here to comment in any way on the means by which they might or should be opposed by countries other than the United States. Nor is it intended to suggest that any of these activities that carry into this country should not be met by anything less than the full rigor of the law. On the contrary, one could wish the laws were even more rigorous in this respect. But when it comes to governmental operations—or disguised operations—beyond our borders, we Americans have a problem.

In the years immediately following the Second World War the practices of the Stalin regime in this respect were so far-reaching, and presented so great an apparent danger to a Western Europe still weakened by the vicissitudes of war, that our government felt itself justified in setting up facilities for clandestine defensive operations of its own; all available evidence suggests that it has since conducted a number of activities under this heading. As one of those who, at the time, favored the decision to set up such facilities, I regret today, in light of the experience of the intervening years, that the decision was taken. Operations of this nature are not in character for this country. They do not accord with its traditions or with its established procedures of government. The effort to conduct them involves dilemmas and situations of moral ambiguity in which the American statesman is deprived of principled guidance and loses a sense of what is fitting and what is not. Excessive secrecy, duplicity and clandestine skullduggery are simply not our dish—not only because we are incapable of keeping a secret anyway (our commercial media of communication see to that) but, more importantly, because such operations conflict with our own traditional standards and compromise our diplomacy in other areas.

One must not be dogmatic about such matters, of course. Foreign policy is too intricate a topic to suffer any total taboos. There may be rare moments when a secret operation appears indispensable. A striking example of this was the action of the United States in apprehending the kidnappers of the *Achille Lauro*. But such operations should not be allowed to become a regular and routine feature of the governmental process, cast in the concrete of unquestioned habit and institutionalized bureaucracy. It is there that the dangers lie.

One may say that to deny ourselves this species of capability is to accept a serious limitation on our ability to contend with forces now directed against us. Perhaps; but if so, it is a limitation with which we shall have to live. The success of our diplomacy has always depended, and will continue to depend, in its inherent honesty and openness of purpose and on the forthrightness with which it is carried out. Deprive us of that and we are deprived of our strongest armor and our most effective weapon. If this is a limitation, it is one that reflects no discredit on us. We may accept it in good conscience, for in national as in personal affairs the acceptance of one's limitations is surely one of the first marks of a true morality.

V

So much, then, for the negative imperatives. When we turn to the positive ones there are, again, two that stand out.

The first of them is closely connected with what has just been observed about the acceptance of one's limitations. It relates to the duty of bringing one's commitments and undertakings into a reasonable relationship with one's real possibilities for acting upon the international environment. This is not by any means just a question of military strength, and particularly not of the purely destructive and ultimately self-destructive sort of strength to be found in the nuclear weapon. It is not entirely, or even mainly, a question of foreign policy. It is a duty that requires the shaping of one's society in such a manner that one has maximum control over one's own resources and maximum ability to employ them effectively when they are needed for the advancement of the national interest and the interests of world peace.

A country that has a budgetary deficit and an adverse trade balance both so fantastically high that it is rapidly changing from a major creditor to a major debtor on the world's exchanges, a country whose own enormous internal indebtedness has been permitted to double in less than six years, a country that has permitted its military expenditures to grow so badly out of relationship to the other needs of its economy and so extensively out of reach of political control that the annual spending of hundreds of billions of dollars on "defense" has developed into a national addiction—a country that, in short, has allowed its financial and material affairs to drift into such disorder, is so obviously living beyond its means, and confesses itself unable to live otherwise—is simply not in a position to make the most effective use of its own resources on the international scene, because they are so largely out of its control.

This situation must be understood in relationship to the exorbitant dreams and aspirations of world influence, if not world hegemony—the feeling that we must have the solution to everyone's problems and a finger in every pie—that continue to figure in the assumptions underlying so many American reactions in matters of foreign policy. It must also be understood that in world affairs, as in personal life, example exerts a greater power than precept. A first step along the path of morality would be the frank recognition of the immense gap between what we dream of doing and what we really have to offer, and a resolve, conceived in all humility, to take ourselves under control and to establish a better relationship between our undertakings and our real capabilities.

The second major positive imperative is one that also involves the husbanding and effective use of resources, but it is essentially one of purpose and policy.

Except perhaps in some sectors of American government and opinion, there are few thoughtful people who would not agree that our world is at present faced with two unprecedented and supreme dangers. One is the danger not just of nuclear war but of any major war at all among great industrial powers—an exercise which modern technology has now made suicidal all around. The other is the devastating effect of modern industrialization and overpopulation on the world's natural environment. The one threatens the destruction of civilization through the recklessness and selfishness of its military rivalries, the other through the massive abuse of its natural habitat. Both are relatively new problems, for the solution of which past experience affords little guidance. Both are urgent. The problems of political misgovernment, to which so much of our thinking about moral values has recently related, is as old as the human species itself. It is a problem that will not be solved in our time, and need not be. But the environmental and nuclear crises will brook no delay.

The need for giving priority to the averting of these two overriding dangers has a purely rational basis—a basis in national interest—quite aside from morality. For short of a nuclear war, the worst that our Soviet rivals could do to us, even in our wildest worst-case imaginings, would be a far smaller tragedy than that which would assuredly confront us (and if not us, then our children) if we failed to face up to these two apocalyptic dangers in good time. But is there not also a moral component to this necessity?

Of all the multitudinous celestial bodies of which we have knowledge, our own earth seems to be the only one even remotely so richly endowed with the resources that make possible human life—not only make it possible but surround it with so much natural beauty and healthfulness and magnificence. And to the degree that man has distanced himself from the other animals in such things as self-knowledge, historical awareness and the capacity for creating great beauty (along, alas, with great ugliness), we have to recognize a further mystery, similar to that of the unique endowment of the planet—a mystery that seems to surpass the possibilities of the purely accidental. Is there not, whatever the nature of one's particular God, an element of sacrilege involved in the placing of all this at stake just for the sake of the comforts, the fears and the national rivalries of a single generation? Is there not a moral obligation to recognize in this very uniqueness of the habitat and nature of man the greatest of our moral responsibilities, and to make of ourselves, in our national personification, its guardians and protectors rather than its destroyers?

This, it may be objected, is a religious question, not a moral-political one. True enough, if one will. But the objection invites the further question as to whether there is any such thing as morality that does not rest, consciously or otherwise, on some foundation of religious faith, for the renunciation of self-interest, which is what all morality implies, can never be rationalized by purely secular and materialistic considerations.

VI

The above are only a few random reflections on the great question to which this paper is addressed. But they would seem to suggest, in their entirety, the outlines of an American foreign policy to which moral standards could be more suitably and naturally applied than to that policy which we are conducting to-day. This would be a policy founded on recognition of the national interest, reasonably conceived, as the legitimate motivation for a large portion of the nation's behavior, and prepared to pursue that interest without either moral pretension or apology. It would be a policy that would seek the possibilities for service to morality primarily in our own behavior, not in our judgment of others. It would restrict our undertakings to the limits established by our own traditions and resources. It would see virtue in our minding our own business wherever there is not some overwhelming reason for minding the business of others. Priority would be given, here, not to the reforming of others but to the averting of the two apocalyptic catastrophes that now hover over the horizons of mankind.

But at the heart of this policy would lie the effort to distinguish at all times between the true substance and the mere appearance of moral behavior. In an age when a number of influences, including the limitations of the electronic media, the widespread substitution of pictorial representation for verbal communication, and the ubiquitous devices of "public relations" and electoral politics, all tend to exalt the image over the essential reality to which that image is taken to relate—in such an age there is a real danger that we may lose altogether our ability to distinguish between the real and the unreal, and, in doing so, lose both the credibility of true moral behavior and the great force such behavior is, admittedly, capable of exerting. To do this would be foolish, unnecessary and self-defeating. There may have been times when the United States could afford such frivolity. This present age, unfortunately, is not one of them.

NOTE

1. *American Diplomacy 1900–1950*. Chicago: University of Chicago Press, 1951.

*George F. Kennan was a diplomat and historian, who helped shape foreign policy toward the Soviet Union. At the time of this writing, he was professor emeritus at the Institute for Advanced Study, Princeton, NJ.

Kennan, George. "Morality and Foreign Policy." *Foreign Affairs*, Winter 1985/86, 205–212.

The Triumph of Just War Theory—And the Dangers of Success

*by Michael Walzer**

1. Some political theories die and go to heaven; some, I hope, die and go to hell. But some have a long life in this world, a history most often of service to the powers-that-be, but also, sometimes, an oppositionist history. The theory of just war began in the service of the powers. At least that is how I interpret Augustine's achievement: he replaced the radical refusal of Christian pacifists with the active ministry of the Christian soldier. Now pious Christians could fight on behalf of the worldly city, for the sake of imperial peace (in this case, literally, *pax Romana*); but they had to fight justly, only for the sake of peace, and always, Augustine insisted, with a downcast demeanor, without anger or lust.[1] Seen from the perspective of primitive Christianity, this account of just war was simply an excuse, a way of making war morally and religiously possible. And that was indeed the function of the theory. But its defenders would have said, and I am inclined to agree, that it made war possible in a world where war was, sometimes, necessary.

From the beginning, the theory had a critical edge: soldiers (or, at least, their officers) were supposed to refuse to fight in wars of conquest and to oppose or abstain from the standard military practices of rape and pillage after the battle was won. But just war was a worldly theory, in every sense of that term, and it continued to serve worldly interests against Christian radicalism. It is important to note, though, that Christian radicalism had more than one version: it could be expressed in a pacifist rejection of war, but it could also be expressed in war itself, in the religiously driven crusade. Augustine opposed the first of these; the medieval scholastics, following in Aquinas's footsteps, set themselves against the second. The classic statement is Vitoria's: "Difference of religion cannot be a cause of just war." For centuries, from the time of the Crusades to the religious wars of the Reformation years, many of the priests and preachers of Christian Europe, many lords and barons (and even a few kings), had been committed to the legitimacy of using military force against unbelievers: they had their own version of jihad. Vitoria claimed, by contrast, that "the sole and only just cause for waging war is when harm has been inflicted."[2] Just war was an argument of the religious center against pacifists, on the one side, and holy warriors, on the other, and because of its enemies (and even though its proponents were theologians), it took shape as a secular theory—which is simply another way of describing its worldliness.

So the rulers of this world embraced the theory, and did not fight a single war without describing it, or hiring intellectuals to describe it, as a war for peace and justice. Most often, of course, this description was hypocritical: the tribute that vice pays to virtue. But the need to pay the tribute opens those who pay it to the criticism of the virtuous—that is, of the brave and virtuous, of whom there have been only a few (but one could also say: at least a few). I will cite one heroic moment, from the history of the academic world: sometime around 1520, the faculty of the University of Salamanca met in solemn assembly and voted that the Spanish conquest of Central America was a violation of natural law and an unjust war.[3] I have not been able to learn anything about the subsequent fate of the good professors. Certainly, there were not many moments like that one, but what happened at Salamanca suggests that just war never lost its critical edge. The theory provided worldly reasons for going to war, but the reasons were limited—and they had to be worldly. Converting the Aztecs to Christianity was not a just cause; nor was seizing the gold of the Americas or enslaving its inhabitants.

Writers like Grotius and Pufendorf incorporated just war theory into international law, but the rise of the modern state and the legal (and philosophical) acceptance of state sovereignty pushed the theory into the background. Now the political foreground was occupied by people we can think of as Machiavellian princes, hard men (and sometimes women), driven by "reason of state," who did what (they said) they had to do. Worldly prudence triumphed over worldly justice; realism over what was increasingly disparaged as naive idealism. The princes of the world continued to defend their wars, using the language of international law, which was also, at least in part, the language of just war. But the defenses were marginal to the enterprise, and I suspect that it was the least important of the state's intellectuals who put them forward. States claimed a right to fight whenever their rulers deemed it necessary, and the rulers took sovereignty to mean that no one could judge their decisions. They not only fought when they wanted; they fought how they wanted, returning to the old Roman maxim that held war to be a lawless activity: *inter arma silent leges*— which, again, was taken to mean that there was no law above or beyond the decrees of the state; conventional restraints on the conduct of war could always be overridden for the sake of victory.[4] Arguments about justice were treated as a kind of moralizing, inappropriate to the anarchic conditions of international society. For this world, just war was not worldly enough.

In the 1950s and early 1960s, when I was in graduate school, realism was the reigning doctrine in the field of "international relations." The standard reference was not to justice but to interest. Moral argument was against the rules of the discipline as it was commonly practiced, although a few writers defended interest as the new morality.[5] There were many political scientists in those years who preened themselves as modern Machiavellis and dreamed of whispering in the ear of the prince; and a certain number of them, enough to stimulate the ambition of the others, actually got to whisper. They practiced being cool and tough-minded; they taught the princes, who did not always need to be taught, how to get results through the calculated application of force. Results were understood in terms of "the national interest," which was the objectively determined sum of power and wealth here and now plus the probability of future power and wealth. More of both was almost always taken to be better; only a few writers argued for the acceptance of prudential limits; moral limits were, as I remember those years, never discussed. Just war theory was relegated to religion departments, theological seminaries, and a few Catholic universities. And even in those places, isolated as they were from the political world, the theory was pressed toward realist positions; perhaps for the sake of self-preservation, its advocates surrendered something of its critical edge.

Vietnam changed all this, although it took a while for the change to register at the theoretical level. What happened first occurred in the realm of practice. The war became a subject of political debate; it was widely opposed, mostly by people on the left. These were people heavily influenced by Marxism; they also spoke a language of interest; they shared with the princes and professors of American politics a disdain for moralizing. And yet the experience of the war pressed them toward moral argument. Of course, the war in their eyes was radically imprudent; it could not be won; its costs, even if Americans thought only of themselves, were much too high; it was an imperialist adventure unwise even for the imperialists; it set the United States against the cause of national liberation, which would alienate it from the Third World (and significant parts of the First). But these claims failed utterly to express the feelings of most of the war's opponents, feelings that had to do with the systematic exposure of Vietnamese civilians to the violence of American war-making. Almost against its will, the left fell into morality. All of us in the antiwar camp suddenly began talking the language of just war—though we did not know that that was what we were doing.

It may seem odd to recall the '60s in this way, since today the left seems all too quick to make moral arguments, even absolutist moral arguments. But this description of the contemporary left seems to me mistaken. A certain kind of politicized, instrumental, and highly selective moralizing is indeed increasingly common among leftist writers, but this is not serious moral argument. It is not what we learned, or ought to have learned, from the Vietnam years. What happened then was that people on the left, and many others too, looked for a common moral language. And what was most available was the language of just war. We were, all of us, a bit rusty, unaccustomed to speaking in public about morality. The realist ascendancy had robbed us of the very words that we needed, which we slowly reclaimed: aggression, intervention, just cause, self-defense, noncombatant immunity, proportionality, prisoners of war, civilians, double effect, terrorism, war crimes. And we came to understand that these words had meanings. Of course, they could be used instrumentally; that is always true of political and moral terms. But if we attended to their meanings, we found ourselves involved in a discussion that had its own structure. Like characters in a novel, concepts in a theory shape the narrative or the argument in which they figure.

Once the war was over, just war became an academic subject; now political scientists and philosophers discovered the theory; it was written about in the journals and taught in the universities—and also in the (American) military academies and war colleges. A small group of Vietnam veterans played a major role in making the discipline of morality central to the military curriculum.[6] They had bad memories. They welcomed just war theory precisely because it was in their eyes a critical theory. It is, in fact, doubly critical—of war's occasions and its conduct. I suspect that the veterans were most concerned with the second of these. It is not only that they wanted to avoid anything like the My Lai massacre in future wars; they wanted, like professional soldiers everywhere, to distinguish their profession from mere butchery. And because of their Vietnam experience, they believed that this had to be done systematically; it required not only a code but also a theory. Once upon a time, I suppose, aristocratic honor had grounded the military code; in a more democratic and egalitarian age, the code had to be defended with arguments.

And so we argued. The discussions and debates were wide-ranging even if, once the war was over, they were mostly academic. It is easy to forget how large the academic world is in the United States: there are millions of students and tens of thousands of professors. So a lot of people were involved, future citizens and army officers, and the theory was mostly presented, though this presentation was also disputed, as a manual for wartime criticism. Our cases and examples were drawn from Vietnam and were framed to invite criticism (the debate over nuclear deterrence also used, in part, the language of just war, but this was a highly technical debate and engaged far fewer people than did Vietnam). Here was a war that we should never have fought, and that we fought badly, brutally, as if there were no moral limits. So it became, retrospectively, an occasion for drawing a line—and for committing ourselves to the moral casuistry necessary to determine the precise location of the line. Ever since Pascal's brilliant denunciation, casuistry has had a bad name among moral philosophers; it is commonly taken to be excessively permissive, not so much an application as a relaxation of the moral rules. When we looked back at the Vietnamese cases, however, we were more likely to deny permission than to grant it, insisting again and again that what had been done should not have been done.

But there was another feature of Vietnam that gave the moral critique of the war special force: it was a war that we lost, and the brutality with which we fought the war almost certainly contributed to our defeat. In a war for "hearts and minds," rather than for land and resources, justice turns out to be a key to victory. So just war theory looked once again like the worldly doctrine that it is. And here, I think, is the deepest cause of the theory's contemporary triumph: there are now reasons of state for fighting justly. One might almost say that justice has become a military necessity.

There were probably earlier wars in which the deliberate killing of civilians, and also the common military carelessness about killing civilians, proved to be counterproductive. The Boer war is a likely example. But for us, Vietnam was the first war in which the practical value of *jus in bello* became apparent. To be sure, the "Vietnam syndrome" is generally taken to reflect a different lesson: that we should not fight wars that are unpopular at home and to which we are unwilling to commit the resources necessary for victory. But there was in fact another lesson, connected to but not the same as the "syndrome": that we should not fight wars about whose justice we are doubtful, and that once we are engaged we have to fight justly so as not to antagonize the civilian population, whose political support is necessary to a military victory. In Vietnam, the relevant civilians were the Vietnamese themselves; we lost the war when we lost their "hearts and minds." But this idea about the need for civilian support has turned out to be both variable and expansive: modern warfare requires the support of different civilian populations, extending beyond the population immediately at risk. Still, a moral regard for civilians at risk is critically important in winning wider support for the war . . . for any modern war. I will call this the usefulness of morality. Its wide acknowledgement is something radically new in military history.

Hence the odd spectacle of George Bush (the elder), during the Persian Gulf war, talking like a just war theorist.[7] Well, not quite: for Bush's speeches and press conferences displayed an old American tendency, which his son has inherited, to confuse just wars and crusades, as if a war can be just only when the forces of good are arrayed against the forces of evil. But Bush also seemed to understand—and this was a constant theme of American military spokesmen—that war is properly a war of armies, a combat between combatants, from which the civilian population should be shielded. I do not believe that the bombing of Iraq in 1991 met just war standards; shielding civilians would certainly have excluded the destruction of electricity networks and water purification plants. Urban infrastructure, even if it is necessary to modern war-making, is also necessary to civilian existence in a modern city, and it is morally defined by this second feature.[8] Still, American strategy in the Gulf war was the result of a compromise between what justice would have required and the unrestrained bombing of previous wars; taken overall, targeting was far more limited and selective than it had been, for example, in Korea or Vietnam. The reasons for the limits were complicated: in part, they reflected a commitment to the Iraqi people (which turned out not to be very strong), in the hope that the Iraqis would repudiate the war and overthrow the regime that began it; in part, they reflected the political necessities of the coalition that made the war possible. Those necessities were shaped in turn by the media coverage of the war—that is, by the immediate access of the media to the battle and of people the world over to the media. Bush and his generals believed that these people would not tolerate a slaughter of civilians, and they were probably right (but what it might mean for them not to tolerate something was and is fairly unclear). Hence, although many of the countries whose support was crucial to the war's success were not democracies, bombing policy was dictated in important ways by the demos.

This will continue to be true: the media are omnipresent, and the whole world is watching. War has to be different in these circumstances. But does this mean that it has to be more just or only that it has to look more just, that it has to be described, a little more persuasively than in the past, in the language of justice? The triumph of just war theory is clear enough; it is amazing how readily military spokesmen during the Kosovo and Afghanistan wars used its categories, telling a causal story that justified the war and providing accounts of the battles that emphasized the restraint with which they were being fought. The arguments (and rationalizations) of the past were very different; they commonly came from outside the armed forces—from clerics, lawyers, and professors, not from generals—and they commonly lacked specificity and detail. But what does the use of these categories, these just and moral words, signify?

Perhaps naively, I am inclined to say that justice has become, in all Western countries, one of the tests that any proposed military strategy or tactic has to meet—only one of the tests and not the most important one, but this still gives just war theory a place and standing that it never had before. It is easier now than it ever was to imagine a general saying, "No, we can't do that; it would cause too many civilian deaths; we have to find another way." I am not sure that there are many generals who talk like that, but imagine for a moment that there are; imagine that strategies are evaluated morally as well as militarily; that civilian deaths are minimized; that new technologies are designed to avoid or limit collateral damage, and that these technologies are actually effective in achieving their intended purpose. Moral theory has been incorporated into war-making as a real constraint on when and how wars are fought. This picture is, remember, imaginary, but it is also partly true; and it makes for a far more interesting argument than the more standard claim that the triumph of just war is pure hypocrisy. The triumph is real: what then is left for theorists and philosophers to do?

This question is sufficiently present in our consciousness that one can watch people trying to respond. There are two responses that I want to describe and criticize. The first comes from what might be called the postmodern left, which does not claim that affirmations of justice are hypocritical, since hypocrisy implies standards, but rather that there are no standards, no possible objective use of the categories of just war theory.[9] Politicians and generals who adopt the categories are deluding themselves—though no more so than the theorists who developed the categories in the first place. Maybe new technologies kill fewer people, but there is no point in arguing about who those people are and whether or not killing them is justified. No agreement about justice, or about guilt or innocence, is possible. This view is summed up in a line that speaks to our immediate situation: "One man's terrorist is another man's freedom fighter." On this view, there is nothing for theorists and philosophers to do but choose sides, and there is no theory or principle that can guide their choice. But this is an impossible position, for it holds that we cannot recognize, condemn, and actively oppose the murder of innocent people.

A second response is to take the moral need to recognize, condemn and oppose very seriously and then to raise the theoretical ante—that is, to strengthen the constraints that justice imposes on warfare. For theorists who pride themselves on living, so to speak, at the critical edge, this is an obvious and understandable response. For many years, we have used the theory of just war to criticize American military actions, and now it has been taken over by the generals and is being used to explain and justify those actions. Obviously, we must resist. The easiest way to resist is to make noncombatant immunity into a stronger and stronger rule, until it is something like an absolute rule: all killing of civilians is (something close to) murder; therefore any war that leads to the killing of civilians is unjust; therefore every war is unjust. So pacifism reemerges from the very heart of the theory that was originally meant to replace it. This is the strategy adopted, most recently, by many opponents of the Afghanistan war. The protest marches on American campuses featured banners proclaiming, "Stop the Bombing!" and the argument for stopping was very simple (and obviously true): bombing endangers and kills civilians. The marchers did not seem to feel that anything more had to be said.

Since I believe that war is still, sometimes, necessary, this seems to me a bad argument and, more generally, a bad response to the triumph of just war theory. It sustains the critical role of the theory vis-à-vis war generally, but it denies the theory the critical role it has always claimed, which is internal to the business of war and requires critics to attend closely to what soldiers try to do and what they try not to do. The refusal to make distinctions of this kind, to pay attention to strategic and tactical choices, suggests a doctrine of radical suspicion. This is the radicalism of people who do not expect to exercise power or use force, ever, and who are not prepared to make the judgments that this exercise and use require. By contrast, just war theory, even when it demands a strong critique of particular acts of war, is the doctrine of people who do expect to exercise power and use force. We might think of it as a doctrine of radical responsibility, because it holds political and military leaders responsible, first of all, for the well-being of their own people, but also for the wellbeing of innocent men and women on the other side. Its proponents set themselves against those who will not think realistically about the defense of the country they live in and also against those who refuse to recognize the humanity of their opponents. They insist that there are things that it is morally impermissible to do even to the enemy. They also insist, however, that fighting itself cannot be morally impermissible. A just war is meant to be, and has to be, a war that it is possible to fight.

But there is another danger posed by the triumph of just war theory—not the radical relativism and the near absolutism that I have just described, but rather a certain softening of the critical mind, a truce between theorists and soldiers. If intellectuals are often awed and silenced by political leaders who invite them to dinner, how much more so by generals who talk their language? And if the generals are actually fighting just wars, if inter arma the laws speak, what point is there in anything we can say? In fact, however, our role has not changed all that much. We still have to insist that war is a morally dubious and difficult activity. Even if we (in the West) have fought just wars in the Gulf, in Kosovo, and in Afghanistan, that is no guarantee, not even a useful indication, that our next war will be just. And even if the recognition of noncombatant immunity has become militarily necessary, it still conflicts with other, more pressing, necessities. Justice still needs to be defended; decisions about when and how to fight require constant scrutiny, exactly as they always have.

At the same time, we have to extend our account of "when and how" to cover the new strategies, the new technologies, and the new politics of a global age. Old ideas may not fit the emerging reality: the "war against terrorism," to take the most current example, requires a kind of international cooperation that is as radically undeveloped in theory as it is in practice. We should welcome military officers into the theoretical argument; they will make it a better argument than it would be if no one but professors took an interest. But we cannot leave the argument to them. As the old saying goes, war is too important to be left to the generals; just war even more so. The ongoing critique of war-making is a centrally important democratic activity.

2. Let me, then, suggest two issues, raised by our most recent wars, that require the critical edge of justice.

First, risk-free war-making. I have heard it said that this is a necessary feature of humanitarian interventions like the Kosovo war: soldiers defending humanity, in contrast to soldiers defending their own country and their fellow-citizens, will not risk their lives; or, their political leaders will not dare to ask them to risk their lives. Hence the rescue of people in desperate trouble, the objects of massacre or ethnic cleansing, is only possible if risk-free war is possible.[10] But, obviously, it is possible: wars can be fought from a great distance with bombs and missiles aimed very precisely (compared with the radical imprecision of such weapons only a few decades ago) at the forces carrying out the killings and deportations. And the technicians/soldiers aiming these weapons are, in all the recent cases, largely invulnerable to counterattack. There is no principle of just war theory that bars this kind of warfare. So long as they can aim accurately at military targets, soldiers have every right to fight from a safe distance. And what commander, committed to his or her own soldiers, would not choose to fight in this way whenever he or she could? In his reflections on rebellion, Albert Camus argues that one cannot kill unless one is prepared to die.[11] But that argument does not seem to apply to soldiers in battle, where the whole point is to kill while avoiding getting killed. And yet there is a wider sense in which Camus is right.

Just war theorists have not, to my knowledge, discussed this question, but we obviously need to do so. Massacre and ethnic cleansing commonly take place on the ground. The awful work might be done with bombs and poison gas delivered from the air, but in Bosnia, Kosovo, Rwanda, East Timor, and Sierra Leone, the weapons were rifles, machetes, and clubs; the killing and terrorizing of the population was carried out from close up. And a risk-free intervention undertaken from far away—especially if it promises to be effective in the long run—is likely to cause an immediate speed-up on the ground. This can be stopped only if the intervention itself shifts to the ground, and this shift seems to me morally necessary. The aim of the intervention, after all, is to rescue people in trouble, and fighting on the ground, in the case as I have described it, is what rescue requires. But then it is no longer risk-free. Why would anyone undertake it?

In fact, risks of this sort are a common feature of *jus in bello*, and while there are many examples of soldiers unwilling to accept them, there are also many examples of their acceptance. The principle is this: when it is our action that puts innocent people at risk, even if the action is justified, we are bound to do what we can to reduce those risks, even if this involves risks to our own soldiers. If we are bombing military targets in a just war, and there are civilians living near these targets, we have to adjust our bombing policy—by flying at lower altitudes, say—so as to minimize the risks we impose on civilians. Of course, it is legitimate to balance the risks; we cannot require our pilots to fly suicidal missions. They have to be, as Camus suggests, prepared to die, but that is consistent with taking measures to safeguard their lives. How the balance gets worked out is something that has to be debated in each case. But what is not permissible, it seems to me, is what NATO did in the Kosovo war, where its leaders declared in advance that they would not send ground forces into battle, whatever happened inside Kosovo once the air war began. Responsibility for the intensified Serbian campaign against Kosovar civilians, which was the immediate consequence of the air war, belongs no doubt to the Serbian government and army. They were to blame. But this was at the same time a foreseeable result of our action, and insofar as we did nothing to prepare for this result, or to deal with it, we were blameworthy too. We imposed risks on others and refused to accept them for ourselves, even when that acceptance was necessary to help the others.[12]

The second issue concerns war's endings. On the standard view, a just war (precisely because it is not a crusade) should end with the restoration of the status quo ante. The paradigm case is a war of aggression, which ends justly when the aggressor has been defeated, his attack repulsed, the old boundaries restored. Perhaps this is not quite enough for a just conclusion: the victim state might deserve reparations from the aggressor state, so that the damage the aggressor's forces inflicted can be repaired—a more extensive understanding of restoration, but restoration still. And perhaps the peace treaty should include new security arrangements, of a sort that did not exist before the war, so that the status quo will be more stable in the future. But that is as far as the rights of victims go; the theory as it was commonly understood did not extend to any radical reconstitution of the enemy state, and international law, with its assumptions about sovereignty, would have regarded any imposed change of regime as a new act of aggression. What happened after World War II in both Germany and Japan was something quite new in the history of war, and the legitimacy of occupation and political reconstitution is still debated, even by theorists and lawyers who regard the treatment of the Nazi regime, at least, as justified. Thus, as the Gulf war drew to a close in 1991, there was little readiness to march on Baghdad and replace the government of Saddam Hussein, despite the denunciation of that government in the lead-up to the war as Nazi-like in character. There were, of course, both military and geopolitical arguments against continuing the war once the attack on Kuwait had been repulsed, but there was also an argument from justice: that even if Iraq "needed" a new government, that need could only be met by the Iraqi people themselves. A government imposed by foreign armies would never be accepted as the product of, or the future agent of, self-determination.[13]

The World War II examples, however, argue against this last claim. If the imposed government is democratic and moves quickly to open up the political arena and to organize elections, it may erase the memory of its own imposition (hence the difference between the western and eastern regimes in post-war Germany). In any case, humanitarian intervention radically shifts the argument about endings, because now the war is from the beginning an effort to change the regime that is responsible for the inhumanity. This can be done by supporting secession, as the Indians did in what is now Bangladesh; or by expelling a dictator, as the Tanzanians did to Uganda's Idi Amin; or by creating a new government, as the Vietnamese did in Cambodia. In East Timor, more recently, the UN organized a referendum on secession and then worked to set up a new government. Had there been, as there should have been, an intervention in Rwanda, it would certainly have aimed at replacing the Hutu Power regime. Justice would have required the replacement. But what kind of justice is this? Who are its agents, and what rules govern their actions?

As the Rwandan example suggests, most states do not want to take on this kind of responsibility, and when they do take it on, for whatever political reasons, they do not want to submit themselves to a set of moral rules. In Cambodia, the Vietnamese shut down the killing fields, which was certainly a good thing to do, but they then went on to set up a satellite government, keyed to their own interests, which never won legitimacy either within or outside of Cambodia and brought no closure to the country's internal conflicts. Legitimacy and closure are the two criteria against which we can test war's endings. Both of them are likely to require, in almost all the humanitarian intervention cases, something more than the restoration of the status quo ante—which gave rise, after all, to the crisis that prompted the intervention. Legitimacy and closure, however, are hard tests to meet. The problems have to do in part with strategic interests, as in the Vietnamese-Cambodian case. But material interests also figure in a major way: remaking a government is an expensive business; it requires a significant commitment of resources—and the benefits are largely speculative and nonmaterial. Yet we can still point to the usefulness of morality in cases like these. A successful and extended intervention brings benefits of an important kind: not only gratitude and friendship, but an increment of peace and stability in a world where the insufficiency of both is costly—and not only to its immediate victims. Still, any particular country will always have good reasons to refuse to bear the costs of these benefits; or it will take on the burden, and then find reasons to perform badly. So we still need justice's critical edge.

The argument about endings is similar to the argument about risk: once we have acted in ways that have significant negative consequences for other people (even if there are also positive consequences), we cannot just walk away. Imagine a humanitarian intervention that ends with the massacres stopped and the murderous regime overthrown; but the country is devastated, the economy in ruins, the people hungry and afraid; there is neither law nor order nor any effective authority. The forces that intervened did well, but they are not finished. How can this be? Is it the price of doing well that you acquire responsibilities to do well again … and again? The work of the virtuous is never finished. It does not seem fair. But in the real world, not only of international politics, but also of ordinary morality, this is the way things work (though virtue, of course, is never so uncomplicated). Consider the Afghan-Russian war: the American government intervened in a major way, fighting by proxy, and eventually won a big victory: the Russians were forced to withdraw. This was the last battle of the cold war. The American intervention was undoubtedly driven by geopolitical and strategic motives; the conviction that the Afghan struggle was a war of national liberation against a repressive regime may have played a part in motivating the people who carried it out, but the allies they found in Afghanistan had a very restricted idea of liberation.[14] When the war was over, Afghanistan was left in a state of anarchy and ruin. At that point, the Americans walked away and were certainly wrong, politically and morally wrong, to do so; the Russians withdrew and were right to do so. We had acted (relatively) well, that is, in support of what was probably the vast majority of the Afghan people, and yet we were bound to continue acting well; the Russians had acted badly and were off the hook; even if they owed the Afghan people material aid (reparations), no one wanted them engaged again in Afghan affairs. This sounds anomalous, and yet I think it is an accurate account of the distribution of responsibility. But we need a better understanding of how this works and why it works the way it does, a theory of justice-in-endings that engages the actual experience of humanitarian (and other) interventions, so that countries fighting in wars like these know what their responsibilities will be if they win. It would also help if there was, what there is not yet, an international agency that could stipulate and even enforce these responsibilities.

This theory of justice-in-endings will have to include a description of legitimate occupations, regime changes, and protectorates—and also, obviously, a description of illegitimate and immoral activity in all these areas. This combination is what just war has always been about: it makes actions and operations that are morally problematic possible by constraining their occasions and regulating their conduct. When the constraints are accepted, the actions and operations are justified, and the theorist of just war has to say that, even if he sounds like an apologist for the powers-that-be. When they are not accepted, when the brutalities of war or its aftermath are unconstrained, he has to say that, even if he is called a traitor and an enemy of the people.

It is important not to get stuck in either mode—defense or critique. Indeed, just war theory requires that we maintain our commitment to both modes at the same time. In this sense, just war is like good government: there is a deep and permanent tension between the adjective and the noun, but no necessary contradiction between them. When reformers come to power and make government better (less corrupt, say), we have to be able to acknowledge the improvement. And when they hold on to power for too long, and imitate their predecessors, we have to be ready to criticize their behavior. Just war theory is not an apology for any particular war, and it is not a renunciation of war itself. It is designed to sustain a constant scrutiny and an immanent critique. We still need that, even when generals sound like theorists, and I am sure that we always will.

NOTES

1. Augustine's argument on just war can be found in *The Political Writings of St. Augustine* (1962: 162–183); modern readers will need a commentary: see Dean (1963: 134–171).

2. See Vitoria (1991: 302–304), and for commentary, Johnson (1975: 150–171).

3. See Boswell (1952:129), quoting Dr. Johnson: "'I love the University of Salamanca, for when the Spaniards were in doubt as to the lawfulness of conquering America, the University of Salamanca gave it as their opinion that it was not lawful.' He spoke this with great emotion. . . ."

4. With some hesitation, I cite my own discussion of military necessity (and the references there to more sympathetic treatments): Walzer (1977: 144–151, 239–242, 251–255).

5. The best discussion of the realists is Smith (1986); chapter 6, on Hans Morgenthau, is especially relevant to my argument here.

6. Anthony Hartle is one of those veterans, who eventually wrote his own book on the ethics of war: *Moral Issues in Military Decision Making* (1989).

7. See the documents collected in Sifry and Cerf (1991: 197–352), which include Bush's speeches and a wide range of other opinions.

8. I made the case against attacks on infrastructural targets immediately after the war (but others made it earlier) in DeCosse (1992: 12–13).

9. Stanley Fish's op-ed piece in *The New York Times* (October 15, 2001) provides an example of the postmodernist argument in its most intelligent version.

10. This argument was made by several participants at a conference on humanitarian intervention held at the Zentrum fur interdisziplinare Forschung, Bielefeld University, Germany, in January 2002.

11. "A life is paid for by another life, and from these two sacrifices springs the promise of a value." Camus (1956: 169). See also the argument in act I of *The Just Assassins*. Camus (1958, esp. pp. 246–247).

12. For arguments in favor of using ground forces in Kosovo, see Buckley (2000: 293–294, 333–335, 342).

13. Bush's statement on stopping the American advance, and his declaration of victory, can be found in Sifry and Cerf (1991: 449–451); arguments for and against stopping can be found in DeCosse (1992: 13–14, 29–32).

14. Artyom Borovik (1990) provides a useful, though highly personal, account of the Russian war in Afghanistan; for an academic history, see Goodson (2001).

REFERENCES

Augustine. *The Political Writings of St. Augustine*. Ed. Henry Paolucci. Chicago: Henry Regnery Company, 1962.

Borovik, Artyom. *The Hidden War: A Russian Journalist's Account of the Soviet War in Afghanistan*. London: Faber and Faber, 1990.

Boswell, James. *Life of Samuel Johnson LL.D. Great Books of the Western World*. Vol. 44. Ed. Robert Maynard Hutchins. Chicago: Encyclopedia Britannica, 1952.

Buckley, William Joseph. *Kosovo: Contending Voices on Balkan Interventions*. Grand Rapids: William B. Eerdmans Publishing Company, 2000.

Camus, Albert. *The Rebel*. Trans. Anthony Bower. New York: Vintage, 1956.

———. *Caligula and Three Other Plays*. Trans. Stuart Gilbert. New York: Vintage, 1958.

Dean, Herbert A. *The Political and Social Ideas of St. Augustine*. New York: Columbia University Press, 1963.

DeCosse, David E., ed. *But Was It Just? Reflections on the Morality of the Persian Gulf War*. New York: Doubleday, 1992.

Goodson, Larry P. *Afghanistan's Endless War: State Failure, Regional Politics, and the Rise of the Taliban*. Seattle: University of Washington Press, 2001.

Hartle, Anthony E. *Moral Issues in Military Decision Making*. Lawrence: University Press of Kansas, 1989.

Johnson, James Turner. *Ideology, Reason, and the Limitation of War: Religious and Secular Concepts, 1200–1740*. Princeton: Princeton University Press, 1975.

Sifry, Micah L., and Cerf, Christopher, eds. *The Gulf War: History, Documents, Opinions*. New York: Times Books, 1991.

Smith, Michael Joseph. *Realist Thought from Weber to Kissinger*. Baton Rouge: Louisiana State University Press, 1986.

Vitoria, Francisco de. *Political Writings*. Eds. Anthony Pagden and Jeremy Lawrance. Cambridge: Cambridge University Press, 1991.

Walzer, Michael. *Just and Unjust Wars*. New York: Basic Books, 1977.

*Michael Walzer, a political philosopher, is a professor emeritus at the Institute for Advanced Study, Princeton, NJ, and a coeditor of *Dissent*. Among his many books are *On Toleration* (2000) and *Spheres Justice: A Defense of Pluralism and Equality* (1983).

Michael Walzer, "The Triumph of Just War Theory—And the Dangers of Success," *Social Research* 69 (2002): 925–944. Copyright 2002. Reproduced with permission of SOCIAL RESEARCH: AN INTERNATIONAL QUARTERLY.

Part 2: Going to War: *Jus ad Bellum*

The just war tradition separates thinking on what conditions would legitimize the resort to war (*jus ad bellum*) and what acts are legitimate in the course of war (*jus in bello*). The hope is that even if a war is unjustly begun, warring parties would still feel obligated, and incentivized, to behave justly in conducting warfare. This chapter will focus on questions of *jus ad bellum*: when may a state rightfully resort to armed force? Are there any situations or triggers that might justify a state responding with force regardless of the consequences for surrounding states or for individuals caught up in the war? A consequentialist might argue that war would be justified if failure to go to war would result in a worse outcome than not doing so. But given the unpredictability and destructiveness of war, how would one ever reliably make the argument that war will certainly result in a better outcome? And how would one balance the relative harm or good of war in any single instance against the perhaps more compelling need for the international system to restrain uses of force and the resort to war overall?

The most commonly accepted (and, some would argue, the sole) rationale for going to war is self-defense, following an attack or imminent threat of one. However, in recent decades, the increasing threats posed by failed states and non-state actors, the immediacy of modern-day threats, and a greater focus on human rights and humanitarian protection have renewed debate about other justifications for using armed force. These include humanitarian intervention; pre-emptive, or preventive, self-defense; and coercive regime change. Have modern conflict dynamics changed the way we view these rationales? Do states have a right or a responsibility to intervene when severe human rights abuses are being perpetrated in other states?

Jus ad Bellum: Criteria for a Just War

States have gone to war for territorial conquest, to acquire sources of wealth or resources, to control trade routes, to aggrandize their own power, or even to annihilate a particular population or group. Leaders have led their countries into war motivated out of revenge, money, religion, bigotry, or even mistaken information. Though it is possible to think of many bad reasons to go to war, it is more challenging to come up with the *right* reasons to go to war.

In an excerpt from his book, *The Morality of War*, Brian Orend discusses six factors that are commonly discussed as necessary for a state to justly go to war.

1. There must be just cause for resorting to force.

2. States must be acting out of the "right intentions," good or "morally appropriate" reasons for going to war.

3. States must have the right authority to go to war, for example, authorized by the public declaration of a proper authority, like the United Nations.

4. War must be a last resort.

5. The resort to force must have a chance of being successful.

6. The decision to go to war must be "proportionate," meaning the costs must be worth the benefits. This must include not only the costs and benefits of the state considering whether to go to war, but the costs versus benefits for the international community as a whole.

Many of these factors would appear to be common sense had they not been so frequently violated during the history of warfare. Though *jus ad bellum* theories, like Orend's, have certainly advanced in time, enforcement of these principles is still a problem. What mechanisms would ensure that states abide by these principles? Orend suggests that some procedural requirements may be necessary. For example, he recommends that states be required to publicly declare their reason for going to war, confining themselves to only one, main motivating rationale. This would help the international community judge whether the reasons were just and were carried out under good intentions. Orend also suggests that according to the ethical principle that states be acting under the proper authority, they seek authorization from the UN Security Council, as stipulated in the UN Charter.

"Just Cause" for Resort to War

Although all six criteria elaborated by Orend are important in evaluating whether the resort to armed force is just, much of the debate in both academic and popular literature focuses on the first criterion of just cause. Given the long history of this school of thought, and even longer history of warfare, one might assume such questions would be well settled. However, in the past several decades changes in the international system and the rise in prominence of non-state actors—both as aggressors and as rights-holding victims—have renewed debate over what is a just cause for war. The right to self-defense is still unchallenged, but the boundaries of what constitutes self-defense are unclear. When states may act in self-defense of others is even murkier.

The Theory of Aggression and the Right to Self-Defense

One of the most important foundations for current thinking on *jus ad bellum* justifications is Michael Walzer's seminal 1977 *Just and Unjust Wars*. In the excerpt included for this section, "The Legalist Paradigm," Walzer lays out his "theory of aggression" and the rationale for self-defense. In Walzer's view, the only just reason to go to war is in response to an act of an aggression, which is any "violation of the territorial integrity and political sovereignty of an independent state."[1]

Walzer asks us to imagine a society of states "more or less like a society of individuals."[2] However, unlike in societies of individuals, in the international system there is no law enforcement. States must rely on themselves and on each other, Walzer argues. Thus, when an act of aggression—a violation of a state's sovereignty or territorial integrity, or an imminent threat to do so—occurs, each state not only has the right to defend itself but an obligation. Each act of aggression or conflict undermines the peacefulness of the overall system, and so in responding to an act of force, a state not only upholds its own rights but the principles of independence and noninterference that keep the international system operating peacefully. Because it is so important for the principle of aggression to be enforced, and for states that violate it to be punished, states that are not themselves attacked may respond with or on behalf of the victim state in repelling and punishing the aggressor state.

Pre-emptive Self-Defense

Walzer argues that a right to self-defense could be triggered either by an actual attack on a state's sovereignty or territory or by the imminent threat of such an attack. While many would acknowledge that some degree of pre-emption is allowed, how imminent need the attack be? What evidence should be required to substantiate that an attack is imminent?

Traditional interpretations of when states might use force in anticipation of an attack were limited. The most broadly accepted international legal definition of anticipatory self-defense arose from a dispute between the United States and royalist Canadian forces in 1837, the so-called *Caroline* dispute. Though the incident itself—which involved the cross-border firing on a U.S. vessel, including the killing of one U.S. citizen—was relatively minor, the diplomatic negotiations that followed set out the principle that anticipatory, or pre-emptive, self-defense is permissible only when the "necessity of that self-defence is instant, overwhelming, and leaving no choice of means, and no moment for deliberation."[3]

But should a 19th century standard for imminence still apply to 21st century threats? Some states have argued that the limitations on anticipatory attacks are outmoded. They argue that today's threats come from nonstate actors such as terrorist groups, who rely almost exclusively on surprise attacks and try to use states' adherence to just war considerations against them. Moreover, given the greater lethality of modern weaponry, waiting for an attack to materialize before responding in self-defense might result in unacceptable levels of harm. A nuclear attack on Israel, a small state, could wipe it off the map. A biological weapon attack in the subway in New York City could kill millions.

The third piece, "The Slippery Slope to Preventative War" by Neta C. Crawford, admits that there might be a cause for pre-emptive strikes but argues that they cannot be based on an amorphous fear that a strike might happen. We must think not only about the threat to the individual state but also about the danger of living in a world in which such strikes were freely permitted. "If all states reacted to potential adversaries as if they faced a clear and present danger of imminent attack, security would be destabilized."[4] Not only would such strikes destabilize the international system, but if not based on clear intelligence about a potential adversary's capabilities and intentions, they might wrongly presume aggressive intentions, leading to an unjust use of force.

Humanitarian Intervention

So far we have discussed the justice of aggressive versus defensive wars. A self-interested "act of aggression" by one state is unjust, while generally a self-defense response to an act of aggression is considered justified. But what if a state initiated a war—an act of aggression—not out of its own self-interest, but altruistically to stop a larger evil, for example, a mass human rights violation happening in a neighboring state? Would the use of armed force be justified if it saved thousands, perhaps millions of civilian lives?

Walzer, and many others in the just war tradition, have argued that it would be just to have a narrow exception for states to intervene on humanitarian, or human rights, grounds—a humanitarian intervention. Yet even if this principle is broadly accepted, what threshold of human rights violations might trigger a justified humanitarian intervention is not always clear. War is costly and often results in extreme rights deprivations, not the least of which is the killing of noncombatants. Thus, humanitarian intervention has typically only been considered just under extreme circumstances of mass human rights violations—rising to the level of genocide, the massacre of high numbers of civilians, mass displacement, or mass rape—such that the overall benefit of stopping such mass abuses would outweigh the inevitable costs of using armed force.

Though such arguments have existed for many decades, they gained greater traction after the end of the Cold War. The 1990s saw a number of urgent situations that seemed to cry out for international intervention—from the displacement of millions following the dissolution of the former Yugoslavia in 1991 to acts of genocide in Rwanda in 1994 and in Srebrenica, Bosnia, in May 1995. The concept of a legitimate humanitarian intervention gained such wide currency that in 2000, the Canadian government established an independent, international commission to review what was seen as an emerging norm of "responsibility to protect." The commission's findings argued that where a state fails to protect its citizens from mass human rights abuses, it loses some of its sovereignty rights. In cases of extreme violations of such rights, the international community not only may intervene legitimately but has the responsibility to do so, first diplomatically, or economically, and then using armed force as a last resort.

Many credit the human rights movement, and its greater prominence in international affairs, with championing humanitarian intervention.[5] But in the final article in this section, "Intervention and State Failure," Michael Ignatieff argues that increasing acceptance of humanitarian intervention has as much to do with security interests following the Cold War as with human rights concerns. In a world of eroding borders and increasing interconnections among states, internal threats and disturbances in one country can quickly become the problems of the world.

> Whereas the abuses of the cold war period came from strong tyrannical
> states, the ones in the post-cold war world chiefly originate in weak or
> collapsing states. . . . since the 1990s began, intervening has also become
> an urgent state interest: to rebuild failed states so that they cease to be
> national security threats.[6]

Ignatieff admits that humanitarian intervention driven by state interests may have some downsides. It might lead to intervention only when weak states are abusing domestic rights or when other self-interested motives are at play. However, he argues that in such cases, additional self-interested motivations might not be such a bad thing if they lead to a needed humanitarian intervention. "Moral perfectionism is the enemy of the possible and the practical."[7]

As you read through the excerpts in this section, consider the following questions:

- One could argue that acts of war in the course of an unjustified aggres-

sion can never be justified. Do you agree? Do you think the division between resort to war and conduct in war makes sense? Does the ability to
"behave justly" once war has begun undermine the deterrent to initiating
unjust wars? Why or why not?

• Brian Orend suggests certain procedural requirements for states to
justify publicly their decision to go to war. Neta Crawford's discussion
of pre-emption, too, illustrates that *how* a state demonstrates a credible
threat may be as important as the fact that there is one. How much do
you think states should have to publicly justify their actions? Which
requirements would you endorse?

• In the discussion of pre-emption, we note that some states have
argued that the nature of some of today's threats—the severity of threats
from weapons of mass destruction or the nature of terrorist attacks—
might justify the use of armed force before the threat actually material-
izes. Do you find such arguments convincing? Why or why not? What is
different about today's threats versus threats of the past?

• Neta Crawford argues that pre-emptive strikes might be justifiable if
they respond to inevitable, imminent attacks (as in days or weeks away).
Where would you draw the line on how imminent an attack must be?
Does it matter if the potential attacker is a state or a nonstate actor?
What is your ethical reasoning behind why you draw that distinction?

• Do you think the concept of a "responsibility to protect"—the idea
that states not only *may* intervene in another country in the case of mass
human rights violations but *have an obligation* to do so—would work in
practice? Why or why not? And how would such calls balance against
the overall fear that any intervention—no matter how well intended—
will only result in more suffering?

• Michael Ignatieff argues that ethical dilemmas resulting from humanitarian intervention—for example, that states might be more motivated
by self interest than humanitarian motives—should not stop us from
intervening at all. Do you agree with his argument? Why or why not?

NOTES

1. Many of the concepts about when it is just to go to war, including Walzer's theory of aggression
are premised on a conception of state sovereignty dating to the 17th century. In 1648, a series
of treaties, collectively known as the Peace of Westphalia, negotiated an end to the bloody
Thirty Years War. More importantly, the Peace of Westphalia established a consensus that
the principles of territorial integrity and state sovereignty would be respected—a step that
many consider to be the founding of the modern international system. Implicit in this idea

of territorial sovereignty is that states should be free from interference by other states, in particular from other states using armed force against them or within their borders. Any use of armed force against a state's territory, or against their citizens, has been considered a just cause for responding with force, from an inherent right to self-defense.

2. Michael Walzer, *Just and Unjust Wars*, 3rd. ed. (New York: Basic Books, 2000), 58.

3. Letter from Daniel Webster, U.S. Secretary of State, to Alexander Baring, 1st Baron Ashburton, August 6, 1842, http://avalon.law.yale.edu/19th_century/br-1842d.asp#web1 (accessed Nov. 9, 2011).

4. Neta C. Crawford, "The Slippery Slope to Preventative War," *Ethics and International Affairs* 17, no. 1 (2003): 36.

5. Since the 1970s, the developing international human rights movement pushed for human rights concerns of individuals to be more prominent in both foreign policy discussions and in stronger emerging international legal mechanisms. Ad hoc tribunals like the International Criminal Tribunal for Yugoslavia and the International Criminal Tribunal for Rwanda and the creation of the International Criminal Court in 2002 demonstrated a greater willingness on the international community's part to call state actors to account for violations of their citizens' human rights. International sanctions against regimes that had repeatedly abused citizens' rights, for example, in Zimbabwe, Syria, or Iran, further illustrated states' willingness to breach the nonintervention policy to stop other states' domestic human rights abuse.

6. Michael Ignatieff, "Intervention and State Failure," *Dissent* (Winter 2002): 115, http://www.dissentmagazine.org/article/?article=641 (accessed Nov. 9, 2011).

7. Ibid., 122.

Jus ad Bellum #1: Resisting Aggression

*by Brian Orend**

---

*"[N]o just war can be waged except for the purpose of punishment or repelling
enemies."* Cicero[1]

The core proposition of just war theory, uniting all its theorists, is this: *sometimes, it is at least morally permissible for a political community to go to war.* This is to say that there *can* be such a thing as a morally justified war; and World War II, on the part of the Allies is often trotted out as the definitive modern example. Some even refer to this conflict as "The Good War."[2]

The goal of just war theory is to restrain both the incidence and destructiveness of warfare. Just war theory seeks to minimize *the reasons* for which it is permissible to fight, and seeks to restrain and limit *the means* with which communities may fight. Just war theory is *not* pro-war. It is, rather, a doctrine deeply aware of war's frightful dangers and brutal inhumanities. It seeks, accordingly, to reduce those dangers, and purge those inhumanities, by insisting that belligerents respect human rights as best they can during the grim circumstances of war.

While there are disagreements between just war theorists—no tradition or discipline generates unanimity—the clear majority endorse some version of the following principles. There is thought to be a fundamental division between the ethics of *resorting* to force—or in Latin *"jus ad bellum"* (literally "the justice *of* war") and the ethics of conduct *during* armed conflict (or *"jus in bello,"* literally "justice *in* war"). Most just war theorists insist that *jus ad bellum* and *jus in bello* are, in a salient sense, separate. The notion is that a war can be begun for just reasons, yet prosecuted in an unjust fashion. (For instance, while World War II is called "The Good War" in terms of its cause, many still raise critical doubts about some Allied tactics, notably the use of atomic weapons.) Similarly, though perhaps much less commonly, a war begun for unjust reasons might (conceivably) still be fought with strict adherence to *jus in bello*. The categories are at least logically or conceptually distinct, and so we must consider them separately, each with their own rules and considerations. For example, the *jus ad bellum* criteria are thought to be the preserve and responsibility of political leaders whereas the *jus in bello* criteria are thought to be the province and responsibility of military commanders, officers and soldiers. Ultimately in this book, I am going to argue that there is a robust connection between *jus ad bellum* and *jus in bello*. This defies tradition. Even so, I admit that one category can be *focused upon one*, and then the other (without admitting they are literally separate). And so that is what we shall do.

A state resorts to war justly only if it satisfies *each of six major rules:* just cause, right intention, public declaration by proper authority, last resort, probability of success and proportionality.

JUST CAUSE

International law allows countries to defend themselves with force if they are victimized by an armed attack; it also allows them to so defend other countries should *they* be attacked. These entitlements commonly get referred to, respectively, as "self-defence from aggression" and "other-defence from aggression" (also called a "war of law enforcement"). These are the two most elemental just causes for war in international law and just war theory. No other kinds of warfare are allowed in international law unless explicitly authorized and endorsed by the United Nations' Security Council (UNSC).

The UNSC is empowered by the UN Charter to try to keep war from breaking out. It has 5 permanent members, who can veto any resolution. These are: America, Britain, China, France, and Russia. It also features 10 non-permanent members, who hold rotating two year terms and can propose, and vote on, resolutions—but can never veto them. This means that there are 15 UNSC members at any given time and a resolution on war and peace, to pass, must enjoy majority support with no vetos.

Self-defence and other-defence are referred to as "inherent rights" (even, in French, as natural rights) of states by Article 51 of the UN Charter. Note that what is being defended against is aggression and *aggression is an armed attack against another country who is a member of the UN*. A bit more on the "armed attack" part: suppose that you are a small country, C, next to a big neighbour, N. In response to domestic lobby groups, the government of N decides to close its border to your forestry exports (trees, lumber, etc.). You are devastated, because your forestry sector is your economy's biggest and your economy is going to suffer severely (lost trade, layoffs, plant shut-downs, a recession). This is pretty tough treatment by N against C: it is not nice; it is completely undiplomatic; and it might even violate a trade treaty. But international law, and just war theory, insist that, rough as it may be, it is not treatment severe enough to merit warfare in response. It is only when the tough treatment in question *is coupled with physical violence* that we can begin to contemplate armed conflict. This makes clear sense in interpersonal life (e.g., we do not think getting fired is a sufficient reason to retaliate with violence, even if the firing sharply harms our interests). The loss—the danger—is merely economic. But most of us do think that, when someone physically attacks us (or those we love) with brute violence, we may employ physical force in response, seeking to resist the attacker, force him to stop and to protect ourselves or others from even deeper hurt. So for an international act to count as aggression, it must not merely be objectionable or even damaging to a country's interests. It must, at the same time, involve the infliction of serious, direct physical force. Almost always in international affairs, this involves the deployment of a country's armed forces—by land, sea or air—into the territory and/or against the people or government of another country. The classic example of international aggression is when one country uses its armed forces to launch an invasion into another country, with the objective being military, political and economic conquest, such as Nazi Germany did to Poland in 1939 or Iraq did to Kuwait in 1990.

International law only stipulates *that* aggression is wrong and punishable with war *in* response; it does not explain *why*. Similarly, international law only dictates that states *have* the right not to be subject to aggression; it fails to explain *why*. It is the job of just war theory to fill in these gaps. Let's start with the issue of state rights. Why do states—like the government of the US—have rights? Which rights do they have? What are the underlying principles here?[3]

[…]

Right Intention

Having finished (for now) with the many complexities of just cause, we turn to the other five rules co-constitutive of *jus ad bellum*. Let us begin with Augustine's obsession with right intention. It is commonly thought, by just war theorists, that it is not enough to have an *objectively* just cause for going to war (like resisting aggression); you must also have the proper *subjective* intention, or state of mind, for your act to be moral. Why? Consider an analogy from personal life: say a child Billy steals a bicycle. Ethically, he must return it. But most of us think it is much better, morally, if Billy returns it because he is sincerely sorry (and not, say, because his parents order him or threaten him). His intentions and state of mind matter to our evaluation. Or suppose Sally drives through a red light, killing a pedestrian. We would evaluate that act very differently if we knew it was not an accident but, rather, brimming hatred and score-settling, that triggered the crash. Same physical act but different intention and thus a different moral evaluation: the latter is clearly worse than the former. Legally, for instance, the intention marks the difference between first-degree murder and mere manslaughter. A comprehensive system of morality seems not only to require the proper *external* behaviour but also *internal* reflection and the right attitude. It is more demanding to include right intention, true, but the whole point of morality is to demand a certain standard from people and the institutions they form.

Considering this rule's application to international affairs, Walzer observes soberly that "a pure good will [is] . . . a political illusion." He also notes a vagueness in the just war tradition regarding whether this rule can be fulfilled only if there is *purity* of intention to secure the just cause, or whether it is possible to satisfy it, provided only that right intention is *present amongst the mix* of motives which usually animates state behaviour. Walzer himself opts for the latter course: he believes it is possible, and meaningful, to criticize some of the non-moral motives which states can have in going to war while still endorsing the moral motive. But that motive *must* be present: Walzer concurs that right orientation towards just cause is a necessary aspect of the justice of resorting to war. *This* is to say that it must be part of a state's subjective intention in pursuing war that it secure and fulfil the objective reason which gives it justification for fighting.[16]

A related question, which Walzer does not answer, is this: must the moral motivation merely be *present* in the mix of motives, or need it be *the main animating force* in the mix? Consider, for example, the *mix* of motives that the Allied coalition, led by the United States, might have had in 1991 for launching the first Persian Gulf War against Iraq: the repulsion of Iraq from Kuwait; the punishment of Iraqi aggression; the desire to secure the oil supply of the Persian Gulf region; President Bush Sr. wanting to demonstrate toughness in the run-up to the 1992 election; the desire by the United States to prove its superiority following the end of the Cold War with the Soviet Union; and the drive of the US military to test out its latest weaponry in real battlefield conditions, and perhaps to vanquish some ghosts left over from Vietnam. There are serious difficulties involved in discerning which motive dominates. Different parts of the American government, after all, might be seen as having had different intentions: which one would then count as the overall "dominant," or conclusive, one? Short-term aims might also have differed from medium- and long-term ones: which was the definitive motivation? This makes it more plausible, though less interesting, to conclude that the moral motive need *only be real and present* amongst the various non-moral motives for this criterion to be fulfilled.[17]

Perhaps the difficulty in discerning correct motivation is one reason why the right intention rule—unlike just cause—is nowhere to be found in the international law of armed conflict. This is interesting, and in my view an unfortunate omission, for several reasons. First, it is clearly part of common moral discourse surrounding war to speculate on, and judge, a state's resort to war based on its supposed motives. Both the first Iraq war (1991), and the second (2003), were labelled unjust by some people on grounds that America's motives supposedly revolved around oil, and/or imperialism, and/or chauvinism against Arabs and Muslims. Purists might object that an agent's intentions are a "mere" matter of ethics, whereas an agent's *conduct* is all that justice is, and can be, concerned with. But this fails to persuade. It is, for instance, part of justice systems the world over to include considerations of intention and motive when it comes to people on trial for such crimes as murder. Moreover, such trials also give indication as to how one might gain reliable knowledge of another's intent. *We know an agent's intent through his conduct.* Intentions can be, and ought to be, discerned through a reasoned examination of publicly accessible evidence, relying on behaviour, consideration of incentives and explicit avowals of intent. Intentions are neither infinitely redescribable nor irreducibly private and mysterious. They are connected to patterns of evidence, as well as constrained by norms of logical coherence, and so right intention is not an empty criterion for moral judgment during war. Though difficult, it is possible to tell whether a state is prosecuting a war out of ethnic hatred, for example, as opposed to vindicating its right of self-defence. Dark motivations produce distinctive and noticeable results, such as torture, massacres, mass rapes, and large-scale displacements. We have the civil wars, in the 1990s, in the former Yugoslavia to offer as historical evidence. We will take a closer look at Bosnia next chapter.

Perhaps a deeper critical question should be raised here: can collective agents, like states, have intentions at all? Implicit here is a systematic analogy between the behaviour of states and the behaviour of individual persons. But does it make sense to speak of state "rights" and "intentions"? To refer to "crimes" which states commit against each other, like aggression, which should be "punished"? Of states acting for the right reasons, out of the proper motives? This is "the domestic analogy".[18] This analogy, which also infuses international law, implies that one of the most *useful* ways to understand how states behave vis-à-vis each other is to liken such behaviour to the way in which individuals behave vis-à-vis each other. It is important to note that this analogy need *not* involve any kind of "statism": I have already said states are merely political associations, and their rights are derived from, and delimited by, the human rights of their individual members. The domestic analogy, rather, draws its vitality from the sheer difficulty of speaking about the behaviour of complex entities like states without employing simplifying assumptions—such as that they have a discernible identity, have intentions, face choices between alternatives, are thus responsible for their choices, and so on. It should also be emphasized that the domestic analogy is merely that: it is only generally persuasive and *neither* precludes the existence of important disanalogies *nor* commits us to a monolithic, naturalized and homogenous conception of the state. The main point here is interpretive: we have *always* employed the domestic analogy in our moral and legal discourse about the ethics of war and peace; it is inherent in the deepest structure of our talk about morality and war; and we all understand what is meant by it. It is an irreplaceable aid to understanding in this regard.

Linking the Categories and Calling Your Shot

One interesting aspect of right intention is whether it should be part of the justice of the resort to war that a state commit itself, both publicly and in advance, to adhering to the other rules of war, contained in *jus in bello* (the justice of conduct in war) and *jus post bellum* (the justice of peace treaties ending war). The idea here, first proposed by Kant, is that a state should commit itself to certain rules of conduct, and appropriate war termination, *as part of its original decision to begin the war*. Why? Because if it cannot so commit, it ought never to start the process. Unless a state pledges to fight in accord with the Hague and Geneva Conventions, and to terminate its war according to proportionate principles, it should never involve itself in such morally serious business as warfare. This seems an important and forward-looking way in which one could, so to speak, run a bright red thread through each of the three just war categories, *tying them into a coherent whole*.[19] This addition is compelling not only because of the moral import of an agent's intent but, moreover, to ensure consistency of just behaviour throughout all three phases of a military engagement. Thus, in addition to having one's subjective intentions (in going to war) be consistent with one's objectively just cause, one must also clearly and publicly commit, in advance of the war starting, to adhering to the other rules of just war theory.[20]

In other words, I propose we understand the three just war categories as ultimately linked. We can separate them out for the purpose of focusing on different issues which different phases of war raise. But that just highlights things for the sake of analysis and perspective; it is not actually splitting the categories. I prefer to think of just war theory as forming one long procedure according to which each preceding step must be satisfied before setting on to the next one. This way of thinking stresses the value of each rule yet also properly emphasizes *just cause as the crucial opening note, which sets the tone for everything which follows.*

Another proposal I wish to make here is this: you have to call your shot, as in billiards. To tie it into the next rule: you have to declare publicly not merely your resorting to war but your *main reason* for resorting to war. This proposal is needed to block the "scatter-shot" approach to justifying war, where you throw out every possible argument in favour of war, hoping some will stick in terms of persuading the public or attracting evidence which will stand the test of time and scrutiny. This addition is needed for both historical and conceptual reasons.

In recent history, the "scatter-shot" approach has been prominent, particularly in terms of America's 2003 Iraq attack and forcible regime change. Such was justified, we were told, because: 1) Saddam had WMDs, some of which could be deployed within forty-five minutes; 2) Saddam intended to give some of its WMDs to al-Qaeda, for use against America; 3) Saddam was actually involved with al-Qaeda in the 9/11 attacks; 4) Saddam needed to be overthrown as an act of humanitarian intervention on behalf of the Iraqi people; 5) Saddam posed a threat to regional security, especially regarding Israel and the Saudi oil fields; 6) Saddam kicked out the UN weapons inspectors in 1998 violating the Persian Gulf War treaty, which specified possible violent consequences for doing so; and 7) Saddam needed to be overthrown so as to create forcibly the first Arab democracy, which would serve as a Trojan Horse for better values throughout the Islamic world.[21]

Now, there's nothing wrong with having multiple reasons for going to war if these multiple reasons are all real and backed with evidence. What is wrong is mixing strong ones with weak ones so as to create a false impression of an "overwhelming pro-war case." Even if you do have multiple reasons, you have the right intention issue of whether you can plausibly intend them all. Human attention, and intention, is finite and needs to be focused. In my view, you need to focus on your main reason for going to war, have your intentions disciplined accordingly, and be prepared to be judged for how well you called your shot. (This focus will also increase your probability of success, since achievement requires concentration and commitment, as opposed to running off in all directions.) This leads into the conceptual reason here: the "scatter-shot approach" is objectionable because war is such a serious and destructive business. You must know what you're doing. And the "scatter-shot" approach, frankly, conveys the impression you do not. You're just letting it all hang out, hoping at least some of it will gather the support you need. But to unleash the terrible "black dogs of war," you need clear proof of a rock-solid reason for doing so, such as self-defence from actual aggression.

Public Declaration of War by a Proper Authority

War must be declared publicly by a proper authority. Why a *public* declaration? To inform the target, or enemy, country that they now face war and its substantial hazards. This also gives the enemy one last chance, prior to hostilities commencing, to cease aggression and begin a process of atonement. Such entitlement to public notification is codified in the Hague Convention III, which mandates that signatory countries must not commence conflict without ". . . previous and explicit warning, in the form either of a reasoned declaration of war or of an ultimatum with conditional declaration of war."[22] Public declaration also alerts one's own citizens to the government's intentions and plans. If state prerogatives in times of war are to be kept reasonably in line with the human rights of their members—which ground such state rights in the first place—we cannot lose sight of this just war criterion. The people must, in some public procedure, meaningfully consent to the launching of a war on their behalf.[23] More on the fuller meaning of this consent dimension later. For now, we continue to ask what "public" means. It means that the target country and one's own citizens can reasonably be expected to be informed of a declaration of war. Whether that be done through an official press conference, a formal speech, or a vote in an elected assembly is not that material. Delivering an official notice of hostilities, say to the enemy country's ambassador, is in my view nice (so to speak) but not required. What would fail to meet the meaning of a genuinely public declaration would be: burying a war declaration within another piece of legislation; or being insincerely cryptic in one's language surrounding the military steps one is about to take; or, more plausibly and expectedly, to refuse to admit that a war is on when a *de facto* unleashing of armed force is already on display. Recall, from the Introduction, that war is an actual, intentional and widespread armed conflict between political communities wherein the ultimate objective is to force the other side to accept one's will regarding governance.

The public declaration and domestic consent criteria need not preclude, or hamper the effectiveness of, rapid-fire responses to "blitzkrieg" attacks from dangerous aggressors. There are defensible procedures which can be put in place for just such reasons: for instance, empowering the executive branch of the national government to command the armed services to ensure rapid deployment, and then requiring legislative branch oversight and eventually approval (or not) of the executive's actions.[24]

[...]

International Authorization?

We know, from our just cause discussions, that Article 51 of the UN Charter famously proclaims that, should an armed attack occur against a member state of the UN, both the victim and any vindicators have "inherent rights" (or "natural rights") to self-defence and other-defence. So most international law experts agree that a United Nations Security Council (UNSC) vote is *not* needed to ground wars of self-defence or other-defence against obvious acts of cross-border aggression. That's clear. But what about wars where such is *not* the case: the aggression is *not* clear-cut; or the violence stays *within* borders and does not cross them (i.e., civil wars or humanitarian catastrophes); or indeed no aggression has *even occurred yet* (as in anticipatory attacks or "pre-emptive strikes")? Many international lawyers argue that, with these latter cases, UNSC authorization is absolutely necessary because: 1) they are not covered by the "inherent right" reference to self- and other-defence in the face of armed attack; 2) they are clearly more controversial than straightforward defence against an act of aggression which has already happened; and 3) the background ideals of the Charter include substantial UN and UNSC responsibilities for war and peace. (Indeed, the very first article of the UN Charter declares that one of the UN's core purposes is to "maintain international peace and security," and Articles 23–54 detail exhaustive procedures and powers for the UNSC to deploy in pursuit of this ideal.) So, a pro-UNSC vote for action in any of these controversial cases is a must.[30]

This was the position of most of the world in the run-up to America's 2003 Iraq attack. America was engaging in a pre-emptive strike (i.e., aggression had not yet happened), moreover one aiming to forcibly change the regime of a UN member. Thus, it needed a UNSC vote. It did not get one, and so the war was illegal and unjust. The official American line was different. While the UNSC did not vote explicitly in favour of "war" or an "American attack," it *did* demand Saddam resume UN weapons inspections or else face "serious consequences." Bush Jr. asserted that the war power was contained within the phrase "serious consequences" and so argued that UNSC authorization was in fact given. In any event, the Americans continued, the terms of the 1991 Persian Gulf War treaty (which was ratified by the UNSC in 1991) pledged Iraq to complete compliance with post-war measures, and also threatened a possible return to hostilities should complete compliance not be forthcoming. Since Saddam booted out the UN weapons inspectors in 1998, he was in violation of that UNSC resolution, which contained this explicit warning of, and authorization for, armed force. Failing all that, America said, the Iraq attack was needed to defend America from future acts of terrorism, and self-defence is indeed recognized by the Charter as an "inherent right."[31]

So who was right? It is not so clear if by "right" you mean "has the best interpretation of international law." Believe it or not, both sides have serious and strong legal arguments; and it is not obviously the case that one side is more powerful; and there's no overriding global legal authority to render a decision. Indeed I venture to say this is one of the reasons why international law is not completely satisfying in connection with *jus ad bellum*. Not only does it not directly deal with the hardest cases—like pre-emptive attacks, terrorist strikes, humanitarian crises and civil wars—the principles which it enumerates are not clear. Indeed, they are predictably vague because international law is the product of state consensus and it is very hard to get that on such controversial issues. The vagueness, in turn, allows for indeterminacy and for opposing sides to present strong arguments with little prospect of resolution. Thus, just war theory is stronger and more insightful on *jus ad bellum* than are the laws of armed conflict. (But note that the reverse is probably true in connection with *jus in bello*, where the detail of international law achieves incredible sophistication. See Chapter 4.) But if by "right" you mean who is morally correct, then please consult the next chapter for an investigation into the justice of the Iraq attack, where I think answers can be had.

Should we buy into UN claims about its sweeping authority in connection with international peace and security, which get asserted throughout the Charter and other documents in a very robust way? I personally believe that it is a very *desirable* thing to get UN authorization to go to war but I hesitate to say it is strictly *morally necessary*. On the one hand, requiring international authorization would represent one more barrier to overcome in any pro-war move, and so would make the resort to war more difficult. Isn't that a good thing? I guess so, but against that very point is that requiring international authorization might consume precious hours, days and weeks, with the result being that the aggressor gets entrenched and becomes more difficult to resist. We can easily imagine cases where the international community does not know enough, or care enough, about a local or regional war to get involved: so why give it authority in that regard? Let's leave it to the people with their fundamental interests and rights actually at stake.

There's also the very fitness and legitimacy of the UN and the UNSC themselves to consider. At any given time, only fifteen members are on the UNSC and, of those, only five hold vetos and permanent seats. These five form the world's most exclusive club, and they are all rich, northern, nuclear powers, and all but one is Western. What gives such an exclusive club the right to legislate on war and peace for the world—especially in regions they know quite little about? Second, it is important not to succumb to naive and romantic ideas about what the UN *is*, based on visions of what it *might ideally become*. The UN is not a world government; it is merely a voluntary association of states. It has, over the years, faced searing questions about its competence, efficiency, treatment and oversight of staff, and even over its integrity. (The UN has recently been embroiled in a huge corruption scandal alleging thefts and kickbacks in its administration of the Oil-for-Food program in Iraq in the late 1990s.) And the UNSC record authorizing wars and peacekeeping missions is spotty at best. While the UN has had real success—over Suez, over East Timor—it has had many controversies and failures, such as Cyprus and Congo. UN peacekeepers were so ineffective in Bosnia they were actually taken hostage by the Serbs and, most notoriously, the UNSC failed to intervene at all in the near-genocidal civil war in Rwanda in the summer of 1994. *This*, we might ask, is the institution to which international lawyers would have us hand over ultimate authority on war and peace issues?

There is also the most important fact that, in spite of globalization, the state remains the crucial scene of political action in our lives. Recall that the UN is a voluntary association of states, and thus is ultimately their creature. The UN Charter itself enshrines state rights to political sovereignty and territorial integrity. And states remain, in terms of causal impact, the best poised to do serious harm to, or serious good for, their citizens. No wonder in recent history so many national groups have sought their own independent state, and why so much attention is paid to the legitimacy or moral quality of state structures. We still experience political life first and foremost as members of nation-states—Americans, Brazilians, Canadians, etc.—and only secondarily (or even less) as citizens of the globe. We strongly prefer to live in groups; and while this fact never justifies shoddy treatment of other groups, it is a reality which must be accommodated by any theory of international justice.[32]

My overall view on international authorization of war is this: it is certainly not required in straightforward cases of defence (whether of self or others) from actual aggression: no UNSC fiat could overturn those pre-existing rights of people. In more contested cases—humanitarian intervention and especially anticipatory attack involving regime change—the desirability of international authorization increases very considerably but might not even then, pending the details, strictly be required. I do not wish to be completely dismissive: at the very least, the UNSC always provides an on-going forum for countries to discuss and debate these issues and to present their cases for going to war on a formal basis, and that is always going to be worth something indeed.

LAST RESORT

Winston Churchill once said, memorably, that it was far better to 'jaw jaw" than to "war war" (i.e., to try to talk a problem over through diplomacy before fighting). Walzer concurs, observing that: "It is obvious that measures short of war are preferable to war itself." He continues: "One always wants to see diplomacy tried before the resort to war, so that we are sure that war is the last resort." In spite of this endorsement of the traditional last resort criterion, which is codified in Articles 2(4) and 33–40 of the UN Charter,[33] Walzer is quick with some helpful caveats. First, he points out that, strictly speaking, there is no such thing as a *last* resort. No matter how fearful the situation, there is always something else which can be tried—yet another round of diplomatic negotiations, for instance—prior to the resort to war. So it would be absurd, in this literal sense, to say that states may turn to war only as a last resort.[34] A second caveat concerns the fact that negotiations, threats and economic sanctions are frequently offered as morally better means of international problem-solving than the use of force. At face value, this claim is indisputable: if a reasonable resolution to the crisis in question can be had through a credible and permissible threat, or through a negotiating session, or perhaps through sanctions, then surely that is preferable to running the sizeable risks, and certain destructions, of war. Upon closer inspection, however, much depends on the nature of the particular act of aggression and the nature of the aggressive regime itself. Sometimes threats, diplomacy and sanctions will not work. The incidents leading up to the 1991 Persian Gulf War are instructive: Saddam Hussein, in the face of all three, refused to be budged from his ill-gotten Kuwaiti gains.[35] Care must be taken that appeals to last resort do not end up rewarding aggression, by giving the aggressor extra time to entrench himself inside the victim. Finally, Albert Pierce and Lori Damrosch have pointed out that the levelling of systematic economic sanctions on an aggressor often violates the *jus in bello* principle of non-combatant immunity, since it is most often innocent civilians (often the poorest and most vulnerable) who bear the brunt of sweeping economic embargoes levelled on their country. In the absence of force directed against them, outlaw regimes always seem to find a way, within their own borders, to take care of themselves. The Hussein regime in Iraq, once more, offers lessons—surviving twelve years in the teeth of sweeping sanctions, which were then given up after the March 2003 US-led strike, that forcibly removed the regime from power. How much innocent civilian deprivation had to be endured while waiting for the sanctions to do their job—which they never did? I direct the reader to the relevant literature on the effects of the Iraqi sanctions in the 1990s.[36]

It seems much more plausible to contend *not* that war be the literal last resort—after all other imaginable means have been totally exhausted—but, rather, that states *ought not to be hasty in their resort to force*. There ought to be a strong presumption against the resort to force. Article 2(4) of the UN Charter is clear evidence of our deep commitment to such a presumption. It reads that all UN Members "shall refrain . . . from the threat or use of force against . . . any state."[37] But beyond this general principle, much depends on the concrete details of the actual situation in question. It is critically important, for example, when the aggressor is mounting a swift and brutal invasion, to respond effectively before all is lost. It is also relevant to consider the nature of the territory of the victim of aggression; if it is a tiny country, like Israel, the need for a speedy and effective response against aggression will likely be much greater than that required by a country the size and strength of the United States. Any response from the international community is likewise relevant. But attention must always be focused on the nature and severity of the aggressor and its actions, for frequently the international community is sluggish in mounting an effective response to aggression. The key question this criterion demands to be always asked, and then answered in the affirmative, is this: is the proposed use of force *reasonable*, given the situation and the nature of the aggression?

PROBABILITY OF SUCCESS

Probability of success is another *jus ad bellum* rule for which only general principles can be convincingly conveyed. Its prudential flavour explains this: probability of success is always a matter of circumstance, of taking reasonable options within the constraints and opportunities presented by the world. The traditional aim of this criterion—which, like right intention, is actually *not* contained within international law—is to bar lethal violence which is known in advance to be futile. As such, the principle is laudable and necessary for any comprehensive just war theory. Great care, however, needs to be exercised that this criterion, like last resort, does not amount to rewarding aggression, and especially that by larger and more powerful nations. This is so because smaller and weaker nations will face a comparatively greater task when it comes to fulfilling this criterion (which I think explains its absence from international law). And the calculation of expected probability of success for resorting to war is difficult. The vicissitudes of war are, as we know from history, sometimes among the most difficult phenomena to predict. Even when the odds seemed incredibly long, remarkable successes have sometimes, somehow, been achieved. Such are the stuff of military legend, like the ancient Greeks fending off the onslaught of Persians or perhaps even the American revolutionaries overthrowing the rule of the mighty lion of the British Empire. The lack of predictability, though, does not always turn out for the better. A notorious example is that the armies of Europe expected, in September 1914, to be home to celebrate Christmas.[38] Walzer also suggests that there are considerations of self-respect here, according to which victims of aggression ought to be permitted at least some resistance, should they decide on it, as an expression of their strong objection to the aggression and as an affirmation of their rights. It thus seems reasonable to judge that, given an act of aggression and given that the other *jus ad bellum* criteria are met, there is a presumption in favour of permitting some kind of armed response, even when the odds of military success (however defined) seem long. At the same time, this rule is not dormant: it remains important that communities contemplating war in response to aggression still consider whether such an extreme measure has any reasonable probability of success. That is the least, we might say, that they owe themselves.

PROPORTIONALITY

Proportionality, codified at Articles 22–3 of the Hague Convention III, is one of the most contentious and challenging *jus ad bellum* criteria, ranking close to just cause itself. It mandates that a state considering a just war must weigh the expected *universal* (not just selfish national) benefits of doing so against the expected *universal* costs. Only if the projected benefits, in terms of securing the just cause, are at least equal to, and preferably greater than, such costs as casualties may the war action proceed. Walzer wrestles at length with the considerable difficulties presented by this otherwise sensible rule. On the one hand, the unchecked triumph of aggression is for him "a greater evil" than war. He also comments that "prudence can be, and has to be, accommodated within the argument for justice." On the other hand, Walzer comments on "the terrible presumption" behind the cost-benefit comparisons implicit in appeals to proportionality. He declares that "we have no way that even mimics mathematics" of making such proportionality judgments. He asks rhetorically: "How do we measure the value of a country's independence against the value of defeating an aggressive regime?"[39] In other words, how can we pretend to measure, on the same scale of value, the benefits of defeating aggression against the body count needed to achieve it? For example, it sounds ridiculous—literally, groundless— to say things like: "My country's freedom from aggression is worth $300 million dollars and 245,000 casualties." The numbers appear completely arbitrary, and the comparison between an abstract, like independence, and a concrete, like cash and casualties, seems as ill-conceived as one between apples and exchange rates—they are simply different things.

The challenges of proportional "calculation" explode, in both number and complexity, as soon as one puts further thought to the question. What things actually count as costs and benefits in wartime? Only elements we can *quantify*, like the body count and economic expenditures? But usually we also want to appeal to *qualitative* elements, like the value of sovereignty and not enduring life as slaves to a foreign invader. Is there a distinction between explicit and implicit costs, such as costs of mobilization on the one hand and, on the other, what else besides war might we have done with our time and treasure? Is there a difference between short-term and long-term benefits? Is it only the costs and benefits of prudence that matter, or do those of morality count as well? How to weigh the "universal" costs and benefits against each other when, usually during war, those who pay the costs *are not the same group* as those who enjoy the benefits, as when soldiers pay the present price for the future independence of their fellow countrymen? The manifest, and manifold, difficulties involved in proportionality calculations cause vexation for just war theorists, and rightly so. The calculations needed are simply too complex and wide-ranging. It is wildly improbable that we could ever devise a completely satisfying set of cost-benefit formulae with regard to wartime action. Far better, I believe, to stick to a firm set of clear and universal rules to guide conduct, which is what the rest of just war theory strives to offer.

Walzer's final judgment on this issue, which seems sound, is that there is *some* truth in the proportionality maxim. But he insists that "it is a gross truth," an unrefined and imprecise truth, which can only point to obvious considerations of prudence and utility *as limiting conditions* on the pursuit of rights-respecting justice in wartime. Proportionality, at best, provides some checks and balances, *some outside constraints*, on the drive to secure a just cause. In other words—and with some irony—we know much better what disproportionality is than proportionality. We can usually recognize the former but frankly have trouble precisely defining the latter. We know when a war is a disproportionate (i.e., exaggerated, harmful and inappropriate) response to a problem, just like we know that, within the context of a marriage, threatening divorce over a disagreement over what to have for dinner is disproportionate. Proportionality has, so to speak, negative content: it does not really positively add anything except to remind us that the problem in question has to be so severe (like unjust armed invasion) that war is, in fact, an appropriate response—and to suggest that the good to be gained from the war must be better than the substantial costs and evils we know war always brings in train.

Providing some war examples, Walzer says that, even though justice may have permitted otherwise, it was appropriate on grounds of proportionality that the United States did not go to war against the Soviet Union after the latter invaded Hungary in 1956, or Czechoslovakia in 1968. The real threat of a broad-based nuclear exchange between the superpowers was simply greater, and more universally fearful, than allowing Soviet expansion at the particular expense of the independence of these nations.[40] Slightly different, more obvious, examples—deeper in history—include some of the old European wars sparked by marriage (or failure to marry) or failure to agree on who would succeed to the throne, or simply by some personal slight delivered to one monarch by another. None of these reasons balance with something as deadly as war as a "solution." To go even farther back, if the Trojan War really was fought over Helen—"the woman whose face launched a thousand ships"—then we can certainly ask questions of justice whether ordering all that fighting and killing was truly proportionate to the problem.

SUMMARY

This is a contemporary updating of the classical account of *jus ad bellum*. Any state, seeking to go to war against any other state, must show that its resort to armed force fulfils *each* of the six rules explained above: just cause; right intention; public declaration by a proper authority: last resort; probability of success; and proportionality. Failure to fulfill *even one* rule renders the resort to force unjust, and thus subject to criticism, resistance and punishment. This allows us to appreciate just how *demanding and stringent* is just war theory. The laws of armed conflict make much the same claims, except that they: 1) do not endorse the rules of right intention and probability of success; 2) are more vague; and 3) are based on a looser conception of political legitimacy. Just war theory is thus *even more demanding than international law*, which is predictable since, quite often, morality sets itself a higher standard than law.

Since *jus ad bellum* is the province of those exercising the war power—often, but not always, heads of state or the executive branch of government—it is their responsibility to ensure that its standards are fulfilled. By the same token, it is they who must answer for any *jus ad bellum* violations, for instance in war crimes trials after the war is over. As an illustration, consider that the Nazi high command, or what was left of it, was charged—among other things—with "crimes against peace" by the prosecutors during the Nuremberg war crimes trials after World War II. This is to say that they were accused—and many eventually convicted—of violating *jus ad bellum* (i.e., of committing aggression, of having waged an unjust war).[41]

The ultimate concepts and values underlying contemporary just war theory are the idea of a minimally just and therefore legitimate political community and the human rights of its individual citizens. It is for the sake of defending a minimally just state, and the human rights of its citizens, that we can morally contemplate the use of measures as forceful and destructive as those of war. We have this moral permission as a result of what aggression means—how it attacks the most basic values and possibilities of human civilization, of the need to respond to it with effective resistance.

NOTES

1. Cicero, *De Re Publica*, (III, 23), trans. R. Regan at p. 16 of his *Just War: Principles and Cases* (Washington, DC: Georgetown University Press, 1996).

2. M. Walzer, "World War II: Why Was This War Different?" *Philosophy and Public Affairs* (1971/72), 3–21.

3. For the laws of armed conflict themselves, see Appendix A. Consult also W. Reisman and C. Antoniou, eds. *The Laws of War* (New York: Vintage, 1994); A. Roberts and R. Guelff, eds. *Documents on the Laws of War* (Oxford: Oxford University Press, 1999) and G. Best, *War and Law since 1945* (Oxford: Clarendon, 1994).

[...]

16. Walzer, *Wars*, xix.

17. Walzer, *Wars*, xix–xx.

18. Walzer, *Wars*, 58; H. Suganami, *The Domestic Analogy and World Order Proposals* (Cambridge: Cambridge University Press, 1989).

19. Thanks to Thomas Pogge for the image.

20. For more on this proposed addition to right intention, and the original Kant scholarship, see Orend, *Kantian Perspective*.

21. Woodward, *Plan*; W. Murray and R. Scales, *The Iraq War* (Cambridge, MA: Harvard University Press, 2003).

22. Reisman and Antoniou, eds., *Laws*, 40.

23. Walzer, *Wars*, 34–40 and 138–43.

24. This is not to say that only Western-style constitutional democracies can fulfil this rule: clearly different regime types can and should publicly declare war. But that fact will not stop me from discussing issues of special importance to Western societies, such as the division of war powers.

[...]

30. Reisman and Antoniou, eds. *Laws*, 3–35; Regan, *Principles*, 20–47 and 213–31.

31. Woodward, *Plan*.

32. M. Walzer, *Thick and Thin* (New Haven: Yale University Press, 1995).

33. Reisman and Antoniou, eds., *Laws*, 3–9.

34. Walzer, *Wars*, 84, xiv.

35. Walzer, *Wars*, xiii–xiv.

36. Walzer, *Wars*, xxv–xxxii; A. Pierce, "Just War Principles and Economic Sanctions," *Ethics and International Affairs* (1996), 99–113; L.F. Damrosch, "The Collective Enforcement of International Norms Through Economic Sanctions," *Ethics and International Affairs* (1994), 60–80; G. Simons, *The Scourging of Iraq* (New York: Macmillan, 2nd ed., 1996); R. Clark, *The Impact of Sanctions on Iraq* (London: World View Forum, 1996) and A. Arnove and A. Abunimah, eds. *Iraq Under Siege* (London: South End Press, 2000).

37. Regan, *Cases*, 214; and Reisman and Antoniou, eds., *Laws*, 5–9.

38. Walzer, *Wars*, 67–74.

39. Walzer, *Wars*, xv–xxi.

40. Walzer, *Wars*, xv–xxi.

41. J. Persico, *Nuremberg: Infamy on Trial* (New York: Penguin, 1995).

*Brian Orend is the director of international studies and a professor of philosophy at the University of Waterloo in Waterloo, Ontario.

Brian Orend, "*Jus ad Bellum* #1: Resisting Aggression," Chap. 2 in *The Morality of War* (Peterborough, NH: Broadview Press, 2006), 31–33, 46–51, 54–62.

The Legalist Paradigm

by Michael Walzer*

If states actually do possess rights more or less as individuals do, then it is possible to imagine a society among them more or less like the society of individuals. The comparison of international to civil order is crucial to the theory of aggression. I have already been making it regularly. Every reference to aggression as the international equivalent of armed robbery or murder, and every comparison of home and country or of personal liberty and political independence, relies upon what is called the *domestic analogy*.[9] Our primary perceptions and judgments of aggression are the products of analogical reasoning. When the analogy is made explicit, as it often is among the lawyers, the world of states takes on the shape of a political society the character of which is entirely accessible through such notions as crime and punishment, self-defense, law enforcement, and so on.

These notions, I should stress, are not incompatible with the fact that international society as it exists today is a radically imperfect structure. As we experience it, that society might be likened to a defective building, founded on rights; its superstructure raised, like that of the state itself, through political conflict, cooperative activity, and commercial exchange; the whole thing shaky and unstable because it lacks the rivets of authority. It is like domestic society in that men and women live at peace within it (sometimes), determining the conditions of their own existence, negotiating and bargaining with their neighbors. It is unlike domestic society in that every conflict threatens the structure as a whole with collapse. Aggression challenges it directly and is much more dangerous than domestic crime, because there are no policemen. But that only means that the "citizens" of international society must rely on themselves and on one another. Police powers are distributed among all the members. And these members have not done enough in the exercise of their powers if they merely contain the aggression or bring it to a speedy end—as if the police should stop a murderer after he has killed only one or two people and send him on his way. The rights of the member states must be vindicated, for it is only by virtue of those rights that there is a society at all. If they cannot be upheld (at least sometimes), international society collapses into a state of war or is transformed into a universal tyranny.

From this picture, two presumptions follow. The first, which I have already pointed out, is the presumption in favor of military resistance once aggression has begun. Resistance is important so that rights can be maintained and future aggressors deterred. The theory of aggression restates the old doctrine of the just war: it explains when fighting is a crime and when it is permissible, perhaps even morally desirable.* The victim of aggression fights in self-defense, but he isn't only defending himself, for aggression is a crime against society as a whole. He fights in its name and not only in his own. Other states can rightfully join the victim's resistance; their war has the same character as his own, which is to say, they are entitled not only to repel the attack but also to punish it. All resistance is also law enforcement. Hence the second presumption: when fighting breaks out, there must always be some state against which the law can and should be enforced. Someone must be responsible, for someone decided to break the peace of the society of states. No war, as medieval theologians explained, can be just on both sides.[10]

There are, however, wars that are just on neither side, because the idea of justice doesn't pertain to them or because the antagonists are both aggressors, fighting for territory or power where they have no right. The first case I have already alluded to in discussing the voluntary combat of aristocratic warriors. It is sufficiently rare in human history that nothing more need be said about it here. The second case is illustrated by those wars that Marxists call "imperialist," which are not fought between conquerors and victims but between conquerors and conquerors, each side seeking dominion over the other or the two of them competing to dominate some third party. Thus Lenin's description of the struggles between "have" and "have-not" nations in early twentieth century Europe: " . . . picture to yourselves a slave-owner who owned 100 slaves warring against a slave-owner who owned 200 slaves for a more 'just' distribution of slaves. Clearly, the application of the term 'defensive' war in such a case . . . would be sheer deception . . ."[11] But it is important to stress that we can penetrate the deception only insofar as we can ourselves distinguish justice and injustice: the theory of imperialist war presupposes the theory of aggression. If one insists that all wars on all sides are acts of conquest or attempted conquest, or that all states at all times, would conquer if they could, then the argument for justice is defeated before it begins and the moral judgments we actually make are derided as fantasies. Consider the following passage from Edmund Wilson's book on the American Civil War:[12]

> I think that it is a serious deficiency on the part of historians that they
> so rarely interest themselves in biological and zoological phenomena.
> In a recent . . . film showing life at the bottom of the sea, a primitive

organism called a sea slug is seen gobbling up small organisms through a large orifice at one end of its body; confronted with another sea slug of an only slightly lesser size, it ingurgitates that, too. Now the wars fought by human beings are stimulated as a rule . . . by the same instincts as the voracity of the sea slug.

There are no doubt wars to which that image might be fit, though it is not a terribly useful image with which to approach the Civil War. Nor does it account for our ordinary experience of international society. Not all states are sea-slug states, gobbling up their neighbors. There are always groups of men and women who would live if they could ill peaceful enjoyment of their rights and who have chosen political leaders who represent that desire. The deepest purpose of the state is not ingestion but defense, and the least that can be said is that many actual states serve that purpose. When their territory is attacked or their sovereignty challenged, it makes sense to look for an aggressor and not merely for a natural predator. Hence we need a theory of aggression rather than a zoological account.

The theory of aggression first takes shape under the aegis of the domestic analogy, I am going to call that primary form of the theory the *legalist paradigm*, since it consistently reflects the conventions of law and order. It does not necessarily reflect the arguments of the lawyers, though legal as well as moral debate has its starting point here.[13] Later on, I will suggest that our judgments about the justice and injustice of particular wars are not entirely determined by the paradigm. The complex realities of international society drive us toward a revisionist perspective, and the revisions will be significant ones. But the paradigm must first be viewed in its unrevised form; it is our baseline, our model, the fundamental structure for the moral comprehension of war. We begin with the familiar world of individuals and rights, of crimes and punishments. The theory of aggression can then be summed up in six propositions.

1. *There exists an international society of independent states.* States are the members of this society, not private men and women. In the absence of an universal state, men and women are protected and their interests represented only by their own governments. Though states are founded for the sake of life and liberty, they cannot be challenged in the name of life and liberty by any other states. Hence the principle of non-intervention, which I will analyze later on. The rights of private persons can be recognized in international society, as in the UN Charter of Human Rights, but they cannot be enforced without calling into question the dominant values of that society: the survival and independence of the separate political communities.

2. *This international society has a law that establishes the rights of its members—above all, the rights of territorial integrity and political sovereignty.* Once again, these two rest ultimately on the right of men and women to build a common life and to risk their individual lives only when they freely choose to do so. But the relevant law refers only to states, and its details are fixed by the intercourse of states, through complex processes of conflict and consent. Since these processes are continuous, international society has no natural shape; nor are rights within it ever finally or exactly determined. At any given moment, however, one can distinguish the territory of one people from that of another and say something about the scope and limits of sovereignty.

3. *Any use of force or imminent threat of force by one state against the political sovereignty or territorial integrity of another constitutes aggression and is a criminal act.* As with domestic crime, the argument here focuses narrowly on actual or imminent boundary crossings: invasions and physical assaults. Otherwise, it is feared, the notion of resistance to aggression would have no determinate meaning. A state cannot be said to be forced to fight unless the necessity is both obvious and urgent.

4. *Aggression justifies two kinds of violent response: a war of self-defense by the victim and a war of law enforcement by the victim and any other member of international society.* Anyone can come to the aid of a victim, use necessary force against an aggressor, and even make whatever is the international equivalent of a "citizen's arrest." As in domestic society, the obligations of bystanders are not easy to make out, but it is the tendency of the theory to undermine the right of neutrality and to require widespread participation in the business of law enforcement. In the Korean War, this participation was authorized by the United Nations, but even in such cases the actual decision to join the fighting remains a unilateral one, best understood by analogy to the decision of a private citizen who rushes to help a man or woman attacked on the street.

5. *Nothing but aggression can justify war.* The central purpose of the theory is to limit the occasions for war. "There is a single and only just cause for commencing a war," wrote Vitoria, "namely, a wrong received."[14] There must actually have been a wrong, and it must actually have been received (or its receipt must be, as it were, only minutes away). Nothing else warrants the use of force in international society—above all, not any difference of religion or politics. Domestic heresy and injustice are never actionable in the world of states: hence, again, the principle of non-intervention.

6. *Once the aggressor state has been militarily repulsed, it can also be punished.* The conception of just war as an act of punishment is very old, though neither the procedures nor the forms of punishment have ever been firmly established in customary or positive international law. Nor are its purposes entirely clear: to exact retribution, to deter other states, to restrain or reform this one? All three figure largely in the literature, though it is probably fair to say that deterrence and restraint are most commonly accepted. When people talk of fighting a war against war this is usually what they have in mind. The domestic maxim is, punish crime to prevent violence; its international analogue is, punish aggression to prevent war. Whether the state as a whole or only particular persons are the proper objects of punishment is a harder question, for reasons I will consider later on. But the implication of the paradigm is clear: if states are members of international society, the subjects of rights, they must also be (somehow) the objects of punishment.

*I shall say nothing here of the argument for nonviolent resistance to aggression, according to which fighting is neither desirable nor necessary. This argument has not figured much in the development of the conventional view. Indeed, it poses a radical challenge to the conventions: if aggression can be resisted, and at least sometimes successfully resisted, without war, it may be a less serious crime than has commonly been supposed. I will take up this possibility and its moral implications in the Afterword.

NOTES

[...]

9. For a critique of this analogy, see the two essays by Hadley Bull, "Society and Anarchy in International Relations," and "The Grotian Conception of International Society," in *Diplomatic Investigations*, chs. 2 and 3.

10. See Vitoria, *On the Law of War*, p. 177.

11. Lenin, *Socialism and War* (London, 1940), pp. 10–11.

12. Edmund Wilson, *Patriotic Gore* (New York, 1966), p. xi.

13. It is worth noting that the United Nations' recently adopted definition of aggression closely follows the paradigm: see the *Report of the Special Committee on the Question of Defending Aggression* (1974). General Assembly Official Records, 29th session, supplement no. 19 (A/9619), pp. 10–13. The definition is reprinted and analyzed in Yehuda Melzer, *Concepts of Just War* (Leyden, 1975), pp. 26ff.

14. *On the Law of War*, p. 170.

***Michael Walzer,** a political philosopher, is a professor emeritus at the Institute for Advanced Study, Princeton, NJ, and a coeditor of *Dissent*. Among his many books are *On Toleration* (2000) and *Spheres Justice: A Defense of Pluralism and Equality* (1983).

Walzer, Michael. *Just and Unjust Wars: A Moral Argument with Historical Illustrations*. New York: Basic Books, 1977, 58–63.

The Slippery Slope to Preventive War

*by Neta C. Crawford**

The Bush administration's arguments in favor of a preemptive doctrine rest on the view that warfare has been transformed. As Colin Powell argues, "It's a different world . . . it's a new kind of threat."[1] And in several important respects, war has changed along the lines the administration suggests, although that transformation has been under way for at least the last ten to fifteen years. Unconventional adversaries prepared to wage unconventional war can conceal their movements, weapons, and immediate intentions and conduct devastating surprise attacks.[2] Nuclear, chemical, and biological weapons, though not widely dispersed, are more readily available than they were in the recent past. And the everyday infrastructure of the United States can be turned against it as were the planes the terrorists hijacked on September 11, 2001. Further, the administration argues that we face enemies who "reject basic human values and hate the United States and everything for which it stands."[3] Although vulnerability could certainly be reduced in many ways, it is impossible to achieve complete invulnerability.

Such vulnerability and fear, the argument goes, means the United States must take the offensive. Indeed, soon after the September 11, 2001, attacks, members of the Bush administration began equating self-defense with preemption:

> There is no question but that the United States of America has every
> right, as every country does, of self-defense, and the problem with terror-
> ism is that there is no way to defend against the terrorists at every place
> and every time against every conceivable technique. Therefore, the only
> way to deal with the terrorist network is to take the battle to them. That
> is in fact what we're doing. That is in effect self-defense of a preemptive
> nature.[4]

The character of potential threats becomes extremely important in evaluating the legitimacy of the new preemption doctrine, and thus the assertion that the United States faces rogue enemies who oppose everything about the United States must be carefully evaluated. There is certainly robust evidence to believe that al-Qaeda members desire to harm the United States and American citizens. The National Security Strategy makes a questionable leap, however, when it assumes that "rogue states" also desire to harm the United States and pose an imminent military threat. Further, the administration blurs the distinction between "rogue states" and terrorists, essentially erasing the difference between terrorists and those states in which they reside: "We make no distinction between terrorists and those who knowingly harbor or provide aid to them."[5] But these distinctions do indeed make a difference.

Legitimate preemption could occur if four necessary conditions were met. First, the party contemplating preemption would have a narrow conception of the "self" to be defended in circumstances of self-defense. Preemption is not justified to protect imperial interests or assets taken in a war of aggression. Second, there would have to be strong evidence that war was inevitable and likely in the immediate future. Immediate threats are those which can be made manifest within days or weeks unless action is taken to thwart them. This requires clear intelligence showing that a potential aggressor has both the capability and the intention to do harm in the near future. Capability alone is not a justification. Third, preemption should be likely to succeed in reducing the threat. Specifically, there should be a high likelihood that the source of the military threat can be found and the damage that it was about to do can be greatly reduced or eliminated by a preemptive attack. If preemption is likely to fail, it should not be undertaken. Fourth, military force must be necessary; no other measures can have time to work or be likely to work.

A Defensible Self

On the face of it, the self-defense criteria seem clear. When our lives are threatened, we must be able to defend ourselves using force if necessary. But self-defense may have another meaning, that in which our "self " is expressed not only by mere existence, but also by a free and prosperous life. For example, even if a tyrant would allow us to live, but not under institutions of our own choosing, we may justly fight to free ourselves from political oppression. But how far do the rights of the self extend? If someone threatens our access to food, or fuel, or shelter, can we legitimately use force? Or if they allow us access to the material goods necessary for our existence, but charge such a high price that we must make a terrible choice between food and health care, or between mere existence and growth, are we justified in using force to secure access to a good that would enhance the self? When economic interests and vulnerabilities are understood to be global, and when the moral and political community of democracy and human rights are defined more broadly than ever before, the self-conception of great powers tends to enlarge. But a broad conception of self is not necessarily legitimate and neither are the values to be defended completely obvious.

For example, the U.S. definition of the self to be defended has become very broad. The administration, in its most recent Quadrennial Defense Review, defines "enduring national interests" as including "contributing to economic wellbeing," which entails maintaining "vitality and productivity of the global economy" and "access to key markets and strategic resources." Further, the goal of U.S. strategy, according to this document, is to maintain "preeminence."[6] The National Security Strategy also fuses ambitious political and economic goals with security: "The U.S. national security strategy will be based on a distinctly American internationalism that reflects the fusion of our values and our national interests. The aim of this strategy is to help make the world not just safer but better." And "today the distinction between domestic and foreign affairs is diminishing."[7]

If the self is defined so broadly and threats to this greater "self" are met with military force, at what point does self-defense begin to look like aggression? As Richard Betts has argued, "When security is defined in terms broader than protecting the near-term integrity of national sovereignty and borders, the distinction between offense and defense blurs hopelessly. . . . Security can be as insatiable an appetite as acquisitiveness—there may never be enough buffers."[8] The large self-conception of the United States could lead to a tendency to intervene everywhere that this greater self might conceivably be at risk of, for example, losing access to markets. Thus, a conception of the self that justifies legitimate preemption in self-defense must be narrowly confined to immediate risks to life and health within borders or to the life and health of citizens abroad.

THRESHOLD AND CONDUCT OF JUSTIFIED PREEMPTION

The Bush administration is correct to emphasize the United States' vulnerability to terrorist attack. The administration also argues that the United States cannot wait for a smoking gun if it comes in the form of a mushroom cloud. There may be little or no evidence in advance of a terrorist attack using nuclear, chemical, or biological weapons. Yet, under this view, the requirement for evidence is reduced to a fear that the other has, or might someday acquire, the means for an assault. But the bar for preemption seems to be set too low in the Bush administration's National Security Strategy. How much and what kind of evidence is necessary to justify preemption? What is a credible fear that justifies preemption?

As Michael Walzer has argued persuasively in *Just and Unjust Wars*, simple fear cannot be the only criterion. Fear is omnipresent in the context of a terrorist campaign. And if fear was once clearly justified, when and how will we know that a threat has been significantly reduced or eliminated? The nature of fear may be that once a group has suffered a terrible surprise attack, a government and people will, justifiably, be vigilant. Indeed they may, out of fear, be aware of threats to the point of hypervigilance—seeing small threats as large, and squashing all potential threats with enormous brutality.

The threshold for credible fear is necessarily lower in the context of contemporary counterterrorism war, but the consequences of lowering the threshold may be increased instability and the premature use of force. If this is the case, if fear justifies assault, then the occasions for attack will potentially be limitless since, according to the Bush administration's own arguments, we cannot always know with certainty what the other side has, where it might be located, or when it might be used. If one attacks on the basis of fear, or suspicion that a potential adversary may someday have the intention and capacity to harm you, then the line between preemptive and preventive war has been crossed. Again, the problem is knowing the capabilities and intentions of potential adversaries.

There is thus a fine balance to be struck. The threshold of evidence and warning cannot be too low, where simple apprehension that a potential adversary might be out there somewhere and may be acquiring the means to do the United States harm triggers the offensive use of force. This is not preemption, but paranoid aggression. We must, as stressful as this is psychologically, accept some vulnerability and uncertainty. We must also avoid the tendency to exaggerate the threat and inadvertently to heighten our own fear. For example, although nuclear weapons are more widely available than in the past, as are delivery vehicles of medium and long range, these forces are not yet in the hands of dozens of terrorists. A policy that assumes such a dangerous world is, at this historical juncture, paranoid. We must, rather than assume this is the present case or will be in the future, work to make this outcome less likely.

On the other hand, the threshold of evidence and warning for justified fear cannot be so high that those who might be about to do harm get so advanced in their preparations that they cannot be stopped or the damage limited. What is required, assuming a substantial investment in intelligence gathering, assessment, and understanding of potential advisories, is a policy that both maximizes our understanding of the capabilities and intentions of potential adversaries and minimizes our physical vulnerability. While uncertainty about intentions, capabilities, and risk can never be eliminated, it can be reduced.

Fear of possible future attack is not enough to justify preemption. Rather, aggressive intent, coupled with a capacity and plans to do immediate harm, is the threshold that may trigger justified preemptive attacks. We may judge aggressive intent if the answer to these two questions is yes: First, have potential aggressors said they want to harm us in the near future or have they harmed us in the recent past? Second, are potential adversaries moving their forces into a position to do significant harm?

While it might be tempting to assume that secrecy on the part of a potential adversary is a sure sign of aggressive intentions, secrecy may simply be a desire to prepare a deterrent force. After all, potential adversaries may feel the need to look after their own defense against their neighbors or even the United States. We cannot assume that all forces in the world are aimed offensively at the United States and that all want to broadcast their defensive preparations—especially if that means they might become the target of a preventive offensive strike by the United States.

The conduct of preemptive actions must be limited in purpose to reducing or eliminating the immediate threat. Preemptive strikes that go beyond this purpose will, reasonably, be considered aggression by the targets of such strikes. Those conducting preemptive strikes should also obey the *jus in bello* limits of just war theory, specifically avoiding injury to noncombatants and avoiding disproportionate damage. For example, in the case of the plans for the September 11, 2001, attacks, on these criteria—and assuming intelligence warning of preparations and clear evidence of aggressive intent—a justifiable preemptive action would have been the arrest of the hijackers of the four aircraft that were to be used as weapons. But, prior to the attacks, taking the war to Afghanistan to attack al-Qaeda camps or the Taliban could not have been justified preemption.

THE RISKS OF PREVENTIVE WAR

Foreign policies must not only be judged on grounds of legality and morality, but also on grounds of prudence. Preemption is only prudent if it is limited to clear and immediate dangers and if there are limits to its conduct—proportionality, discrimination, and limited aims. If preemption becomes a regular practice or if it becomes the cover for a preventive offensive war doctrine, the strategy then may become self-defeating as it increases instability and insecurity.

Specifically, a legitimate preemptive war requires that states identify that potential aggressors have both the capability and the intention of doing great harm to you in the immediate future. However, while capability may not be in dispute, the motives and intentions of a potential adversary may be misinterpreted. Specifically, states may mobilize in what appear to be aggressive ways because they are fearful or because they are aggressive. A preemptive doctrine which has, because of great fear and a desire to control the international environment, become a preventive war doctrine of eliminating potential threats that may materialize at some point in the future is likely to create more of both fearful and aggressive states. Some states may defensively arm because they are afraid of the preemptive-preventive state; others may arm offensively because they resent the preventive war aggressor who may have killed many innocents in its quest for total security.

In either case, whether states and groups armed because they were afraid or because they have aggressive intentions, instability is likely to grow as a preventive war doctrine creates the mutual fear of surprise attack. In the case of the U.S. preemptive-preventive war doctrine, instability is likely to increase because the doctrine is coupled with the U.S. goal of maintaining global preeminence and a military force "beyond challenge."[9]

Further, a preventive offensive war doctrine undermines international law and diplomacy, both of which can be useful, even to hegemonic powers. Preventive war short-circuits nonmilitary means of solving problems. If all states reacted to potential adversaries as if they faced a clear and present danger of imminent attack, security would be destabilized as tensions escalated along already tense borders and regions. Article 51 of the UN Charter would lose much of its force. In sum, a preemptive-preventive doctrine moves us closer to a state of nature than a state of international law. Moreover, while preventive war doctrines assume that today's potential rival will become tomorrow's adversary, diplomacy or some other factor could work to change the relationship from antagonism to accommodation. As Otto von Bismarck said to Wilhelm I in 1875, "I would . . . never advise Your Majesty to declare war forthwith, simply because it appeared that our opponent would begin hostilities in the near future. One can never anticipate the ways of divine providence securely enough for that."[10]

One can understand why any administration would favor preemption and why some would be attracted to preventive wars if they think a preventive war could guarantee security from future attack. But the psychological reassurance promised by a preventive offensive war doctrine is at best illusory, and at worst, preventive war is a recipe for conflict. Preventive wars are imprudent because they bring wars that might not happen and increase resentment. They are also unjust because they assume perfect knowledge of an adversary's ill intentions when such a presumption of guilt may be premature or unwarranted. Preemption can be justified, on the other hand, if it is undertaken due to an immediate threat, where there is no time for diplomacy to be attempted, and where the action is limited to reducing that threat. There is a great temptation, however, to step over the line from preemptive to preventive war, because that line is vague and because the stress of living under the threat of war is great. But that temptation should be avoided, and the stress of living in fear should be assuaged by true prevention—arms control, disarmament, negotiations, confidence-building measures, and the development of international law.

NOTES

1. Colin Powell, "Perspectives: Powell Defends a First Strike as Iraq Option," interview, *New York Times*, September 8, 2002, sec. 1, p. 18.

2. For more on the nature of this transformation, see Neta C. Crawford, "Just War Theory and the U.S. Counterterror War," *Perspectives on Politics* 1 (March 2003), forthcoming.

3. "The National Security Strategy of the United States of America September 2002," p. 14; available at www.whitehouse.gov/nsc/nss.pdf.

4. Donald H. Rumsfeld, "Remarks at Stakeout Outside ABC TV Studio," October 28, 2001; available at www.defenselink.mil/news/Oct2001/t10292001_t1028sd3.html.

5. "National Security Strategy," p. 5.

6. Department of Defense, "Quadrennial Defense Review" (Washington, D.C.: U.S. Government Printing Office, September 30, 2001), pp. 2, 30, 62.

7. "National Security Strategy," pp. 1, 31.

8. Richard K. Betts, *Surprise Attack: Lessons for Defense Planning* (Washington, D.C.: Brookings Institution, 1982), pp. 14–43.

9. Department of Defense, "Quadrennial Defense Review," pp. 30, 62; and "Remarks by President George W. Bush at 2002 Graduation Exercise of the United States Military Academy, West Point, New York," June 1, 2002; available at www.whitehouse.gov/news/releases/2002/06/20020601-3.html.

10. Quoted in Gordon A. Craig, *The Politics of the Prussian Army, 1640–1945* (Oxford: Oxford University Press, 1955), p. 255.

*Neta C. Crawford is a professor of political science and African American studies. She also serves as co-director of the Eisenhower Study Group "Costs of War" study.

Crawford, Neta C. "The Slippery Slope to Preventative War." *Ethics & International Affairs* 17, no. 1 (Spring 2003): 30–36.

Intervention and State Failure

by Michael Ignatieff*

As we begin a new century, what is most striking about the human rights challenges we face is how different they are from those of the cold war era. Whereas the abuses of the cold war period came from strong tyrannical states, the ones in the post–cold war world chiefly originate in weak or collapsing states. We have not come to terms with this changed situation. Our current debate about humanitarian intervention continues to construe intervening as an act of conscience, when in fact, since the 1990s began, intervening has also become an urgent state interest: to rebuild failed states so that they cease to be national security threats.

To understand how the human rights situation has changed, we need to go back to the end of the Second World War. From 1945 until the end of the cold war, human rights remained subordinate to state sovereignty within the framework of the United Nations Charter. Articles 2.1 and 2.7 of the charter define sovereignty in terms of inviolability and non-interference. The prohibition on internal interference is peremptory, while the language that urges states to promote human rights is permissive. States are encouraged to promote human rights, not commanded to do so.

The UN Charter's bias against intervention reflects the chapter of European history the drafting powers believed they had been lucky to escape. Even in death and defeat, Adolf Hitler remained the ghost at the drafters' feast. Yet it was Hitler the warmonger, not Hitler the architect of European extermination, who preoccupied the drafters. For them, aggressive war across national frontiers was a more salient risk than the extermination of peoples within states. This fact illuminates the degree to which both the Holocaust and the Red Terror existed in suspended animation during the cold war. They were not the all-defining crimes they were to become in the modern moral imagination of the 1970s.

The central problem of the cold war world, from the Western point of view, was to consolidate state order and guarantee that these new states remained in the Western camp. Accordingly, the human rights performance of states mattered much less to the West than their allegiance to the Western camp. Human rights was also given a subordinate place in the UN system. UN bodies, such as the Human Rights Commission, for example, had no power to investigate member states, and after the successful passage of the Universal Declaration of the Rights of Man in 1948, no formal human rights conventions were ratified until the 1970s.

The marginal place of human rights in the institutional order of the cold war also related to the ambiguous light that human rights standards cast on the behavior of superpowers. Universal commitments, even if only rhetorical, can be embarrassing. The Americans had Jim Crow to hide. The Russians' dirty secret was the Gulag. When the Americans and the Russians used the universalistic creed to lecture developing nations, they discovered how easily their own language could be turned against them. Newly emerging nations in Africa and Asia proved adept at using the vocabulary of self-determination to ward off or ignore external scrutiny of their domestic rights records.

What broke this conspiracy of state silence was the emergence of mass-based human rights groups, beginning with Amnesty International in 1961. These organizations transformed human rights into the most powerful critique of the non-interference rule in postwar state relations.

The simultaneous historical rediscovery of the Red Terror and the Holocaust in the 1970s proved important here. The rediscovered memory of these terrible events focused the moral imagination of activists, intellectuals, and foreign policy specialists on sovereignty as an instrument and an alibi for extermination.

Another factor in the renaissance of human rights in the 1970s was the weakening of the Soviet empire. Until 1968, it was able to counter demands for freedom by sending in the tanks. By the mid 1970s, it became dependent for its survival on Western trade and investment. The Helsinki Final Act of 1975, adopted at the Conference on Security and Co-operation in Europe, institutionalized the process by which foreign assistance to an ailing empire was made conditional on human rights concessions. Helsinki marked the moment in which the rulers of the Soviet empire conceded that there were not two human rights languages—one socialist, one capitalist—but one to which all nations, at least in theory, were obliged to conform.

By conceding the right of their own citizens to form human rights organizations—a feature of the Helsinki Act—the Soviets set in train the process that led first to Charter 77 in Prague, Solidarity in Poland, and Memorial in the Soviet Union. The gathering wave of underground civic activism sapped the self-confidence of the Gorbachev-era elite and slowly but surely undermined the empire from within. Andrei Sakharov, Lech Walesa, and Vaclav Havel drew legitimacy away from the regime to the human rights movement, and in doing so, dug the grave of the empire.

With the collapse of the Soviet Union in 1991, human rights ceased to be subordinate to sovereignty. The new nations that emerged after the dissolution of the Soviet empire wrote rights guarantees into their new constitutions and accepted human rights oversight from Western governments as the price of rejoining Europe and the West. As the cold war order disintegrated, human rights became the condition of entry to the emerging security architecture of NATO and the European Union. Turkey, for example, discovered that it could not hope to gain entry to the EU unless it abolished the death penalty. Peace, combined with the emergence of the EU, diluted the exercise of Westphalian sovereignty in the continent that had been its home. With peace at home, European powers found a new overseas role for themselves promoting human rights abroad. Western aid agencies, international banks, and UN organizations increasingly "mainstreamed" human rights in their aid and lending packages for developing nations. These nations, some of which had depended entirely on Soviet support, now felt obliged to comply.

As this summary suggests, the ascendancy of human rights in the post–cold war world has complex causes. Those who see its rise as the simple story of progress, of an idea whose time finally came, are missing the key political dimensions: the weakness and collapse of the Soviet Union, the emerging salience of governance—and therefore of human rights—as development issues in the states of Africa and Asia, and finally, the pacification of Europe and its search for a new legitimizing ideology. A final feature was the coming to power of the sixties generation, nurtured in anti-Vietnam War politics, disillusioned with socialism and Marxism, awakening to the moral reality of the Holocaust and the Red Terror, and discovering in human rights a redemptive cause.

Yet, for all this change, states do not accept that their legitimacy—internal or external—is conditional on their human rights performance. The greatest champion of human rights overseas, the United States, is simultaneously an uncompromising defender of a unilateralist definition of its own sovereignty. American leaders of all political stripes regard foreign criticism of its domestic human rights norms—the persistence of capital punishment, for example—as either irrelevant or impudent.

At this point, we are in a halfway house, no longer in the world of 1945, where sovereignty was clearly privileged over human rights, and yet nowhere near the world desired by human rights activists, in which sovereignty is conditional on being good international citizens. We are somewhere in between, negotiating the conflicts between state sovereignty and international human rights as they arise, case by case.

For all their new prestige and power, human rights concerns have not essentially changed the international law governing recognition between states. In the customary practice that governs recognition of new regimes, legitimacy continues to be defined by whether a particular regime has effective control over a given territory. All states have an interest in ensuring that territories remain under the effective control of a government, regardless of its human rights record. Indeed, some states perceive that the promotion of democracy and human rights, especially in fragile, newly emerging states with complex mixtures of minorities and religions, may actually promote secession, fragmenting the international state system still further. This preference for order has been reinforced by the disintegration of multi-ethnic states like the former Yugoslavia. When democracy came to the Balkans, it came in the form of demands for self-determination on ethnic lines, with catastrophic consequences for the state order left behind by Marshal Tito. Wherever democracy means self-determination for the ethnic majority, state formation all too often means "ethnic cleansing" and massacre for the minority.

Mention of Yugoslavia brings into focus the chief reason why the conflict between sovereignty and human rights came into the open in the 1990s: the process of state fragmentation convulsed the international system. Triumphant apologists for globalization are usually also prophets of an age beyond sovereignty. These fantasies can be indulged in Europe or in the North American free trade area, but they ring especially hollow in Africa and Asia. There effective sovereignty—defined as a monopoly over the means of violence and as the capacity to deliver basic needs to a population—is the precondition for any kind of successful entry into the world economy. It is also the precondition for any kind of human rights observance.

Calling the international order of the post–cold-war era a "system" obscures the reality that it has broken down altogether in the poorer parts of the world. States that are fighting losing battles against insurgents, states where civil wars have become endemic, or where state authority has broken down altogether, radiate instability around them. Failing states are more than problems for themselves. They create what Myron Weiner memorably called "bad neighborhoods." These bad neighborhoods include

Latin America: Colombia, Ecuador, and Peru
South Balkans: Macedonia, Montenegro, and Kosovo
South Caucasus: Georgia, Ossetia, Azerbaijan, Nagorno, and Karabakh
West Africa: Liberia and Sierra Leone
Central Africa: Congo

Southern Africa: Angola
East Africa: Sudan and Somalia
South Asia: Sri Lanka
Central Asia: Pakistan, Afghanistan, Uzbekistan, and Tajikistan

Some of these—Colombia and Sri Lanka—are capable states that are fighting a losing battle against insurgents and terror. Others—Congo, Angola, and Sudan—are resource-rich states whose elites are incapable or unwilling to use resource revenue to develop their countries and end civil wars. Still others—Afghanistan, Somalia, and Sierra Leone—are weak states, with poor resource endowments, and have proved incapable of providing effective governance at all. What all of these have in common, though, is an inability to maintain a monopoly of the internal means of violence. Violence is eating away these societies from within. It would be impossible to assemble all the reasons why this convulsion is underway, but it represents a widening tear in the system of state order, analogous to the tear in the global ozone layer. Historically, this episode of state fragmentation recalls at least four previous periods:

- 1919: The dismantling of the European empires after Versailles
- 1945: The creation of the so-called people's democracies in Eastern Europe
- 1947–1960: The decolonization of Africa and Asia
- 1989–1991: The independence of former Soviet satellites

In these four periods, the dominant process was state formation and the dismantling of defeated empires. In the fifth and current wave, processes of disintegration predominate. In part, these processes represent an attempt to correct the failure of the previous episodes of state formation. Yugoslavia, for example, figures in three of these four previous episodes of state formation. It was a Versailles state after 1919. It re-emerged as a people's democracy after 1945. In the wake of 1991, it was a satellite of the Soviet system whose component parts set out to create a nation on the basis of popular sovereignty. Each time, these efforts failed. Once democracy returned, each dominant ethnic majority set itself the task of abolishing both the Versailles and the Titoist versions of the federal state. Doing so led them to expel, terrorize, and massacre their minorities. This process is still not completed.

Many of the disintegrative state conflicts in Africa—Congo and Angola, for example—represent the continuing struggle of competing tribal and regional groups to consolidate state authority on the ruins of colonial regimes. Scholars remain divided as to whether state failure is to be blamed on the colonial legacy or on what successor regimes did with that legacy. The Portuguese left behind a weak colonial inheritance, but the Angolan civil war has destroyed what was left of it. In Congo, Belgium left behind little that independent regimes could build upon. In Sierra Leone, however, it could be argued that the British left a decent colonial inheritance, which was then squandered by successor elites. What these examples have in common is state failure, although the extent of the failure differs in each case. Sometimes the state is struggling; sometimes disintegrating; in a few cases—Somalia, for instance—it has collapsed altogether. Sometimes the cause is the colonial legacy; sometimes it is maladministration by an indigenous elite; sometimes, failure is a legacy first of interference by outside powers, and then abandonment. Afghanistan has been devastated both by interference—first by the Soviets, then by the Americans—and then by neglect—the American withdrawal and strategic disinterest after the defeat of the Soviets. Finally, and most important, many failed or failing states are poor and have suffered from the steadily more adverse terms of trade in a globalized economy. An adverse situation is then made worse by corruption, bad planning choices, or ideological dogma. As the developed world has accelerated into the fourth industrial revolution of computers and information technology, sub-Saharan Africa, for example, remains stuck at the bottom of the international division of labor as primary producers.

Given the unrelenting pressure of poverty—made worse by mismanagement—it is unsurprising that state institutions begin to break down. As the tax revenue base shrinks, ruling elites lose their capacity to buy off or conciliate marginal regions or minorities. When these minorities pass from disobedience to rebellion, the elites lack the resources to quell revolts. As these revolts spread, the central government loses the monopoly of the means of violence. Where state order disintegrates, basic economic infrastructure also begins to collapse and a new economic order begins to take root. Armed ethnic groups, bandits, and guerilla forces take over, using violence to secure the forced allegiance of the local population and to extract the remaining surplus. As the weakening government struggles to regain control, it engages in more and more egregious attempts to terrorize the population into obedience, and rebel groups use more and more drastic forms of counterterror to demoralize government forces. This process of fission may then spread beyond the borders of the state itself, as refugee populations flee across the border, and as insurgent groups use frontier zones for their base camps. A collapsing state thus has the capacity to metastasize and to spread its problems through the region. These poor neighborhoods present a cluster of human rights catastrophes: forced population displacement, ethnic or religious massacre, genocide, endemic banditry, enslavement, and forced recruitment of child soldiers. All these proceed from the incapacity of a state to secure and maintain order.

This is a different profile of human rights abuse from the ones in the cold war. These were not caused by weak or collapsing states, but by strong, intolerant, and oppressive ones. To be sure, the problem of tyranny remains: China, North Korea, Iraq, and Libya are strong states, not weak ones, and their human rights abuses fit into a more classical pattern: arrest of activists, detention without trial, extra-judicial murder, torture, and disappearances. The Rwandan genocide could not have occurred without the existence of a strong and effective administrative structure—the burgomaster system—left over from the colonial period. Yet even if some strong states remain a menace to their own people, the worst abuse now occurs not where there is too much state power, but too little. The human rights dilemmas of the twenty-first century derive more from anarchy than tyranny.

If chaos rather than tyranny is the chief cause of human rights abuse, then activists will have to rethink their traditional suspicion of the state and of the exercise of sovereignty. In the Balkans, as well as west, central, and southwestern Africa, the chief prerequisite for the creation of a basic rights regime for ordinary people is the re-creation of a stable national state capable of giving orders and seeing them carried out throughout the territory, a state with a classic Weberian monopoly on the legitimate means of force. Without the basic institutions of a state, no basic human rights protection is possible. As long as populations are menaced by banditry, civil war, guerrilla campaigns, and counter-insurgency by beleaguered governments, they cannot be secure. In such conditions, international human rights and humanitarian organizations can do no more than bind up the wounded and protect the most vulnerable. These Hobbesian situations teach the message of the Leviathan itself: that consolidated state power is the very condition for any regime of rights whatever. In this sense, state sovereignty, instead of being the enemy of human rights, has to be seen as their basic precondition. Protecting human rights in zones where state order is embattled or had collapsed has to mean consolidating or re-creating a legitimate state. Nation building thus becomes, for the first time since the Allied occupation of Germany and Japan, a critical instrument for the creation of rights regimes. In Japan and Germany, however, total defeat and unconditional surrender gave the Allies the authority to create new democratic institutions from scratch, while the conditions for modern nation building in states recovering from civil war are much less auspicious.

If state fragmentation and collapse are the chief sources of human rights abuse, the debate over humanitarian intervention needs to be rethought. This debate conceives the challenge of intervention as a response to a series of essentially unrelated moral crises, in which differing populations of civilians in desperate need appeal to us for rescue. But the crises themselves are not unrelated, and they are not just humanitarian or moral in their claim on our attention. A crisis of order in a single state risks creating "bad neighborhoods" in a whole region. Pakistan, for example, has been "Talibanized" by nearby Afghanistan. These bad neighborhoods in turn present direct threats to the national interest of states. For bad neighborhoods harbor terrorists, produce drugs, and generate destabilizing refugee flows. Afghanistan is the best example of a failing state that was perceived as a distant humanitarian crisis, when it ought to have been seen as a clear and present national security threat.

As long as the chief motive for intervention is conscience alone, we can only expect sporadic action from a few responsible actors. Once it is realized that we are looking at a crisis in the international order, a tear in the ozone layer of global governance, states that would otherwise remain uninvolved might understand that their long-term interest in stability and order compel them to commit resources to the problem. Putting national interest criteria into the debate also helps with the problem of triage. There are many failed and failing states. The ones that will actually receive sustained international attention will be those that directly threaten the national interest and national security of powerful states.

The debate about humanitarian intervention strikes many people from poorer countries as a lurid exercise in emotional self-gratification—an attempt to demonstrate the power of conscience when the real tasks that rich Western nations need to address are much harder: helping states regain a monopoly over the means of violence, increasing the competence of local institutions, conciliating ethnic conflict, and building up a functioning economy.

The way the academy divides up the debate also enfeebles it. The international lawyers who dominate the humanitarian intervention debate spend more time thinking about intervention criteria than how to rebuild failed states once intervention has occurred. The development strategists who do know something about how to set off self-sustaining paths to growth and institutional competence have no place in the debate. The human rights activists who document the increasingly catastrophic rights abuses in failing states often have no strategy other than denunciation and a perfectionist reluctance to use force to end these abuses. All of these divisions further fragment our capacity to craft strategies of intervention that actually succeed.

Another problem is the way humanitarian intervention is actually done. Most strategies of humanitarian rescue, particularly UN peacekeeping and conflict mediation, are premised on staying neutral in zones of conflict. In reality, as

Bosnia cruelly showed, neutrality can become discreditable as well as counter-productive. Once the decision is taken to introduce humanitarian aid into a war zone, backed up with peacekeepers to aid in its delivery, the aid itself becomes a focus of combat, and its provision—even to unarmed combatants—becomes a way not to damp down the fighting but to keep it going. Neutral humanitarian assistance can have the perverse effect of sustaining the fighting it seeks to reduce.

All victims have some claim to mercy, assistance, and aid from those bystanders who can provide it. But if that is all that bystanders do, they may help to keep civil wars going, by sustaining the capacity of a civilian population to absorb still more punishment. Moreover, when neutralist mediators impose a cease-fire in an ongoing civil war, they invariably draw the line in such a way as to reward the side that has waged the conflict with the most aggression and the most success. That is why, when peacekeepers are deployed to enforce the cease-fire, they are usually viewed by the party that has lost most in the conflict as colluders in aggression. Such cease-fires rarely hold.

Neutral humanitarianism, when viewed more cynically, is a kind of hedged bet, in which intervening parties salve their consciences while avoiding the difficult political commitments that might actually stop civil war. For the key dilemma in civil wars is which side to back. Unless one side is helped to win, and win quickly, nothing serious can be done to reduce the violence. The basic choice is whether external intervention should be aimed at preserving the existing state or at helping a self-determination claim succeed. In Bosnia, Western interveners thought they were intervening to keep warring parties apart. They failed to understand that a recognized member of the UN—Bosnia Herzegovina—was being torn apart by a self-determination claim, aided and abetted by outside powers, chiefly Serbia, but also Croatia. The crisis was seen as an internal affair, when in fact its chief determinants were illicit foreign subversion: the arming and training of insurgents and the provision of safe bases of operation in both Serbia and Croatia. The war within Bosnia was brought to an end only when foreign intervention was directed not at the internal combatants but at the chief external instigator, Serbia. It was only when outside interveners took sides and bombed Serbian installations, forcing the Serb government to exert pressure on its internal proxies, that the civil war stopped. In other words, the international community finally intervened to sustain the unity of a state and to *defeat* a self-determination claim by the Bosnian Serbs.

The case of Afghanistan illustrates the dilemmas of taking sides. Prior to September 11, the dilemma was this: if Western powers recognized the Taliban, they would help consolidate Taliban rule over the entire territory and thus help bring an end to a devastating civil war. Order would prevail, but it would be the despotism of rural Islam at its most obscurantist. In such a situation, Afghan women would pay the price of a Western preference for order over justice. If, on the other hand, Western support continued to reach the Taliban's opponents, the civil war would continue, and Afghanistan would continue to bleed to death.

Until September 11, Western powers placed a two-way bet, supporting the Northern Alliance just enough to keep it in business, while refusing to normalize relations with the Taliban. The United States allowed the Pakistani secret service to funnel support to the Taliban, while at the same time American officials denounced the regime for its treatment of women and the destruction of religious monuments. This double game has now come apart, and in the wake of September 11, it is apparent that it was bound to. Having washed its hands of Afghanistan after the Soviet departure, the United States spent the 1990s conceiving of Afghanistan as a humanitarian or human rights disaster zone, failing to notice that it was rapidly becoming a national security nightmare, a training ground for terror. Nothing enfeebled American policy more in the 1990s than the refusal to notice that untended human rights and humanitarian crises have a way of becoming national security threats. Afghanistan is the most dramatic example of this tendency. Now, finally, the United States and its allies will take sides, but once they defeat the Taliban, the same problem they have avoided— namely how to rebuild a nation state there—will recur.

Taking sides is not the only dilemma. There is also the problem of triage. Given the fact that resources of will power, diplomatic skill, and economic aid are always finite, there have to be criteria to determine which conflicts to take on and which ones to ignore. Intervention occurs, in general, where states are too weak, too friendless, to resist. The Chinese occupation of Tibet goes unsanctioned. The Russians reduce Grozny to rubble with impunity. Yet the Serbs are bombed for seventy-eight days. These inconsistencies mean that intervention in the domestic affairs of states will never rest on unassailable grounds. Yet the fact that we cannot intervene everywhere is not a justification for not intervening where we can.

Nor is the experience of intervention as nation building entirely negative. The UN Mission in Cambodia managed to oversee peaceful elections and the creation of democratic rule in a country ravaged by genocide. NATO, the UN, and the EU have joined forces to put

Bosnia into a transitional trusteeship. It is a state in which internal peace and security are guaranteed by foreign troops. Resettling of refugees and rebuilding are both funded from the outside. The process is costly, but violence has not returned, and peace in Bosnia has hastened democratic transitions in Croatia and Serbia next door. Further south in Kosovo, another trusteeship experiment is underway. A former province of a state is being prepared for substantial autonomy and self-government. The UN administration has written the constitutional rules for a gradual handover of power to elected local elites, and there is even a chance that eventually the Serb minority will take their places at the table. Finally, in East Timor, a transitional UN administration is handing a new country over to its elected leaders. All of these experiences are fraught with difficulty, but all indicate that an inchoate practice of state building, under UN auspices, is emerging. The next obvious candidate for treatment is Afghanistan.

An intervention strategy that takes sides, that uses force, and that sticks around to rebuild is very different from one premised on neutrality, casualty-avoidance, and exit strategies. It is also based on different premises. These premises have been outlined recently in "The Responsibility to Protect," a report sponsored by the Canadian government and delivered to the UN secretary-general in December 2001. Building on ideas of good citizenship and human security, the commission has argued that all states have a responsibility to protect their citizens. In certain limited cases, where states are unwilling or unable to do that, and where the resulting human rights situation is catastrophic, other states have a responsibility to step in and provide the protection instead. The international responsibility to protect is a residual obligation that comes into play only when a domestic state proves incapable or unwilling to act and where the resulting situation is genuinely catastrophic.

The idea of a responsibility to protect also implies a responsibility to prevent and a responsibility to follow through. Action, especially of a coercive kind, lacks legitimacy unless every effort has been made to avert the catastrophe; once action is taken, its legitimacy depends on staying the course until the situation is on the mend. Thus the responsibility to protect is intended to provide a rationale for constructive engagement by rich countries through an intervention continuum that begins with prevention and ends with sustained follow-up.

All of these exercises in nation building represent attempts to invent, for a postimperial, postcolonial era, a form of temporary rule that reproduces the best effects of empire (inward investment, pacification, and impartial administration), without reproducing the worst features (corruption, repression, confiscation of local capacity). Unlike the empires of the past, these UN administrations are designed to serve and enhance the ideal of self-determination rather than suppress it.

Taking responsibility without confiscating it is the balance international administrators have to strike. The trick in nation building is to force responsibility—for security, for co-existence—back to local elites. This is not easy. The spectacle of disgruntled locals, sitting in cafes, watching earnest young internationals speeding around to important meetings in Toyota Land Cruisers has been repeated in every nation-building experiment of the 1990s. The most successful transitional administrations are ones that try to do themselves out of a job. This is not always possible. The legacy of bitterness in places like Kosovo and Bosnia is so intense that international administration has to remain in place, simply in order to protect minorities from vengeance by the victorious yet previously victimized majority. Controlling the culture of vengeance usually takes longer than the time frame dictated by most modern exit strategies. Once Western forces intervene they are usually committed to rebuild or at least patrol post-conflict societies for a long period of time. It takes time to create responsible political dialogue in shattered communities, still longer to create shared institutions of police and justice, and longest of all to create the molecular social trust between warring communities necessary for economic development and community co-existence. The initiative for these developments has to come from the local people. Internationals can provide impartial administration, some inward investment, and some basic security protection, but the work has to be done by the political elites who inherit the intervention. Nation building takes time, and it is not an exercise in social work. Its ultimate purpose is to create the state order that is the precondition for any defensible system of human rights and to create the stability that turns bad neighborhoods into good ones.

This survey of what has happened to the interaction between sovereignty and human rights since 1945, and how the theory and practice of humanitarian intervention has developed in response to the epidemic of state failure since the end of the cold war, necessarily ends with skeptical conclusions. If we survey the interventions of the recent past, the story is decidedly mixed. In Bosnia, intervention prevented the full realization of Serbian war aims, but it did not prevent the deaths of more than three hundred thousand people and the expulsion of nearly a million from their homes. In Kosovo, intervention put a stop to a civil war that, had intervention not occurred, might still be claiming lives. In East Timor, intervention delivered self-determination to the people, but not before more than a thousand people were massacred for seeking their rights. In Iraq, Kurds remain under the protection of Allied air power, but they do not have the resources to become genuinely self-governing. In places like Cambodia and Haiti, democracy has been restored, but power remains in the hands of corrupt elites. In other places, such as Angola, where the UN intervened with high hopes of moving the society out of a civil war, it has now withdrawn altogether. In still other places, ranging from Chechnya to Tibet, no intervention took place, and the failure showed that universal principles still lack consistent enforcement. Worst of all, eight hundred thousand dead Rwandans remain testimony to our incapacity—even when no insurmountable obstacle exists, either in state sovereignty or Security Council veto—to do the right thing. The most that can be said about the emerging practice of intervention is that at its best it prevents the worst from happening; at its worst, it compromises and betrays the very values it purports to defend.

Yet through it all, an inchoate practice of nation building—in Kosovo, Bosnia, East Timor, and Cambodia—is showing that state order can be successfully rebuilt if wealthy and powerful states are prepared to invest the time and money. More generally, this survey seems to demonstrate something important about legitimacy itself. Intervening to defend human rights will never have anything more than conditional legitimacy, even when the cause is just and the authority right. We all aspire to perfect legitimacy. We want to live in a world in which we do the right thing, and know we are doing the right thing, and believe that the whole world will accept that we have done the right thing. There is no such possibility. Indeed, it is a dangerous utopia. Moral perfectionism is always the enemy of the possible and the practical. Doing the right thing appears to require the tenacity to do it when half the world thinks you are wrong.

Acknowledgments

Michael Ignatieff would like to thank many colleagues at the Kennedy School of Government, especially Monica Toft and Robert Rotberg, for reading and commenting on earlier drafts of this essay.

*Michael Ignatieff is director of the Carr Center for Human Rights Policy, Kennedy School of Government, Harvard University. He is the author of *Human Rights as Politics and Idolatry*, a trilogy of books on ethnic war and humanitarian intervention, and a biography of the liberal philosopher Isaiah Berlin.

Ignatieff, Michael. "Intervention and State Failure." *Dissent*, Winter 2002, 115–123. Dissent by the Foundation for the Independent Study of Ideas Copyright © 2002 Reproduced with permission of UNIVERSITY OF PENNSYLVANIA PRESS–JOURNALS

Part 3: Who Merits Protection in Warfare? *Jus in Bello*

This section moves from *jus ad bellum* considerations, when is it right to go to war, to *jus in bello*, what ethical guidelines should govern conduct once war has begun. As Part 1 noted, a pacifist objection to the basic premise of just war theory is that it requires rationalizing killing, something that is not possible from an absolutist view. However, the just war theorist accepts that war is sometimes necessary, even though war inevitably results in killing and destruction. The difficult question then becomes who may be killed (or otherwise harmed) and in what circumstances?

Most just war theorists agree that those who are not participating in warfare, and who are less morally culpable, should be spared to the extent possible. Thus, a broad consensus exists on sparing innocent civilians. While these general principles offer a helpful starting point, objections to them redound, often due to the difficult situations that arise in war; the difficulty of generalizing or assigning moral culpability when many people, including some civilians, have dirty hands in war; and the often extreme life-or-death justifications that balance against absolute prohibitions. What if civilians are not as innocent as presumed? Even if combatants have more of a direct blame for fighting, a combatant is still a human being with a right and a desire to live. Why should the lives of enemy civilians be prioritized above theirs? Finally, while protections for those who are morally blameless for war (whether civilians or, in some circumstances, combatants) are to be respected as a general principle, are there exceptional situations in warfare that might justify the violation of these rules?

CONSEQUENTIALIST VERSUS ABSOLUTE VIEWS ON PROTECTION OF CIVILIANS IN WARFARE

The principle limitations in *jus in bello*, both among ethical schools of thought and in modern international law, relate to the deliberate killing of noncombatants and other acts that cause unnecessary suffering or inhumane treatment. Although a full exploration of these prohibitions is beyond the scope of this compendium, most just war thinkers generally agree that because civilians are not engaged in waging war, and thus are presumed to be less morally culpable, they should not be deliberately killed or harmed. There is a broad consensus that torture or inhumane treatment of individuals, including detained enemy combatants, is morally reprehensible and never justified. It is generally argued that mass destruction of civilians or property in conflict, above what is necessary or proportionate to the success of a military objective, is wrong. Many international law provisions have been heavily influenced by this just war thinking and reflect the above limitations on war. [1]

Yet for all the unanimity on these rules, violations of these principles occur routinely. The first reading revisits the mass killing of civilians by Allied air operations during World War II. Aerial fire-bombing of German cities like Dresden led to the deliberate death, injury, and displacement of millions of German civilians. The use of nuclear weapons on Japanese cities Hiroshima and Nagasaki killed or injured an estimated 135,000 and 64,000 civilians respectively, roughly 52 percent and 33 percent of the cities' populations. Such actions were defended at the time under a theory of "total war"—that all sectors and individuals of an enemy belligerent, including the civilian population, were involved in supporting the war efforts and thus were legitimate targets. Additionally, many politicians, military leaders, and commentators at the time justified large-scale attacks on Japanese and German cities as necessary to break the will of the Japanese and German publics, and thus end the war more quickly. General Curtis LeMay, who led the U.S. bombing campaign against Japan in 1945, argued, "I think it's more immoral to use less force than necessary, than it is to use more. If you use less force, you kill off more of humanity in the long run because you are merely protracting the struggle."[2]

In a public letter titled "Mr. Truman's Degree," G. E. M. Anscombe objects to concepts like total war, or consequentialist justifications for killing civilians. She argues that though war is unquestionably bad, there are limits, and killing large numbers of innocent civilians deliberately (or foreseeably) is one of them. "For men to choose to kill the innocent as a means to their ends is always murder, and murder is one of the worst of human actions," she writes.[3]

Anscombe's discussion is an appropriate introduction to the broader topic of the absolute nature of certain protections within just war theory. Though many discussions of jus in bello are context-specific, lawyers and ethicists have identified some acts that are so morally illegitimate that no circumstances can justify them, including the deliberate killing of civilians, rape as a weapon of war, or the use of torture or cruel or inhumane treatment against prisoners of war. These are deemed to be absolutely prohibited, not justifiable by any greater good such acts might achieve.

As Alex J. Bellamy discusses in "Supreme Emergencies and the Protection of Non-Combatants in War," though just war theorists and policymakers alike frequently declaim attacks on innocent civilians, some extraordinary circumstances may make disregarding absolute prohibitions seductive. In 1940, the UK Prime Minister Winston Churchill argued that the bombing of German cities was justified given the "supreme emergency" confronting Britain at the time. The phrase "supreme emergency" has gained a second life in theoretical *jus in bello* debates. No less than the leading just war theoretician, Michael Walzer has argued that in the face of such a supreme emergency, the deliberate killing of civilians might be justified.[4]

Bellamy argues that the supreme exception doctrine undermines overall just war principles. He maintains that it is either a thinly disguised form of realist thinking—states will/can violate these principles when it suits their strategic thinking—or a consequentialist weighing of costs and benefits that ignores the importance of absolutist prohibitions within just war thinking. Just war theory recognizes that war is inevitable, as is the death and destruction that comes with war, but it attempts to take the moral high road by setting outer limits on what is permissible conduct. Permitting those outer limits to be broken in certain circumstances defeats the whole purpose of setting them and undermines the premise of just war thinking, Bellamy argues. Unthinkable acts are simply unthinkable acts and cannot be justified based on the ends they serve.

Bellamy's piece points out a number of contradictions in the ethics of war—a critique reminiscent of some of the overarching issues laid out in Part 1. Because just war theory straddles the realist's recognition that war is inevitable and the pacifist's moral repulsion at the killing and destruction implicit in war, it often has a somewhat schizophrenic position on the absolute nature of any given right. Once one has opened the door for killing or destruction in war to be potentially morally justifiable, drawing the line on what types of killing can be justified becomes difficult.

Moral Culpability and Targeting in War: Civilians versus Combatants

Anscombe and Bellamy's pieces consider whether the deliberate killing of innocent civilians can be justified by extreme circumstances and answer the question by balancing the legitimacy of absolute versus consequentialist thinking in just war restrictions. But we might also challenge the more basic definitions underlying the prohibition on killing civilians: what if the civilians are not actually innocent, or at least no more innocent than some combatants?

Some just war theorists have argued that particularly in a democracy, in which civilians might have greater control over war-making, many civilians might be considered at least as morally culpable as the average foot soldier. In modern conflict, civilians play an increasingly prominent and decisive role in the execution of war. Insurgent campaigns depend on population support ranging from providing food and shelter to fighters, to acting as look-outs or information sources, to providing transport or propaganda. In national militaries the mobilization of civilian persons and industries—from telecommunications technologies to munitions factories to civilian transport lines—is often as important to fighting and winning wars as ground forces. Who is to say that these individuals, who knowingly play a decisive role in war-fighting or simply support the overall war effort, are not as morally guilty, and therefore as justly targeted, as the average soldier?

Just as not all civilians may be "innocent," it follows that perhaps not all combatants are "guilty." Even if all combatants have some level of culpability by virtue of participating in the conflict, does that mean that they have forfeited all rights to life? In answering this question, James M. Dubik argues that recognition of individuals' inherent right to life has played a strong role in shaping just war thinking, including in Walzer's seminal *Just and Unjust Wars*. The right to life—like the right of populations to self-determination—is considered to be universal and inalienable. If so, Dubik argues, how is it that a combatant's inherent right to life is dispensed with so easily?

The final author, Emanuel Gross, also pushes against the way that combatant lives are valued in just war ethics by thinking through the very real trade-off in lives in modern combat situations. In "Use of Civilians as Human Shields," Gross explores how we value civilian versus combatant lives in situations in which insurgent groups deliberately contravene ethical codes. Gross argues that the dominant trends of modern warfare fundamentally shift traditional assumptions about what is ethical in warfare: "The laws of war are not designed for wars conducted against terrorist organizations. [. . .] Accordingly, even were one to agree that the law is the binding expression of social and public morality, [. . .] one would not be able to find a positive objective solution to the moral dilemmas which arise within the context of this war."[5]

A strong example of this occurs when terrorists deliberately take "human shields." The taking of human shields can describe a variety of situations. A common example would be a group of fighters hiding among an urban population on the assumption that the opposing party will not bomb the entire city in order to kill the relatively small number of terrorists hiding in it. Or, in the post-2001 Afghanistan conflict, Taliban fighters have frequently fired on U.S. forces from civilian homes, often using threats of force to prevent the civilians from fleeing.

Such actions pose a moral dilemma for the opposing party: Are a warring party's moral duties different when the opponent's actions deliberately place the civilian lives at risk? Gross argues that it is not always possible to think in terms of absolutes in situations that force us to choose the least reprehensible of a series of immoral acts. Some people will die, and tough choices have to be made as to who this will be, Gross argues. Civilians have a right to life, but so do combatants, even if it is a somewhat compromised right given their participation in war-fighting. The broader population also has a right to life and an expectation that their sovereign state will protect them from future attacks. Would it be right to fire on a house in which civilians were being held as human shields, knowing that they would be killed? Would it be right to ask the soldiers involved to take on extra risk storming the house (rather than firing on it remotely) if the civilians were in some way complicit? Would it be right to walk away and let the terrorists live to fight another day, knowing that they would later harm the broader population? Gross offers his own thinking on such dilemmas but these overall issues are far from settled.

As you read the arguments in each of the excerpts think through the following questions:
- How do you view a civilian's right to life in wartime? Is it such an absolute right that no deliberate or foreseeable killing of civilians would be justified, regardless of the overall benefits of such an action? What if it was certain to bring to an end an otherwise lengthy war that would surely result in more killing?
- Some ethicists and lawyers argue that civilian lives should be spared wherever possible, regardless of the expense to combatant lives. Do you agree with this position? Why or why not? How would you argue against it?
- Given that the killing of innocent civilians is a near certain consequence of military conflict, how should we think about the imperative that civilian lives be protected at all cost? Does this mean that, as pacifists argue, we should abandon military conflict once and for all? Why or why not?
- James M. Dubik and Emanuel Gross argued that combatants do retain

a right to life, even if it may be less stringent than that of innocent civilians. Do you find their arguments convincing? Why or why not? How would you balance a soldier's right to life in situations in which sparing him risk would put civilians at additional risk, or certain death?

• There may be many situations in which soldiers have to choose not to fire and to fight another day, or else risk their own lives or the lives of civilians. How would you reconcile that dilemma with Gross' point that states have a *higher* duty to prevent attacks against their citizens?

• Is a military justified in violating ethical practice in war when its enemy is doing so? What if the consequence of remaining committed to ethical practice in war means certain defeat?

Notes

1. For example, among the key relevant provisions, international law prohibits the deliberate killing of civilians, attacks that do not take due care to avoid civilian harm, or attacks that cause a level of civilian harm that is disproportionate to the military advantage gained.

2. Editorial, "Using Our Total Strength," *Lewiston Daily Sun*, December 7, 1965, 4.

3. Elizabeth Anscombe, "Mr. Truman's Degree," in *Nuclear Weapons: A Catholic Response*, ed. Walter Stein (New York: Sheed and Ward, 1961), reprinted in *The Collected Philosophical Papers of G. E. M. Anscombe*, vol. 3, *Ethics, Religion and Politics* (Oxford: Blackwell, 1981), 62–71.

4. How one would distinguish a supreme emergency from the general emergency situation of war is not clear, but Walzer has argued that such a supreme emergency would have to be beyond the ordinary risks of warfare, and the danger would have to be imminent. Michael Walzer, *Just and Unjust Wars: A Moral Argument with Historical Illustrations* (New York: Basic Books, 1977), 267–268; "Emergency Ethics," in *Arguing About War* (New Haven: Yale University Press, 2004), 46.

5. Emanuel Gross, "Use of Civilians as Human Shields: What Legal and Moral Restrictions Pertain to a War Waged by a Democratic State against Terrorism?" *Emory International Law Review* 16, no. 2 (Fall 2002): 469.

Mr. Truman's Degree

*by G. E. M. Anscombe**

I.

In 1939, on the outbreak of war, the President of the United States asked for assurances from the belligerent nations that civil populations would not be attacked.

In 1945, when the Japanese enemy was known by him to have made two attempts toward a negotiated peace [...], the President of the United States gave the order for dropping an atom bomb on a Japanese city; three days later a second bomb, of a different type, was dropped on another city. No ultimatum was delivered before the second bomb was dropped.

Set side by side, these events provide enough of a contrast to provoke enquiry. Evidently development has take[n] place; one would like to see its course plotted. It is not, I think, difficult to give an intelligible account:

(1) The British Government gave President Roosevelt the required assurance, with a reservation which meant "If the Germans do it we shall do it too." You don't promise to abide by the Queensbury Rules even if your opponent abandons them.

(2) The only condition for ending the war was announced to be unconditional surrender. Apart from the "liberation of the subject peoples," the objectives were vague in character. Now the demand for unconditional surrender was mixed up with a determination to make no peace with Hitler's government. In view of the character of Hitler's regime that attitude was very intelligible. Nevertheless some people have doubts about it now. It is suggested that defeat of itself would have resulted in the rapid discredit and downfall of that government. On this I can form no strong opinion. The important question to my mind is whether the intention of making no peace with Hitler's government necessarily entailed the objective of unconditional surrender. If, as may not be impossible, we could have formulated a pretty definite objective, a rough outline of the terms which we were willing to make with Germany, while at the same time indicating that we would not make terms with *Hitler's* government, then the question of the wisdom of this latter demand seems to me a minor one; but if not, then that settles it. It was the insistence on unconditional surrender that was the root of all

evil. The connection between such a demand and the need to use the most ferocious methods of warfare will be obvious. And in itself the proposal of an unlimited objective in war is stupid and barbarous.

(3) The Germans did a good deal of indiscriminate bombing in this country. It is impossible for an uninformed person to know how much, in its first beginnings, was due to indifference on the part of pilots to using their loads only on military targets, and how much to actual policy on the part of those who sent them. Nor do I know what we were doing at the same time. But certainly anyone would have been stupid who had thought in 1939 that there would not be such bombing, developing into definite raids on cities.

(4) For some time before war broke out, and more intensely afterwards, there was propaganda in this country on the subject of the "indivisibility" of modern war. The civilian population, we were told, is really as much combatant as the fighting forces. The military strength of a nation includes its whole economic and social strength. Therefore the distinction between the people engaged in prosecuting the war and the population at large is unreal. There is no such thing as a non-participator; you cannot buy a postage stamp or any taxed article, or grow a potato or cook a meal, without contributing to the "war effort." War indeed is a "ghastly evil," but once it has broken out no one can "contract out" of it. "Wrong" indeed must be being done if war is waged, but you cannot help being involved in it. There was a doctrine of "collective responsibility" with a lugubriously elevated moral tone about it. The upshot was that it was senseless to draw any line between legitimate and illegitimate objects of attack.—Thus the court chaplains of democracy. I am not sure how children and the aged fitted into this story: probably they cheered the soldiers and munitions workers up.

(5) The Japanese attacked Pearl Harbor and there was war between America and Japan. Some American (Republican) historians now claim that the acknowledged fact that the American Government knew an attack was impending some hours before it occurred, but did not alert the people in local command, can only be explained by a purpose of arousing the passions of American people. However that may be, those passions were suitably aroused and the war was entered on with the same vague and hence limitless objectives; and once more unconditional surrender was the only condition on which the war was going to end.

(6) Then came the great change: we adopted the system of "area bombing" as oppose[d] to "target bombing." This differed from even big raids on cities, such as had previously taken place in the course of the war, by being far

more extensive and devastating and much less random; the whole of a city area would be systematically plotted out and dotted with bombs. "Attila was a Sissy," as the *Chicago Tribune* headed an article on this subject.

(7) In 1945, at the Potsdam conference in July, Stalin informed the American and British statesmen that he had received two requests from the Japanese to act as a mediator with a view to ending the war. He had refused. The Allies agreed on the "general principle"—marvellous phrase!—of using the new type of weapon that the Americans now possessed. The Japanese were given a chance in the form of the Potsdam Declaration, calling for unconditional surrender in face of overwhelming force soon to be arrayed against them. The historian of the Survey of International Affairs considers that this phrase was rendered meaningless by the statement of a series of terms; but of these the ones incorporating the Allies' demands were mostly of so vague and sweeping a nature as to be rather a declaration of what unconditional surrender would be like than to constitute conditions. It seems to be generally agreed that the Japanese were desperate enough to have accepted the Declaration but for their loyalty to their Emperor: the "terms" would certainly have permitted the Allies to get rid of him if they chose. The Japanese refused the Declaration. In consequence, the bombs were dropped on Hiroshima and Nagasaki. The decision to use them on people was Mr. Truman's.

* * * * * *

For men to choose to kill the innocent as a means to their ends is always murder, and murder is one of the worst of human actions. So the prohibition on deliberately killing prisoners of war or the civilian population is not like the Queensbury Rules: its force does not depend on its promulgation as part of positive law, written down, agreed upon, and adhered to by the parties concerned.

When I say that to choose to kill the innocent as a means to one's ends is murder, I am saying what would generally be accepted as correct. But I shall be asked for my definition of "the innocent." I will give it, but later. Here, it is not necessary; for with Hiroshima and Nagasaki we are not confronted with a borderline case. In the bombing of these cities it was certainly decided to kill the innocent as a means to an end. And a very large number of them, all at once, without warning, without the interstices of escape or the chance to take shelter, which existed even in the "area bombing" of the German cities.

I have long been puzzled by the common cant about President Truman's courage in making this decision. Of course, I know that you can be cowardly without having reason to think you are in danger. But how can you be courageous? Light has come to me lately: the term is an acknowledgement of the truth. Mr. Truman was brave because, and only because, what he did was so bad. But I think the judgement unsound. Given the right circumstances (*e.g.* that no one whose opinion matters will disapprove), a quite mediocre person can do spectacularly wicked things without thereby becoming impressive.

I determined to oppose the proposal to give Mr. Truman an honorary degree here at Oxford. Now, an honorary degree is not a reward of merit: it is, as it were, a reward for being a very distinguished person, and it would be foolish to enquire whether a candidate deserves to be as distinguished as he is. That is why, in general, the question whether so-and-so should have an honorary degree is devoid of interest. A very distinguished person will hardly be also a notorious criminal, and if he should chance to be a non-notorious criminal it would, in my opinion, be improper to bring the matter up. It is only in the rather rare case in which a man is known everywhere for an action, in fact of which it is sycophancy to honor him, that the question can be of the slightest interest.

I have been accused of being "high-minded." I must be saying "You may not do evil that good may come," which is a disagreeably high-minded doctrine. The action was necessary, or at any rate it was thought by competent, expert military opinion to be necessary; it probably saved more lives than it sacrificed; it had a good result, it ended the war. Come now: if you had to choose between boiling one baby and letting some frightful disaster befall a thousand people—or a million people, if a thousand is not enough—what would you do? Are you going to strike an attitude and say "You may not do evil that good may come"? (People who never hear such arguments will hardly believe they take place, and will pass this rapidly by.)

"It pretty certainly saved a huge number of lives." Given the conditions, I agree. That is to say, if those bombs had not been dropped the Allies would have had to invade Japan to achieve their aim, and they would have done so. Very many soldiers on both sides would have been killed; the Japanese, it is said—and it may well be true—would have massacred the prisoners of war; and large numbers of their civilian population would have been killed by "ordinary" bombing.

I do not dispute it. Given the conditions, that was probably what was averted by that action. But what were the conditions? The unlimited objective, the fixation on unconditional surrender. The disregard of the fact that the Japanese were desirous of negotiating peace. The character of the Potsdam Declaration— their "chance." I will not suggest, as some would like to do, that there was an exultant itch to use the new weapons, but it seems plausible to think that the consciousness of the possession of such instruments had its effect on the manner in which the Japanese were offered their "chance."

We can now reformulate the principle of "doing evil that good may come." Every fool can be as much of a knave as suits him.

I recommend this history to undergraduates reading Greats as throwing a glaring light on Aristotle's thesis that you cannot be or do any good where you are stupid.

I informed the Senior Proctor of my intention to oppose Mr. Truman's degree. He consulted the Registrar to get me informed on procedure. The Vice-Chancellor was informed; I was cautiously asked if I had got up a party. I had not; but a fine House was whipped up to vote for the honour. The dons at St. John's were simply told "The women are up to something in Convocation; we have to go and vote them down." In Worcester, in All Souls, in New College, however, consciences were greatly exercised, as I have heard. A reason was found to satisfy them: *It would be wrong to try to PUNISH Mr. Truman!* I must say I rather like St. John's.

The Censor of St. Catherine's had an odious task. He must make a speech which should pretend to show that a couple of massacres to a man's credit are not exactly a reason for not showing him honour. He had, however, one great advantage: he did not have to persuade his audience, who were already perfectly convinced of that proposition. But at any rate he had to make a show.

The defence, I think, would not have been well received at Nuremberg.

We do not approve the action; no, we think it was a *mistake*. (That is how communists now talk about Stalin's more murderous proceedings.) Further, Mr. Truman did not make the bombs by himself, and decide to drop them without consulting anybody; no, he was only responsible for the decision. Hang it all, you can't make a man responsible just because "his is the signature at the foot of the order." Or was he not even responsible for the decision? It was not quite clear whether Mr. Bullock was saying that or not; but I never heard anyone else seem to give the lie to Mr. Truman's boasts. Finally, an action of this sort is, after all, only one episode: an incident, as it were, in a career. Mr. Truman has done some good.

I know that in one way such a speech does not deserve scrutiny; after all, it was just something to say on its occasion. And he had to say something. One must not suppose that one can glean anything a man actually thinks from what he says in such circumstances. Professor Stebbing exposing the logical fallacies in politicians' speeches is a comic spectacle.

II.

Choosing to kill the innocent as a means to your ends is always murder. Naturally, killing the innocent as an end in itself is murder too; but that is no more than a possible future development for us:* [* This will seem a preposterous assertion; but we are certainly on the way, and I can think of no reasons for confidence that it will not happen.] in our part of the globe it is a practice that has so far been confined to the Nazis. I intend my formulation to be taken strictly; each term in it is necessary. For killing the innocent, even if you know as a matter of statistical certainty that the things you do involve it, is not necessarily murder. I mean that if you attack a lot of military targets, such as munitions factories and naval dockyards, as carefully as you can, you will be certain to kill a number of innocent people; but that is not murder. On the other hand, unscrupulousness in considering the possibilities turns it into murder. I here print as a case in point a letter which I received lately from Holland:

> "We read in our paper about your opposition to Truman. I do not like him either, but do you know that in the war the English bombed the dykes of our province Zeeland, an island where nobody could escape anywhere to. Where the whole population was drowned, children, women, farmers working in the field, all the cattle, everything, hundreds and hundreds, and we were your allies! Nobody ever speaks about that. Perhaps it were well to know this. Or, to remember."

That was to trap some fleeing German military. I think my correspondent has something.

It may be impossible to take the thing (or people) you want to destroy as your target; it may be possible to attack it only by taking as the object of your attack what includes large numbers of innocent people. Then you cannot very well say they died by accident. Here, your action is murder.

"But where will you draw the line? It is impossible to draw an exact line." This is a common and absurd argument against drawing any line; it may be very difficult, and there are obviously borderline cases. But we have fallen into the way of drawing no line and offering as justifications what an uncaptive mind will find only a bad joke. Wherever the line is, certain things are certainly well to one side or the other of it.

Now who are "the innocent" in war? They are all those who are not fighting and not engaged in supply[ing] those who are with the means of fighting. A farmer growing wheat which may be eaten by the troops is not "supplying them with the means of fighting." Over this, too, the line may be difficult to draw.

But that does not mean that no line should be drawn, or that, even if one is in doubt just where to draw the line, one cannot be crystal clear that this or that is well over the line.

"But the people fighting are probably just conscripts! In that case they are just as innocent as anyone else." "Innocent" here is not a term referring to personal responsibility at all. It means rather "not harming." But the people fighting are "harming," so they can be attacked; but if they surrender they become in this sense innocent and so may not be maltreated or killed. Nor is there round for trying them on a criminal charge; not, indeed, because a man has no personal responsibility for fighting, but because they were not the subjects of the state whose prisoners they are.

There is an argument which I know from experience it is necessary to forestall at this point, though I think it is visibly captious. It is this: on my theory, would it not follow that a soldier can only be killed when he is actually attacking? Then, *e.g.*, it would be impossible to attack a sleeping camp. The answer is that "what someone is doing" can refer to what he is doing at the moment or to his rôle in a situation. A soldier under arms is "harming" in the latter sense even if he is asleep. But it is true that the enemy should not be attacked more ferociously than is necessary to put them *hors de combat*.

These conceptions are distinct and intelligible ones; they would formerly have been said to belong to the Law of Nations. Anyone can see that they are good, and we pay tribute to them by our moral indignation when our enemies violate them. But in fact they are going, and only fragments of them are left. General Eisenhower, for example, is reported to have spoken slightingly once of the notion of chivalry towards prisoners—as if that were based on respect for their virtue or for the nation from which they come, and not on the fact that they are now defenceless.

It is characteristic of nowadays to talk with horror of killing rather than of murder, and hence, since in war, since you have committed yourself to killing—*i.e.* "accepted an evil"—not to mind whom you kill. This seems largely to be the work of the devil; but I also suspect that it is in part an effect of the existence of pacifism, as a doctrine which many people respect though they would not adopt it. This effect would not exist if people had a distinct notion of what makes pacifism a false doctrine.

It therefore seems to me important to show that for one human being deliberately to kill another is not inevitably wrong. I may seem to be wasting my time, as most people do reject pacifism. But it is nevertheless important to argue the point because if one does so one sees that there are pretty severe restrictions on legitimate killing. Of course, people accept this within the state, but when it comes to war they have the idea that any restrictions are something like the Queensbury Rules—instead of making the difference between being guilty and not guilty of murder.

I will not discuss the self-defence of a private person. If he kills the man who attacks him who [sic] someone else, it ought to be accidental. To aim at killing, even when one is defending oneself, is murderous. (I fear even this idea is going. A man was acquitted recently who had successfully set a lethal booby trap to kill a thief in his absence.)

But the state actually has the authority to order deliberate killing in order to protect its people or to put frightful injustices right. (For example, the plight of the Jews under Hitler would have been a reasonable cause of war.) The reason for this is pretty simple: it stands out most clearly if we first consider the state's right to order such killing within its confines. I am not referring to the death penalty, but to what happens when there is rioting or when violent malefactors have to be caught. Rioters can sometimes only be restrained, or malefactors seized, by force. Law without force is ineffectual, and human beings without laws miserable (though we, who have too many and too changeable laws, may easily not feel this very distinctly). So much is indeed fairly obvious, though the more peaceful the society the less obvious it is that the force in the hands of the servants of the law has to be force up to the point of killing. It would become perfectly obvious any time there was rioting or gangsterism which had to be dealt with by the servants of the law fighting.

The death penalty itself is a completely different matter. The state is not fighting the criminal who is condemned to death. That is why the death penalty is not indispensable. People keep on discussing whether the point of it is deterrence or vengeance; it is neither. Not deterrence, because nobody has proved anything about that, and people think what they think in accordance with their prejudices. And not vengeance, because that's nobody's business. Confusion arises on this subject because the state is said, and correctly said, to *punish* the criminal, and "punishment" suggests "vengeance." Therefore many humane people dislike the idea and prefer such notions as "correction" and "rehabilitation." But the action of the state in depriving a man of his rights, up to his very life, has to be considered from two sides. First, from that of the man himself. If he could say "Why have you done this to me? I have not deserved it," then the state would be acting with injustice. Therefore he must be proved guilty, and only as punishment has the state the right to inflict anything on him. The concept of punishment is our one safeguard against being done "good" to, in ways involving a deprivation of rights, by impudent powerful people. Second, from the side of the state, divine retributive justice is not its affair: it only has to protect its people and restrain malefactors. The ground of its right to deprive of liberty and even life is only that the malefactor is a nuisance, like a gangrenous limb. Therefore it can cut him off entirely, if his crime is so bad that he could not justly protest "I have not deserved *this*." But when I say that the sole ground of state's right to kill him is that he is a nuisance, I only mean that he is a nuisance *qua* malefactor. The lives of the innocent are the actual point of society, so the fact that in some other way they may be a nuisance (troublesome to look after, for example) does not justify the state in getting rid of them. Though that is another thing we may yet come to. But the blood of the innocent cries to heaven for vengeance.

Thus the malefactor who has been found guilty is the only defenceless person whom the state may put to death. It need not; it can choose more merciful laws. (I have no prejudice in favour of the death penalty.) Any other defenceless person is as such innocent, in the sense "not harming." And so the state can only order to kill others of its subjects besides convicted criminals if they are rioting or doing something that has to be stopped, and can only be stopped by the servants of the law fighting them.

Now, this is also the ground of the state's right to order people to fight external enemies who are unjustly attacking them or something of theirs. The right to order to fight for the sake of other people's wrongs, to put right something affecting people who are not actually under the protection of the state, is a rather more dubious thing obviously, but it exists because of the common sympathy of human beings whereby one feels for one's neighbour if he is attacked. So in an attenuated sense it can be said that something that belongs to, or concerns, one is attacked if anybody is unjustly attacked or maltreated.

Pacifism, then, is a false doctrine. Now, no doubt, it is bad just for that reason, because it is always bad to have a false conscience. In this way the doctrine that it is a bad act to lay a bet is bad: it is all right to bet what it is all right to risk or drop in the sea. But I want to maintain that pacifism is a harmful doctrine in a far stronger sense than this. Even the prevalence of the idea that it was wrong to bet would have no particularly bad consequences; a false doctrine which merely forbids what is not actually bad need not encourage people in anything bad. But with pacifism it is quite otherwise. It is a factor in the loss of the conception of murder which is my chief interest in this pamphlet.

I have very often heard people say something like this: "It is all very well to say 'Don't do evil that good may come.' But *war* is evil. We all know that. Now, of course, it is possible to be an Absolute Pacifist. I can respect that, but I can't be one myself, and most other people won't be either. So we have to accept the evil. It is not that we do not see the evil. And once you are in for it, you have to go the whole hog."

This is much as if I were defrauding someone, and when someone tried to stop me I said: "Absolute honesty! I respect that. But of course absolute honesty really means having no property at all . . ." Having offered the sacrifice of a few sighs and tears to absolute honesty, I go on as before.

The correct answer to the statement that "war is evil" is that it is bad—*i.e.*, a misfortune—to be at war. And no doubt if two nations are at war at least one is unjust. But that does not show that it is wrong to fight or that if one does fight one can also commit murder.

Naturally my claim that pacifism is a very harmful doctrine is contingent on its being a false one. If it were a true doctrine, its encouragement of this non-sensical "hypocrisy of the ideal standard" would not count against it but given that it is false, I am inclined to think it is also very bad, unusually so for an idea which seems as it were to err on the noble side.

When I consider the history of the events from 1939 to 1945, I am not surprised that Mr. Truman is made the recipient of honours. But when I consider his actions by themselves, I am surprised again.

Some people actually praise the bombings and commend the stockpiling of atomic weapons on the ground that they are so horrible that [a] nation. . . will be afraid ever again to make war. "We have made a covenant with death, and with hell we are at an agreement." There does not seem to be good ground for such a hope for any long period of time.

Pacifists have for long made it a point in their propaganda that men must grow more murderous as their techniques of destruction improve, and those who defend murder eagerly seize on this point, so that I imagine by now it is pretty well accepted by the whole world. Of course, it is not true. In Napoleon's time, for example, the means of destruction had much improved since the time of Henry V; but Henry, not Napoleon, was a great massacre of civilians, saying when he did particularly atrocious things that the French were a sinful nation and that he had a mission from God to punish them. And, of course, really large scale massacre up to now has belonged to times with completely primitive methods of killing. Weapons are now manufactured whose sole point is to be used in massacre of cities. But the people responsible are not murderous because they have these weapons; they have them because they are murderous. Deprived of atomic bombs, they would commit massacres by means of other bombs.

Protests by people who have not power are a waste of time. I was not seizing an opportunity to make a "gesture of protest" at atomic bombs; I vehemently object to *our* action in offering Mr. Truman honours, because one can share in the guilt of a bad action by praise and flattery, as also by defending it. When I puzzle myself over the attitude of the Vice-Chancellor and the Hebdomadal Council, I look round to see if any explanation is available why so many Oxford people should be willing to flatter such a man.

I get some small light on the subject when I consider the productions of Oxford moral philosophy since the first world war, which I have lately had occasion to read. Its character can easily be briefly demonstrated. Up to the second world war the prevailing moral philosophy in Oxford taught that an action can be "morally good" no matter how objectionable the thing done may be. An instance would be Himmler's efforts at exterminating the Jews: he did it from the "motive of duty" which has "supreme value." In the same philosophy—which has much pretence of moral seriousness, claiming that "rightness" is an objective character in acts, that can be discerned by a moral sense—it is also held that it might be right to kill the innocent for the good of the people, since the "prima facie duty" of securing some advantage might outweigh the "prima facie duty" of not killing the innocent. This sort of philosophy is less prevalent now, and in its place I find another, whose cardinal principle is that "good" is not a "descriptive" term, but one expressive of a favourable attitude on the part of the speaker. Hand in hand with this, though I do not know if there is any logical connection, goes a doctrine that it is impossible to have any quite general moral laws; such laws as "It s wrong to lie" or "Never commit sodomy" are rules of thumb which an experienced person knows when to break. Further, both his selection of these as the rules on which to proceed, and his tactful adjustments of them in particular cases, are based on their fitting together with the "way of life" which is his preference. Both these philosophies, then, contain a repudiation of the idea that any class of actions, such as murder, may be absolutely excluded. I do not know how influential they may have been or be; they are perhaps rather symptomatic. Whether influential or symptomatic, they throw some light on the situation.

It is possible still to withdraw from this shameful business in some slight degree; it is possible not to go to Encaenia; if it should be embarrassing to someone who would normally go to plead other business, he could take to his bed. I indeed should fear to go, in case God's patience suddenly ends.

*G. E. M. (Elizabeth) Anscombe** was a professor of philosophy at Cambridge University from 1970 to 1986. Her writings on morality helped change the course of moral philosophy.

G. E. M. Anscombe, "Mr. Truman's Degree," in Walter Stein (ed.), *Nuclear Weapons: A Catholic Response*, Sheed and Ward, 1961 (reprinted in *The Collected Philosophical Papers of G. E. M. Anscombe*, vol. III, Ethics, Religion and Politics. Blackwell, Oxford: 1981, 62–71).

Reproduced with permission of Blackwell Publishing Ltd.

Supreme Emergencies and the Protection of Non-combatants in War

by Alex J. Bellamy*

Is it ever justifiable deliberately to target non-combatants in war? If so, under what circumstances? The history of warfare is littered with cases where non-combatants were deliberately targeted. Such cases include, *inter alia*, the massacre of the Melians at the hands of Athens in 416 BC, the fire-bombing of German cities by the British Royal Air Force (RAF) during the Second World War, the Nazi and Soviet atrocities in the same war, the atomic attacks on Hiroshima and Nagasaki at the end of that war, and the genocide and ethnic cleansing witnessed in Bosnia and Rwanda in the 1990s.[1] All too often, war has deteriorated into generalized slaughter, leading some to argue that it is always thus.[2] When this has happened, the perpetrators justify their actions through a mixture of arguments. The Athenians famously argued that 'right, as the word goes, is only in question between equals in power, while the strong do what they can and the weak suffer what they must'.[3] In other words, it cannot be unjust for the strong to massacre the weak because questions of justice apply only between equals. In the 1990s, Rwandan Hutu and Bosnian Serb butchers insisted that what they did was necessary to preserve the security of their own nations. The British and American governments during the Second World War argued that targeting German and Japanese non-combatants was necessary to save lives and prevail in the struggle against fascism.

It is this last idea, that it is sometimes necessary to suspend the moral restrictions on targeting non-combatants, that is investigated in this article. Although it was Winston Churchill who first put the idea forward, when he argued that the 'supreme emergency' confronting Britain in 1940 necessitated the bombing of German cities, it was Michael Walzer who developed it fully in his doctrine of the 'supreme emergency' exception. Since Walzer, the exception has not received the attention it deserves, though John Rawls used it to condemn the atomic attacks on Japan, Terry Nardin criticized it, and Brian Orend has offered a reformulation based on the idea that the supreme emergency is a moral tragedy in the proper sense of the term.[4]

After outlining Walzer's case, I argue that there are at least four major problems with it. First, it contradicts Walzer's own deontological account of the just war tradition. It flirts with realism and succumbs to utilitarianism, both perspectives that Walzer himself denounces. Second, creating exceptions to the prohibition on direct attacks on non-combatants weakens arguably the most significant element of the just war tradition's constraints on contemporary war.[5] It is particularly problematic because, by countenancing the deliberate targeting of non-combatants, it undermines the Augustinian insistence that outward acts of violence in war are legitimate only if accompanied by an inward disposition of love. Third, Walzer's case is based on a 'thought experiment' that is historically problematic.[6] Fourth, Walzer's thought experiment is also strategically flawed. That is, the direct targeting of non-combatants cannot be required by military necessity because the strategic principles of war demand that one's forces be orientated towards the accomplishment of political goals, unified in their approach, and directed against the enemy's military.

I argue that as a result of these four problems the existence of a 'supreme emergency' cannot justify overriding non-combatant immunity. According to Brian Orend, however, this position should be colloquially labelled the 'let justice be done though the heavens fall' position.[7] He argues that demanding compliance with non-combatant immunity in supreme emergencies is both unrealistic and unreasonable.[8] These are important criticisms that challenge the practical utility and morality of complying with non-combatant immunity at all times. According to Orend, the supreme emergency exemption demonstrates the moral tragedy of war—that in some cases, no matter what one does, it will be wrong. It is a moral tragedy in the full sense of the term, because 'each viable option you face involves a severe moral violation'.[9]

In the final part of the article, I will seek to defend the view that non-combatant immunity should not be violated even in supreme emergencies, and that this is not an unrealistic position: on the contrary, I argue, there are always morally better alternatives and these alternatives are also often strategically better as well. The proportionality principle allows political and military leaders considerable room for manoeuvre that permits them to meet the threat with significant military force without violating the principle of non-combatant immunity. When confronted with a supreme emergency, proportionality allows leaders to take greater risks with the lives of enemy non-combatants without violating the principle of discrimination so long as their deaths are only the foreseen consequences of attacks on military targets. This distinction is important, because on the one hand it preserves the idea, first found in Ambrose and Augustine, that it is one's intent in war that shapes the justice of a particular action; and on the other hand, much more importantly, it protects non-combatants from some of the worst excesses of war.

WALZER'S SUPREME EMERGENCY EXCEPTION

Walzer's ethics of the conduct of war is based on a deontological conception of human rights. He argues that a thin veneer of rules derived from legal norms, religious and philosophical ideas, professional codes, reciprocal agreements and public dialogue establishes a 'war convention' that permeates all international society.[10] According to Walzer, the second principle of the war convention is that non-combatants may never be attacked.[11] The principle of non-combatant immunity plays an important role in most of the major religious perspectives on the ethics of war, is grounded in customary international law, and has been a part of the just war tradition in one form or another since the nineteenth century.[12] Walzer agrees that anyone who is not engaged in making war is immune from attack. Non-combatants, he emphatically argues, 'cannot be attacked at any time. They can never be the objects or targets of military activity.'[13] For Walzer, this is not a matter of granting special privileges to certain classes on the basis of their social or economic function in peacetime,[14] but a fundamental moral right that cuts across time and space.

To overcome the pacifist argument that it is incongruent for a just war theory to justify war yet demand non-combatant immunity, since non-combatants are always killed in wartime, Walzer deploys a somewhat revised doctrine of the double effect.[15] The doctrine of double effect, first articulated in the thirteenth century by Thomas Aquinas (see below), holds that an act carried out with good intentions may nevertheless have evil consequences such as the killing of non-combatants.[16] This leaves it open to the charge that the difference between *intending* harm and merely *foreseeing* it—which is integral to the doctrine—is a facile one that does not in practice afford protection to non-combatants.[17] Walzer agrees that this is a problem and argues that leaders must not only desist from intentionally targeting non-combatants but must also take measures to reduce the risks faced by non-combatants as far as possible. As Walzer put it, "simply not to intend the death of civilians is too easy . . . What we look for in such cases is some sign of a positive commitment to save civilian lives . . . And if saving civilian lives means risking soldiers' lives, the risks must be accepted." [18] For Walzer, this obligation even overrides the proportionality principle that the good accomplished outweighs the evil inflicted, because it is derived from the fundamental (deontological) rights held by non-combatants.

Although Walzer sets up the principle of non-combatant immunity in strict deontological terms, he allows two possible exceptions. The first, which there is no space to explore here, concerns reprisals. Walzer argues that belligerents may sometimes legitimately conduct reprisals against prisoners if doing so persuades one's enemies to cease committing the unjust acts that prompted the reprisals.[19] The second is the idea that non-combatant immunity may be waived during supreme emergencies.

According to Walzer, there are situations "Where the danger confronted in war is so great that it requires the use of measures expressly forbidden by the 'war convention.'"[20] An emergency becomes supreme when two conditions are satisfied. First, the danger must be imminent. In this context, 'imminence' carries two connotations. The danger must be present and real (the fear of future danger is not sufficient); and the danger must be so imminent that leaders are left with *no alternative* but to waive the rights of enemy non-combatants.[21] This latter point is crucial for the discussion that follows here, because its practical application, I believe, actually undermines the idea of a supreme emergency exception. Walzer states that a threat 'neither compels, nor permits attacks on the innocent, *so long as other means of fighting and winning are available*'.[22] I argue that there is good reason to think that there are always better alternatives.

The second element of the supreme emergency is the nature of the threat. In wartime, every nation believes that it is confronting a supreme danger. This is not enough, however. The danger, Walzer tells us, 'must be of an unusual and horrifying kind'; it must, in other words, shock the conscience of humanity.[23] Most wars, according to Walzer, are not concerned with the defence of 'ultimate values' but instead involve questions of relative gains. Nations face a supreme emergency only when the costs of losing are catastrophic—when massacre on a large scale would be the result.

Walzer demonstrates his point by considering Britain's decision to begin targeting German population centres in 1940. For Walzer, the threat posed by Nazism constituted the ultimate supreme emergency. His analysis of the decision to bomb German cities is based on two convenient fictions, which he acknowledges as such. The first is that, in the second half of 1940, Britain stood alone against Germany. This is utterly untrue. Not to mention the partisan soldiers who opposed Germany throughout Europe, Britain in 1940 received considerable assistance from the Commonwealth (Australia, Canada and India especially).[24] Second, Walzer acknowledges that he is conducting a thought experiment, since it was not the case that the strategic bombardment of cities was the only possible course of action open to the British in the final months of 1940, an issue to which I will return later. However, on the basis of these two assumptions, Walzer proceeds to argue that Britain was justified in bombing Germany cities from 1940 until 1942 when the imminence of the Nazi threat receded with the entry of the United States and Soviet Union into the war and

Germany's first reversals on the battlefield. The continuation of city bombing thereafter and the destruction of Japanese cities by the US air force were, in Walzer's eyes, unjustifiable because the supreme emergency had passed.

According to Walzer, although Britain was justified in breaking the rules, its decision to do so was a moral tragedy and the political leadership was quite correct to refuse to honour Arthur Harris, the head of the RAP's Bomber Command, at the end of the war. The decision to bomb was legitimate because 'utilitarian calculation can force us to violate the rules of war only when we are face-to-face not merely with defeat but with defeat likely to bring disaster to the political community'.[25] In such cases, Walzer seems to suggest, leaders lose their agency: they are simply compelled to do whatever they can to defend the political community against a supreme danger. Leaders who refuse to take this decision err by placing their own moral values above the well-being of the political community they have a responsibility to protect.

The case for a supreme emergency exception appears convincing at first glance, particularly when the war against Nazism is used as a case in point. It is very difficult to argue that Churchill should have risked defeat to maintain his own moral purity. To do so would have been an abrogation of his responsibilities to the British people *and* a betrayal of his duty to humanity. Indeed, Augustine argued that failing to protect the innocent against grave injustice when one is able to do so is as much a crime as committing the injustice itself.[26] More recently, the Dutch peacekeepers at Srebrenica in 1995 were rightly condemned for their failure to protect the town's civilian population.[27] On closer inspection, however, the concept is fundamentally flawed. In particular, it is inconsistent with the rest of Walzer's theory of the ethics of war, it is historically and strategically untenable, and it is out of step with contemporary western understandings of legitimate conduct in wartime.

Four Objections

This section identifies four principal flaws in Walzer's supreme emergency exception to non-combatant immunity. Taken together, I argue, they make it clear that the case for an exception cannot be sustained. However, the case for an absolute ban on the intentional targeting of non-combatants then has to be defended against the charge that it is both unrealistic (that is, so idealistic that it is out of step with what a political community ought to expect its leaders to do) and irresponsible (that is, it demands that a political leader sacrifice the welfare of the political community to satisfy his or her own moral beliefs). I shall go on to present such a defence in the remainder of the article.

Realism and Utilitarianism

The first problem with Walzer's supreme emergency exception is that it contradicts the deontological basis of his own theory of the ethics of war. As noted above, Walzer's ethics of war is based on neither theology nor law (either natural or positive), but the 'war convention', which is by and large a product of custom. Within this customary convention, however, there are some basic principles that are founded on the fundamental human rights enjoyed by all people as a result of their very humanity. The most fundamental of these deontological rules, grounded in human rights not customary practice, is the principle of non-combatant immunity. This principle states not that non-combatants may never be killed in war, but that they may never be *intentionally* targeted. We use the doctrine of the double effect to judge the difference between unjustified (intentional) killing and justified (unintended but foreseen) killing. However, Walzer countenances the abrogation of these rights in supreme emergencies. This brings his overall theory dangerously close to two perspectives on the ethics of war that he expressly rejects elsewhere: realism and utilitarianism. Although the supreme emergency exception can be distinguished from realism (though not wholly satisfactorily), it is very difficult to distinguish it from utilitarianism because at its heart is the idea that the defence of a political community is more important than the fundamental rights of individuals.

Realists hold that the defence of the state and its vital national interests are reason enough to go to war, and that when the state's vital interest or very survival is at stake the only constraint on state action should be prudential considerations. Thus, classical realists tend to be conservative about supporting the use of force. Clausewitz's famous dictum that 'war is nothing but the continuation of policy by other means' does not so much give statesmen a free hand to wage war as implore them to calibrate their use of the military tool with precise policy objectives.[28] The politics of prudence calls for the application of traditional *jus ad bellum* criteria such as proportionality of ends, last resort (because waging war is always more costly than other measures) and likelihood of success. In relation to the conduct of war, realists argue that leaders may do anything to ensure victory. In limited wars, prudence may dictate that measures be taken to protect enemy non-combatants. In other wars, however, the protection of non-combatants must not be allowed to compromise the chances of success. As Steven Forde has put it, 'acting in accordance with the international common good when others refuse to do so is harmful, and perhaps even immoral, considering the state's obligation to the safety of its members'.[29]

The idea that good statesmen sometimes have to get their hands dirty is one of the central characteristics of realism, particularly the Christian realism of Reinhold Niebuhr.[30] The Niebuhrian inflection of some of Walzer's thinking was evident prior to *Just and unjust wars* in his discussion of the 'dirty hands' principle. Here, Walzer argued that it is impossible to govern without occasionally overriding basic moral principles to accomplish a greater political good. Indeed, he insisted that there are instances where a ruler has a *duty* to do so, though doing so incurs moral guilt.[31]

Despite the similarities between Walzer and Niebuhr, *Just and unjust wars* begins with a denunciation of realism. He argues that an interests-based concept of war offers no coherent way of talking about war.[32] Moreover, he points out that the discourse of war is an inherently moral discourse and that war is not an inevitable part of international life. Thus Walzer dismisses each of the cornerstones of realism: the idea that international life is amoral and interests-driven; that 'moralism' in world politics is dangerous; and that war is inevitable in an anarchical system.[33]

However, the realist prescriptions that Walzer rejects sound very similar to his supreme emergency exception. Most realists accept the view that states will find it prudent broadly to follow the main elements of the laws of war in all but the most extreme of circumstances, owing to the power of reciprocity and the desire for foreign alliances. However, whenever necessity dictates, leaders would and indeed should override the rules. According to this view, all the supreme emergency does is offer a guide to the types of circumstances in which leaders will reject the rules. Any political leader, a realist would argue, can construct a plausible case that what he or she is facing is a supreme emergency.[34] Read this way, the 'exception' could be cast so broadly that the 'rule' of non-combatant immunity would cease to offer much protection.

Although the supreme emergency exception seems to have much in common with realism, there are important grounds for rejecting the idea that they are synonymous. First, Wheeler argues that Walzer is careful when defining the supreme emergency to distinguish between threats to all humanity and threats to individual states. Where the threat is felt only by a particular state, leaders should be more circumspect about breaking the rules.[35] However, Walzer is, as we have seen, quite clear on the point that a single political community may feel a supreme emergency when that community is under dire threat. While it may be *easier* to invoke the exception when the threat confronts all humanity, this argument does not really provide a clear distinction between Walzer's position and realism, for both concur that when a political community confronts a horrific danger, the exception may be invoked.

A second and more fundamental distinction is that in his discussion of the supreme emergency Walzer still holds that there are binding moral constraints on leaders which may be temporarily overridden in extreme cases but may never be ignored. This qualification reveals Walzer's discomfort with his own argument. Realists would feel no such discomfort because they argue that in such cases there are no binding moral constraints, and so no need for state leaders to justify their actions as warranted by a supreme emergency: military necessity and prudential arguments would suffice. However, although this argument may provide a clear intellectual distinction, it is not at all clear that it makes a difference in practice.

It is more difficult for Walzer to defend himself against the charge that the doctrine of the supreme emergency is a utilitarian doctrine and that it therefore contradicts *his* own denunciation of utilitarianism. In the preface to the second edition of *Just and unjust wars*, Walzer emphatically rejected utilitarianism, arguing that 'considerations of utility play into the scenario on many points, but they cannot account for it as a whole. Their part is subsidiary to that of rights; it is constrained by right'; and, he continues, 'at every point, the judgments we make are best accounted for if we regard life and liberty as something like absolute values'.[36] In war, Walzer argued, there are certain rights that are inalienable. Specifically, he identifies the prohibition of rape as one such inalienable right, and we can suppose that non-combatant immunity is another.[37] 'A legitimate act of war', Walzer concludes, 'is one that does not violate the rights of the people against whom it is directed.' Moreover, 'no one can be threatened with war or warred against, unless *through some act of his own* he has surrendered or lost his rights' to life and liberty.[38] Thus Walzer clearly repudiated the utilitarian idea that if a cause is just one may use whatever means are necessary to secure victory, thereby securing the greatest good of the greatest number.[39] Indeed, in his discussion of supreme emergencies he concedes that 'to kill 278,966 civilians (the number is made up) in order to avoid the deaths of an unknown but probably larger number of civilians and soldiers is surely a fantastic, godlike, frightening and horrendous act'.[40]

But does not the doctrine of the supreme emergency force us to make such utilitarian calculations? Is it not founded on the very idea that in certain circumstances state leaders should prioritize the greater good over the (supposedly inalienable) rights of non-combatants? Walzer concedes that it does, and uses a utilitarian analysis to defend the British decision to bomb German cities in 1940 and criticize the American decision to launch an atomic attack on Japan in 1945: Britain faced defeat in 1940, the US did not face defeat in 1945. According to the doctrine of supreme emergency, utilitarian calculations do come into play and may override the rules when defeat and disaster are imminent, but not in other circumstances.[41]

It is clear that Walzer cannot avoid the charge of utilitarianism when it comes to the supreme emergency; and thus his ethics of war are inconsistent. More troubling, however, is the effect that permitting a limited right to override the rules has on the moral and legal quality of the rules. Seen in this light, the rights of non-combatants are conditional, not inalienable. They may be breached when a political community justifiably believes that it confronts a supreme emergency. Such an argument could have been used to justify Serbian tactics in both Bosnia and Kosovo. From a Serbian perspective there was every reason to believe that defeat in Bosnia and Kosovo would lead to massacre and forced expulsion, however misplaced that belief. It would be quite feasible to argue that the Serbs believed that they faced a supreme emergency in the 1990s and that the defence of Serbian Bosnia and Kosovo required that the rights of Bosnians and Kosovars be overridden. However plausible we find this argument (I do not find it very plausible), we must accept that Walzer's formulation of the supreme emergency doctrine allows the possibility of making it. Moreover, the supreme emergency argument assumes that rule-breaking behaviour *will* produce the desired effect. How would we regard the terror bombing of cities in response to a supreme emergency if, in the end, the side conducting the terror bombing did not prevail?[42] In this sense, the utility of a supreme emergency decision can only be assessed retrospectively; it cannot provide a moral guide to state leaders at the time of confronting the emergency.

The first problem with Walzer's doctrine of supreme emergency, therefore, is that it contradicts his broader ethics of war. Although it can be defended against the charge that it resembles realism, it has to be conceded that it is an essentially utilitarian doctrine. However limited the occasions where a valid supreme emergency argument can be made, it nevertheless has the effect of rendering conditional what Walzer elsewhere describes as fundamental rights. According to the supreme emergency doctrine, non-combatants lose their immunity because of the actions of others. This contradicts Walzer's claim—which underpins his concept of the double effect—that utilitarian claims are secondary to the deontological rights held by all non-combatants.

The Rule of Non-combatant Immunity

The second reason for rejecting the supreme emergency argument flows from our discussion of utilitarianism: namely, the ethics and laws of war impose a complete ban on the direct intentional targeting of non-combatants. Moreover, under the Rome Statute of the International Criminal Court (ICC), the leaders of almost one hundred states would face criminal charges if they ordered the direct targeting of non-combatants, for whatever reason.[43]

The idea that non-combatants should be immune from direct targeting is one of the fundamental elements of the 'war convention', however conceived. Sun Tzu, the renowned Chinese strategist of the fifth century, insisted that armies should treat prisoners and non-combatants with respect.[44] The ancient Hindu, Egyptian and Hebrew civilizations all produced customs relating to the humane treatment of prisoners and non-combatants in wartime.[45] In the western tradition, Plato insisted that armies refrain from burning habitations and should kill only those who are directly foes, and not all the men, women and children of the enemy state.[46] Although Augustine was ambivalent about the treatment of non-combatants,[47] virtually every other key member of the just war tradition forbade the direct killing of non-combatants. Medieval canon law prohibited the use of force against certain classes of people who performed important peacetime roles and played no role in hostilities (clerics, farmers, merchants), while the chivalric tradition forbade violence against the weak.[48]

The principle of non-combatant immunity is arguably the most clearly understood and widely accepted element of the contemporary laws of war. The idea is enshrined in all four of the Geneva Conventions concluded on 12 August 1949. The central concern of all four conventions was the protection of the victims of war. Many of the specific articles were derived from proposals formulated by the International Committee of the Red Cross (ICRC) between 1945 and 1948. Because of the large number of signatories, these conventions are assumed to hold the status of customary international law—a point recognized by the UN Secretary General in 1993. The conventions were also embodied in the founding statutes of the criminal tribunals for former Yugoslavia and Rwanda, which also confirmed that they formed part of customary law.[49] Crucially, common article 3 of the conventions, which clearly sets out the rule of non-combatant immunity, is a peremptory rule of war. It demands that: 'Persons taking no active part in the hostilities, including members of armed forces who have laid down their arms, and those placed hors de combat by sickness, wounds, detention or any other cause, shall in all circumstances be treated humanely, without any adverse distinction founded on race, colour, religion or faith, sex, birth, or wealth.'[50]

According to Colm McKeogh, the ethical and legal principle of non-combatant immunity is important for at least seven reasons. First, non-combatants have committed no wrong and therefore they may not have war waged upon them.

Second, non-combatants are not participating in the fighting. Third, a reason developed from the chivalric tradition of the Middle Ages, non-combatants are unable to defend themselves. Fourth, killing non-combatants is militarily unnecessary. Fifth, maintaining non-combatant immunity reduces the casualties of war (a particularly pertinent question in the contemporary era when many more non-combatants than combatants die in war). Sixth, sparing women and children (and, we may add, those who perform essential peacetime services such as farmers) is important for species survival. Seventh, killing non-combatants is contrary to the 'war convention', however undersrood.[51]

It is not necessary to labour this point. Suffice it to say that the supreme emergency exception endorses the suspension of one of the most fundamental rights permitted by the ethics and laws of war. Importantly, none of the sources cited here suggest that the right is conditional on the demands of military necessity.

The Historical Fallacy of the Fateful Choice

The third problem with the supreme emergency exception is that it is based on a fictitious worst-case scenario, from which it extrapolates a moral exception with practical import. The fallacy, I argue, is the claim that political and military leaders confront one of two possibilities in supreme emergencies: refuse to break the rules of war and face destruction; or directly target enemy non-combatants. The case that Walzer uses to make his point is the British decision to target German cities at the end of 1940. According to Walzer, 'the more certain a German victory appeared to be in the absence of a bomber offensive the more justifiable was the decision to launch the offensive'.[52] This view is problematic for two reasons. First, it overlooks the extent to which British thinking had incorporated the targeting of non-combatants into its air strategy a long time before 1940. Acknowledging this suggests that the choice presented itself in 1940 not in the light of a moral tragedy, but because it reflected dominant thinking in British strategic circles. Second, by presenting the choice in an 'either-or' fashion, it overlooks the range of alternative strategies that Britain could have used to defend itself without terrorizing German civilians.

The idea of using the strategic bombing of cities and mass killing of non-combatants to achieve positive outcomes in war indirectly was a cornerstone of British thinking a long time before 1940. In 1918, the Chief of the British Air Staff, Major-General Frederick Sykes, supported the strategic bombardment of cities, insisting that 'the aim of such attacks would be to sow alarm, set up nervous tension, check output, and generally tend to bring military, financial, and industrial interests into opposition . . . The wholesale bombing of densely-populated industrial centres would go far to destroy the morale of the operatives.'[53] After the war, the first head of the RAF, Hugh Trenchard, was a keen advocate of terror bombing. Immediately after the First World War, he complained that the only reason why he had been unable to destroy Germany's industrial centres had been the lack of resources.[54] Four years later, he made the same point more emphatically: 'Why is it that your [the RAF's] policy of attack from the air is so different from the policy of the Army, whose policy is to attack the enemy's army, while yours is *to attack the civilian population* . . . The Army policy was to defeat the enemy army—ours is to defeat the enemy nation.'[55]

Prior to the outbreak of the Second World War, Trenchard continued to insist that the RAF develop its ability to strike enemy population centres, even at the expense of other arms of the military.[56] Once war broke out, he argued that it was not the role of the RAF to provide close air support to the British Expeditionary Force in Belgium. This view stood at odds with the Luftwaffe's close relationship with the German army and its role in combat support.[57] The air force, Trenchard argued, should be deployed against the enemy's industrial and civilian centres in order to destroy production and morale.[58] Crucially, Trenchard's view was echoed across the RAF. A Staff College manual produced in 1922 discussed the crucial role played by strategic campaigns aimed at undermining the will of the populace through direct attack;[59] and Brigadier General Groves heralded the new air power that replaced the 'war of lines' with the 'war of areas', supporting strategic bombardment for its ability to have a significant psychological effect on the enemy population.[60]

My point here is that by 1939–40 strategic thinking in the RAF was strongly predisposed towards the use of air power for the strategic bombardment of industrial and civilian population centres. Although none of the writers cited above actually called for the demolition of cities, each commended the psychological impact of strategic bombardment. Such psychological effects, Douhet had observed, are brought about by the direct targeting of civilian population centres.[61] Thus, it is not the case that the strategic bombardment of German cities was a choice forced upon the British government by the supreme emergency it confronted. Indeed, one of the principal advocates of this policy, Trenchard, confessed that he was unsure whether strategic bombardment would be successful.[62] However, he wielded what has been described as 'absolute' power over the RAF, and for more than two decades before the outbreak of war his focus had been on the importance of the offensive ability of the air force to attack civilian and industrial centres. It is unsurprising, therefore, that British politicians were presented with the tragic choice of either bombarding German cities or 'doing nothing' to reduce the likelihood of British defeat. That choice, however, was a product not of the essential moral tragedy of war, but of the strategic preferences of the RAF elite.

Were there alternatives to the strategic bombardment of German cities? It is certainly the case that the bombardment was ineffective: German production in July 1944 was more than three times that of February 1942.[63] Perhaps the most innovative and forward-thinking strategist in the RAF, Wing Commander John Slessor, believed that air power could be used more effectively. In a series of lectures to the Army Staff College between 1931 and 1934, Slessor argued that strategic bombardment was not a suitable way of supporting Britain's expeditionary land forces. Reflecting on scenarios similar to the First World War (a land war in Europe), he argued that air power could be most effectively used to isolate enemy forces in the field by attacking the enemy's military supply lines, its communications, transportation and headquarters, and by providing close air support to land forces. In place of the rigid separation of air and land commands supported by the focus on strategic bombing and Trenchard's belief that the army and air force had different objectives in war, Slessor argued that the two components had the same objective and should share command centres.[64] Slessor's ideas were not merely preferable in theory. His preferred strategy of targeting enemy supply lines was used with great effect by the US Air Force immediately before D-Day in 1944.

Had Slessor, not Trenchard, been the dominant figure in the RAF, and had the unfounded belief that strategic bombing of population centres produced significant and positive effects not become so integral to top-level thinking, the British government would not have confronted quite the same 'fateful choice' in late 1940. There would have been a much wider selection of options, including many that did not require the direct targeting of non-combatants. The so-called 'fateful choice', I argue, was a product not of the supreme emergency in "Which Britain undoubtedly found itself, but of the RAF's preferences. It presented itself in the terms it did because, at least twenty years earlier, the RAF leadership had taken the moral decision that it was legitimate to target non-combatants to make a psychological and economic impact upon the enemy. 'Fateful choices' are similarly constructed in other supreme emergencies. However, a military that refuses to countenance the direct targeting of non-combatants does not resign itself to inevitable defeat, but develops alternative strategies. Such strategies, the following section suggests, are consistent with modern ideas about the essentials of successful military strategy.

The Strategic Fallacy of the Fateful Choice

The fourth problem with the supreme emergencies exception is that, rather than being predicated on hard-nosed military reality, the idea that armed force should be used against non-combatants runs contrary to key aspects of contemporary strategic thinking, particularly those derived from Jomini. Specifically, using force against non-combatants contradicts the idea that militaries should employ an 'economy of force', should endeavour to defeat the enemy's armed forces and should attack the enemy's military 'centres of gravity'. Thus, with the exception of three notable approaches to strategy (Douhet's air strategy adopted by the RAF, Mao Zedong's 'people's war' strategy, and counter-city nuclear strategy[65]), military strategy tends to reject the direct targeting of non-combatants on prudential grounds.

Both of the most renowned strategic theorists, Sun Tzu and Clausewitz, placed important prudential limits on the conduct of war. For both, the conduct of war should be determined by its objectives, and each act of war orientated towards its conclusion. Sun Tzu, for instance, emphasized the importance of the non-military aspects of war and argued that the enemy's army should always be given a road down which to retreat once victory had been secured.[66]

Although Clausewitz was not very interested in the non-military aspects of war, his strategic ideas were based on two fundamental ideas. First, war is the continuation of policy by other means: that is, war is a means to an end and not an end in itself, and 'no other possibility exists, then, than to subordinate the military point of view to the political'.[67] Second, the way to prevail in war is to defeat the enemy's military forces. War, Clausewitz recognized, does not take place in isolation but within a wider political context. The way one fights has a direct bearing on that wider context. Fighting in an unrestrained fashion, by killing non-combatants, makes it much more difficult to accomplish the political goals that the war is being fought to achieve. As Colonel Kuhn observed, 'the quickest way of achieving and maintaining a lasting peace is to conduct hostilities humanely . . . it is evident that humanitarian considerations cannot be disassociated from the strategic concept of military leaders'.[68] The conduct of war should be limited to accomplishing one's political goals by defeating the enemy's military forces. Moving beyond these limitations carries with it the risk of losing allies, raises the danger that the enemy will reciprocate in kind, and makes it much more difficult to build a lasting peace once the war is over.

There is an important question mark, however, over whether these prudential restraints on war are relevant in supreme emergencies. Sun Tzu argued that as a last resort it was legitimate to attack the enemy's cities, while Clausewitz argued that the destruction of the enemy's army was the foremost goal; and, although he acknowledged that the enemy's public opinion played an important part in shaping the outcome of war, Clausewitz did not argue that the destruction of cities would be necessary. The problem with Sun Tzu's position, as both Clausewitz and his Swiss predecessor Jomini implicitly recognized, is that targeting non-combatants in cities does little to diminish the fighting capacity of the enemy's fielded army. Indeed, firepower directed at cities is firepower not directed at the enemy's army, and unless one has firepower to spare (which is never the case in a supreme emergency), attacking the enemy's non-combatants cannot be the most effective way of inflicting military defeat.

Jomini, arguably the most influential strategist of the modem era, put forward a number of principles to guide the conduct of war, principles that still guide the planning process in many western militaries. The first is to take the initiative and attack the enemy's 'feeble' points. The second is to 'direct our movement against the most advantageous feeble part . . . the one whose occupation will ensure us the most favourable opportunities and results'.[69] The third is to bring a combined effort to bear upon a single target. In the contemporary era, this means mounting joint operations that simultaneously combine land, air and sea components. The last of Jomini's principles relevant to this discussion is the requirement to follow up a military victory in order to deny the enemy an opportunity to regroup.

If we accept the proposition that these four principles contribute to the success of a military operation, it becomes apparent that directly targeting noncombatants in a supreme emergency is consonant with none of them and therefore not conducive to military success. Attacking the enemy's cities rather than its army awards the military initiative to the enemy. Once an army has been raised and deployed, such a strategy allows the enemy to marshal, organize and manoeuvre its forces with fewer restrictions than would be the case if military rather than non-combatant targets were given priority. Second, the 'advantage' to be gained by bombing the enemy's cities is at best indirect. It assumes, first, that it will damage the enemy's morale (whereas evidence from the Second World War suggests that the contrary is true) and, second, that it will have a negative impact on the war-fighting capacity of the enemy's army. While there is evidence to suggest that in the long run the destruction of cities and industrial centres has a negative impact on a state's war-fighting capacity, it is unlikely to diminish the capacity of the enemy's army in the short term and thereby avert the immediate supreme emergency. It was the Luftwaffe's inability to achieve command of the skies over Britain, not the destruction of German cities and industries, that averted the supreme emergency in 1940–41. Thankfully for Britain, Germany never massed an invasion army in northern Europe in preparation for an invasion. If it had done so (and recognizing the danger of counterfactual arguments), Britain's strategic choices would have been shown lacking, because the bombardment of German cities would have done nothing to reduce the potency of the invading army.

Third, as noted in the previous section, the decision to use RAF Bomber Command for strategic purposes dramatically reduced the potential for improving operational effectiveness through joint and combined activities. Indeed, Trenchard advocated the complete separation of army and air force, insisting that the two fight *different* wars. Today, most advanced militaries follow the idea of 'joint warfare' implied by Jomini, the idea being that the greatest effect is accomplished when the different arms of the military operate simultaneously to achieve common goals.[70] Activating the supreme emergency exception means denying yourself the potential advantages of joint warfare. Finally, by its nature it is difficult to follow up successful strategic bombing attacks. Factories can be rebuilt and production sites can be moved.

There is therefore a good case to be made that it does not make strategic sense to violate the rights of enemy non-combatants when a state confronts a supreme emergency. A strategy of targeting non-combatants has very little effect on the immediate ability of the enemy to inflict the impending calamity, and may even reduce the capacity of the defenders to resist by drawing their fire away from the enemy's military forces and dividing the different components of the military.

Given these four problems, the idea that it is legitimate to suspend the principle of non-combatant immunity in supreme emergencies is brought into serious question. First, although it can be defended against the charge of realism, it is a clearly utilitarian doctrine that contradicts Walzer's rights-based approach to the ethics of war. There is a real danger that making what are otherwise considered to be fundamental rights conditional on criteria beyond the control of those in line to lose their immunity will have the effect of making rights secondary to utilitarian considerations. As in previous centuries, the right of non-combatant immunity would become instead a privilege bestowed by the opposing military on the condition that it did not contravene military necessity. Second, contemporary legal and moral thinking flatly rejects the direct targeting of non-combatants, in all circumstances. The idea that non-combatants may be intentionally targeted is simply not countenanced by contemporary international society.[71] Third, Walzer's thought experiment, which suggests that governments face 'either-or' choices in supreme emergencies, is a historical fallacy. There are always alternative courses of action, and where those alternatives have been foreclosed, it is usually because of the prior moral choices of the people or institutions involved. This is clearly demonstrated by the British decision to bomb German cities in 1940, which was not a decision 'forced' upon the RAF by necessity but a direct product of over two decades of strategizing. Finally, the idea that the direct killing of non-combatants can be *essential* to successful defence during a supreme emergency is strategically untenable. There is no evidence that the bombing of German cities staved off defeat or hastened victory. Indeed, it is difficult to recall a single case where killing non-combatants has won a war. In the 1990s, Bosnian Serbs and Rwandan Hutus both suffered military defeats in part because they directly attacked non-combatants. There is therefore good reason to reject Walzer's supreme emergencies exception to non-combatant immunity.

PROPORTIONALITY AND DISCRIMINATION IN SUPREME EMERGENCIES

Despite this, my claim that the principle of non-combatant immunity should be upheld remains vulnerable to the dual charge that it is unrealistic to expect leaders to do this and that to ask them to do so is to ask them to place their responsibility to their own political community second to their (or our) personal moral preferences. As Sidney Axinn put it, 'in order to govern an institution one must sometimes do things that are immoral', and 'we do not want leaders who are so concerned with their own personal morality that they will not do what is necessary to . . . win the battle'. What is more, 'we have an inept leader if we have a person who is so morally fastidious that he or she will not break the law when that is the only way to success.'[72]

Similarly, Brian Orend has argued that there are two principal flaws with the demand for strict adherence to non-combatant immunity. First, he argues that it is 'unrealistic'. In the real world, Orend argues, political leaders will not respond to supreme emergencies 'with one hand tied behind their back'. Second, echoing the 'dirty hands' doctrine discussed above, 'it is fundamentally irresponsible on the part of the victim country's government, which has a foremost duty to protect its country's citizens from massacre and enslavement'.[73] To fail to discharge that responsibility would be to fiddle while Rome burned.

Orend, Axinn, Walzer and others are correct to argue that political leaders will not respond to supreme emergencies with one hand tied behind their back and, more important, that they *should* not. It is one thing to use all necessary means to overcome the supreme emergency, however, and quite another directly to attack non-combatants. The latter two of my four criticisms of the supreme emergency exception suggest that the 'fateful choice' between defeat and revoking non-combatant immunity is a false one. Killing non-combatants is certainly not an essential component of military success and it seems strange that it is deemed to become so in supreme emergencies.

The problem is that the victim of a supreme emergency is often hard-pressed. By the time it confronts such an emergency, a political community is under immense stress. Its military, economy and vital networks are all heavily damaged. In this situation, it would be imprudent for military commanders to insist on strict adherence to non-combatant immunity, for doing so would place military personnel and equipment in greater peril, reducing the chances of a successful defence. This may be acceptable in a 'war of choice' or another type of 'normal' war, but not in supreme emergencies where men and *materiél* cannot be spared. In such circumstances, it is surely justifiable for victims to prioritize the safety of their soldiers over that of enemy non-combatants. This is a compelling argument, but one can accept it without countenancing the deliberate targeting of non-combatants. The key to doing so lies in the distinction between the principle of discrimination, which places an absolute prohibition on the intentional targeting of non-combatants, and the principle of proportionality, which places limits on the number of foreseen but unintentional non-combatant casualties. It is possible, I argue, to defeat a supreme emergency by deploying overwhelming force without breaking either the discrimination or proportionality principles.

The principle of proportionality has its roots in Thomas Aquinas's discussion of double effect. Aquinas argued that:

> Nothing hinders one act from having two effects, only one of which is intended, while the other is beside the intention. Now moral acts take their species according to what is intended . . . accordingly the act of self-defence may have two effects, one is the saving of one's life, the other is the slaying of the aggressor. Therefore this act, since one's intention is to save one's own life, is not unlawful, seeing that it is natural to everything to keep itself in being . . . And yet, though proceeding from good intention, an act may be rendered unlawful, if it be out of proportion to the end. Wherefore if a man, in self-defence, uses more than necessary violence, it will be unlawful: whereas if he repel force with moderation his defence will be lawful . . . But as it is unlawful to take a man's life, except for the public authority acting for the common good, as stated above, it is not lawful for a man to intend killing a man in self-defence, except for such as have public authority, who while intending to kill a man in self-defence refer this to the public good.[74]

As formulated by Aquinas, the doctrine of double effect has two fundamental elements. The first is that any act may have two consequences: one that is intended and one that is not. The first question that anyone who kills another (either within or without war) needs to answer is: 'What is my intent?' There are only two legitimate responses to this. If the question is asked of an individual, the only legitimate intent that one may have is self-preservation. Even then, it is incumbent upon the killer to demonstrate through his actions that he did not intend the death of his assailant. If the question is put in relation to a government and a war, the government must demonstrate that its intent is to promote the common good and that its cause is just. The second element of double effect focuses on the objective consequences of the action. Even if we intend good, we must be sure that the good achieved outweighs the possible negative consequences. As Ramsey put it, 'the evil, secondary effect . . . must not be out of proportion to the good effect one intends to obtain'.[75]

The principle of double effect went through many revisions before it developed into the coherent moral theory that Walzer cites approvingly. According to Ramsey, the principle legitimizes the use of force if four conditions are met:

1. The desired end must be good in itself.

2. The good effect and not the evil effect must be intended.

3. The good effect must not be produced by means of the evil effect.

4. The good of the good effect must outweigh the evil of the evil effect.[76]

The principle of double effect therefore offers ways of responding to supreme emergencies that are both morally and strategically preferable to revoking non-combatant immunity.

In a supreme emergency, the protection of one's forces is paramount. In such a situation it makes no sense to insist that leaders place their soldiers and airmen at greater risk to protect enemy non-combatants. Thus, for example, leaders might insist that pilots fly at higher altitudes to avoid anti-aircraft fire, even though this makes it more difficult for them to hit their target and more likely that inaccurate bombs will kill enemy non-combatants. To compensate for the lack of accuracy, a leader may assign more aircraft and more bombs to attack a particular military target, increasing the collateral devastation. In a supreme emergency, such a strategy may be extended across the whole range of military activities: soldiers will not be required to ensure that there are no non-combatants in an area before firing and whenever in doubt they may be required to assume that someone is a combatant until proven otherwise. Through strategies such as these, leaders can maximize the security of their own soldiers. The cost is that more enemy non-combatants will die, because the lives of 'our' soldiers are prioritized over the lives of 'their' non-combatants. In a supreme emergency, the proportionality principle would permit almost any degree of collateral damage, so long as the destruction were a foreseen but unintended consequence of an attack on legitimate military targets, those targets were of sufficient importance, and the collateral damage was not the means of victory. According to this approach, a soldier is not required to place himself in danger to save enemy non-combatants as required by Walzer in cases other than supreme emergencies. However, neither is a soldier permitted to kill non-combatants intentionally.

To what extent does this tie the hands of political and military leaders confronting a threat to the very existence of their political community? Insisting that non-combatant immunity be upheld at all times does place important limits on the types of force that may be used. It rules out the fire-bombing of city centres and the use of weapons of mass destruction on populated areas. However, it may permit the use of small nuclear devices in areas where enemy troops are concentrated or aerial attacks on military sites housed in civilian areas where the destruction of significant military targets is the objective. As Paul Ramsey put it, 'this distinction is not determined by the amount of the devastation or the number of deaths, but by the direction of the action itself, i.e. by what is deliberately intended and directly done. This permits there to be foreseeable evil consequences acceptable among the multiple effects of military action.'[77] In a supreme emergency, the devastation that may be wrought proportionally but without intentionally targeting non-combatants is significant. Because the stakes are so high, soldiers may do whatever necessary to attack a military target. They are prohibited only from intentionally killing non-combatants.

Given the relative nature of proportionality and double effect, it is difficult to maintain the view that it is 'unrealistic' to suppose that non-combatant immunity could and should be upheld even in supreme emergencies. To justify an exception to non-combatant immunity it is necessary to demonstrate that the exception is essential to the success of the defender. Given the theoretical, legal, historical and strategic flaws with the supreme emergencies exception and the room for manoeuvre afforded by the proportionality principle, it is clear that the supreme emergency exception does not pass the 'essentialness' test.

There is, however, one final problem. Pacifists and others argue that there is little difference between non-combatant deaths that are intended and those that are merely foreseen. In both cases, non-combatants are killed in large numbers. By making the proportionality principle so permissive, there is a danger that the end result would be the same, in terms of non-combatant deaths, as if the supreme emergencies exception were applied. This is a powerful argument, and it is certainly not possible to prove that fewer non-combatants would be killed if these prescriptions were fulfilled. However, there are at least three reasons to support the practical efficacy and moral worth of abandoning the supreme emergency exception. First, it is certainly *likely* that fewer non-combatants would be killed, simply because some of the reckless carnage of strategic bombardment would be avoided. Furthermore, as Walzer's own account of the Second World War attests, once the decision is taken to strike cities, it creates a cycle of attack and revenge attack that is very difficult to break. Had non-combatant immunity not been revoked in 1940, some of the worst excesses of the war, such as the bombardment of Dresden, might have been avoided.[78] Second, by removing an exception to the rule of non-combatant immunity, we help to strengthen the rule as it comes under attack once again, this time by so-called 'new wars' and new forms of terrorism.[79] Finally, it challenges the realist teaching, evident in Walzer's rendition of the supreme emergency doctrine, that war is a moral tragedy in which soldiers and politicians are forced to choose between a variety of morally bad options. Contrary to this, I suggest that there are always morally better and worse choices, and that it is certainly not the case that there is a zero-sum relationship between good morality and good strategy.

Acknowledgments

I would like to thank Rod Lyon, Brian Orend, Nick Wheeler and especially Sara Davies for sharing their ideas with me.

NOTES

1. Thucydides, *The Peloponnesian war*, trans. C. F. Smith (London: Loeb Classical Library, 1923), bk 4, p. 98. On terror bombing, see Hermann Knell, *To destroy a city: strategic bombing and its human consequences in World War II* (Cambridge: De Capo Press, 2003). On the atomic attacks on Japan, see J. Samuel Walker, *Prompt and utter destruction: Truman and the use of atomic bombs against Japan* (Chapel Hill: University of North Carolina Press, 1997). On Rwanda, see Linda Melvern, *A people betrayed: the role of the West in Rwanda's genocide* (London: Zed, 2000). On the wars in former Yugoslavia, see James Gow, *The Serbian war project and its adversaries: a strategy of war crimes* (London: Hurst, 2003).

2. This argument is put forward by Martin Shaw, *War and genocide* (Cambridge: Polity, 2003).

3. Thucydides, *The Peloponnesian war*, bk 4, p. 98.

4. John Rawls, *The law of peoples* (Cambridge, MA: Harvard University Press, 1999), p. 98; Terry Nardin, *Law, morality and the relations of states* (Princeton, NJ: Princeton University Press, 1983), pp. 292–5; Brian Orend, *Michael Walzer on war and justice* (Cardiff: University of Wales Press, 2000), pp. 127–34; Brian Orend, 'Is there a supreme emergency exemption?', MS, 2003,

to be published as Brian Orend, 'Is there a supreme emergency exemption?', in M. Evans, ed., *Revisiting just war theory* (Edinburgh: Edinburgh University Press, forthcoming). I am very grateful to Brian Orend for permission to cite this paper.

5. The writings of Paul Ramsey certainly seem to suggest that he believed the concept of non-combatant immunity from direct targeting to be the cornerstone of the just war tradition. See Paul Ramsey, *War and the Christian conscience: how shall modern war be conducted justly?* (Durham, NC: Duke University Press, 1961), pp. 34–59.

6. Walzer describes it as a 'morally important fantasy': Michael Walzer, *Just and unjust wars*, 2nd edn (New York: Basic Books, 1991 [first publ. 1977]), p. 259.

7. Orend, 'Is there a supreme emergency exemption?', p. 10.

8. Ibid., p. 11.

9. Ibid., p. 14.

10. Walzer, *Just and unjust wars*, p. 44. We know that this must be a *thin* community of rules because Walzer argues elsewhere that 'thick' systems of rule are possible only within political communities housed in states. See Michael Walzer, *Thick and thin: moral arguments at home and abroad* (Notre Dame, IL: University of Notre Dame Press, 1996).

11. The first principle is that, once war starts, opposing soldiers may intentionally attack one another: Walzer, *Just and unjust wars*, p. 138.

12. On the presence of non-combatant immunity in major religious perspectives, see Paul Robinson, ed., *Just war in comparative perspective* (Dartmouth: Ashgate, 2003). Non-combatant immunity is integral to the 1949 Geneva Conventions and is set out in common article 3: see Adam Roberts and Richard Guelff, *Documents on the laws of war*, 3rd edn (Oxford: Oxford University Press, 2000), pp. 195–365.

13. Walzer, *Just and unjust wars*, p. 151.

14. Early canon laws articulating the principle of non-combatant immunity tended to limit it to those groups, such as fanners and clerics, whose work was essential for the peacetime functioning of the society. The prohibition on killing non-combatants was often therefore based on instrumentalism rather than deontological principle. *See* Frederick Russell, *The just war in the Middle Ages* (Cambridge: Cambridge University Press, 1975) and Maurice Keen, *The laws of war in the Middle Ages* (London: Routledge & Kegan Paul, 1965).

15. The pacifist case in this respect is put forward most persuasively by Robert Holmes, *On the morality of war* (Princeton, NJ: Princeton University Press, 1992).

16. Walzer, *Just and unjust wars*, p. 153.

17. This argument is made throughout Colm McKeogh, *Innocent civilians: the morality of killing in War* (London: Palgrave, 2002). For an alternative critique of the doctrine of double effect, see Alison McIntyre, 'Doing away with double-effect', *Ethics* III: I, 2001, pp. 219–55.

18. Walzer, *Just and unjust wars*, pp. 155–6.

19. Ibid. Brian Orend has convincingly challenged Walzer on this: see Orend, *Michael Walzer on war and justice*, pp. 87–9.

20. Walzer, *Just and unjust wars*, p. 251.

21. Ibid, pp. 254–5.

22. Ibid., p. 255 (emphasis added).

23. Ibid., *Just and unjust wars*, p. 253.

24. This point has been made by both Nardin, *Law, morality and the relations of states*, p. 292 and Orend, *Michael Walzer on war and justice*, p. 197.

25. Walzer, *Just and unjust wars*, p. 268.

26. See Herbert A. Deane, *The political and social ideas of St Augustine* (New York: Columbia University Press, 1963), pp. 154–8.

27. See Jan Willem Honig and Norbert Both, *Srebrenica: record of a war crime* (London: Penguin, 1997).

28. Carl von Clausewitz, *On war*, ed. and trans. Michael Howard and Peter Paret (London: Everyman's Library, 1993), p. 77.

29. Forde, 'Classical realism', in Terry Nardin and David R. Mapal, eds, *Traditions of international ethics* (Cambridge: Cambridge University Press, 1992), p. 79.

30. Reinhold Niebuhr, *Christianity and power politics* (New York: Charles Scribner's Sons, 1940), and *Moral man and immoral society* (New York: Macmillan, 1960).

31. Michael Walzer, 'Political action: the problem of dirty hands', in Marshall Cohen, Thomas Nagel and Thomas Scanlon, eds, *War and moral responsibility* (Princeton, NJ: Princeton University Press, 1974), pp. 63–83.

32. Walzer, *Just and unjust wars*, p. 14.

33. This assessment mirrors, but differs from, Brian Orend's. See Orend, *Michael Walzer on war and justice*, pp. 62–3.

34. This type of argument is put most eloquently in relation to sovereignty and intervention by Stephen D. Krasner, *Sovereignty: organized hypocrisy* (Princeton NJ: Princeton University Press, 1999).

35. See Nicholas J. Wheeler, 'Dying for "Enduring Freedom": accepting responsibility for civilian casualties in the war against terrorism,' *International Relations* 16: 2, 2002, p. 223, n. 55.

36. Walzer, *Just and unjust wars*, p. xxii.

37. Ibid., p. 134.

38. Walzer, *Just and unjust wars*, p. 135 (emphasis added).

39. This utilitarian argument can be found in some of the earliest attempts to outline a theory of justified war. It is even implied in some medieval canon law, which spent much more time explicating the conditions by which a war may be waged justly than it did exploring restraints on the conduct of war. See Russell, *The just war in the Middle Ages*, p. 71.

40. Walzer, *Just and unjust wars*, p. 262.

41. Ibid., p. 168.

42. I am very grateful to Sara Davies for raising this point.

43. See Alex J. Bellamy and Marianne Hanson, 'Justice beyond borders? Australia and the International Criminal Court', *Australian Journal of International Affairs* 56: 3, 2002, pp. 417–33.

44. Sun Tzu, *The art of war*, trans. Samuel Griffith (Oxford: Oxford University Press, 1963), pp. 76–8.

45. Paul Christopher, *The ethics of war and peace: an introduction to legal and moral issues* (Englewood Cliffs, NJ: Prentice-Hall, 1994), pp. 9–10.

46. Plato, *The republic*, ed. Robin Waterfield (Oxford: Oxford University Press, 1998), bk V, p. 471.

47. Richard Shelly Hartigan, 'Saint Augustine on war and killing: the problem of the innocent', *Journal of the History of Ideas* 27: 2, 1966, pp. 195–204.

48. See Russell, *The just war in the Middle Ages*; Keen, *The laws of war in the late Middle Ages* (London: Routledge & Kegan Paul, 1965); Richard Barber, *The knight and chivalry*, rev. edn (Woodbridge: Boydell, 1974); Richard W. Kaeuper, *Chivalry and violence in medieval Europe* (Oxford: Oxford University Press, 1999).

49. See G. J. Bass, *Stay the hand of vengeance: the politics of war crimes tribunals* (Princeton, NJ: Princeton University Press, 2000).

50. Common article 3 of the Geneva Conventions in Roberts and Guelff, *Documents on the laws of war*.

51. McKeogh, *Innocent civilians*, pp. 7–11.

52. Walzer, *Just and unjust wars*, p. 259.

53. Cited by Sir Charles Webster and Noble Frankland, *The strategic air offensive against Germany 1939–1945*, vol. I (London: HMSO, 1961), p. 46.

54. Ibid., p. 46.

55. Webster and Frankland, *Strategic air offensive*, vol. 4, p. 66 (emphasis added).

56. H. W. Koch, 'The strategic air offensive against Germany', *Historical Journal* 34: I, 1991, p. 123.

57. Ibid., p. 127. This view is supported by John Terraine, *The right of the line: the Royal Air Force in the European war 1939–1945* (London: Sceptre, 1988), p. 144.

58. See Philip S. Meilinger, 'The historiography of airpower: theory and decline', *The Journal of Military History* 64: 2, 2000, p. 481.

59. Allan D. English, 'The RAF Staff College and the evolution of British strategic bombing policy', *Journal of Strategic Studies* 16: 3, 1993, pp. 408–31.

60. Brigadier General P. R. C. Groves, *Our future in the air: a survey of the vital question of British air power* (London: Hutchinson, 1922).

61. Giulio Douhet, *Command of the air*, trans. Dino Ferrari (London: Coward-McCann, 1942). There is evidence to suggest that Douhet's ideas were very popular in the UK. See Louis A. Sigaud, *Douhet and aerial warfare* (New York: Putnam's, 1941).

62. Koch, 'The strategic air offensive', p. 127.

63. Kenneth P. Werrell, 'The strategic bombing of Germany in World War II: costs and accomplishments', *Journal of American History* 73: 3, 1986, p. 711.

64. His central ideas are set out in John C. Slessor, *Air power and armies* (London: Oxford University Press, 1936).

65. See Douhet, *Command of the air*, John Shy and Thomas Collier, 'Revolutionary war', in Peter Paret, ed., *Makers of modern strategy from Machiavelli to the nuclear age* (Princeton, NJ: Princeton University Press, 1986), pp. 845–52; Herman Kahn, *Thinking about the unthinkable* (New York: Horizon, 1962).

66. Sun Tzu, The *art of war*, pp. 109–10.

67. Clausewitz, *On war*, p. 607.

68. Cited by Justin Morris and Hilaire McCoubrey, 'Law, politics and the use of force', in John Baylis, James Wirtz, Eliot Cohen and Colin S. Gray, eds, *Strategy in the contemporary world: an introduction to strategic studies* (Oxford: Oxford University Press, 2002), p. 54.

69. Antoine-Henri Jomini, *Treatise on grand military operations*, trans. S. B. Holabird (New York: Van Nostrand, 1965), p. 448.

70. Roger Beaumont, *Joint military operations: a short history* (London: Greenwood, 1993).

71. And it is the direct targeting of non-combatants that forms the basis for the global consensus against terrorism.

72. Sidney Axinn, *A moral military* (Philadelphia, PA: Temple University Press, 1989), p. 189.

73. Orend, 'Is there a supreme emergency exemption?', p. 11.

74. Thomas Aquinas, cited by Ramsey, *War and the Christian conscience*, pp. 39–40.

75. Ibid., p. 43.

76. Ibid., pp. 48–9.

77. Paul Ramsey, 'The case for making "just war" possible', in Paul Ramsey, *The just war: force and political responsibility* (Lanham, MD: Rowman & Littlefield, 1983), p. 154.

78. Kenneth Hewitt, 'Place annihilation: area bombing and the fate of urban places', *Annals of the Association of American Geographers* 73: 2. 1983, pp. 257–84.

79. On the former see James Turner Johnson, *Morality and contemporary warfare* (New Haven, CT: Yale University Press, 1999); on the latter see Richard Devetak, 'Violence, order and terror', in Alex J. Bellamy, ed., *International society and its critics* (Oxford: Oxford University Press, 2004).

*Alex J. Bellamy is professor of peace and conflict studies at the University of Queensland.

Bellamy, A. J. (2004), Supreme emergencies and the protection of non-combatants in war. International Affairs 80: 829–850. Doi: 10.1111/j.1468-2346.204.00421.x

Used by permission.

Human Rights, Command Responsibility, and Walzer's Just War Theory

*by James M. Dubik**

Walzer's just war theory, as presented in *Just and Unjust Wars*, is based on the following proposition: the single justification for going to war is the defense of two basic human rights—the right to life and the right to liberty.[1] He demonstrates that in just war theory the problem of *jus ad bellum*, the justification for going to war, and the problem of *jus in bello*, the justification for specific actions in war, are separate though related. I find the way in which Walzer relates them particularly interesting. The protection of rights, which by Walzer's account is the only justification for going to war, also plays a vital role in determining individual moral responsibilities, and in justifying acts committed in war.

Nevertheless, I will show that Walzer's relation of these two issues has an important shortcoming. That is, if the rights Walzer uses as the basis for his just war theory are basic human rights,[2] how can he claim that citizens lose or exchange them when they become soldiers?[3] It is my opinion that Walzer's answer to this question is incomplete and inconsistent; furthermore, this inconsistency seems to lead to difficulty in fully accounting for a most important aspect of *jus in bello*; the officer's command responsibility in war.

In the preface to *Just and Unjust Wars* Walzer says that his moral theory of war "is focused on the tensions within the theory that make it problematic and that make choice in wartime difficult and painful. The tensions are summed up in the dilemma of winning and fighting well."[4] Walzer's inconsistent answer to the above question, however, prevents him from fully analyzing the tensions present in the war-time decisions required of military commanders. In this paper I hope to show that an answer consistent with the balance of the theory presented in *Just and Unjust Wars* can be provided, and that a richer account of the officer's command responsibility in war will result. This richer account will present command responsibility as the moral responsibility which requires commanders to balance "due care" owed to civilians and "due risk" expected of soldiers. Furthermore, it will show that these competing and sometimes conflicting responsibilities flow from a common source. This clarification will significantly enhance the power of Walzer's just war theory.

I

Civilians, according to Walzer, have two rights the value of which he labels "something like absolute": the rights to life and liberty.[5] This claim is the most basic and most important claim he makes in *Just and Unjust Wars*. It is the most basic because it is the foundation of the moral theory according to which he analyzes both *jus ad bellum* and *jus in bello*. In the first case, the defense of the two rights is seen as the only reason to wage war.[6] In the latter case, Walzer defines a legitimate act of war as one which does not violate the rights (life and liberty) of the people against whom the act is directed.[7] This claim is important just because it plays a vital role in Walzer's theory. Therefore, I shall analyze in detail Walzer's account of the rights to life and liberty in order to discover the precise nature of these rights.

The "something like absolute" rights to life and liberty are, for Walzer, somehow founded in what it means to be a human being.[8] They are not rights a citizen acquires by becoming a member of any particular civil state. On the contrary, they are independent of the state:

> Individual rights may well derive, as I am inclined to think, from our ideas of personality and moral agency, without reference to political processes and social circumstances.[9]

Walzer, in *Just and Unjust Wars*, is hesitant to label the rights of life and liberty natural.[10] However, I think it is the proper label since he says these are rights each of us has merely by virtue of the fact that we are human beings. The label also appears appropriate in light of the fact that Walzer's description of the rights to life and liberty satisfies the two conditions Hart sets down for natural rights in "Are There Any Natural Rights?": a right all men have qua men, and a right which is not conferred or created by any voluntary action.[11]

Walzer uses "something like absolute" as an adjectival phrase describing these "natural" rights for good reason. On one hand, he does not want to call them absolute rights because such a description would be too strong. There would be no case where one could justify the violation of an absolute right. Since Walzer concludes in *Just and Unjust Wars* that taking another's life is, in certain specific circumstances, justified, it would be inconsistent for him to say that the right is absolute. On the other hand, it cannot be said to result merely from arbitrary conventions either because it would be too easy to justify the violation of a right of this kind. Taking another's life would in this case need too little justification. Walzer wishes to avoid the pitfalls of justifying actions performed in combat by mere appeal to military necessity, utility, or realism. He wants to arrive at a description which would allow violation of these rights but only under specific circumstances, for example, war. In describing the rights to life and liberty as "something like absolute" and admitting that they may justifiably be violated, Walzer's description again corresponds with Hart's theory of natural rights. Hart says:

It is quite obvious that my view is not as ambitious as the traditional view of natural rights; for . . . no man has an absolute or unconditional right to do or not to do any particular thing or to be treated in any particular way; coercion or restraint of any action may be justified in special conditions. . . .[12]

Some philosophers have argued that Walzer's theory of just war is based primarily upon states' rights and not upon the rights of individuals.[13] However, I think that this interpretation is mistaken. In *Just and Unjust Wars* Walzer makes the claim that the rights of states, namely territorial integrity and political sovereignty, are based upon the individual rights of citizens.[14] Though this claim is not everywhere made explicit, it is Walzer's firm position. My interpretation seems correct in light of Walzer's recent article "The Moral Standing of States: A Response to Four Critics." In this article, Walzer restates the position first expounded in *Just and Unjust Wars*:

The real subject of my argument is not the state at all but the political community that (usually) underlies it. And I will compound my putative conservatism by saying at the outset that that community rests most deeply on a contract. . . . Contract, as I wrote in the book, is a metaphor. The moral understanding on which the community is founded takes shape over a long period of time. But the idea of a communal integrity derives its moral and political force from the rights of contemporary men and women to life as members of a historic community.[15]

It is true, Walzer might say, that a just war theory is concerned with the rights of states to territorial integrity and political sovereignty, but it must always be remembered that these rights are founded upon each individual's right to life and liberty. In Walzer's view, when a community is formed, whatever communal rights it has are derived from those rights possessed by each individual who comprises that community. "Hence," Walzer writes, "the distinction of states' rights and individual rights is simplistic and wrongheaded. Against foreigners, individuals have a right to a state of their own. Against state officials, they have a right to political and civil liberty. Without the first of these rights, the second is meaningless. . . ."[16] By this account, individual rights seem to be manifested on two levels—an intranational level against state officials and an international level against foreigners. One seems warranted in concluding, therefore, that

Walzer's position is that a state has rights only by virtue of those of its citizens. Thus Walzer holds that the state exists to protect the individual and the individual's "natural" rights to life and liberty.[17]

Furthermore, we may conclude Walzer thinks that when state A violates the political sovereignty and territorial integrity of state B, state A is committing a crime[18]—that is, it is violating the rights of individual members of state B. And, when state B declares war on state A, it seems consistent with what Walzer says that (1) the rights which citizens of state B have against their state officials remain intact (these are the intranational manifestation of individual rights); and (2) the government of state B may require its citizens to become soldiers in order to protect the international manifestation of their individual rights. What prima facie seems to be a violation of an individual right to life may plausibly be understood as no violation at all. Rather, governments may be seen as the orchestrators and coordinators of the efforts of the citizens to protect the international manifestation of their own individual rights to life and liberty. Thus, Walzer says: "The citizens defend one another and their common life; the government is merely their instrument"[19] and "states exist to defend the rights of their members."[20]

In sum, Walzer's position with respect to the "something like absolute" rights that form the basis of his theory of both *jus ad bellum* and *jus in bello*, seems to be that each of us has "natural," individual rights to life and liberty which are manifested on two levels; and that these rights are the foundation of and are only enforceable within political communities.

However, Walzer presents a most troubling claim in *Just and Unjust Wars* concerning these rights: that a person's right to life is lost when he becomes a soldier, that it is somehow exchanged for soldier's rights.[21] In view of his theory that these are individual, "natural" rights, this claim is prima facie dubious. It is dubious because one is warranted in asking, If the rights to life are "natural," individual rights, how can they be "lost" or "exchanged"? Because Walzer understands these rights as he does, it does not appear that one may lose them.

This intuition—that there is something dubious in suggesting that one may lose or exchange one's individual, "natural" rights to life and liberty—must be examined in detail. To do so, I will interest myself only in Walzer's account of the right to life. I will not be concerned with the right to liberty, interesting and problematic as it may be. My chief concern centers on the answer to the question, Can Walzer consistently hold that one's right to life may be lost or exchanged given his understanding of the nature of that right?

II

It seems quite clear that a right one has merely by virtue of the fact that one is a human being cannot simply be lost. Soldiers, whatever their vices, remain human beings; how could they conceivably lose a right they have qua human beings? The interesting claim, therefore, must be that this right is somehow exchanged for soldiers' rights. Walzer explains the exchange as follows:

> . . . soldiers who do the fighting . . . lose the rights they are supposedly defending. They gain war rights as combatants and potential prisoners . . . .[22]

One naturally asks, Under what conditions does Walzer think the right to life is exchanged? Walzer provides three answers. First, he says "simply by fighting" soldiers lose their right to life.[23] Second, he claims that by becoming a "dangerous man," one who "bears arms effectively," a soldier loses his right to life.[24] Finally, he holds that soldiers lose their right to life when they become members of a class of people who are able to be attacked at any time.[25] It seems, however, that these three answers do not form a consistent set. For example, Fred may be a soldier who is not fighting. By the second and third answers, he has lost his right to life; by the first, he has not. Or, he may be a soldier who, having just been inducted into the service, has not yet learned to bear arms effectively. By the first and second answers, Fred has not lost his right; by the third, he has. Which of these answers, then, consorts best Walzer's overall theory? It is, I shall suggest, the last.

The first answer, that a soldier exchanges his right to life merely by fighting, is shown to be inadequate by the conclusions Walzer reaches from examples which he calls "naked soldier examples":

> At this moment a man, presumably carrying a message to an officer, jumped out of the trench and ran along the top of the parapet in full view. He was half-dressed and was holding up his trousers with both hands as he ran. I refrained from shooting at him. It is true that I am a poor shot and unlikely to hit a running man at a hundred yards . . . . Still, I did not shoot partly because of that detail about his trousers. I had come here to shoot at Fascists; but a man who is holding up his trousers isn't a Fascist, he is visibly a fellow-creature, similar to yourself, and you don't feel like shooting at him.[26]

One of the things Walzer says concerning this and other like examples is that it is morally permissible to kill a "naked soldier." That is, killing a soldier such as the one described does not violate the rules of war. Walzer says: "It is not against the rules of war as we currently understand them to kill soldiers who look funny, who are taking a bath, holding up their pants, reveling in the sun, smoking a cigarette."[27] The fact that "naked soldiers" may be legitimately killed though they are not actually fighting indicates that Walzer's first answer does not hold up.

Walzer's second answer, that soldiers exchange their right to life when they become dangerous men, also fails under close scrutiny. Walzer admits that, "when it is militarily necessary, workers in a tank factory can be attacked and killed, but workers in a food processing plant not."[28] The former workers, Walzer goes on to explain, are assimilated to a degree into the class of soldiers. They can be attacked "only in their factory (not in their homes), when they are actually engaged in activities threatening and harmful to their enemies."[29] The latter workers are doing nothing specifically warlike, hence they do not lose their immunity from attack. Innocent people, Walzer concludes, are those "who have done nothing and are doing nothing that entails their loss of rights."[30]

But what of soldiers in a training camp? Can they be attacked and killed? It seems they can as they have done and are doing something which is directly threatening and harmful to their enemy in that they are learning how to bear arms effectively. However, in a training camp, they are not yet dangerous men. Although they are just learning how to bear arms effectively, they have lost, by Walzer's account, their right to life already. Thus, it appears that his second answer also fails.

The conclusion, therefore, seems to be that one exchanges one's right to life as soon as one becomes a soldier. This is the only answer that will accomplish what Walzer has set out to accomplish—that is, to explain how it is that citizens lose their right to life when they become soldiers. However, even this explanation is problematic in that the notion of exchanging one's individual, "natural" right seems as dubious as losing it altogether.

Walzer, in conceiving of an exchange of rights, seems to forget that the right to life is not a right that "goes with the job," so to speak. One does not possess that right by being a civilian; one possesses it on his own account merely by being human. To exchange means to give up one thing for something else. If the individual right to life is a right one has merely by virtue of the fact that one is a living human being, that is, a natural right, it does not seem correct to say that one may give up the right under any circumstances.

At this point, I must conclude that it seems that one's individual, "natural" right to life, as Walzer conceives it, is neither lost nor exchanged. This conclusion results from the inconsistencies I have shown to develop in Walzer's position concerning the "natural" right to life. On one hand, he holds that the individual right to life is a right one possesses merely by virtue of being human and not as a result of any social or political arrangement. On the other hand, he holds that this right may be lost or exchanged. I will now argue that this conclusion also follows from another source: Walzer's belief that individual rights should not be distinguished from states' rights.[31]

As was previously shown, Walzer believes that it is "simplistic and wrongheaded" to make the distinction between individual and state rights. "Without the first of these rights," Walzer says, "the second is meaningless: as individuals need a home, rights require a location."[32] Individual rights form the foundation of and give meaning to states' rights; and, without the state, individual rights would not have a home and could not be enforced.

To diminish the distinction between individual and state rights pursuant to Walzer's suggestion, I have previously suggested that individual rights be understood as being manifested on two separate levels: an intranational level and an international level. Individual rights manifested on the intranational level are, to use Walzer's words, "against states officials, they (individuals) have a right to political and civil liberty." Individual rights manifested on the international level are, again to quote Walzer, "against foreigners, individuals have a right to a state of their own." Intranational rights are the rights to life and liberty. On the international level, these rights become a state's rights to political sovereignty and territorial integrity. Now, which of these manifestations of individual rights are those which, by Walzer's theory, are lost or exchanged when a citizen becomes a soldier?

It does not seem possible to say that the international manifestation can be lost or exchanged as it is to preserve or reestablish the state's political sovereignty or territorial integrity which justifies one state declaring war on another. Nor does it seem possible that the intranational manifestation of individual rights can be lost or exchanged either. This manifestation is in regard to state officials: when a citizen becomes a soldier, he remains a citizen. It appears, then, that neither manifestation of one's individual rights is lost or exchanged. Again, the conclusion that one's individual right to life is neither lost nor exchanged appears warranted.

However, I cannot deny that something happens when a citizen becomes a soldier. Before a citizen becomes a soldier, he may not legitimately be killed by a foreigner or a national; but, after becoming a soldier, his demise at the hands of his enemies may be quite legitimate. I think that it is possible to show how this change might be explained using Walzer's theory without claiming any loss or exchange of rights.

We have seen that Walzer holds that governments exist to protect the rights of their citizens at both the international and intranational levels.[33] This position seems to imply that a government is obligated to enforce and protect its citizens' rights. Traditionally, the primary agents for discharging the government's responsibility at the intranational level are its judicial, legislative, and police organizations while its primary executing agents at the international level are its diplomatic and military officer corps. I shall suggest therefore that when a citizen becomes a member of the class of citizens called soldiers, the change that occurs can be seen in terms of the following claims: (1) he retains his individual, "natural" right to life; (2) his government retains its responsibility to ensure that his rights are protected while he serves as a soldier; and (3) he accepts increased risk and may legitimately be killed by enemy soldiers because he is actively defending his and each community member's individual right to life as manifested at the international level, that is, the right to political sovereignty and territorial integrity.[34] The change in status from citizen to soldier cannot be, as I have shown, due to any loss or exchange of one's individual right. It would be better viewed as resulting from an increased obligation that occurs when a citizen becomes a soldier. That is, when one becomes a soldier, regardless of one's reasons for becoming a soldier, one is fighting for the individual rights of one's community. In so doing, one is defending the rights of each community member. Perhaps it is the case that in becoming a soldier, in defending one's community, one incurs the additional obligation of increased risk? This suggestion, although not fully developed here, appears at least both consistent and plausible. Furthermore, it seems to correspond with Walzer's position that: "The rules of fighting well (the war convention) are simply a series of recognitions of men and women who have a moral standing independent of and resistent to the exigencies of war."[35] Isn't having a "moral standing independent of and resistent to the exigencies of war" having some sort of right? It seems possible, then, to suggest that the War Convention exists to protect the rights of those fighting the war.

The foregoing claims are significant because they indicate a most important shortcoming in one aspect of Walzer's analysis of *jus in bello*. Walzer holds that soldiers are a specific subclass of citizens, a class whose members I have shown retain their right to life. When this fact is coupled with Walzer's belief that the very purpose of governments is to protect the rights of its citizens, it appears to be the case that the government should retain its responsibility toward its "citizens-now-soldiers." I think I have shown that this is exactly the case.

Furthermore, I have suggested that military officers are traditionally considered as those agents of the government charged with executing the government's responsibility to protect the rights of its citizens while they are soldiers. Because Walzer holds that soldiers lose or exchange their right to life, he is blind to this most significant fact. Therefore, his explication of command responsibility lacks an important element. A fresh look at command responsibility is in order.

III

Walzer admits that "being an officer is not at all like being a common soldier."[36] "Officers," he goes on to explain, "take on immense responsibility . . . unlike anything in civilian life, for they have in their control the means of death and destruction."[37] Because of this fact, Walzer points out three obligations or responsibilities officers incur with their position: First, officers must train their soldiers to fight with restraint and be mindful of the rights of the innocent;[38] officers are expected to devote a great deal of "time and attention to the discipline and control of the men with guns they have turned loose in the world."[39] Second, officers must attend carefully in their planning to take positive steps to limit "even unintended civilian death."[40] Last, officers must take positive steps to "enforce the war convention and hold men under their command to its standards."[41]

With these requirements I have little difficulty. They indicate true and important command responsibilities. Commanders are responsible to ensure that due care is afforded to civilians. But, this is not an exhaustive list. It lacks recognition of the fact that soldiers are men—a subclass of citizens. They are not just dangerous people to be held in check by discipline, punishment, and training. These aspects—discipline, training and punishment—are surely present in the commander's responsibilities, but it must be remembered that in addition to being responsible for the control of the means of death and destruction, officers are directly responsible to the state and to the soldier to protect the soldiers' right to life. General Stilwell emphasized this point:

> The average general envies the buck private; when things go wrong, the private can blame the general, but the general can only blame himself. The private carries the woes of one man; the general carries the woes of all. He is conscious always of the responsibility on his shoulders, of the relatives of the men entrusted to him, of their feelings. He must act so that he can face those fathers and mothers without shame or remorse.[42]

Walzer is not unaware that commanders are responsible for the lives of their men. But, for him, this responsibility is considered different from the responsibility of protecting the rights of civilians. Citizens must be protected, afforded "due care," because they possess rights. This does not appear to be the case with soldiers. Walzer views soldiers as losing or exchanging their right to life once they become soldiers. Therefore, Walzer says that while it is morally permissible for soldiers to die in battle, it is wrong that their lives be wasted. Wrong for what reason?

It seems that Walzer's answer to this question would go something like this: Soldiers are assets, among many others, which are entrusted to the commander. Commanders are required to make prudent use of all assets. Therefore, it is wrong that commanders waste their assets. This hypothetical answer seems consistent with the following comments Walzer made at the 1980 War and Morality Symposium:

> . . . (a commander) is also responsible . . . to each and everyone of them (his soldiers). His soldiers are in one sense instruments with which he is supposed to win victories, but they are also men and women whose lives, because they are entrusted to his *use*, are also in his care. He is bound not to waste their lives, that is, not to persist in battles whose cost overwhelm their military value, and so on (my emphasis).[43]

The commander's responsibility toward soldiers, implied in *Just and Unjust Wars* and stated above, is quite different from his responsibility toward civilians.

It seems that Walzer's view of the commander's responsibility to his soldiers is best described as a corporate responsibility." Soldiers are assets that a commander controls and uses. The commander is responsible, therefore, to manage his assets correctly. Inefficient or sloppy management procedures—for example, persisting in battles that can't be won—are not permitted. Other comments at the War and Morality Symposium make this conclusion explicit. First, Walzer describes two sorts of military responsibility: hierarchical (upward toward one's military commanders and downward toward one's subordinates) and nonhierarchical (outward toward civilians on the battlefield). Given this description of the types of military responsibility, I think it is most consistent with the ideas Walzer has developed elsewhere to say that a commander has only "corporate responsibility" on the hierarchical side while moral responsibility resides on the nonhierarchical side. Second, Walzer again shows that he thinks soldiers are best considered assets when he says: "I don't think it can ever be impermissible for an officer to send his soldiers into battle: that is what he is for and that is what they are for."[44]

For Walzer, then, the foundation of a commander's responsibility toward his soldiers seems to be the principles of efficient management. This foundation is contrasted with that of a commander's responsibility toward civilians where Walzer holds that commanders are responsible to ensure civilians are afforded due care because they have rights.[45]

However, when soldiers are understood to retain their right to life and officers are understood as agents designated by the government to protect these rights, then the picture changes drastically; commanders are morally responsible not to waste lives of their soldiers because they are charged to protect soldiers' rights to life. It is this moral responsibility to which General Stilwell refers in the passage quoted above. Richard A. Gabriel and Paul L. Savage, analyzing the performance of the officer corps in Vietnam, refer in their book *Crisis in Command* to this moral responsibility. They claim that soldiers cannot be managed to their death; rather, that officers have a moral responsibility to lead their soldiers.[46]

By missing this aspect of command responsibility, Walzer loses sight of the fact that one of the most troublesome aspects of *jus in bello* is this: Commanders are expected to balance, simultaneously, their responsibility to ensure due care is afforded to civilians with their responsibility to ensure due risk is required of their soldiers. Additionally, Walzer is unaware of the fact that these two conflicting responsibilities stem from a common source: the right to life.

This added feature of command responsibility seems to make some difference in the casuistry of just war theory. Because we are now aware of the fact that commanders are morally responsible to protect the rights of their soldiers, we must reopen cases Walzer has considered closed. We must return to reexamine war situations in order to discover the moral realities Walzer overlooks. That the feature I have added to the understanding of command responsibility does make a significant difference in the casuistry of war can be seen by looking at an example Walzer introduced concerning bombardment in Korea.

A battalion of American troops advanced slowly, without opposition, under the shadow of low hills. "We were well into the valley now, halfway down the straight . . . strung out along the open road, when it came, the harsh stutter of automatic fire sputtering the dust around us." The troops stopped and dove for cover. Three tanks moved up, "pounding their shells into the . . . hillside and shattering the air with their machine guns. It was impossible in this remarkable inferno of sound to detect the enemy, or to assess his fire." Within fifteen minutes, several fighter planes arrived, "diving down upon the hillside with their rockets." This is the new technique of warfare, writes the British journalist, "born of immense productive and material might. . . . the cautious advance, the enemy small arms fire, the halt, the close support air strike, artillery, the cautious advance, and so on." It is designed to save the lives of soldiers, and it may or may not have that effect. "It is certain that it kills civilian men, women, and children, indiscriminately and in great numbers, and destroys all that they have. . . . At last, after more than an hour . . . a platoon from Baker Company began working their way through the scrub just under the ridge of the hill." But the first reliance was always on bombardment.[47]

In his analysis of this situation, Walzer correctly points out that the American commander may not be justified in placing first reliance on such inordinate amounts of firepower. The commander was clearly wrong. He did not seem to attend to his responsibility to ensure that due care was afforded to civilians whose lives were endangered. Walzer then suggests that another option was available. A patrol could have been sent to flank the enemy's position. His claim is that this action should have been taken at the outset of the engagement, not used as a last resort. Further, Walzer implies that the patrol in this situation should not have used the available firepower. This position is implicit in Walzer's claim that "if saving civilian lives means risking soldiers' lives, the risks must be accepted."[48] Even though Walzer admits that there is a limit to the risks that can be required—what he labels due risk—the revised principle of double effect he proposes seems to preclude the use of indirect firepower in this situation and many others like it.[49]

It is with this last claim that Walzer's theory of command responsibility clashes with mine. Walzer does not realize that a commander is not only responsible for protecting the rights of civilians, but also for protecting the rights of soldiers, to ensure that they are only exposed to due risk. For Walzer, a soldier is an asset, an asset which should be employed wisely and efficiently. Therefore, any limit set on the amount of risk to which this asset may be exposed is set by virtue of the principles of efficient management. Walzer's theory is devoid of a dimension of command responsibility which lies dormant in his concept of rights: that commanders are morally responsible for protecting the rights citizens retain when they become soldiers.

The proper analysis of the Korean situation seems to lie between two extremes, massive bombardment used by the American commander in Walzer's example and no fire support implied by Walzer's situation. It seems plausible to say that the American commander, pursuant to fulfilling his responsibility to protect his soldiers' rights, is quite justified in providing his maneuvering troops with appropriate amounts of supporting fire during their movement to the enemy. "Appropriate" in this context means sufficient to suppress the enemy's fire thus allowing his soldiers to maneuver successfully. By employing his available firepower in this way, the commander will ensure that due care is afforded to civilians in the battle area. Soldiers would enhance their own security at the expense of some civilians in this situation; however, civilians would be afforded due care and soldiers exposed only to *due* risk.

A *jus in bello* theory that neglects the aspect of a commander's moral responsibility I have presented is incomplete and inadequate. Understanding that the commander is morally responsible to protect both the right to life of civilians while he employs the means of death and destruction at his disposal and the right to life of soldiers because they are entrusted to his care as an agent of the government provides an added dimension to the *jus in bello* theory which is unavailable to Walzer because of his claim that soldiers lose their right to life. The understanding of command responsibility developed in this paper is a more accurate portrayal of the "tensions within the theory that make it problematic and that make choice in wartime difficult and painful."[50] The tension results, at least to a large degree, from the dual nature of command responsibility explained above.

The richer understanding of a commander's responsibility I have presented seems to enhance the power of Walzer's *jus in bello* theory significantly by providing: (1) an analysis of a commander's responsibility which is more consistent with the concept of rights Walzer uses to ground his just war theory; (2) a tool with which one can more accurately interpret the moral realities of battle; and (3) a guide or standard that individuals may use in making moral decisions in war—a task that is, or should be, in the forefront of moral philosophy.

Acknowledgments

I would like to thank Dr. Lester Hunt of The Johns Hopkins University, with whom I worked through the problems presented in this paper.

Notes

1. Michael Walzer, *Just and Unjust Wars* (New York: Basic Books, 1977), p. 72.

2. Ibid., p. xvi.

3. Ibid., pp. 136–37.

4. Ibid., p. xvi.

5. Ibid.

6. Ibid., pp. 60, 72.

7. Ibid., p. 135.

8. Ibid., p. 56; idem, "The Moral Standing of States: A Response to Four Critics," *Philosophy & Public Affairs* 9, no. 3 (Spring 1980): 226.

9. Walzer, "A Response," p. 226.

10. Walzer, *Just and Unjust Wars*, p. 54.

11. Hart, "Are There Any Natural Rights?" in *Rights*, ed. David Lyons (Belmont, CA: Wadsworth Publishing Company, 1979), p. 15.

12. Ibid.

13. See Gerald Doppelt, "Walzer's Theory of Morality in International Relations," *Philosophy & Public Affairs* 8, no. 1 (Fall 1978); and David Luban, "Just War and Human Rights," *Philosophy & Public Affairs* 9, no. 2 (Winter 1980).

14. Walzer, *Just and Unjust Wars*, pp. 53–54, 59.

15. Walzer, "A Response," pp. 210–11.

16. Ibid., p. 228.

17. Ibid., p. 211.

18. Walzer, *Just and Unjust Wars*, pp. 51, 53.

19. Walzer, "A Response," p. 211.

20. Walzer, *Just and Unjust Wars*, p. 136.

21. Ibid., pp. 136–37.

22. Ibid., pp. 136, 145.

23. Ibid., p. 136.

24. Ibid., p. 145.

25. Ibid., p. 138.

26. Ibid., p. 140.

27. Ibid., p. 142.

28. Ibid., p. 146.

29. Ibid.

30. Ibid.

31. Walzer, "A Response," p. 226.

32. Ibid.

33. Walzer, *Just and Unjust Wars*, pp. 60, 136.

34. The following chart depicts the change that occurs when a citizen becomes a soldier:

Individual Rights Manifested on	CITIZEN	Enforcement or Legal Code	SOLDIER	Enforcement or Legal Code
International Level	Foreigners may not kill nationals	International Agreements, Conventions	Some foreigners may kill some nationals (i.e. soldiers may kill soldiers and some civilians)	War Convention (See footnote 36.)
International Level	Nationals may not kill nationals	Positive Law	Nationals may not kill nationals	Code of Military Law
Primary Executing Agents	Legislative, Judicial, and Police Organizations; Diplomatic Corps		Diplomatic Corps and Military Officer Corps	

35. Walzer, *Just and Unjust Wars*, p. 44. The War Convention, Walzer explains, consists of the "set of articulated norms, customs, professional codes, legal precepts, religious and philosophical principles and reciprocal arrangements that shape our judgments of military conduct."

36. Ibid., p. 316.

37. Ibid.

38. Ibid., pp. 151, 317.

39. Ibid., p. 321.

40. Ibid., p. 317.

41. Ibid.

42. Anton Myrer, *Once An Eagle* (New York: Holt, Rinehart and Winston of Canada, Ltd., 1968), introductory comment.

43. CPT Roger A. Rains and CPT Michael J. McRea, eds., *The Proceedings of the War and Morality Symposium* (West Point, New York: United States Military Academy, 1980), p. 20.

44. Ibid., pp. 20–21.

45. Walzer may be tempted to claim that an officer's responsibility as he explains it is a kind of moral responsibility—that is, a moral responsibility based on utilitarian grounds. By this interpretation, an officer would maximize the well being of his soldiers insofar as it is consistent with other constraints; or insofar as officers should take care, as best as possible, of this, his most valuable asset. However, this interpretation does not seem open to Walzer in that in the preface to *Just and Unjust Wars* he claims to be expounding a moral theory of war based on human rights.

46. Richard A. Gabriel and Paul L. Savage, *Crisis in Command: Mismanagement in the Army* (New York: Hill and Wang, 1978), pp. 3–28, especially p. 23.

47. Walzer, *Just and Unjust Wars*, pp. 154–55.

48. Ibid., p. 156.

49. Ibid., pp. 155, 305. Walzer revised the traditional principle of double effect by adding the

following condition: "The intention of the actor is good, that is, he aims narrowly at the acceptable effect; the evil effect is not one of his ends, nor is it a means to his ends, and, aware of the evil involved, he seeks to minimize it, accepting cost to himself." The American commander would be precluded from using the kind of supporting fire I describe because: (1) he could not be said to be aiming "narrowly at the acceptable effect" with artillery; and (2) he is enhancing his soldier's security at the expense of civilians.

50. Walzer, *Just and Unjust Wars*, p. xvi.

*Lt. Gen. James M. Dubik (U.S. Army, Ret.) is a senior fellow at the Institute for the Study of War.

"Human Rights, Command Responsibility, and Walzer's Just War Theory," James M. Dubik, *Philosophy and Public Affairs* 11, no. 4 (1982): 354–365. Copyright © 1982 by Princeton University Press.

Use of Civilians as Human Shields: What Legal and Moral Restrictions Pertain to a War Waged by a Democratic State against Terrorism?

by Emanuel Gross*

[…]

III. The Moral Dilemma—Protection of Civilians versus Refusal to Surrender to Terrorists and the Soldiers' Right to Self-Defense: What Is the Balancing Formula?

A democratic state fighting terrorism is required to conduct this process in accordance with principles and values which derive from its democratic nature. Respect for human rights, the right to life, and the right to dignity are the principle characteristics of a democratic state. At the same time, human rights are not a staging post for national destruction. The state must supply its citizens with the conditions that will enable them to implement their rights, i.e., national security. The purpose of the democratic state's duty to provide security for its citizens is to protect the most basic right and value, namely, human life. It follows that the concern here is with the moral duty of a democratic state to protect its citizens and to make use of appropriate measures to preempt dangers to their security: "The moral duty of the democratic state is therefore to fight, to exercise force, to overcome the enemy, so long as it is not possible to properly protect the lives of citizens in another way, without the exercise of force."[36]

In circumstances where the enemy of the democratic state is terrorism—an enemy which, as noted, violates the rules of war—there is a strong likelihood that the duty of a democratic state to vanquish the enemy to meet its moral duty to protect its citizens will clash with other legal obligations and moral concepts of the democratic state and its soldiers. In particular, we may identify a clash with two obligations: The obligation to avoid, as much as possible, harm to citizens of the enemy, and the obligation to protect the lives of the state's soldiers during the course of the conflict. This clash exposes moral dilemmas which shall be discussed in this part. First, however, I shall explain, in general terms, what constitutes a "moral dilemma," and how one is resolved. Thereafter, I shall apply these principles to the circumstances under discussion here.

A. Moral Dilemmas

In practice, a moral dilemma consists of a clash of values that makes it difficult to act, since choosing any of the alternatives will be inconsistent with the decision-maker's obligations and values. "Dilemmas are not situations in which a person must do something which he is forbidden to do, but where he must do something bad."[37] In other words, it refers to a situation in which a person is required to perform a particular act (to protect the lives of the citizens of his state) and must also refrain from doing it (because if he protects the lives of his citizens he will be required to harm innocent civilians of the adverse party). In a situation in which two clashing obligations occur, there are those who believe that one of the options—which one depends on the circumstances—is not a duty.[38]

However, this type of solution is too comfortable. Clashes between moral obligations occur frequently. If it is agreed that in every such case one of the duties does not apply, then most of the moral obligations shall be deprived of their effect. Accordingly, the solution must be more complex and it is difficult to guarantee that the solution to a moral dilemma will be a moral solution *per se*. Each of the possible avenues of action entails the doing of something bad.

> Most, if not all, the cases used as examples of moral dilemmas are cases of a choice between evils. They are cases of being in a situation in which whatever one does either one will wrong people, or one will fail in some binding duty. . . . [I]t is of the essence of dilemmas that those facing them have no morally acceptable option.[39]

These remarks possess added weight in the types of dilemmas with which we are concerned here: moral dilemmas that require us to choose between the lives of different groups—the citizens of the defending state and the citizens of the enemy and soldiers. The value of human life is a commonly held value which is expressed in the clash between the duty of a democratic state to protect the lives of its citizens and soldiers versus its duty to avoid injuring civilians of the enemy. Immanuel Kant opined that dilemmas of this type are insoluble as there is a moral imperative stating that human beings are equal in value, and every person must be treated as having his own value and being an end in himself.[40] Accordingly, if we succeed in proving not all human beings are equal in value, then we shall be able to choose which persons to protect and thereby achieve the solution to the dilemma.

Moreover, Kant's approach is an absolute one, and as such, is problematic. If the value of human life always prevailed in any clash, doctors would be able to save all their patients and people would not die in road accidents because the state would provide authorities with the entire budget necessary to minimize traffic accident fatalities. Reality urges us to refrain from absolute concepts and exercise discretion within the decision making process. On occasion, other considerations outweigh the value of human life.[41]

True, the argument that human life is not an absolute value and that, in particular circumstances, it is possible to prefer the life of one person to that of another does not necessarily release us from a sense of moral guilt. This sense may be a sign of having committed a wrongful act which one may regret. Alternatively, the feeling of regret and guilt may relate not to the violation of a duty in circumstances where the act was the only proper act from a moral point of view, but rather to the undesirable results of that violation.[42] The sense of moral guilt reflects moral character, but it does not reflect the absolute nature of a moral duty.

> To say that act X is in the nature of a moral obligation is not to say that the validity of this obligation is not dependent on competing moral considerations. The reason for this is that on occasion moral obligations clash and in a particular situation two opposing obligations are imposed on the actor. If we had assumed that all the moral obligations are absolute in the sense that they override all competing considerations, including competing moral considerations, then in cases of conflict each of the obligations would have overridden the other, something which of course is impossible . . . the validity of a moral obligation is contingent upon the validity and force of other obligations which clash with it.[43]

In our case, in a clash between the duty to protect the citizens of the state from terrorist attacks as well as to protect soldiers' lives and the duty to avoid harm to innocent civilians themselves held by the terrorists, the former is likely to prevail. It is true that the killing of innocent persons is an act which is legally prohibited and morally reprehensible.

> However, it would seem that only a few would be willing to accept in simple terms the duty never to kill innocent persons. Someone who is not a pacifist and who is not blind to the modern reality of war which inevitably entails injury to the innocent, will find it difficult to argue in favor of the principle that the killing of innocent persons is always absolutely prohibited.[44]

As shall be seen below, moral and legal justification may be found for the killing of innocent persons within the context of military operations.[45] If we agree there are no absolute moral obligations, we might ask which approach we ought to use to determine which moral obligation prevails. This Article focuses on two primary moral approaches: the utilitarian-consequential approach versus the deontological approach.

According to the utilitarian approach, the moral value of an act is determined in accordance with its impact on happiness in the world. If the actor's actions brought about the greatest happiness, he fulfilled his one and only obligation, and all is proper from a moral point of view.[46] It follows that if injury to civilians who provide a human shield will lead to injury to the terrorists and comprise an essential measure in the war against terror, significantly eroding the force and capabilities of the terrorists, the injury to the innocent civilians will, in effect, lead to better results than avoiding harm to them. The latter course of action (avoiding harm) will lead to continued terror and further harm the state's citizens. This alone is justification for causing harm to the innocent civilians.

In contrast, adherence to the deontological approach does not confer moral legitimacy upon a wrongful act by reason of the beneficial results which derive from it. According to this approach, there is a certain threshold up to which considerations of outcome are irrelevant[47] and certainly are not sufficiently strong to negate a strict moral prohibition against harming innocent persons. These two approaches to resolving moral dilemmas will assist us to resolve the dilemma we shall consider in this part, and analyze in the context of the circumstances relevant to a democratic state's war against terror.

However, it should first be clarified that the starting point for the discussion on the moral dilemmas arising in this type of war rejects the argument that war is *per se* morally reprehensible. "(1) Murder is the intentional and uncoerced killing of the innocent. (2) Murder is by definition morally wrong. (3) Modern war by its very nature involves the intentional killing of innocent people. Therefore, modern war is morally wrong."[48]

We are concerned with a war that is consistent with the "theory of just war" by virtue of the fact that it is a war of self-defense.[49] The terror which we seek to fight is not a one-time passing phenomenon. It consists of a series of prolonged, numerous and brutal attacks which threaten the existence of states of the free world, and thereby affords these states the legal and moral right to self-defense.[50]

I reject the argument justifying terrorism and presenting it as the weapon of the weak fighting for their freedom, using terrorism not out of choice, but out of a lack of choice, as the only weapon available to them.[51] The terrorism against which we fight is not the only means available to the weak. Rather, it is the objective of a strong enemy that threatens the entire world; an enemy which does not fight for freedom but against it. Terrorists kill solely for the sake of killing.

The determination of the moral dilemmas to which we shall now turn is likely to equalize the balance of power and confer an advantage to terrorism over democracy. If a democratic state decides that its obligation to protect the lives of its citizens and soldiers overrides its moral obligation not to injure innocent persons among whom the terrorists operate, there is a great likelihood that this decision will attract a heavy international political price from the defending state.

As noted, I believe war is not a morally reprehensible state of affairs. On the contrary, it is the duty of a democratic state to go to war if such war is the only possible way to protect its citizens. "Governments have moral responsibilities to act in self-defense, in protection of innocents, in protection of the common good, and in protection of *tranquilitas ordinis*, the safety and civic peace which allows citizens to go about their daily lives."[52] The fact that this duty exists does not testify to its nature. The moral duty of the state to protect its citizens is not an absolute duty.[53] The hesitation shown by a democratic state regarding the means that should appropriately be taken to fulfill this duty proves the duty is not conclusive and unqualified. It is conceivable that we shall be required to choose means which express the balance between this duty and another moral duty.

The dilemmas with which we are dealing arise within the framework of war against an enemy, which is motivated by profound hatred, possessing a religious, cultural and national character. Terrorism is characterized by the threat to engage in the daily mass killing of civilians and the refusal to resolve disputes in other manners, such as negotiation or compromise. To suggest to a state whose citizens are victims of this terror, that it refrain from taking combative action, is immoral.

> Can a nation be asked, on moral grounds, to sacrifice itself—or one of its allies—rather than engage in hostilities which will produce an unpredictable (though certainly great) amount of bloodshed on both sides? The possibility that surrender would be more moral than war is not even conceded a probability.[54]

In our opinion, it would be even more morally reprehensible if the state were to choose to remain indifferent to the risks posed to its citizens.[55] The dilemma, therefore, does not concern whether one should or should not go to war. The dilemma relates to the means chosen within the framework of the war. The principal question is, therefore, that even on the assumption that the moral force and binding nature of the moral duty of a democratic state to exercise force against terrorists to protect its citizens causes it to override other moral duties, are all acts which fall within that moral duty permissible?

Currently, the laws of war do not supply an answer to this question or to the moral dilemmas derived from it, as such laws are constructed on the principle of reciprocity, whereby the adverse parties respect and abide by these principles. The laws of war are not designed for wars conducted against terrorist organizations.[56] Accordingly, even were one to agree that the law is the binding expression of social and public morality,[57] one would not be able to find a positive objective solution to the moral dilemmas which arise within the context of this war. The solution, therefore, to every dilemma is a subjective solution, which is adjusted to a varying reality and to the diverse situations which comprise this reality.

In the aftermath of the events of September 11, 2001, and President Bush's declaration of war against terror,[58] many observers emphasized the just and essential objectives of this war concurrently with the importance of abiding by the legal rules of war and the moral principles guiding a democratic state. "We must respond to the September 11 tragedy in the spirit of the laws: seeking justice, not vengeance; applying principle, not merely power. We must respond according to the values embodied in our domestic and international commitments to human rights and the rule of law."[59]

Below, we shall explain why not every action taken in the name of protecting one's citizens is permitted, but that some action may nevertheless be taken without being tainted by allegations of legal and moral impropriety. The rules of war are not absolute inflexible prohibitions which can never justifiably be violated.

In our view, one must reject the approach asserting that soldiers fighting a just war are entitled to do everything useful in that war, on the ground that it is the enemy which is responsible for the war. Such unrestricted freedom of action is dangerous and morally improper. Its purpose is the absolute transfer of responsibility onto the shoulders of the enemy, and improperly regards as unqualified the rights of the just so that any resulting wrongdoing is the sole responsibility of the adverse party.[60] Even when the enemy is terrorism and the war against it is a just war, not every wrongdoing performed by the democracy is the responsibility of the terrorist opponent.

As a rule, killing during the course of a war is permitted when it is an essential means of self-defense. Legal and moral principles require us to distinguish between soldiers and civilians where only the former may be harmed. According to theorist Michael Walzer, civilians who are not combatants are in a certain sense innocent and therefore entitled to a moral immunity to which soldiers are not.[61] This distinction between civilians and soldiers is a basic rule of the laws of war and has special importance in a war being waged by a democratic state against terror.

> There must be no resort to general indiscriminate repression. The government must show that its measures against terrorism are solely directed at quelling the terrorists and their active collaborators and at defending society against the terrorists. A slide into general repression would destroy individual liberties and political democracy and may indeed bring about a ruthless dictatorship even more implacable than the terrorism the repression was supposed to destroy.[62]

In contrast, there are those who believe there is no moral basis for the distinction between civilians and soldiers, only a consensual basis. In other words, the distinction reflects the common desire of the parties to limit the destructive consequences of the war. It expresses mutual consent to avoid inflicting harm upon the civilian population.[63] According to this approach, if one of the parties deviates from the principle of mutuality, the other party will also be released from the duty to abide by the distinction. I do not agree with this approach where the circumstances involve a war in which one of the parties is a democratic state. We have seen that according to international law[64] and, in particular, according to moral imperatives, a democratic state is not discharged from its duty to avoid inflicting harm upon the civilian population merely because the adverse party—the terrorists—deliberately target civilians.

B. Moral Dilemmas in the War against Terror

Dilemma 1: We have seen that terrorists use civilians as a human shield for their own protection; operating out of civilian population centers and against them. The military forces of the democratic state, which are required to defend the citizens of the state, are forced to contend with very difficult battle conditions requiring them, in the name of moral and practical concepts, to adhere to the laws of just war and pay the price at a very real risk to their own lives. Is it proper to require them to pay this price?

Perhaps we should rather say, for example, in the case of the State of Israel, which faces an existential risk from terrorist acts directed at it, as part of the declared and open plan of the terrorist leaders to destroy it, that:

> A nation fighting a just war, which is in a desperate situation and whose very existence is in danger, will necessarily have to have recourse to soldiers who do not have moral inhibitions or an understanding of morals; and when it will no longer need them, it must repudiate them.[65]

It would be impossible for the State of Israel, a Jewish and democratic state, to repudiate moral values based on respect for human life, because such action would be contrary to its nature. Accordingly, it is not inconceivable that soldiers be required to risk their lives for a moral imperative which directs them to avoid harm to the innocent. This is a justified risk, "a risk which is required to preempt an existing risk . . . the army of a democratic state recognizes two types of situations in which a soldier is permitted to risk his own life and the lives of his soldiers: in the face of the enemy and to save human life."[66] Is there a parallel between terrorism posing a risk to the citizens of the democratic state, which requires the state's protection, putting soldiers' lives at risk, and terrorism posing a risk to the citizens of their own state, which also compels the democratic state to risk its soldiers' lives, this time to protect the citizens of the enemy? Can one speak of a justified risk in both these cases?

The two situations are not fully analogous. A democratic state must exercise the force needed to overcome the military might of the enemy, even when this poses a risk to its forces attempting to vanquish the enemy. Remember, the harm suffered by the citizens of the enemy has been generated by the terrorists themselves. Endangering our own forces to avoid injury to civilians, but consequently failing to harm the terrorists, allows the sinners to reap the benefit of their sins. The military forces of the democratic state would be injured; the threat to its citizens would continue. The moral duty to avoid injury to civilians would absolutely override the duty to protect the democracy's own citizens and the lives of its soldiers. In other words, the state would not be able to conduct effectively, if at all, the just war it set out to pursue: "In principle, it is possible for a nation to avoid killing noncombatants, but such a policy would seriously weaken its military position, not to mention the advantage it would give to a less morally scrupulous adversary."[67]

There are those who contend that "we are not subject to any moral duty to endanger the lives of our soldiers within the framework of military action to defend against the enemy, the attacker or potential attacker, merely to save the attacker from fatalities or property damage."[68]

In combat against an enemy operating from a civilian population which supports it, it may be argued: "If the guerrilla fighters and the population that supports them do not keep the distinction between combatants and noncombatants, why should the enemy be committed to this distinction?"[69]

As explained, there are no absolute duties: No duty not to endanger the lives of our soldiers to protect the citizens of the enemy, and no duty to refrain from injuring those citizens. There is a correct balance within the circumstances of each case. As a rule, aerial bombardment is too destructive a tactic to use against places housing terrorists alongside innocent civilians. It is necessary to choose less lethal means, even if these are less certain and may endanger the state's military forces. The operation must aspire to pinpoint accuracy to distinguish between civilians and terrorists; more precisely, between innocent civilians and terrorists.[70]

Guilty Civilians versus Innocent Civilians

The classic approach entails a distinction between combatants and noncombatants. Protection of "innocents" is actually protection of all those who are not called "combatants." A more accurate approach, legally and morally, distinguishes between the guilty and the innocent.[71] According to this approach, in some cases civilians may be deemed guilty. The effort must be directed at distinguishing between civilians who have lost their rights by their involvement in the war, and those who have not. The relevant distinction for this Article is not between those who do and do not contribute to the war effort, but between those who supply the soldiers with tools to fight and those who supply them with provisions to live.[72] The innocent are those who have done nothing which would deprive them of their rights. On the other hand, "[w]hat is required for the people attacked to be non-innocent in the relevant sense, is that they should themselves be engaged in an objectively unjust proceeding which the attacker has the right to make his concern."[73]

This occurs when civilians freely choose to provide shelter and protection to terrorists and allow them to operate from their homes. These civilians are collaborators with the terrorists and, as such, lose their immunity from harm. Is it conceivable to demand the soldiers of the democratic state to risk their own lives to avoid injuring civilians who have sheltered and protected terrorists, even permitting them to shoot at and operate against the soldiers from their homes? This pattern of civilian behavior serves the policy of terror. Accordingly, it would be improper to demand the protection of such civilians, merely because they hide under the title "civilian," and are not officially active in any particular terrorist organization.

The title "civilian" is not an empty phrase. Though protection of enemy civilians is a legal rule with moral weight deriving from the respect due human life, the rule is subject to an exception. The exception applies when civilians collaborate and assist in bringing about the objectives of the terrorists who pose an imminent danger to the democratic state. As such, the civilians become participants in the actual fighting and are a danger to the forces of the democratic state and, indirectly, to that state's citizens. "Thus: combatants may be viewed as all those in the territory or allied territory of the enemy of whom it is reasonable to believe that they are engaged in an attempt to destroy you."[74]

In practice, this is merely a *prima facie* exception, because civilians assisting terrorists are manifestly not innocent, "in fact, they [are] more 'guilty' than ordinary soldiers. And if indiscriminatory attacks against civilians are wrong because they express a lack of respect for human life, then no such lack of respect is expressed when civilians themselves are the main perpetrators of these acts."[75] The concern is not with civilians who are not entitled to protection, but rather from whom it is necessary to seek protection. Recognition of a state's right to self-defense enables it to defend itself against those who threaten or attack it—those such as the terrorists and civilians who collaborate in achieving terrorist objectives.

Nonetheless, it is not necessary to attack the involved civilians if it is possible to stop their activities without creating great risk to our forces. Only when such an option does not exist, and the civilians pose a risk, will the obligation of a democratic state to avoid harm to these civilians be cancelled and these civilians will lose their rights.

Article 52 of the Additional Protocol to the Geneva Convention defines military objectives, which are legal objectives for attack, as objects which by their nature, location, purpose or use make an effective contribution to military action and whose total or partial destruction, capture or neutralization, in the circumstances ruling at the time, offers a definite military advantage. The definition is flexible and highly relative.[76] The same objective may be regarded as both civilian and military. Accordingly, the Article provides that in case of doubt whether an object normally dedicated to civilian purposes is being used to make an effective contribution to military action, it shall be presumed to remain civilian. However, this is a rebuttable presumption that only arises in cases of doubt. In the situation under discussion here, it is assumed the military forces have well-founded and reliable information proving a civilian home is being used by terrorists; they together with the "civilians" are operating from that location. In such a case, the home becomes a military target. In this situation, the civilians are not innocent but are tainted by moral guilt. It would not be morally wrong to kill them; the target is not civilian and no legal blame would be attached to an attack upon it.

Two situations occur in war against terror where fighting is conducted on a house-by-house basis in an urban area and the civilians are warned before the attack to leave their homes and vacate the area but chose to remain. In the first, civilians have freely chosen to remain in their homes to make it more difficult for the democratic state to target the terrorists, knowing the democracy is fettered by legal and moral principles which prohibit causing them harm.

> In such fighting, which is conducted from house to house in a built-up area, there is no practical means of distinguishing between combatants and civilians. Accordingly, the assault force need not conduct detailed checks: first one shoots and afterwards one investigates who has been hit. The place of civilians is outside the battle arena. If they stay there and are hit—their blood is on their own heads.[77]

Civilians who shelter terrorists to furnish them with a military advantage over the democratic state, are differentiated in only one way from civilians who are physically involved with the terrorists fighting from their homes. The former are passively involved; the latter are actively involved. However, both their involvement causes loss of their moral immunity from harm. When they choose not to escape from the danger of the battle arena, assuming they had been warned in advance and could have escaped, and yet prefer to supply the terrorists with shelter, they choose a side; moral blame must therefore be attached. Consequently, they risk treatment as combatants under the laws of war, where their death will not be the death of innocents and protecting the lives of the soldiers of the democratic state is more important.

> A person may be *liable* to suffer harm if, through his own culpable action, he has made it inevitable that *someone* must suffer harm. In such a case, it is permissible, and sometimes even obligatory, to harm the morally guilty person rather than to allow his morally culpable action to cause harm to the morally innocent. The interests of the innocent have priority as a matter of justice.[78]

In contrast, when civilians are made hostages by the terrorists—used to shelter terrorists from attack, and their houses used as a staging post to attack the democracy's soldiers—the civilians are innocent persons not posing a threat to the forces of the democracy. Such a case is sufficient to provide moral justification for the democracy's soldiers' risk of their own lives on behalf of the civilians. It is in this context, Walzer comments:

> It is forbidden to kill any person for trivial reasons. Civilians have rights which supersede even this. And if the saving of civilian life means the risking of soldiers' lives, such a risk must be accepted. Nonetheless, there is a limit to the risks which we demand. We are talking, after all, of death caused by mistake and by legitimate military action and the absolute rule against attacking civilians does not apply here. War necessarily endan-

gers civilians; that is another aspect of the inferno. We can only demand of the soldiers that they limit the risks which they impose.[79]

Dilemma II: In the context of this dilemma, I shall consider the moral duty to avoid inflicting harm upon enemy civilians who are innocent as defined above. When terrorists use innocent persons as human shields, the right to self-defense does not provide moral and legal justification for injuring these civilians. The relevant legal defense is the defense of necessity. However, though it will discharge us from criminal liability, it will not necessarily transform the action into a moral action. Our purpose is not to identify the legal defense for an action resulting in injury to innocents. Our purpose, instead, is to focus on moral justification (if one can speak of such justification at all) for harm to innocents in situations that pose a clear danger to the lives of the soldiers and civilians of the democratic state which cannot be avoided, save by harming innocent people. These situations are analogous to those of necessity in criminal law.

A central concept useful in balancing the duty to use one's weapons when necessary to vanquish an enemy of its citizens with the avoidance of injury to civilians, is *Tohar Haneshek*. This Hebrew term, loosely translated as "use of weapons in a virtuous manner" or "moral warfare," focuses on ensuring a moral regime within the battle arena.[80] It recognizes that armed force should not be a supreme value. *Tohar Haneshek* requires the self-restraint of military forces in refraining from the use of more force than necessary. Even when the enemy does not recognize "moral warfare," the democratic state has a duty to limit the blood bath created in its war with terrorism.

> It is a duty to understand and recall that the enemy too is a man, however, hostile, evil and malicious. The moral man will defend himself against the enemy appropriately. He will not concede to him. The democratic state will defend itself against him, by means of its army, as it must, in a moral manner, as is necessary, and not beyond what is necessary. This is one way of explaining the duty to restrain oneself, in the manner of "*Tohar Haneshek*" [moral warfare], the moral duty of the democratic state, with all its structures, and among them the army.[81]

When it is impossible to vanquish the enemy without killing civilians, because distinguishing between civilians and terrorists is difficult or impossible, does use of necessary force include killing civilians? Vitoria, in his book *De jure bellic*,[82] asserts that it is forbidden to deliberately kill innocent civilians, except when there is no other way to vanquish the guilty. This is necessary in the battle now underway. Wasserstrom believes that military necessity is a central concept in the implementation of the laws of war.[83] He offers general justification for the breach of the prohibitions at the basis of these laws. In his view, the doctrine of military necessity transforms the laws of war into a general moral precept, but enables them to be circumvented.[84]

The doctrine of military necessity is similar to the emergency situation Walzer describes as a time in which it is acceptable to trample the right to life—even of innocents.[85] Even John Rawls, who thought "there is never a time when we are free from all moral and political principles and restraints,"[86] recognized emergency situations as an exception to that rule.

> Rawls, following Walzer, argues that "[civilians] can never be attacked directly except in times of extreme crisis."[87] Therefore, we can violate human rights—we can directly attack civilians—if we are sure we can do some "substantial good' by so doing, and if the enemy is so evil that it is better for all well-ordered societies that human rights be violated on this occasion.[88]

There is no doubt terrorism is a brutal and dangerous enemy. A decision during battle, which calls upon soldiers to avoid harming innocents, will have the *de facto* consequence of sacrificing the lives of the soldiers' fellow citizens.[89] In such situations, the sense of moral urgency the soldiers may feel in terms of avoiding harm to innocents may retreat in the face of moral urgency to defend their fellow citizens. In exceptional circumstances, such a retreat may be legally and morally justified. For example, when the most senior wanted terrorists, who plan, send, and carry out horrendous terrorist attacks, hide among innocent civilians and it is not possible to capture or attack them, save by engaging in a collective attack against the entire house and all its occupants. Must we refrain from such an attack? The question is not easy and I tend to think it should be answered in the negative. If indeed the risk posed by the terrorists is unusual, imminent, and has the power to augment the weight and authority of the moral duty to protect the citizens of the state, then the latter duty will prevail in accordance with the principle of proportionality, whereby the benefit of the action (saving the lives of many innocent persons who are threatened by the terrorists) exceeds the damage ensuing from it (harm to innocent persons who are held by the terrorists and damage to the state's image).

This is what distinguishes us from terrorists: The latter's actions are designed to harm the innocent, whereas the democratic state intends to strike at the guilty. Injury to the innocent, even if unavoidable, is certainly not deliberate.

> Thus, if a country engages in acts of war with the intention of bringing about the death of children, perhaps to weaken the will of the enemy, it

would be more immoral than if it were to engage in acts of war aimed at killing combatants but which through error also kill children.[90]

The presumption that there are no absolute moral obligations, and as part of this, that there is also no absolute duty not to kill the innocent,[91] may assist us in removing the moral taint which has adhered to the killing of innocent persons. Every duty may be construed in at least two ways: As an absolute duty or as a *prima facie* or universal duty (one which, in the event of exceptional circumstances, may be breached).[92] The difference between them is that an absolute duty is a duty which will never clash with other duties. The characteristic of a duty as being absolute shows there are no circumstances in which it does not exist. In contrast, a *prima facie* or universal duty may fall into conflict with other duties in certain situations.[93]

In cases where a just war is being waged, such as a war against terrorism, and the duty to avoid harming the innocent and the duty to protect the citizens of the state cannot be implemented simultaneously, the moral duty not to kill the innocent is more compatible with the case of a *prima facie* duty.[94] In exceptional circumstances—such as may be created during the war against terrorism—a *prima facie* duty may be breached, even though we are aware our activities will lead to the death of innocents who are located in the vicinity of the terrorists.

However, our decision to prefer the democratic state's duty to protect its own citizens over its moral and legal duty to avoid causing harm to the innocent does not mean the latter duty should be abandoned. The prohibition on harming the innocent remains a universal moral duty that retreats in the face of another universal moral duty, which has superior status in the specific circumstances precluding us from regarding the duty not to harm the innocent as an absolute duty: "It seems to misunderstand the character of our moral life to claim that, no matter what the consequences, the intentional killing of an innocent person could never be justifiable—even, for example, if a failure to do so would bring about the death of many more innocent persons."[95]

This approach to resolving the dilemma is close to the consequential approach, as soldiers are entitled to kill innocent civilians if the consequence of this act is to achieve the primary goal of killing the terrorists and saving the lives of an entire nation. However, permission to violate the right to life of civilians held by terrorists is not an all-encompassing permission. The decision must be subject to the principle of proportionality: The right to harm civilians is a defined, specific, and limited right, which must refer to the smallest possible number of people, whose sacrifice, to save the lives of many others, is proportional, and thereby dulls the sense of moral guilt which attaches to the action.

Whether it can be permissible to kill everyone in a group knowing that the group contains both guilty and innocent people. The standard response is to claim that it is permissible provided that killing the guilty alone would be justified and that the killing of the innocent is both unintended and not disproportionate to the good that is to be achieved by killing the guilty.[96]

Terrorism, which challenges principles of freedom and democracy, endangers all the nations of the free world. It thereby forces upon us a "regime of necessity" whereby we are compelled to put aside guiding moral principles in favor of a moral duty to protect the lives of the citizens of the free world. The significance of the refusal to concede to this moral shunting is to surrender to the evil of terrorism and a life lived in fear of it taking control.

Notwithstanding this, the deontological approach, which recognizes rights and refrains from mathematical calculations as to the outcome, will find it difficult to justify the killing of innocent persons—a repudiation of the highest moral obligations—irrespective of the purpose of such action. Philosophical approaches at the heart of which stand rights, dignity, and freedom will apparently support the absolute prohibition against killing innocent persons.

[…]

Acknowledgments

Thanks are due to my research assistant Karin Meridor, whose diligence and dedicated work enabled this Article, as well as to Mr. Ranan Hartman of the Academic Center, Kiryat Ono, who assisted in financing the Article.

NOTES

[…]

36. ASSA CASHER, ETIKA TZAVIT [MILITARY ETHICS] 37–38 (1996).

37. DANIEL STATMAN, DILMUT MUSRIUT [MORAL DILEMMAS] 175 (Hebrew University Jerusalem, 1996).

38. R.M. HARE, MORAL THINKING: ITS LEVELS, METHODS, AND POINT 26–27 (Clarendon Press, 1981). Hare distinguishes between the intuitive level and the critical level in relation to moral dilemmas. The intuitive level characterizes those who believe a clash between two moral obligations is insoluble. On the critical level, the situation is regarded as one which can be resolved. According to this view: "If you have conflicting duties, one of them isn't your duty." Id. at 26.

39. JOSEPH RAZ, THE MORALITY OF FREEDOM 359–60 (Clarendon Press, 1986).

40. IMMANUEL KANT, FUNDAMENTAL PRINCIPLES OF THE METAPHYSICS OF ETHICS 108–09 (M. Shefi trans., Magnes Press, 1973).

41. *See infra*, notes 99–113 and accompanying text. There are those who believe that Kant had his own view about war in which the value of human life is not absolute. The emphasis is on the dominant purposes and values underlying the activities performed during the course of war.

42. STATMAN, *supra* note 37, at 164–65. For example, one may think of a doctor on a battlefield forced to choose whom to save, where the equipment and drugs do not suffice to save all. The doctor is faced with the dilemma of whose life to save and how to make that choice.

43. Daniel Statman, *She'elot ha-Mochlatot ha-Mosrit shel ha-Isur le-Anot* [*The Question of Absolute Morality Regarding the Prohibition on Torture*], 4 LAW & GOV'T 161–62 (1997) [hereinafter *She'elot*].

44. *Id.* at 168.

45. For example, the doctrine of double effect dictates that the killing of innocent persons is not absolutely prohibited; only the deliberate killing of innocent persons is prohibited. Furthermore, the killing of innocent persons, which is the unavoidable and undesired corollary of combat, is not prohibited.

46. STATMAN, *supra* note 37, at 168.

47. *She'elot*, *supra* note 43, at 187–88.

48. Jeffrie G. Murphy, *The Killing of the Innocent, in* WAR, MORALITY AND THE MILITARY PROFESSION 343 (Malham M. Wakin ed., 1979). Professor Murphy does not take a stand on this issue; his argument is that you can kill in warfare, but only those trying to kill you. *Id. See also* Donald A. Wells, *How Much Can the 'Just War' Justify, in* WAR, MORALITY AND THE MILITARY PROFESSION (Malham M. Wakin ed., 1979).

49. MICHAEL WALZER, JUST AND UNJUST WARS 133 (1984). *See also* Darrell Cole, *09.11.01: Death Before Dishonor or Dishonor Before Death? Christian Just War, Terrorism, and Supreme Emergency*, 16 NOTRE DAME J.L. ETHICS & PUB POL'Y 81, 86 (2002). The rules of international law in which the primary principle prohibits the use of force as a mode of dispute resolution, recognizes the right of a state to launch a war in one situation only: When the use of force is the outcome of the right to self-defense. *See* UNITED NATIONS CHARTER, art. 51.

50. For further clarification, *see* Emanuel Gross, *Thwarting Terrorist Acts by Attacking the Perpetrators or Their Commanders as an Act of Self-Defense: Human Rights Versus the State's Duty to Protect Its Citizens*, 15 TEMP. INT'L & COMP. L. J. 195 (2001). *See also* Emanuel Gross, *The Laws of War Between Democratic States and Terrorist Organizations*, FLA. J. INT'L L. (forthcoming) [hereinafter *The Laws of War*].

51. *See* Jenny Teichman, *How to Define Terrorism*, 64 PHIL. 505, 515 (1989).

52. Maryann Custimano Love, *Globalization, Ethics, and the War on Terrorism*, 16 NOTRE DAME J.L. ETHICS & PUB POL'Y 65, 69–70 (2002).

53. This is contrary to those who believe in the absolute right of self-defense available to a state defending itself against attack. *See* MOSHE GILBOA, MASA LA-EGOISM SHEL HA-ANOSHUT [JOURNEY TO THE EGOISM OF HUMANKIND] 102–05 (1990).

54. Struckmeyer, *supra* note 4, at 276.

55. In the dilemma whether to die or to kill, a distinction must be drawn between the right of an individual to his life and his decision to not kill and die and the duty of the state and its leaders to protect the state's citizens; that duty negates the possibility of the state deciding to "die," *i.e.*, to sacrifice the lives of its citizens in order to avoid the decision to "kill." "While

I clearly have the prerogative of taking my own life, or of allowing someone else to take it, I do not have the same prerogative where the lives of others are concerned. I cannot compel another man to sacrifice himself if he wishes to defend his life. . . ." *Id.* at 278.

56. *See The Laws of War, supra* note 50.

57. *See also* L. A. HART, CHOK, CHIRUT, VE-MUSAR [LAWS AND MORALITY], 25–37 (1981) (stating the law reflects the morality prevailing in society).

58. President Bush's Declaration of War Following the Attack of September 11th, 2001, at http://www.whitehouse.gov/news/releases/2001/09/20010920-8.html (last visited March 5, 2003).

59. Harold Hongju Koh, *The Spirit of the Laws*, 43 HARV. INT'L L.J. 23, 39 (2002).

60. WALZER, *supra* note 49, at 270.

61. *Id.* at 165.

62. WILLIAM GUTTERIDGE, THE NEW TERRORISM 17 (1986).

63. *See* George I. Mavrodes, *Conventions and the Morality of War*, 4 PHIL. & PUB. AFF. 117 (1975).

64. Protocol I, *supra* note 7, art. 51.

65. WALZER, *supra* note 49, at 380 (describing the cruel policy of Arthur Harris, commander of the strategic aerial bombardment of Germany from February 1942 until the end of the war that claimed the lives of 3,000,000 Germans and injured another 780,000).

66. CASHER, *supra* note 36, at 47.

67. Daniel Statman, *Jus in Bello and the Intifada, in* PHILOSOPHICAL PERSPECTIVES ON THE ISRAELI-PALESTINIAN CONFLICT, 133, 152 (Tomis Kapitan ed., 1997) [hereinafter *Jus in Bello*].

68. CASHER, *supra* note 36, at 158.

69. *Jus in Bello, supra* note 67, at 133, 134.

70. The distinction between combatants and non-combatants is not equivalent to a distinction between innocence and guilt. Various philosophers have argued that from a moral point of view the more accurate distinction lies between "the guilty" and "the innocent," in which there may be soldiers who are innocent and civilians who are guilty. *See, e.g.,* Richard Wasserstrom, *On the Morality of War: A Preliminary Inquiry, in* WAR, MORALITY AND THE MILITARY PROFESSION, *supra* note 4, at 299, 316–17. In the case of the war against terror, reference is not to soldiers in the accepted sense, comparable to soldiers of the democratic state. There can be no terrorist who is not guilty. Accordingly, it is necessary to be satisfied distinguishing civilians who are guilty from civilians who are innocent—only the latter merit protection.

71. Murphy, *supra* note 48, at 344, 346–47, 353. "Why, then, should we worry about killing noncombatants and think it wrong to do so—especially when we realize that among the noncombatants there will be some, at any rate, who are morally and/or legally guilty of various things and that among the combatants there will be those who are morally and/or legally innocent?" *Id. See also* Jeff McMahan, *Innocence, Self-Defense and Killing in War*, 3(3) J. PHIL. 193, 199 (1994).

72. WALZER, *supra* note 49, at 173–74.

73. Elizabeth Anscombe, *War and Murder, in* WAR, MORALITY AND THE MILITARY PROFESSION 285, 288 (Malham M. Wakin ed., 1979).

74. Murphy, *supra* note 48, at 344, 350.

75. *Jus in Bello*, *supra* note 67, at 133, 143. These comments were directed at Palestinian children who threw stones at IDF soldiers during the first *intifada*, who, according to this argument, lost their immunity.

76. *See* Jeanne M. Meyer, *Tearing Down The Facade: A Critical Look at the Current Law on Targeting the Will of the Enemy and Air Force Doctrine*, 51 A.F. L. REV. 143, 164–68, 177–78 (2001).

77. Yoram Dinstein, *Tohar ha-Nashek ba-Dinei ha-Milchama* [*The Theory of Arms in the Laws of War*], *in* TOHAR HA-NASHEK [THE THEORY OF ARMS] (Seminar Issues of Israel's Security) 25, 27 (Yad Tebenkin, 1991).

78. McMahan, *supra* note 71, at 193, 204.

79. WALZER, *supra* note 49, at 186. The status of these "captive" civilians is equivalent to that of innocent hostages, and therefore it is proper to demand that the soldiers risk their lives on their behalf. As in the case of hostages though, there can be no guarantee that they will never be harmed; the outcome depends on the particular circumstances of the case.

80. Me'ir Pa'il, *Marekhet Mosrit ba-Maaseh Hilchima* [*A Moral Regime Within Warfare, Tohar Haneshek*], *in* TOHAR HA-NASHEK [THE THEORY OF ARMS], *supra* note 77, at 9.

81. CASHER, *supra* note 36, at 57.

82. Ronit A. Peleg & Irit M. Tamir, Ha-Tzeley ha-Adom ve-ha-She'elot ha-Mosriut Shemeorerat ha-Milchama [*The Red Cross and the Moral Questions Raised by War*], *in* INTERNATIONAL PROBLEMS: SOCIETY AND STATE] 26 (Marian Mushkat ed., 1987) (quoting FRANCISCO DE VITORIA, DE JURE BELLIC 15:430 (John Pawley Bate trans., Scott ed.)).

83. Richard Wasserstrom, *The Responsibility of the Individual for War Crimes*, *in* PHILOSOPHY, MORALITY, AND INTERNATIONAL AFFAIRS 47, 62 (Virginia Held, Sidney Morgenbessen, & Tomas Nagel eds., 1974).

84. Peleg & Tamir, *supra* note 82, at 13.

85. WALZER, *supra* note 49, at 294.

86. JOHN RAWLS, *Fifty Years After Hiroshima*, *in* COLLECTED PAPERS 565, 572 (Samuel Freeman ed., 1999).

87. Cole, *supra* note 49, at 91 (quoting Rawls, *supra* note 86).

88. Cole, *supra* note 49, at 91.

89. Walzer offers an example of the threat of destruction of a nation in the name of which it is possible to quash the rights of innocents. WALZER, *supra* note 49, at 297.

90. Wasserstrom, *supra* note 70, at 318.

91. Murphy, *supra* note 48, at 357. "Thus I do not think that it has yet been shown that it is always absolutely wrong, whatever the consequences, to kill innocent babies. And thus it has not yet been shown that it is absolutely wrong to kill those innocent in a less rich sense of the term, *i.e.* noncombatant." *Id.*

92. W. DAVID ROSS, THE RIGHT AND THE GOOD 18–19 (1930). *See also* DANIEL STATMAN, MORAL DILEMMAS (1996).

93. MALHAM M. WAKIN, INTEGRITY FIRST, REFLECTION OF A MILITARY PHILOSOPHER 24 (2000).

94. In contrast, there are those who believe that the prohibition on killing innocents is an absolute moral duty to which there are no exceptions. *See* Elizabeth Anscombe, *Modern Moral Philosophy*, 33 PHILOSOPHY 1–11 (1958).

95. Wasserstrom, *supra* note 70, at 318.

96. McMahan, *supra* note 71, at 215.

[…]

*Emanuel Gross** is a professor of law at Haifa University, Israel.

Gross, Emanuel. "Use of Civilians as Human Shields: What Legal and Moral Restrictions Pertain to a War Waged by a Democratic State against Terrorism?" *Emory International Law Review* 16, no. 2 (Fall 2002): 460–485.

Part 4: Who Makes Up the Fighting Forces?

The selections in the previous section asked you to consider the distinction between civilians and combatants in war. In particular, you were asked to think about whether civilians should be protected from the violence wrought by war, and if they were ever legitimate targets in war. In general, the writers concluded that the killing of innocent civilians is an unfortunate, but sometimes inevitable, consequence of even the most just of warfare. The selections in this section ask you to focus specifically on *who* makes up the fighting army that is sent to war. Should militaries be constructed from volunteers who are willing to fight on behalf of their country? Is the hiring of private military companies or mercenaries objectionable from the perspective of just war theory? If one of the military's objectives is to protect its soldiers, should we encourage the development of autonomous weapons systems, which can be controlled from remote locations? Or is the willingness to put the lives of one's soldiers at risk a necessary condition of just war?

THE DRAFT VERSUS THE ALL-VOLUNTEER FORCE

Although the United States abandoned the draft after the Vietnam War and turned instead to an all-volunteer force, many countries continue to demand that their citizens perform military (or, more generally, national) service of some kind. In the last decade as the United States has participated in several demanding military conflicts, there have been increasing calls for a return to conscription. According to one of its advocates, William A. Galston, requiring all citizens to participate provides a way to communicate the meaning of citizenship. To be a citizen means to take responsibility for the actions of the state and to be willing to defend the state with one's life. Citizenship is crucially a collective activity, which citizens pursue together, and which demands that we carry out some obligations in exchange for having our rights protected. In "A Sketch of Some Arguments for Conscription," Galston dismisses claims that requiring citizens to participate in the military is akin to slavery or that it is an abuse of state power. Instead, he says, the turn away from mandatory service has caused fissures in American society. The political leaders who decide to enter the nation into military conflict are less likely than ever to have directly experienced military conflict themselves, and therefore they are less acutely cognizant of the risks to which they are subjecting citizens. More concerning, he says, is that the all-volunteer force, he contends is now disproportionately composed of Republicans and citizens from poor backgrounds who view the military as one of few ways to secure their social advancement (or any employment at all). As a result, the makeup of the military represents a narrow segment of the population rather than the population at large. Galston argues that this has "contributed to a widening gap between the orientation and experience of military personnel and that of the citizenry as a whole."[1]

MERCENARIES

A more pragmatic reason cited in favor of conscription is that in light of ongoing and expansive military commitments the military is in need of additional bodies. Rather than move to a drafted army, however, an alternative is to rely on mercenaries or private military companies to provide some of the services typically supplied by the military. As Cécile Fabre defines it in "In Defence of Mercenarism," a mercenary is

> an individual who offers his military expertise to a belligerent against payment, outside the state's military recruitment and training procedures, either directly to a party in a conflict, or through an employment contract with a private military corporation.[2]

Multiple reasons exist for rejecting the use of mercenaries in military conflicts. For one thing, says Galston, we cannot be sure of mercenaries' loyalty in times of war, since they are motivated solely by financial gain and can thus be predicted to fight for the highest bidder. More than that, however, he writes

> beyond these practical considerations lies a moral intuition: even if a mercenary army were reliable and effective, it would be wrong, even shameful, to use our wealth to get non-citizens to do our fighting for us. This is something we ought to do for ourselves, as a self-respecting people.[3]

Fabre defends the use of mercenaries against Galston's objection and that of several others. For Fabre, so long as the cause of a war is just, we should have no principled objections to the use of mercenaries. To those, like Galston, who worry that mercenaries are only motivated by the prospect of financial gain— the "motivation" objection—she responds that soldiers too are frequently motivated by financial gain. To those who would argue that mercenaries are likely to be victims of shoddy treatment by their employer, since they often are not citizens—the "objectification" objection—she reports that there is no reason *inherent* to the experience of mercenarism, as distinct from employment more generally, that makes this likely.

To those who would argue that mercenaries appear to profit from the suffering of others—the "profiteering" objection—she observes that many people, ranging from weapons makers to army suppliers, profit from war. Some may also worry that the reliance on mercenaries entails a loss of control by the government fighting the war—the "loss of control" objection—since it may appear that "states lose control over the decision to use violence, as well as over the agents by which it is used."[4] In other words, mercenaries could take orders from their employers rather than the state and may therefore be more concerned about protecting their jobs than about the actual outcome of the war. But, says Fabre, governments seek insight from a range of experts during military conflict, not all of whom have a stake in the outcome of the war.

Having argued that nearly all of the objections to mercenarism can be overcome, Fabre contends instead that the historical reluctance to extend the same rights and privileges to mercenaries as are granted to soldiers is objectionable: morally, she writes, they incur the same risks as soldiers, and in support of the same causes, and therefore deserve the same "liabilities, rights and privileges during war."[5] For example, the same rules that dictate when soldiers may kill others and when they should be prosecuted for war crimes should apply equally to mercenaries.

Eliminating Risk in Warfare: The Ethics of Autonomous Weapons Systems

When Fabre justifies her claim that mercenaries and soldiers deserve the same liabilities, rights, and privileges during war, her justification stems in part from the risk that both take in participating in warfare. Mercenarism, like soldiering, requires those participating to risk their lives in support of a state or their employer. Paul W. Kahn's selection, "The Paradox of Riskless Warfare," asks readers to acknowledge that risk is an inherent part of military conflict: to the extent that soldiers are justified in killing each other, they are justified only if they "stand in a relationship of mutual risk."[6]

If the imposition of mutual risk is what justifies soldiers' right of self-defense, which in turn may require the killing of enemy soldiers, then, Kahn asserts, we should question the morality of warfare in which one combatant possesses technology that spares him the battlefield risk. Kahn writes, "A regime capable of targeting and destroying others with the push of a button, with no intervention but only the operation of the ultimate high tech weapon, propels us well beyond the ethics of warfare."[7] By removing oneself from the battlefield, says Kahn, the soldier effectively erases the distinction between combatant and non-combatant; those who remain on the battlefield can no longer be credibly described as a threat against whom legal force can be used in self-defense. And if "combatants are no longer a threat . . . then they are no more appropriate targets than noncombatants."[8] To the extent that just war theory has given us the tools to think through the morality of warfare, the increasingly widespread use of robotic technology forces us to rethink the ethics that guide military conflict.

We may think that the emergence of truly autonomous robots in the battlefield—robots that can absorb information from the battlefield and make decisions about the appropriate actions to take, without human input—is fanciful. However, in the final selection, "How Just Could a Robot War Be?" Peter M. Asaro notes that this technology is being developed and is a concerted goal for many militaries, including the American military. On the surface, the pursuit of these weapons may seem to be morally justified. Doing so serves to reduce the risk to soldiers who will be stationed behind a computer screen rather than the battlefield. If one believes that among a state's central objectives is to protect its own soldiers from harm, the pursuit of weapons that enable conflict without putting soldiers in harm's way seems not only morally justified but in fact morally required. Indeed, in the case of truly autonomous weapons, no actions by soldiers would be needed at all. Where autonomous weapons take the form of robots on the battlefield, they have another potential advantage as well: they may be better at limiting harm in warfare than are soldiers. As a matter of fact, many civilian casualties and many serious misapplications of the laws of war transpire when soldiers believe they are being threatened, often by nonexistent threats, and respond in a "trigger-happy" way. Robots, on the other hand, do not respond from fear, anger, or self-defense and may therefore be better at responding to actual rather than perceived threats. Thus, in addition to the benefit of offering protection to the soldiers who deploy autonomous weapons, the use of these weapons may equally reduce the harm caused to innocent civilians.

Yet the widespread use of these weapons poses multiple ethical problems as well. For one thing, as Kahn suggested above, many people believe that risk is inherently a part of just military conflict, and therefore that the pursuit of weapons that protect one side's soldiers from risk renders the conflict fundamentally unjust. This worry is exacerbated by the fact that these autonomous weapons seem almost certain to be deployed in asymmetrical conflicts, in which one side has a disproportionate military or technical advantage over the other(s). Given the advanced level of technology necessary to produce and deploy autonomous weaponry effectively, it has largely been pursued centrally by the strongest militaries in the world, which, given 21st century conflict dynamics, tend to be pitted against nonstate actors or groups with vastly inferior technology and resources.

Another issue, says Asaro, is the challenge of assigning responsibility for "actions" taken by robotic technologies. To some extent these technologies display features of autonomous decision making—the "capability to sense, decide and act without human intervention."[9] But, they are not fully autonomous entities. We may believe that truly independently acting robots will never emerge—we may feel that soldiers acting from behind computer screens will always be the final decision maker, and thus that the danger of atrocities being committed for which no one is responsible is remote. Even if truly autonomous robots are unlikely, however, their possibility forces us to consider how and whether they can be held responsible for their actions in any meaningful way. Moreover, even now, more and more of the information that soldiers use to make decisions in war is being collected and processed by robots. How should we assign responsibility for crimes committed when a soldier has read the information provided by the robot correctly but the information collected has been inadequately processed? Just war theory does not appear to give us the tools to answer this question.

As you read the articles in this section, consider some of the following questions:

• Should military service be mandatory? Should citizens be permitted to opt out of military service, and if so, for what reasons?

• Do you believe that it is a problem that most political leaders have no direct military experience when they are so frequently responsible for sending soldiers to war?

• If public opinion does not support a particular military conflict in which its government has pledged involvement, should the government withdraw its involvement? Why or why not?

• Is the presence of risk a necessary part of a just war? If so, how do we know which "risk-reducing" tactics may be legitimately pursued?

• Should the roles that mercenaries play in military conflict be limited? If so, how?

• Who or what should be responsible for protecting mercenaries in war? Who or what should be responsible for prosecuting them when they commit war crimes?

• Antiwar arguments often point to the large-scale destruction and indiscriminate killing that accompany war. Remember from Part 2 that these arguments weighed heavily in *jus ad bellum* concerns on restricting force. If less passionate, more precise "riskless" autonomous robots significantly reduce the level of random killing and violence in war, does it or should it impact *jus ad bellum* criteria or decisions?

• If we permit the use of robots or other autonomous weapons systems in war, how should we allocate responsibility when these robots make costly mistakes?

NOTES

1. William A. Galston, "A Sketch of Some Arguments for Conscription," *Philosophy and Public Policy Quarterly* 23, no. 3 (2003).

2. Cécile Fabre, "In Defence of Mercenarism," *British Journal of Political Science* 40, no. 3 (2010): 540.

3. Galston, "A Sketch of Some Arguments for Conscription," 5.

4. Fabre, "In Defence of Mercenarism," 556.

5. Ibid., 547.

6. Paul W. Kahn, "The Paradox of Riskless Warfare," *Philosophy and Public Policy Quarterly* 22, no. 3 (2002): 3.

7. Ibid.

8. Ibid., 5.

9. Peter M. Asaro, "How Just Could a Robot War Be?" in *Proceedings of the 2008 Conference on Current Issues in Computing and Philosophy*, ed. Adam Briggle, Katrinka Waelbers, and Philip A.E. Brey (Amsterdam: IOS Press, 2008), 51.

A Sketch of Some Arguments for Conscription

*by William A. Galston**

In the run up to the war against Iraq, an op-ed by congressional representative Charles Rangel (D-NY) rekindled a debate about the military draft; unexpectedly, because most scholars and an overwhelming majority of senior military leaders regarded this matter as settled. The Vietnam-era draft was regarded as arbitrary and unfair, and it was held responsible for dissension within the military as well as the wider society.

In the immediate wake of its disaster in Vietnam, the United States made an historic decision to end the draft and institute an All-Volunteer Force (AVF). On one level, it is hard to argue with success. The formula of high quality volunteers, combined with intensive training and investment in state of the art equipment has produced by far the most formidable military in history. Evidence suggests that the military's performance, especially since 1990, has bolstered public trust and confidence. For example, a recent Gallup Poll of public opinion trends since the end of the Vietnam war in 1975 indicates that while the percentage of Americans expressing confidence in religious leaders fell from 68 to 45, and from 40 to 29 for Congress, the percentage expressing confidence in the military rose from under 30 to 78. Among 18 to 29 year olds, the confidence level rose from 20 to 64 percent. (Remarkably, these figures reflect sentiment in late 2002, *before* the impressive victory in Iraq.)

These gains in institutional performance and public confidence are impressive and significant, but they hardly end the discussion. As every reader of Machiavelli (or the Second Amendment) knows, the organization of the military is embedded in larger issues of citizenship and civic life. It is along these dimensions that the decision in favor of the AVF has entailed significant costs. First, the AVF reflects, and has contributed to the development of, what I call *optional citizenship*, the belief that being a citizen involves rights without responsibilities and that we need do for our country only what we choose to do. Numerous studies have documented the rise of individual choice as the dominant norm of contemporary American culture, and many young people today believe being a good person—decent, kind, caring, and tolerant—is all it takes to be a good citizen. This duty-free understanding of citizenship is comfortable and undemanding; it is also profoundly mistaken.

Second, the AVF contributes to what I call *spectatorial citizenship*—the premise that good citizens need not be active but can watch others doing the public's work on their behalf. This spectatorial outlook makes it possible to decouple the question of whether we as a nation should do X from the question of whether I would do or participate in X. In a discussion with his students during the Gulf War, philosophy professor Cheyney Ryan was struck by "how many of them saw no connection between whether the country should go to war and whether they would . . . be willing to fight in it." A similar disconnect exists today. Young adults have been more supportive of the war against Iraq than any other age group (with more than 70 percent in favor), but recent surveys have found an equal percentage would refuse to participate themselves.

As a counterweight to this decoupling, Ryan proposes what he calls the Principle of Personal Integrity: You should only endorse those military actions of your country in which you yourself would be willing to give your life. The difficulty is that integrity does not seem to require this kind of personal involvement in other public issues. For example, a citizen of integrity can favor a costly reform of the welfare system without being required to serve as a welfare caseworker. Presumably it is enough if citizens are willing to contribute their fair share of the program's expenses. So one might ask: why is it not enough for citizens to contribute their fair share to maintain our expensive military establishment? Why should integrity require direct participation in the case of the military but not in other situations? This raises the question, to which I shall return, of when monetary contributions are morally acceptable substitutes for direct participation, and why.

Finally, the AVF has contributed to a widening gap between the orientation and experience of military personnel and that of the citizenry as a whole. To be sure, this is an empirically contested area, but some facts are not in dispute. First, since the inauguration of the AVF, the share of officers identifying themselves as Republican has nearly doubled, from 33 to 64 percent. (To be sure, officers were always technically volunteers, but as I can attest from personal experience, the threat of the draft significantly affected the willingness of young men to volunteer for officer candidacy.) Second, and more significantly, the share of elected officials with military experience has declined sharply. From 1900 through 1975, the percentage of members of Congress who were veterans was always higher than in the comparable age cohort of the general population. Since the mid-1990s, the congressional percentage has been lower, and it continues to fall.

Lack of military experience does not necessarily imply hostility to the military. Rather, it means ignorance of the nature of military service, as well as diminished capacity and confidence to assess critically the claims that military leaders make. (It is no accident that of all the post-war presidents, Dwight Eisenhower was clearly the most capable of saying no to the military's strategic assessments and requests for additional resources.)

For these reasons, among others, I believe that as part of a reconsideration of the relation between mandatory service and citizenship, we should review and revise the decision we made thirty years ago to institute an all-volunteer armed force. I hasten to add that I do not favor reinstituting anything like the Vietnam-era draft. It is hard to see how a reasonable person could prefer that fatally flawed system to today's arrangements. The question, rather, is whether feasible reforms could preserve the gains of the past thirty years while enlisting the military more effectively in the cause of civic renewal.

AN ABUSE OF STATE POWER?

My suggestion faces a threshold objection, however, to the effect that any significant shift back toward a mandatory system of military manpower would represent an abuse of state power. In a recent article, Judge Richard Posner drafts nineteenth-century political theorist John Stuart Mill as an ally in the cause of classical liberalism—a theory of limited government that provides an "unobtrusive framework for private activities." Limited government so conceived, Posner asserts, "has no ideology, no 'projects,' but is really just an association for mutual protection." Posner celebrates the recent emergence of what he calls the "Millian center"—a form of politics that (unlike the left) embraces economic liberty and (unlike the right) endorses personal liberty, and he deplores modern communitarianism's critique of untrammeled personal liberty in the name of the common good. High on Posner's bill of particulars is the recommendation of some (not all) communitarians to reinstitute a draft.

Mill misapplied. Before engaging Posner's own argument, I should note that his attempt to appropriate Mill's *On Liberty* to support an anti-conscription stance is deeply misguided. To clinch this point, I need only cite a few of the opening sentences from Chapter Four, entitled "Of the Limits to the Authority of Society Over the Individual":

> [E]veryone who receives the protection of society owes a return for the benefit, and the fact of living in society renders it indispensable that each should be bound to observe a certain line of conduct toward the rest. This conduct consists, first, in not injuring the interests of one another, or rather certain interests which, either by express legal provision

or by tacit understanding, ought to be considered as rights; *and secondly, in each person's bearing his share (to be fixed on some equitable principle) or the labors and sacrifices incurred for defending the society or its members from injury and molestation. These conditions society is justified in enforcing at all costs to those who endeavor to withhold fulfillment.*

Posner's view of Mill would make sense only if Mill had never written the words I have italicized.

The fair share argument. It is not difficult to recast Mill's position in the vocabulary of contemporary liberal political thought. Begin with a conception of society as a system of cooperation for mutual advantage. Society is legitimate when the criterion of mutual advantage is broadly satisfied (versus, say, a situation in which the government or some group systematically coerces some for the sake of others). When society meets the standard of broad legitimacy, each citizen has a duty to do his or her fair share to sustain the social arrangements from which all benefit, and society is justified in using its coercive power when necessary to ensure the performance of this duty. That legitimate society coercion may include mandatory military service in the nation's defense.

A counterargument urged by the late political philosopher Robert Nozick that that we typically do not consent to the social benefits we receive and that the involuntary receipt of benefits does not trigger a duty to contribute. Mill anticipated, and rejected, that thesis, insisting that the duty to contribute does not rests on a social contract or voluntarist account of social membership. Besides, the argument Socrates imputes to the Laws in the *Crito* is a compelling one: if a society is not a prison, if as an adult you remain when you have the choice to leave, then you have in fact accepted the benefits, along with whatever burdens the principle of social reciprocity may impose.

Economist Robert Litan has recently suggested that citizens should be "required to give something to their country in exchange for the full range of rights to which citizenship entitles them." Responding in a quasi-libertarian vein, public policy expert Bruce Chapman charges that this proposal has "no moral justification." Linking rights to concrete responsibilities is "contrary to the purposes for which [the United States] was founded and has endured." This simply is not true. For example, the right to receive GI Bill benefits is linked to the fulfillment of military duties. Even the right to vote (and what could be more central to citizenship than that?) rests on law-abidingness; many states disenfranchise convicted felons for extended periods. As Litan points out, this linkage is hardly tyrannical moralism. Rather, it reflects the bedrock reality that "the rights we enjoy are not free" and that it takes real work—contributions from citizens—to sustain constitutional institutions.

Conscription as slavery. Now on to the main event. Posner contends that "Conscription could be described as a form of slavery, in the sense that a conscript is a person deprived of the ownership of his own labor." If slavery is immoral, so is the draft. In a similar vein, Nozick once contended that "taxation of earnings from labor is on a par with forced labor." (If Nozick were right, then the AVF that Posner supports, funded as it is with tax dollars, could also be described as on a par with forced labor.)

Both Posner's and Nozick's arguments prove too much. If each individual's ownership of his or her own labor is seen as absolute, then society as such becomes impossible, because no political community can operate without resources, which must ultimately come from *someone*. Public choice theory predicts, and all of human history proves, that no polity of any size can subsist through voluntary contributions alone; the inevitable free riders must be compelled by law, backed by force, to ante up.

Posner might object, reasonably enough, that this argument illustrates the difference between taxation and conscription: while political community is inconceivable without taxation, it is demonstrably sustainable without conscription. It is one thing to restrict self-ownership of labor out of necessity, but a very different matter to restrict it out of choice. The problem is that this argument proves too little. Posner concedes that "there are circumstances in which military service is an obligation of citizenship." But there are no circumstances in which slavery is an obligation of citizenship. Moreover, it is not morally impermissible to volunteer for military service. But it is impermissible, and rightly forbidden, to voluntarily place oneself in slavery. Therefore, slavery and military service differ in kind, not degree. And if there are circumstances in which military service is an obligation of citizenship, then the state justified in enforcing that obligation through conscription, which is not impermissible forced labor, let alone a form of slavery. QED. For the purposes of this article, then, I will suppose that a legitimate government would not be exceeding its rightful authority if it chose to move toward a more mandatory system of military recruitment.

Celebrating the cash nexus: four thought experiments. But this is not the end of the argument, because Posner has another arrow in his quiver. He rejects the claim, advanced by Michael Sandel and other communitarians, that substituting market for non-market services represents a degrading "commodification" of social and civic life. Indeed, Posner celebrates what communitarians deplore. "Commodification promotes prosperity," he informs us, "and prosperity alleviates social ills." Moreover, commodification enables individuals to transform burdensome obligations into bearable cash payments: middle-aged couples can purchase both care for their children and assisted living for their parents, and so forth.

Posner charges that communitarian theory is incapable of drawing a line between matters that rightly belong within the scope of the market and those that do not. Posner's celebration of the cash nexus is exposed to precisely the same objection. Rather than scoring rhetorical points, I will offer a series of examples designed to help delimit the proper sphere of non-market relations.

Paying people to obey the law. Suppose we offered individuals a "compliance bonus"—a cash payment at the end of each year completed without being convicted of a felony or significant misdemeanor. It is not hard to imagine situations in which the benefits of this policy (measured in reduced enforcement costs) would outweigh the outlays for bonuses. What (if anything) is wrong with this?

My answer: at least two things. First, it alters for the worse the expressive meaning of law. In a legitimate order, criminal law represents an authoritative declaration of the behavior the members of society expect of one another. The authoritativeness of the law is supposed to be a sufficient condition for obeying it, and internalizing the sense of law as authoritative is supposed to be a sufficient motive for obedience. To offer compliance payments is to contradict the moral and motivation sufficiency of the law.

Second, payment for compliance constitutes a moral version of Gresham's law: lower motives will tend to drive out higher, and the more comfortable to drive out the more demanding. When those who are inclined to obey the law for its own sake see others receiving compensation, they are likely to question the reasonableness of their conduct and to begin thinking of themselves as suckers. Most would end up accepting payment and coming to resemble more closely those who began by doing so.

Paying citizens for jury duty. Consider the analogy (or disanalogy) between national defense and domestic law enforcement. The latter is divided into two subcategories: voluntary service (there is no draft for police officers) and mandatory service (e.g., jury duty). Our current system of military manpower is all "police" and no "jury." If we conducted domestic law enforcement on our current military model we'd have what might be called "The All-Volunteer Jury," in which we'd pay enough to ensure a steady flow of the jurors the law enforcement system requires to function.

There are two compelling reasons not to move in this direction. First, citizens who self-select for jury duty are unlikely to be representative of the population as a whole. Individuals who incur high opportunity costs (those who are gainfully employed, for example) would tend not to show up. The same considerations that militate against forced exclusion of racial and ethnic groups from jury pools should weigh equally against voluntary self-exclusion based upon income or employment status. (We should ask ourselves why these considerations do not apply to the composition of the military.)

Second, it is important for all citizens to understand that citizenship is an *office*, not just a *status*. As an office, citizenship comprises matters of both rights and duties—indeed, some matters that are both. Service on juries is simultaneously a right, in the sense that that there is a strong presumption against exclusion, and a duty, in the sense that there is a strong presumption against evasion. To move jury duty into the category of voluntary, compensated acts would be to remove one of the last reminders that citizenship is more than a legal status.

Paying foreigners to do our fighting for us. Consider: we might do as well or better to hire foreigners (the All-Mercenary Armed Forces) as kings and princes did regularly during the eighteenth century. The cost might well be lower, and the military performance just as high. Besides, if we hire foreigners to pick our grapes, why not hire them to do our fighting?

There is of course a practical problem, discussed by Machiavelli among others: a pure cash nexus suggests the mercenaries' openness to opportunistic side-switching in response to a better offer, as happened in Afghanistan. In addition, what Abraham Lincoln called the "last full measure of devotion" would be less likely to be forthcoming in the handful of extreme situations in which it is required.

Beyond these practical considerations lies a moral intuition: even if a mercenary army were reliable and effective, it would be wrong, even shameful, to use our wealth to get non-citizens to do our fighting for us. This is something we ought to do for ourselves, as a self-respecting people. I want to suggest that a similar moral principle does some real work in the purely domestic sphere, among citizens.

Paying other citizens to do our fighting for us. Consider military recruitment during the Civil War. In April 1861 President Lincoln called for, and quickly received, 75,000 volunteers. But the expectation of a quick and easy Union victory was soon dashed, and the first conscription act was passed in March, 1863. The act contained two opt-out provisions: an individual facing conscription could pay a fee of $300 to avoid a specific draft notice; and an individual could avoid service for the entire war by paying a substitute to volunteer for three years.

This law created a complex pattern of individual incentives and unanticipated social outcomes, such as anti-conscription riots among urban workers. Setting these aside, was there anything wrong in principle with these opt-out provisions? I think so. In the first place, there was an obvious distributional unfairness: the well off could afford to avoid military service, while the poor and working class could not. Second, even if income and wealth had been more nearly equal, there would have been something wrong in principle with the idea that dollars could purchase exemption from an important civic duty.

THE LEGACY OF THE AVF: ECONOMIC AND SOCIAL STRATIFICATION

We can now ask: What is the difference between the use of personal resources to opt *out* of military service and the impact of personal resources on the decision to opt *in*? My answer: as both a practical and a moral matter, less than the defenders of the current system would like to believe. To begin with, the decision to implement an AVF has had a profound effect on the educational and class composition of the U.S. military. During World War Two and the Korean War—indeed, through the early 1960s—roughly equal percentages of high school and college graduates saw military service, and about one third of college graduates were in the enlisted (that is, non-officer) ranks. Today, enlisted men and women are rarely college graduates, and elite colleges other than the service academies are far less likely to produce military personnel of any rank, officer or enlisted. As a lengthy *New York Times* feature story recently put it, today's military "mirrors a working-class America." Of the first twenty-eight soldiers to die in Iraq, only one came from a family that could be described as well off.

Many have argued that this income skew is a virtue, not a vice, because the military extends good career opportunities to young men and women whose prospects are otherwise limited. There is something to this argument, of course. But the current system purchases social mobility at the expense of social integration. Today's privileged young people tend to grow up hermetically sealed from the rest of society. Episodic volunteering in soup kitchens does not really break the seal. Military service is one of the few experiences that can.

In an evocative letter to his sons, Brookings Institution scholar Stephen Hess reflects on his experiences as a draftee and defends military service as a vital socializing experience for children from fortunate families. His argument is instructive: "Being forced to be the lowest rank . . . , serving for long enough that you can't clearly see 'the light at the end of the tunnel,' is as close as you will ever come to being a member of society's underclass. To put it bluntly, you will feel in your gut what it means to be at the bottom of the heap. . . . Why should you want to be deprived of your individuality? You shouldn't, of course. But many people are, and you should want to know how this feels, especially if you someday have some responsibility over the lives of other people." It is a matter, not just of compassion, but of respect: "The middle class draftee learns to appreciate a lot of talents (and the people who have them) that are not part of the lives you have known, and, after military duty, will know again for the rest of your lives. This will come from being thrown together with—and having to depend on—people who are very different from you and your friends."

A modern democracy, in short, combines a high level of legal equality with an equally high level of economic and social stratification. It far from inevitable, or even natural, that democratic leaders who are drawn disproportionately from the upper ranks of society will adequately understand the experiences or respect the contributions of those from the lower. Integrative experiences are needed to bring this about. In a society in which economic class largely determines residence and education and in which the fortunate will not willingly associate with the rest, only non-voluntary institutions cutting across class lines can hope to provide such experiences. If some kind of sustained mandatory service does not fill this bill, it is hard to see what will.

THE IMPORTANCE OF UNIVERSAL SERVICE

The inference I draw from this analysis is far from original: to the extent that circumstances permit, we should move toward a system of universal eighteen-month service for all high school graduates (and in the case of dropouts, all eighteen year olds) who are capable of performing it. Within the limits imposed by whatever ceiling is imposed on military manpower, those subject to this system would be able to choose between military and full-time civilian service. (If all military slots are filled, then some form of civilian service would be the only option.) The cost of fully implementing this proposal (a minimum of $60 billion per year) would certainly slow the pace of implementation and might well impose a permanent ceiling on the extent of implementation. The best response to these constraints would be a lottery to which all are exposed and from which none except those unfit to serve can escape.

It might be argued that a program of this sort would have little if any effect on the armed forces, which would continue to draw their manpower from the current stream of volunteers. That may be the case if the military does not expand during the next decade. But there are reasons to believe that it will. It is fast becoming evident that that the post-war occupation of Iraq will take more troops and last longer than administration officials had predicted. As an interim response, the military has already moved away from the all-volunteer principle. The US Marine Corps has frozen enlistments for all of the 175,000 personnel currently on active duty. Marines whose period of voluntary enlistment has expired are required to remain in the service, on active duty, until the free expires. Other services have imposed similar if more limited freezes. It is likely, moreover, that the prospect of being sent to Iraq as part of a vulnerable long-term occupation force will depress voluntary enlistments, especially in the Army and Marines.

There is evidence suggesting that movement toward a less purely voluntary system of military and civilian service could pass the test of democratic legitimacy. For example, a 2002 survey sponsored by the Center for Information and Research on Civic Learning and Engagement (CIRCLE) found 60 percent-plus support for such a move across lines of gender, race and ethnicity, partisan affiliation, and ideology. Still, it is plausible that intense opposition on the part of young adults and their parents could stymie such a change. Assuming that this is the case, there are some feasible interim steps that could yield civic rewards. Let me mention just two.

First, we could follow the advice of former secretary of the navy John Lehman and eliminate the current bias of military recruiters in favor of career personnel and against those willing to serve for shorter periods. As Lehman puts it, we should "actively seek to attract the most talented from all backgrounds with service options that allow them to serve their country . . . without having to commit to six to ten years' active duty." He makes a strong case that this change would markedly increase the number of young men and women from elite colleges and universities who would be willing to undergo military service.

Second, the Congress could pass legislation sponsored by senators John McCain (R-AZ) and Evan Bayh (D-IN) that would dramatically expand AmeriCorps (the Clinton-era national and community service program) from its current level of 50,000 to 250,000 full-time volunteers each year. Survey evidence shows overwhelming (80 percent-plus) support for the basic tenet of this program, that young people should have the opportunity to serve full-time for a year or two and earn significant post-service benefits that can be used for higher education and advanced technical training. As Sen. McCain rightly puts it, "one of the curious truths of our era is that while opportunities to serve ourselves have exploded . . . [,] opportunities to spend some time serving our country have dwindled." In this context, the ongoing resistance to AmeriCorps in some quarters of Congress verges on incomprehensible.

It would be wrong to oversell the civic benefits that might accrue from the revisions to the AVF that I propose, let alone the more modest steps I have just sketched. Still, some of our nation's best social scientists see a link between World War Two-era military service and that generation's subsequent dedication to our nation's civic life. If reconsidering a decision about military manpower made three decades ago could yield even a fraction of this civic improvement, it would be well worth the effort.

SOURCES

The Gallup Poll referred to is cited by Robin Toner, in "Trust in the Military Heightens Among Baby Boomers' Children," *New York Times* (May 27, 2003); Richard Posner, "An Army of the Willing," *New Republic* (May 9, 2003); John Stuart Mill, *On Liberty* (Viking, 1982); Robert Litan's arguments for compulsory service occur in, among other sources, "September 11, 2001: The Case for Universal Service," *Brookings Review* (Fall 2002), and Bruce Chapman's response, "A Bad Idea Whose Time Is Past: The Case Against Universal Service," occurs in the same issue. David M. Halbfinger and Steven A. Holmes, "Military Mirrors Working Class America," *New York Times* (March 30, 2003); Stephen Hess, "Military Service and the Middle Class: A Letter to My Sons," in *United We Serve: National Service and the Future of Citizenship*, edited by E.J. Dionne, Jr., Kayla Meltzer Drogosz, Robert E. Litan (Brookings, 2003); John Lehman's editorial, "Military Recruiting and Common Sense" has been reprinted variously; for instance, see: www.nwaonline.net/pdfarchive/2003/january/ 28/1-28-03%20A6.pdf; Senator John McCain, "Putting the 'National' in National Service," also has been variously reprinted; see for instance http://www.washingtonmonthly. com/features/2001/0110.mccain.html (the online edition of the *Washington Monthly*, October 2001).

*William A. Galston is Saul I. Stern Professor of Civic Engagement; director, Institute for Philosophy and Public Policy; and director, Center for Information and Research on Civic Learning and Engagement (CIRCLE), School of Public Affairs, University of Maryland.

Galston, William A. "A Sketch of Some Arguments for Conscription." *Philosophy & Public Policy Quarterly*. Vol. 23:3 (Summer 2003): 2–7.

Used by permission.

In Defence of Mercenarism

*by Cécile Fabre**

[...]

FIVE OBJECTIONS TO MERCENARISM

To recapitulate, I have defended the right to enter a mercenary contract by appealing to the importance of enabling just defensive killings. I have also argued that uniformed soldiers and mercenaries should be treated on a par—and that what matters, for deciding whether a combatant is lawful or unlawful, is not the nature (political or economic) of the organization employing him, but rather whether he abides by the principles of the Just War. In this section, I examine and reject five objections to mercenarism: the *motivational objection*; the *objectification objection*; the *profiteering objection*; the *loss of control objection*; and the *neutrality objection*.

The Motivational Objection

The claim that mercenaries are acting wrongly because they fight for financial gain, rather than out of loyalty to their state and/or commitment to a just cause, has a very long pedigree in the intellectual and legal history of warfare. It draws on one of the traditional conditions of the just war, namely, that a war is just only if belligerents wage war with the right intentions (defined as wanting to redress the wrong which justifies the war), and applies the requirement to the individuals who fight in the war. Incidentally, the condition of right intentions is ambiguous, requiring as it does either that belligerents and soldiers act from the right motives, or that they wage, and kill in, a war towards just ends. As applied to mercenaries, the condition is usually interpreted as pertaining to agents' motives; accordingly, it is this particular interpretation that I shall target here.[19]

As has been often noted, any argument for, or against, a particular act that appeals to the agent's motivations is vulnerable to two criticisms: (1) that discerning what those motivations are is not as easy as it might seem; (2) that motives are irrelevant to the permissibility of actions. For what it is worth, I do not find either claim persuasive. But even if the motivational objection's fundamental premises are correct (that motives are discernible and do matter), it is nevertheless vulnerable to the following criticisms. For a start, there is no reason to suppose that a member of the regular armed forces *by definition* is not motivated mostly by financial gain and the social benefits that go with it, or is mainly motivated by loyalty to her state and/or to a just cause. In fact, joining the army is, for many youngsters in many countries, a way out of poverty. It is also, for many of them, a way to channel aggressive tendencies, or to cater for a psychological need for a highly structured and hierarchically-based way of life. By contrast, there is no reason to suppose that a mercenary is, *by definition*, motivated mostly by the lure of financial gain. On the contrary, evidence suggests that a number of private soldiers take up jobs with PMCs after being made redundant by the army or after retirement from combat duties, and see themselves as continuing to act in the defence of their country's interests abroad.[20]

The foregoing points are definitional. So let us suppose, for the sake of argument, that a mercenary, unlike a regular soldier, just *is* someone who is essentially motivated by money. The crucial question, then, is whether those definitional points have any bearing on the right to enter a mercenary contract. Two claims are usually made to the effect that they do. First, it is said that soldiers have the right to kill only if they believe, at least in large part, that the war is just. In so far as mercenaries by definition do not have those motives, mercenarism is morally dubious—whether seen from the standpoint of mercenaries themselves, or of those who procure or hire them.

However, even if motives are decisive for the permissibility of actions, and thus even if mercenaries are guilty of wrongdoing, it does not follow that they lack a claim, or a power, to contract with belligerents. This is because, definitionally speaking, there can be such a thing as a claim, or a power, to act wrongly. Accordingly, the motivational objection can successfully reject the conferral on mercenaries and PMCs of the relevant claim and power only if it can provide an independent justification for the view that this particular wrongdoing ought not to be protected by the law.[21]

Such a justification can only be that mercenaries' and PMCs' interest in, respectively, offering, or procuring, lethal services is not important enough to be protected by a claim or power. However, unless one can show that mercenarism so defined harms more fundamental interests of third parties (a point to which I shall return below), it seems that mercenaries' and PMCs' interests are, in fact, important enough to warrant such protection. Individuals do all sorts of things out of mostly financial motivations. They often choose a particular line of work, such as banking or consulting, rather than others, such as academia, largely because of the money. They often decide to become doctors rather than nurses for similar reasons. Granting that their interest in making such choices, however condemnable their motivation, is important enough to be protected by a claim (against non-interference) and a power (to enter the relevant employment contracts), it is hard to see how one could deny similar protection to mercenaries. *Mutatis mutandis*, the point applies to executives and owners of PMCs, who procure, rather than directly offer, lethal services.

I noted above that the harms accruing to third parties as a result of mercenarism count as a good reason against conferring on mercenaries, PMCs and states the right to contract with one another. Appositely, the second normative worry about mercenarism is that mercenaries, precisely because they are fighting for money, are much more likely to have unjust aims and to commit offences against the laws of war than members of regular armed forces, who are motivated by the belief that their cause is just.[22] However, that claim is less persuasive than may appear at first sight. In the light of the long list of exactions committed against civilian populations by regular forces, precisely on the grounds that their cause was just, the suggestion that armed forces are more likely to abide by the laws of war than mercenaries seems somewhat optimistic. One need only think of the Wehrmacht and the Red Army during the Second World War, the French Army in Algeria during the war of independence (1954–62), the US Army in Japan in the closing months of the Second World War (Hiroshima and Nagasaki come to mind here) and the British Air Force in Germany during that war. It is equally unclear, again judging on the basis of recent interstate wars, whether regular armies are more likely than mercenaries to pursue just aims when making strategic decisions as to whom to target, which kind of infrastructures to destroy, etc.

In any event, those points about unjust aims and exactions are vulnerable to the charge that one may act out of wrong motives but nevertheless have just aims, or conduct oneself justly. More precisely, it is not inherent in the act of offering one's killing services in exchange for money that it should lead the agent to commit atrocities against civilians and to pursue unjust aims. Finally, it is worth noting that the freelance soldier, in so far as he has greater control over the conditions under which he will be deployed, is in a better position than the corporate fighter *or the professional soldier* to ensure that he will not be made to fight for unjust ends or in unjust ways. On that count, making oneself available for hire on a freelance basis might be less morally risky than joining the army and running the risk of having to obey an unjust order on pain of being dishonourably discharged.

Although the motivational objection's main target is mercenaries and PMCs (for obvious reasons), it might nevertheless be thought to apply to states as well, as follows: (a) to hire mercenaries to fight one's war is to countenance a wrong-doing, and (b) to countenance a wrongdoing is itself a moral wrongdoing of a kind that should not be protected by either a claim or a power. Assuming the motivational objection that mercenarism is wrong, I will not take issue with (a). Claim (b), however, is too strong—certainly in those cases where the state that hires mercenaries simply could not conduct its (just) war otherwise, and particularly when its sovereignty and/or territorial integrity are at stake. Perhaps, as Coady suggests in his interesting discussion of mercenarism, we have here a case of dirty hands, where a leader has to choose between the wrongdoing of hiring mercenaries and that of allowing the defeat of one's community by an unjust at-tacker.[23] Be that as it may, even if hiring mercenaries under those circumstances is morally wrong (albeit the lesser of two wrongdoings), this would not in itself count as a reason to deny the state the claim and the power so to act. Here again, absent countervailing arguments, the belligerent's interest in fighting a just war surely is important enough to be protected by a right to enter merce-nary contracts. Consider the following analogy. Even if it is wrong (*arguendo*) for someone to enter the medical profession mostly out of financial motives, and even if it is wrong for a patient to hire him, surely the patient's interest in surviving is important enough to grant him a right to do so. The alternative would be to subject him to criminal sanctions, or to deny him the protection of the law if the doctor breaches the contract (for example, by not providing the medical treatment which the patient paid for). Likewise, the alternative, for the belligerent state, would be to be denied the protection of its own laws if the mercenaries or PMCs it has hired default on their contracts, as well as protec-tion from interference, on the part of other states, with its attempt to secure its own survival. And yet, just as the patient's interest in remaining alive surely deserves the twin protection of a claim and a power, so does the belligerent's interest in its own survival.

The Objectification Objection

The motivational objection, which is the most familiar of those deployed against mercenarism, focuses on mercenaries rather than their employers. By contrast, the objectification objection targets the latter: according to the ob-jection, hiring mercenaries is morally wrong in so far as it consists in treating individuals as little more than both killing machines and cannon fodder. As Kant puts it, 'the hiring of men to kill or to be killed seems to mean using them as mere machines and instruments in the hands of someone else (the state), which cannot easily be reconciled with the rights of man in one's own person.'[24] Similar arguments were raised in Britain at the time of the American War of Independence, when Britain had to decide whether or not to recruit German mercenaries to its cause.[25] Interestingly, the objection is sometimes made against PMCs—with the further twist that those companies, motivated as they are by the search for greater profits, are prone similarly to disregard their employees' welfare. It has thus been alleged by the families of the four Blackwater employees, who were ambushed, killed and dismembered in Fallujah on 31 March 2004, that their employers had assigned them to a highly dangerous mission with hardly any protection.[26]

Although the objectification objection is not always meant to condemn mercenarism while endorsing standing armies, it is nevertheless tempting to suppose that states are less likely to treat their own uniformed soldiers as killing machines and cannon fodder—particularly democratic states whose rulers are accountable to citizens, and particularly in an age where body bags bring home the true horrors of wars fought in far-flung corners of the world. The point, however, should not be overstated, for two reasons. First, nondemocratic regimes are not noted for their respect for the lives of their soldiers: the objection thus applies to those regimes *as well as* to the use by the state of private armies, and there is nothing *distinctively wrong*, with respect to the objectification of soldiers, about the latter.

Secondly, the objectification objection works best against practices that are concomitant to the hiring of private armies—such as the practice of not taking due care with mercenaries' lives. But it does not weaken the claim that states have the right to turn to private soldiers or, for that matter, the claim that PMCs have the right to procure private armies. By analogy, the claim that men who visit prostitutes are likely to treat them in abusive ways does not entail that buying sexual services *per se* ought to be criminalized; nor does it entail that transactions with prostitutes ought to be regarded as null and void.

In fact, all that the objectification objection does (and that is in fact considerable, if off target) is support the view that states have a duty of care to the private soldiers whom they hire—just as they have a duty of care to their armed forces. More specifically, they have a duty to deploy them in accordance with the *jus in bello* requirements of proportionality (whereby the harms done by a particular tactical decision must not exceed the good it brings about) and necessity (whereby states should risk soldiers'—and civilians'—lives if and only if it would serve their (just) ends.) States which fail in that duty are morally guilty of wrongdoing, lack the power to contract with private soldiers if they fail to set out the ways in which they will discharge their duty of care to the latter, and are morally liable for their negligence. States that abide by the aforementioned requirements cannot be charged with moral wrongdoing simply for recruiting private soldiers rather than, or alongside, regular forces. Similar considerations apply to PMCs: those that treat their employees as little more than profit-making and fungible entities lack the right so to employ them, and, thereby, the right to contract with states for their use. However, those that fulfil their duty of care to their employees are left untouched by the objectification objection.

The Profiteering Objection

A third objection to mercenarism invokes the fact that individual mercenaries and PMCs live off the suffering of others. More recently, PMCs have been criticized for profiteering from the devastation brought about by war: they make a profit by sending out private armies that will cause considerable damage and destruction; they then make further profits by offering their protection services to the multinational corporations subsequently entrusted by belligerents with the task of reconstructing the country. Put bluntly, they get paid vast amounts of money for assisting in the reconstruction of countries which they were paid similarly vast amounts of money to help destroy. And even if they do not contribute to causing such destruction in the first instance, they nevertheless profit from the injustices that war victims suffer.

Here again, the objection may well have a point in so far as it targets current practices by states and PMCs, particularly in Iraq.[27] Its point is limited, however, for although it is true that PMCs do benefit from war and its attendant unjust practices, so do weapons manufacturers and firms that supply armies (whether regular or private) with food and protective clothing. In fact, a vast range of private firms benefit from other people's suffering, such as companies that manufacture medical equipment, private medical practices, and firms that provide the means (such as helicopters, life-saving equipment, engineering skills) for humanitarian relief, etc. Indeed, many professions would not exist *but* for the fact that injustices have been committed—foremost amongst which is the legal profession. Yet, to claim that those private firms, therefore, lack the right to contract with states for those goods and services seems rather extreme. By the same token, the fact that PMCs benefit from the suffering and destruction wrought by war cannot alone render their activities morally impermissible. In order to succeed, the objection would have to show that there is something *constitutively* wrong about PMCs' profiteering, which being a lawyer or a manufacturer of medical equipment lacks. Yet, it is not clear how it could establish that. The most obvious move that the objection could make, at this juncture, would be to insist that there is something inherently wrong about making a profit from killing, or helping to kill, others. By contrast (it might say), a factory that manufactures surgical instruments helps to save people's lives without thereby contributing to the deaths of others as a means to do so; likewise, there is nothing inherently unjust in helping people seek rightful redress through the courts. However, that putative move would fail. For surely, a firm that knowingly sells surgical instruments to doctors who practise surgical experimentation on non-consenting patients lacks the right to do so; likewise, a corrupt lawyer who helps his mobster clients defraud the state out of millions of pounds in owed taxes is not acting within his rights. In just the same way, a PMC lacks the right to hire private soldiers and offer their services to contracting states if the war in which it fights is unjust. However, if the war is just, so that the deaths thus caused are not wrongful deaths, there is no reason for concluding on the aforementioned grounds that the medical factories and lawyers have the right to operate while PMCs do not.

The Loss-of-Control Objection

The fourth objection to mercenarism applies neither to individual mercenaries nor to PMCs but, rather, to states. It avers that by contracting with either kind of agents, but especially PMCs, states lose exclusive control over the decision to use violence, as well as over the agents by which it is used. And yet, the objection claims, there are good reasons for granting states that kind of control. For states, in so far as they represent as well as articulate their members' interests, are more likely to resort to, and control, violence for the sake of the common good, rather than in defence of private interests. But when a state entrusts a PMC with the task of fighting its wars or assisting in the prosecution thereof, it is vulnerable to be unduly influenced by the corporation over the conduct of its foreign policy. It is also unable effectively to control the behaviour of the corporation's employees, since the latter are accountable to the corporation, and not to the state itself: by contrast, a regular soldier is liable to being court martialled if, for example, he commits exactions against enemy civilians. Finally, a state that routinely appeals to PMCs as a means to resolve military conflicts is in danger of becoming over-reliant on such firms at the expense of its own forces, which in turn might undermine its ability to promote its own interests when the latter conflict with PMCs' profit-driven goals. In other words, by hiring private armies, the state fails to do that which it is mandated to do, that is to ensure that violence is used abroad only for the sake of the common good, and in compliance with the laws of war. In so doing, it is guilty of a wrongdoing—and one of such magnitude that its interest in so acting can be protected neither by a power to contract with PMCs nor by a claim to do so.[28]

The objection draws considerable strength from the ways in which, in practice, nations such as the United States are alleged to have given private military corporations such as Blackwater some input into American foreign policy. Likewise, Paul Bremer's aforementioned decision to grant Blackwater employees immunity from prosecution for acts perpetrated in Iraq has done little to assuage the worries of opponents to mercenarism. However, proponents of the objection should beware the risk of overstating their case: any potential belligerent, including states, must seek advice from military and security experts when deciding whether or not to resort to war—if only because those experts, whether members of the army or civilians, have a better claim to know whether a particular military course of action has a reasonable chance of success. Including the actors who are not elected leaders into the design of security policy is, therefore, essential. What the objection must show, thus, is that *private* military contractors acquire undue influence over decisions that are the state's alone to take. The difficulty, of course, is that whether they do so is entirely contingent on the facts of the cases. As a result, the objection is vulnerable to the counter-claim that proper regulation might succeed in mitigating the problems arising from belligerents' loss of control over the transnational use of force. Such regulatory measures might include, *inter alia*, clear rules for what constitutes an acceptable mercenary activity, licensing regimes similar to those that already regulate the arms trade, providing adequately for the prosecution and sanction of actors who fail to comply with those measures, as well as publicly funding electoral campaigns so as to deprive corporations of the means of leverage over presidential candidates. Moreover, account should be taken of the fact that PMCs, like all other major corporations, are global in scope, which in turn requires a transnational regulatory framework. Under those conditions, it is hard to see on what grounds one can deny states a right to hire a private army.[29]

Moreover, the objection supposes that states have compliant and effective armed forces at their disposal. Quite often, however, they do not, and are at the mercy either of their own soldiers or of armed minority rebel groups that operate within their borders, more often than not with the assistance or complicity of other states. In such cases, the state's decision to hire a private army will help it strengthen its control over the use of violence, rather than undermine it. Thus, it is often argued that Sierra Leone, which was blighted by civil war in the 1990s, was able to end the war only once they had brought Executive Outcomes in. Likewise, it is also argued that Croatia, when under attack by Serbia, was able to obtain some military successes in 1995 after entrusting Military Professional Resources Inc. with the task of training and restructuring its troops. Under those conditions, and to reiterate a point made earlier against the motivational objection, when a state can defend itself only with the help of private soldiers, denying it, and its people, the right to hire a private army is tantamount to denying it the right to avail itself of the resources it needs for collective self-defence. To insist on doing so *simply* on the basis of the status of such resources is a piece of fetishism.[30]

[...]

Acknowledgments

[...] An earlier version of this article was presented in 2008 in Stirling at the Philosophy Department Seminar, at the UK IVR Conference in Edinburgh and at the Annual Conference for the Society for Applied Philosophy. I am grateful to participants at those events for very useful discussions, and to James Pattison, Guy Sela, Albert Weale and two anonymous *Journal* referees for written comments.

NOTES

[...]

19. For the distinction, in this context, between right motives and just aims (or, as he calls them, intentions), see Pattison, 'Just War Theory and the Privatization of Military Force'. For a comprehensive review of the motivational objection to mercenarism, see Percy, *The History of a Norm in International Relations*, esp. chap. 5. See also F. H. Russell, *The Just War in the Middle Ages* (Cambridge: Cambridge University Press, 1975), chap. 6. Two classical thinkers who condemn mercenaries on motivational grounds are Machiavelli in *The Prince* (ed. by G. Bull) (Harmondsworth, Midx.: Penguin, 1981), chap. XII, esp. pp. 77–8, and Grotius in *The Rights of War and Peace* (ed. by R. Tuck) (Indianapolis, Ind.: Liberty Fund, 2005), Bk II, chap. XXV, §ix, p. 1164. For a powerful rebuttal of the motivational objection along the lines deployed in this paragraph and the next two, see T. Lynch and A. J. Walsh, 'The Good Mercenary?', *Journal of Political Philosophy*, 8 (2000), 133–53.

20. See Scahill, *Blackwater*, esp. chap. 5. Suppose that uniformed soldiers in a given country decide to leave the army *en masse*, unless their pay is significantly raised. Would it be morally wrong of them to do so? I owe this point to Alan Hamlin.

21. I deploy a structurally similar argument regarding organ sales, prostitution and surrogate motherhood in my *Whose Body is it Anyway?* (Oxford: Oxford University Press, 2006, chaps 6–8). To illustrate here: suppose that White becomes a mercenary because he really enjoys killing. If motives are decisive to the permissibility of actions, White is acting wrongly. But that is not enough to show that White ought not to have the right to work as a mercenary— any more than the fact that someone becomes a surgeon because he gets aroused by cutting into the flesh of anaesthetized patients is enough to warrant legally preventing him from being

a surgeon. One would have to show that his perverse motives lead him to provide sub-standard medical care to his patients.

22. In other words, to advert to the aforementioned distinction between two interpretations of the requirement of just intentions, the worry is that, precisely because they have the wrong motives, mercenaries are more likely to act in pursuit of wrongful aims. See Pattison, 'Just War Theory and the Privatization of Military Force', p. 147 and pp. 150–2. To return to the example given in fn. 21, *if* it turned out that White's appetite for killing made him prone to killing indiscriminately, then that would be sufficient warrant for preventing him (forcibly) from doing so. Likewise, if a surgeon's appetite for cutting into sleeping flesh were to lead him to operate without a medical reason, that would be sufficient warrant to withdraw his licence (and put him into jail for inflicting grievous bodily harm on his patients).

23. Coady, *Morality and Political Violence*, pp. 218–19.

24. I. Kant, 'Perpetual Peace', in H. Reiss, ed., *Kant—Political Writings*, 2nd edn (Cambridge: Cambridge University Press, 1991), p. 95. (See also Wilfred Burchett and Derek Roebuck, *The Whores of War* (Harmondsworth: Penguin, 1977), for a similar objection in the context of the use of mercenaries in Africa in the 1970s.) According to Kant, the important difference is not between private and standing armies but, rather, between both kinds of armies on the one hand and occasional citizens' armies on the other. He claims that standing armies should be abolished, because 'they constantly threaten other states with war by the very fact that they are always prepared for it' ('Perpetual Peace', p. 94).

25. See Percy, *Mercenaries*, pp. 152–3 and 160.

26. See Scahill, *Blackwater*, chaps. 5 and 13.

27. This, in effect, is the thrust of Scahill's critique of Blackwater's activities. See his *Blackwater*, esp. chap. 13.

28. For a study of the ways in which PMCs have been able to influence US foreign policy, see Avant, *The Market for Force*, esp. chap. 4, and D. Shearer, *Private Armies and Military Intervention* (Oxford: Oxford University Press, 1998), pp. 34ff. For worries about the loss of accountability attendant on states' decisions to use PMCs, see, e.g., Singer, *Corporate Warriors*, chap. 10, and Pattison, 'Just War Theory and the Privatization of Military Force', pp. 150ff.

29. For examples of ways in which to regulate PMCs, see, e.g., Avant, *The Market for Force*, chap. 4; Singer, *Corporate Warriors*, chap. 15; and Chesterman and Lehnardt, eds, *From Mercenaries to Market*.

30. See Percy, *Mercenaries*, pp. 218–19, and Shearer, *Private Armies and Military Intervention*, chap. 4, for a strong argument along those lines. See Singer, *Corporate Warriors*, chaps 1, 7 and 8 for discussions of the cases of Croatia and Sierra Leone.

[…]

*Cécile Fabre is professor of political philosophy at Oxford University.

Cécile Fabre, "In Defense of Mercenarism," *British Journal of Political Science* 40, no. 3 (2010): pp. 550–557. Copyright © 2010 Cambridge University Press. Reprinted with the permission of Cambridge University Press.

The Paradox of Riskless Warfare

*by Paul W. Kahn**

The fundamental moral fact about war is that the innocent are appropriate targets of physical violence—not, of course, *all* of the morally innocent. The morality of the battlefield distinguishes not between the innocent and the guilty, but between the *combatant* and the *noncombatant*. Combatants, however, cannot be equated with the morally guilty, since opposing combatants are likely to have equally valid claims to moral innocence. Neither has wronged the other, or anyone else. But each is licensed, legally and morally, to try to injure or kill the other. Each possesses this license because each acts in self-defense vis-à-vis the other. The reciprocal imposition of risk creates the space that allows injury to the morally innocent. Yet, every military force also has a compelling ethical obligation to minimize the risk of injury to its own forces. Each strives to create an asymmetrical situation in which the enemy suffers the risk of injury while its own forces remain safe. The paradox of riskless warfare arises when the pursuit of asymmetry undermines reciprocity. Without reciprocal imposition of risk, what is the moral basis for injuring the morally innocent?

In this essay, I argue that riskless warfare, which increasingly characterizes U.S. military policy, pushes up against the limits of the traditional moral justification of combat. If it passes those limits, as it arguably did in Kosovo, *warfare* must become *policing*. Policing is the application of force to the morally guilty. The moral difference between policing and warfare requires not just different rules of engagement but also different institutions to control the decision to use force. A national army is not, and cannot be, an international police force. Effective international policing requires a credible separation of the application of force from national political interests. A failure to adjust military institutions to the moral grounds of combat will likely result in increasing attacks on our own civilian population.

THE MORAL CHARACTER OF COMBATANTS

1. Lack of autonomy. War in the modern age has been fought largely by conscript armies. Conscription makes vivid the contemporary ethical context of soldiering: combatants typically take up the military burden because they have to. That compulsion is likely to rest on physical, political, and legal considerations. The solder's ethos uses the language of political patriotism, of doing one's duty, of obeying the law, and—most importantly—of confronting uncontrollable circumstance. The combatant's primary concern is the survival of himself and his friends. An ethical demand of independent choice is placed on soldiers only when they have some control: they are not personally to commit war crimes.

Combatants are constrained by forces and circumstances that determine what they "must" do. They tend to be young, with little opportunity to develop an educated opinion. Belief in the justice of their cause is likely to be shaped by propaganda, not deliberation. In some cases—certainly in the case of child soldiers—the combatant is yet another victim of the regime in power, rather than a participant in that regime. Combatants are placed in a situation of mortal danger by political decisions over which they have little, if any, control and which they may not even understand. The only alternative to a combatant's own injury or death may be the successful injuring of another—one who is equally likely to be morally innocent. The morality of contemporary combat emphasizes the mutual moral degradation of combatants: they are not free agents. The role-morality of the combatant begins from a recognition of the suspension of the individual's free choice.

2. The separation of political ends from the morality of combat. Since combatants cannot ordinarily remove themselves from combat because of a moral disagreement with the ends for which they are deployed, their moral status is not the same as that of the political leadership. A combatant who complies with the rules of warfare has not done anything for which he deserves punishment, regardless of which side he fights on. Thus, we didn't think that every German soldier committed a moral wrong for which he deserved to be punished at the end of World War II, even though we thought criminal punishment appropriate for the leadership. We didn't think that the soldiers of the Soviet Union shared in the moral guilt we attributed to much of the political leadership. This is a kind of implicit bargain the state strikes with the individual.

The terms "guilt" and "innocence" don't lose all sense on the battlefield. Rather, they refer to a separate moral code that specifies war crimes. After all, the fundamental reality of the battlefield is a kind of license to kill. That which is prohibited in ordinary life is the point from which moral deliberation begins on the battlefield. Nevertheless, the separation of the political ends of warfare from the morality of combat is always tenuous. The more we believe to be at stake in the outcome of a war, the less willing we are to maintain this distinction. If we thought, for example, that loss of the war would mean the slaughter of all the society's males, and the selling off of the women and children into slavery—the consequences of loss in classical times—we would not be willing to respect the distinction of *jus ad bellum* (principles concerning the just resort to war) from *jus in bello* (principles of just conduct in war). Moderation in political ends is a necessary condition of maintaining the distinct morality of the battlefield.

3. The requirement of reciprocity. The right of combatants to injure and kill each other is founded neither on judgments of their own moral guilt nor on judgments of the moral evil of the end for the sake of which their force is deployed. Rather, combatants are allowed to injure each other just as long as they stand in a relationship of mutual risk. The soldier who takes himself out of combat is no longer a legitimate target. The morality of the battlefield, accordingly, is a variation on the morality of individual self-defense. Injury beyond the point required for self-defense is disproportionate and, therefore, prohibited. Defending himself, the combatant advances the political objective for which force is deployed.

The soldier's privilege of self-defense is subject to a condition of reciprocity. Soldiers cannot defend themselves by threatening to injure noncombatants; they are not permitted civilian reprisals. Combatants cannot threaten the family of an enemy soldier, even if the threat would effectively induce surrender, and thus reduce the overall injuries caused by combat.

These limits do not distinguish the morally guilty from the morally innocent. All may be morally innocent; all are in a tragic and dangerous situation. Nor do such limits necessarily minimize the overall suffering in a war. On efficiency grounds alone, we can never dispose of the claim that ruthlessness in the pursuit of war is the most humane method of fighting, for it brings combat to a swift end. Surely we cannot look at the battlefields of the twentieth century and conclude that the morality of *jus in bello*—just conduct in war—has made wars less costly or more humane.

The rule of reciprocal self-defense cannot be justified by appeal to any of our ordinary moral intuitions: it fails the test of utility, and it also fails the test of deontological rules, since it does not support the moral autonomy and dignity of the individual. Rather, *the rule of reciprocal self-defense stands as its own first principle within a circumscribed context in which individuals act in politically compelled roles.*

If the fundamental principle of the morality of warfare is a right to exercise self-defense within the conditions of mutual imposition of risk, then the emergence of asymmetrical warfare represents a deep challenge. A regime capable of targeting and destroying others with the push of a button, with no human intervention but only the operation of the ultimate high tech weapon, propels us well beyond the ethics of warfare. Such a deployment of force might be morally justified—it might be used to promote morally appropriate ends—but we cannot appeal to the morality of warfare to justify this mode of combat.

It would be a mistake to believe that we remain sufficiently far from this high-tech image that the problem does not press upon us practically. Riskless warfare can be a product of technological innovation, but it is also a function of political decisions. In Kosovo, Western forces were reported to be operating under a policy that missions were not to be undertaken if there was a serious risk of casualties. The situation in Afghanistan is less clear. While the losses are few, an outsider at least has the impression of reciprocal risk. The political leadership took a different position from that in Kosovo, warning the public that in this case there would be casualties, that sacrifice would be required. There are, however, likely to be more, not fewer, Kosovos in our future.

ASYMMETRICAL WARFARE AS POLICE ACTION

In a previous essay, I identified a number of problems with riskless warfare. It is an image of warfare without the possibility of chivalry. In situations of humanitarian intervention, it expresses a disturbing inequality in the calculus by which we value different lives. It may take the destructive power of war outside of the boundaries of democratic legitimacy, because we are far more willing to delegate the power to use force without risk to the president than we are a power to commit the nation to the sacrifice of its citizens. It is likely to create international accusations of hypocrisy as we choose to intervene in some conflicts and not others, when all are equally a matter of money spent, not lives lost.

All of these are real practical and political problems, but they do not get to the heart of the moral conundrum. At the heart is a violation of the fundamental principle that establishes the internal morality of warfare: self-defense within conditions of reciprocal imposition of risk. Without the imposition of mutual risk, warfare is not war at all. What is it then? It most resembles police enforcement. The moral condition of policing, however, is that only the morally guilty should suffer physical injury. There may be exceptions to this rule, but there is no wholesale license to target the morally innocent.

The ethos of international policing is the same as that of ordinary criminal law enforcement. Individuals are the targets of police actions because of what they have done, not because of who they are. It is no longer enough to know that someone wears a military uniform to make him an appropriate target. Wearing a uniform is not the same as participation in a criminal conspiracy. It is no longer enough to act within the limits of proportionality; we need to protect the morally innocent. We can no longer speak of acceptable collateral damage; we need to obtain a strict correspondence between injury and guilt. If our high tech weapons, imagined or real, are not limited in their use to the destruction of the morally guilty, then asymmetrical applications of force may satisfy neither the conditions of warfare nor those of policing.

While one can demand of the police that they assume risks in order to protect the morally innocent, there is no moral demand upon the police of symmetrical risk: policing is better to the degree that the police can accomplish their ends without risk to themselves. A perfect technology of justice would achieve a perfect asymmetry: the morally guilty should suffer all the risk and all the injury. This would simultaneously be the ideal technology of policing and the end of warfare.

The motivation to convert traditional political conflicts into matters of law enforcement has not been driven only by the revolution in military technology. The introduction of juridical elements into international relations is one of the great movements of the late twentieth century, ranging across the new activism of the International Court of Justice, the ad hoc tribunals for the former Yugoslavia and Rwanda, and the emerging International Criminal Court. The more we think of international politics under the paradigm of criminal law, the more likely we are to think of the use of force under the paradigm of policing, including its preference for asymmetry. In this sense, asymmetrical warfare represents a sort of moral category confusion.

I don't mean to suggest that there is anything wrong with the movement from warfare to policing. Morally, this can only be seen as progress. The problem is the confusion of the traditional morality of the battlefield with the appropriate morality for contemporary, international policing. If the military is engaged in policing, then it needs to rethink its rules of engagement. When a criminal seizes a hostage, we don't destroy the house in which both are occupants. At least, we don't do so unless we believe there is a virtual certainty that the criminal will injure or kill others if we fail to act immediately. Even then, we demand that every effort be made to protect the innocent hostage. But in many nations, conscripts are little more than hostages—morally speaking—of criminal regimes. We can fight them if we must, but we do not have a license to injure them because of someone else's (or some regime's) wrongdoing. If we cannot adequately discriminate between the morally guilty and the innocent, we may not be able to use force at all. To be sure, many other options remain open: e.g., sanctions, political and financial support of various interests, boycotts, and the pressure of world opinion.

ASYMMETRY AND THE DISTINCTION BETWEEN COMBATANTS AND NONCOMBATANTS

So far I have argued that, absent the reciprocal imposition of risk, there is no warrant for attacking the morally innocent. To make this argument, I explored the source of the soldier's license to kill, but one can reach this same conclusion by beginning the inquiry from the perspective of the victim. What makes the enemy combatant a morally appropriate *target* for the application of force?

In situations of extreme asymmetry, the distinction between combatants and noncombatants loses its value for moral discrimination. This distinction is central to the ethics of warfare not because it separates the morally guilty from the innocent but because it delineates a domain of threat. If combatants are no longer a threat, however, then they are no more appropriate targets than noncombatants. Both may be the victims of a repressive regime. To identify combatants as appropriate targets under these circumstances is not morally different from identifying the winners of a macabre lottery as the appropriate targets.

To see this point more clearly, suppose that the United States decides that Saddam Hussein's regime is an appropriate target for the use of force. If American forces confront Iraqi forces on a battlefield, then the Iraqi forces are appropriate targets as long as they threaten injury. But if the American forces never show up, what makes these Iraqis appropriate targets? They pose no risk to the United States, and many, if not most, have not done anything wrong. To answer that they provide internal support for the regime does not distinguish Hussein's military forces from many other groups he needs to maintain power. Why not target his bankers or his oil resources? To insist that his army remains an appropriate target, one cannot rely on the ethics of warfare. We need a different set of moral principles that delineates the appropriate targets for what we might, in classic fashion, call uses of force "short of war."

There are three possible responses to this argument. First, combatants are appropriate targets because ultimately *they have consented* to their position, which is one of threatening to use force in support of the regime. Second, although there may not be moral grounds for distinguishing combatants from others, *prudential arguments* support the distinction. Third, although combatants may not threaten an asymmetrically powerful intervener, they nevertheless *threaten others* whom we are entitled to use force to protect. I will treat these arguments in turn.

1. Are combatants appropriate targets because they have consented to their position? As many narratives from Afghanistan are beginning to reveal, it is unrealistic to believe that a morally robust idea of consent operates within authoritarian societies. These are stories of men rounded up and sent to the front, often with little training and rarely with any choice. More important, to rely on consent to identify the legitimate targets for harm is an unjustifiable attempt to extend the moral guilt of the political leadership to the ordinary combatant. If consent is the ground for distinguishing legitimate from illegitimate targets, it is because consent represents a kind of active support of, or participation in, the regime's moral guilt. The regime's active supporters and beneficiaries, however, are not likely to correspond to the traditional category of combatants.

Of course, destroying a regime's army may be a way of destabilizing a regime, but so is destroying elements of its civilian infrastructure or any other significant group of its population. It is no longer the ethics of warfare that legitimates the choice of these targets but the moral value of the end in view.

2. Are these prudential grounds for maintaining the distinction between combatants and others? My arguments so far have proceeded from first principles. For both individuals and nations, however, prudence may sometimes require less principled behavior. Nevertheless, much the same conclusion can be reached from an argument that explores the practical consequences of the application of riskless force.

One consequence of an asymmetrical capacity to apply force can be a self-imposed effort strictly to adhere to the legal limits on targets. Those limits can function as a source of self-constraint. They can also offer an invitation to escalation in the face of frustration, as we saw with the steady expansion of targets in the Kosovo campaign. The list of legal targets can be very long. Scrupulous adherence to lawful targets by an asymmetric power is unlikely to support a perception of legitimacy. In the absence of reciprocal risk, what had traditionally been seen as fair is likely to be seen as morally arbitrary and, if arbitrary, then an act of victimization of the powerless.

Further, conditions of asymmetry are unstable because they compel innovation by the disadvantaged side. Military tactics can be changed in hopes of neutralizing the advantage; for example, guerrilla warfare is one response to technological advantage. Equally possible is the infliction of reciprocal injury on a morally innocent, civilian population. Asymmetry may become an invitation to popular resistance and to terrorism. It is no accident that Saddam Hussein has been developing weapons of mass destruction since his defeat in the Gulf War. His strategy is to create symmetrical risk. If he cannot do this on the battlefield, he will do it elsewhere. The same motivations are powering the Intifada. If the Palestinians cannot hope realistically to create a reciprocal risk for the Israeli military, they will direct the risk of injury at civilians. And, of course, the character of the attack on September 11 was itself a response to the asymmetry in conventional forces. For the asymmetrically powerful to insist on the maintenance of the combatant/noncombatant distinction has the appearance of self-serving moralizing.

Just as it is practically intolerable to suffer an asymmetrical use of force, it is intolerable to suffer an asymmetrical risk to a civilian population. There is likely to be a cycle of escalation, as each side responds to the other's infliction of risk upon noncombatants. The bombing of London was followed by the bombing of Berlin. If it became clear, for example, that Iraq was responsible for the release of anthrax in this country, would the American response respect the line separating combatants from noncombatants? The Israelis allegedly threatened Iraq with just such a retaliation when they perceived a threat of attack by chemical weapons during the Gulf War. It is hard to believe that any country would act differently.

This means that the asymmetrical capacities of Western—and particularly U.S. forces—themselves create the conditions for increasing use of terrorism. This, in turn, creates a cycle of destruction outside of the boundaries of the battlefield, with its reliance on the distinction of combatants from noncombatants.

There is no easy, practical answer to this problem. Military forces cannot be asked to assume unnecessary risks. Every army wants to fight in such a way as to impose a maximum threat to the enemy and a minimum threat to itself. Indeed, it would be immoral for the military leadership not to try to minimize the risk of injury to its own forces. That the moral grounds of warfare may shift at the point at which this ideal approaches reality is not an obvious matter of concern for the internal process of military deliberation. Breaking the cycle requires a transition from combat to policing. There must be a general perception that force is used only against the morally guilty and there must be agreement on who are the morally guilty. This is why contemporary deployments of force tend to end with public, criminal trials.

In both its classical and colonialist forms, asymmetrical power has brought with it an ambition for empire. The capacity to realize ends through the application of force without suffering the risk of reciprocal injury is simultaneously a tactical prize and an intolerable political situation. No state will trust other states with this power. Equally, no people should trust their political leadership with this power. The pursuit of national interests through military means is restrained by the expectation of loss. If that expectation disappears, what are the sources of constraint? Even when legitimate objectives are pursued, the fact that they are the political project of a hegemonic power delegitimizes the application of force in the eyes of both those who suffer the intervention and those who are not directly involved. Riskless warfare may be a prescription for short-term success and long-term disaster.

Riskless warfare will be perceived as hegemonic interference unless it is perceived as legitimate policing. But the latter perception depends on institutional developments. Good intentions are not enough. Human rights claims will be seen as only a form of neocolonialism if advanced through a national military with the capacity risklessly to deploy force. Yet we are only just beginning to develop institutions of international law that could imaginably have a power of policing. Until we do so, we are likely to remain in this paradoxical situation in which the military's capacity for riskless application of force makes our own lives substantially riskier.

3. Does the combatants' threat to others distinguish them from noncombatants? While the United States may be able to use force without risk, others—on the ground—are likely to suffer injuries from the combatants against whom we are intervening. Future uses of force are likely to look like interventions in situations of gross violations of human rights. Those violations constitute the moral ground of the combatants' traditional right to deploy force.

This argument suggests that the moral issue here is not different in kind from traditional arguments of "collective self-defense" when one party aids another in a military conflict. It is morally appropriate for one state to come to the aid of another that has suffered an armed attack. Morally, and increasingly legally, the same rule applies when a people has been attacked by its own government. Typically, interventions in the past have involved supply of material resources—particularly weapons. The deployment of asymmetrical force is simply another variation on this sort of aid. Intervention is morally justifiable so long as the side on whose behalf one intervenes faces a reciprocal risk from the target. The recipient of aid is the principal; the state that intervenes is only the agent.

This argument, while powerful, suggests real limits on intervention. First, the asymmetrical application of force morally *depends on a prior and continuing symmetrical application of force*. To target the morally innocent requires an argument of self-defense by those with whom the asymmetric power chooses to ally itself. Second, *the conflict that grounds the intervention must have its own integrity*. It cannot simply be a situation constructed by Western interests—or even by local parties—to create subsequent grounds for an asymmetrical intervention. Third, *asymmetric intervention places considerable pressure on arguments concerning the just resort to war* because the moral grounds for intervention receive no support from any internal dynamic of combatant self-defense.

When the United States chooses intervention, it assumes the moral obligation to make the *right* choice. "Right," here, means more than "supportive of our own political interests." Why and when does the United States have a right to decide the outcome of other peoples' wars? In situations of genuine political dispute, a potential intervener has no such right.

While riskless intervention in support of the victims of gross violations of fundamental human rights is permissible as a form of collective self-defense, this argument is not independent of the sorts of claims considered in the last section. There remains the problem of external perception: why should the rest of the world see intervention by U.S. forces as anything other than a political decision to dictate who will be the winner in a local conflict? Intervention is perceived as neocolonialism in support of that group most likely to advance Western interests. Such perceptions extend the risk to our own civilian population. Internationalization of decisions to use force, within increasingly juridified institutions, is the only possible response to this perception.

CONCLUSION

My argument can be represented with a highly simplified example. Imagine a confrontation between a champion heavyweight and an untrained lightweight. Suppose the heavyweight proposes that the way to solve their disagreements is to have a fight within the traditional rules of the ring. Because of the asymmetry, most people would find this proposal self-serving rather than fair. Now suppose that the lightweight challenges another lightweight. To this, the heavyweight responds by demanding cessation of the challenge, and he backs that demand with a threat of his own intervention. We would not necessarily object to this form of intervention, but we would ask whether the heavyweight is intervening on the *right* side. If the dispute between the two lightweights is genuine, why should the side against whom intervention is threatened agree that this is an appropriate way to end the dispute? From his point of view, we are just back at the first situation of asymmetrical force.

This example suggests that a shift in moral concern occurs in the two situations. In the first case, we question the *asymmetry itself*, while in the second, we question *the uses for which* force is being deployed. Our intuitions about a "fair fight" carry weight independently of our intuitions about the purpose for which force is deployed. But the stylized account also suggests that these two perspectives cannot remain separate: asymmetry places a particular burden on any decision to use force. As the asymmetry increases, so does our need to find the grounds for a common belief in the legitimacy of the deployment.

Viewed abstractly, this example is precisely the Hobbesian story of the origin of the state: there is a need to concede a monopoly on the legitimate use of force to a single heavyweight, who then retains the responsibility, as well as the capacity, to resolve private disputes. In the international arenas, the United States increasingly finds itself with monopoly power. The problem of practical ethics lies in the difference between these two situations: the United States is the heavyweight, but it does not have the legitimacy of the sovereign.

Acknowledgments

This essay is based on a paper originally delivered at the U.S. Army War College's Annual Strategy Conference, April 10–11, 2002. The author thanks the participants for their helpful comments.

SOURCES

At the end of World War II, only twenty-two high-level Nazi officials were indicted at Nuremberg for planning a war of aggression, crimes against humanity and war crimes. Outside of Nuremberg, about 5,000 German soldiers were charged with particular war crimes. Readers interested in the content of the combatants' moral obligations under contemporary humanitarian law should refer to the Statute of the International Criminal Court, Art. 6–8. Concerning the point that the soldier who removes himself from combat is no longer a legitimate target, see Hague Convention IV (1907), Annex of Regulations, Art. 23.; Statute of the International Criminal Court, Art. 8, sec. 2(b)(vi). My earlier discussion of some problems of riskless warfare can be found in Paul W. Kahn, "War and Sacrifice in Kosovo," *Report from the Institute for Philosophy and Public Policy*, vol. 19, no. 2/3 (Spring/Summer 1999). On the expansion of the target list during the air war in Kosovo, see Michael Ignatieff, *Virtual War: Kosovo and Beyond* (Chatto & Windus, 2001). That we might have reason to worry about the moral integrity of an intervention in Iraq is suggested by recent talk of "creating" a Northern-Alliance type operation in Iraq as a predicate to U.S. action. See, e.g., Inter Press Service, Dec. 2, 2001, "Iraq Veers Back into Washington's Crosshairs," by Jim Lobe, *The Independent* (London), April 8, 2002, (quoting Tony Blair).

*Paul W. Kahn is Robert W. Winner Professor of Law and Humanities, Director of the Orville H. Schell Jr. Center for International Human Rights, Yale Law School.

Kahn, Paul W. "The Paradox of Riskless Warfare." *Philosophy & Public Policy Quarterly* Vol. 22:3 (Summer 2002): 2–8.

Used by permission

How Just Could a Robot War Be?

*by Peter M. Asaro**

*Abstract. While modern states may never cease to wage war against one an-
other, they have recognized moral restrictions on how they conduct those wars.
These "rules of war" serve several important functions in regulating the organization and behavior of military forces, and shape political debates, negotiations,
and public perception. While the world has become somewhat accustomed to
the increasing technological sophistication of warfare, it now stands at the verge
of a new kind of escalating technology—autonomous robotic soldiers—and
with them new pressures to revise the rules of war to accommodate them. This
paper will consider the fundamental issues of justice involved in the application of autonomous and semi-autonomous robots in warfare. It begins with a
review of just war theory, as articulated by Michael Walzer [1], and considers
how robots might fit into the general framework it provides. In so doing it considers how robots, "smart" bombs, and other autonomous technologies might
challenge the principles of just war theory, and how international law might be
designed to regulate them. I conclude that deep contradictions arise in the principles intended to govern warfare and our intuitions regarding the application of
autonomous technologies to war fighting.*

1. INTRODUCTION

Just war theory is a broadly accepted theoretical framework for regulating
conduct in war that has been embraced by such esteemed and influential institutions as academia, the US military establishment (including the military
academies[1]), and the Catholic Church. It is also compatible with, if not actually a formulation of, the principles underlying most of the international laws
regulating warfare, such as the Geneva and Hague Conventions.

This paper aims to illuminate the challenges to just war theory posed by
autonomous technologies. It follows Michael Walzer's [1] articulation of the
theory, which has been the most influential modern text on just war theory.
While there are compelling criticisms of Walzer's formulation (*e.g.* [2]), it is his
articulation which has had the most influence on the institutions and international laws regulating war.

Before we begin, I should clarify what I mean by robots and other autonomous systems. "Autonomy" is a rather contentious concept, especially when applied to material technologies, because the term is used with different meanings in the fields of philosophy and robotics. While usually used as an all-or-nothing property, it is more useful to think about a continuum of autonomy along which various technologies fall depending upon their specific capabilities. Most generally, any system with the capability to sense, decide and act without human intervention has a degree of autonomy. This includes simple systems, such as a landmine that "decides" to explode when it senses pressure. Obviously, systems with only the most rudimentary forms of sensors, decision processes and actions lack various aspects of full autonomy. The landmine does not decide where it will be placed, and its physical placement largely determines the consequences of its actions, thus it has much less "autonomy" than systems with more sophisticated means of sensing, deciding and acting. If we were to consider it as a moral agent, we would not be inclined to hold it morally responsible for its actions, but rather hold responsible those who placed and armed it. It thus occupies an endpoint in the continuum of autonomy and moral responsibility.

Certain kinds of "precision" weapons, such as "smart" bombs use global-positioning systems (GPS), laser designation, and sophisticated control mechanisms to deliver them accurately to a target. The selection of a target, the determination of the target's location, and the assessment of its value and risks is still determined by human agents who control the weapons system, however. Thus we might wish to "blame" a smart bomb, or its design, for failing to reach a designated target, but not for the selection of the target. These guided munitions thus represent a point further along this continuum of autonomy. Further down this continuum we find automated anti-ballistic missile defense systems (*e.g.* the Patriot missile system, the Phalanx gun system, and the proposed Star Wars/SDI missile shield), that automatically detect and destroy sensed threats of incoming missiles without immediate human intervention, though are dependent on responsible human decisions as to when it is appropriate to activate such an armed system.

Still more autonomous are systems which use sophisticated sensor analysis to select appropriate targets on their own and make decisions about the appropriateness of various actions in response to its situation. The emerging technologies of robotic weapons platforms incorporate some or all of these features, using image processing to identify targets, and selecting from a broad range of offensive and defensive actions in their engagement of targets. These are technological capabilities which already exist, and are beginning to be implemented in various countries. These systems tend to be designed to seek permission from human authorities before using lethal force against a target, what the US military calls the "human-in-the-loop," but this is not a technological necessity. We can identify the choice to use deadly force against a specific target as a critical threshold along the continuum of autonomy, and one which carries a greater moral burden in the design and use of such a technology. There are, however, systems with more autonomy than this.

As robotic technologies advance, it is possible that they will acquire moral capacities that imitate or replicate human moral capacities. While some systems might merely enact pre-programmed moral rules or principles, autonomous robotic agents might be capable of formulating their own moral principles, duties, and reasons, and thus make their own moral choices in the fullest sense of moral autonomy. There are many possibilities short of replicating a fully autonomous moral subject, such as agents with moral awareness but without the freedom of choice to act upon that awareness. While this still remains in the realm of science fiction, it is not impossible in principle that a robot could achieve autonomy in a Kantian sense, in which it takes responsibility for its actions, reasons about them morally, and identifies itself with the moral quality of its own actions. At some point along the continuum, but probably before Kantian autonomy, will arise various questions about the moral responsibilities of others towards such autonomous systems, and in particular whether these systems have moral rights.

There are many degrees of autonomy along the continuum at which specific systems might fall, so we will consider the implications of these on the interpretation and application of just war theory to various situations. I should also say something at this point about the speculative nature of this work. Many people find the idea of robotic soldiers and robotic moral agents to be somewhat fantastical, the stuff of science fiction and not something that deserves serious consideration. My arguments are meant to cover technological possibilities that do not yet exist, and even some that shall perhaps never exist, yet I believe that it is important to develop our understanding of existing technologies in light of these hypothetical possibilities. There is a very great interest in building autonomous systems of increasing complexity, and a great deal of money is being invested towards this goal. It does not seem to be an unreasonable prediction that within the next decade we will see something very much like a robotic soldier being used.[2] If we consider the amount of time and effort it took moral and legal theorists to come to terms with the atomic bomb, then it makes sense to start thinking about military robots now, before they appear fully formed on the battlefield. Robots may not have the same potential to reshape global politics that the atomic bomb did, though indeed they may. Still, it is not unreasonable to expect that these technologies might find their way into other security applications, such as policing civilian populations. There is thus a definite necessity, and a certain urgency to establishing the moral framework in which we might judge the various applications of such technologies, as well as the ethics of designing and building them. This examination of just war theory is a part of that broader investigation.

As my concern in this analysis is with the general capabilities of technologies, primarily their ability to act autonomously, and not with the specific technologies used, I will not spend much time discussing how these technologies might work, apart from their degree of autonomy. One might also object that there already exist legal restrictions on the use of autonomous systems in combat, and these have succeeded thus far in keeping humans-in-the-loop of the most advanced military systems being developed, at least in the US, and thus there is no need for such an analysis. While it is true that humans are being kept "in the loop," it is not clear to what extent this is only a contingent truth, and whether this restriction can resist pressures to extend the autonomy granted to military systems [3]. It thus seems reasonable to review the fundamental principles which underwrite existing prohibitions on the use of autonomous technologies, as well as to try to anticipate how they may need to be augmented or extended to address new technological possibilities as they begin to appear on the horizon.

[...]

4. AUTONOMOUS TECHNOLOGY AND JUS IN BELLO

Walzer claims that just war theory is largely indifferent to the kinds of technology that are used in battle. As far as he is concerned, there are individuals who have a right not to be killed, the innocent civilians, and those who have given up that right by taking up arms, the uniformed combatants. As it is morally permissible to kill uniformed combatants, it does not matter much how one goes about killing them (assuming that one recognizes their right to surrender, *etc.*). However, there are a number of international conventions which do limit the use of specific kinds of weapons, such as chemical, biological and nuclear weapons, as well as landmines, lasers designed to blind soldiers, and other sorts of weapons. There are various reasons for the existence of these treaties, and several principles which determine what kinds of technologies are permissible as weapons of war. In this section, we will consider how autonomous technologies might challenge the standards of *jus in bello*.

Despite Walzer's claims that his theory does not care about the technologies used for killing, he does discuss several specific technologies in terms of how they changed the conventional standards of war. In particular, the use of submarines, aerial bombing and the atomic bomb, all relatively new technologies at the time, changed the accepted conventions of warfare during World War II.

The clearest example of this is the way in which the specific technologies of submarine warfare in World War II served to repeal a centuries-old naval warfare convention. The convention held that there was a moral duty to rescue the surviving crew of a sinking enemy ship once a battle was over. Over the long history of European naval warfare, this convention made sense to all participants, since combat usually occurred in open seas, often hundreds or even thousands of miles from safe harbors, and disabled or sinking ships generally had significant numbers of survivors. From the development of submarines through World War I, this convention held for submarines as it had for all other ships. It was decided during World War II, however, that this convention no longer applied to submarines. The reason for this was that requiring a submarine to surface and conduct rescue operations would make it too vulnerable to detection from radar and attack from airplanes armed with torpedoes. Additionally, the small submarines (with crews of less than 50) could not spare space for survivors on-board, adequate guards to take officers prisoner, or space to store much rescue equipment (ships sunk by submarines often had more than 1,000 people on board), all of which made rescue efforts challenging and impractical. They could, however, right upset lifeboats and provide food and water, as well as pick up men from the sea and put them in their own lifeboats, but these activities were considered too risky.

While there were some specific and dramatic events that led to the abandonment of this particular convention for submarines, it was largely due to the fact that obedience to the convention was so risky that it would render submarine warfare impractical. The official abandonment of the convention occurred when the German Admiral Doenitz issued the *Laconia* Order in 1942, which expressly directed submarines to not engage in any form of assistance to survivors [1]. Doenitz was tried at Nuremberg for a war crime in issuing this order, but was acquitted of the charge by the judges. The legal decision rested primarily on the fact that because both sides assented to the new convention in practice, the old convention was effectively annulled and submarines no longer had a moral obligation to rescue crews, despite the fact that it was sometimes safe for a submarine to rescue survivors. Walzer believes this is the correct moral interpretation, and accounts for it in his theory as a valid use of the principle of military necessity. That is, it became a military necessity to forgo the convention of rescue in order for submarine warfare to be an effective naval strategy, though this clearly makes naval warfare a more brutal affair.

I believe this deference to military necessity presents a significant weakness in just war theory, as formulated by Walzer, when viewed in the context of technological development. That is, why should we not say that submarines should not be used at all if they cannot be used in a manner which conforms to the conventions of just war? If we cannot argue this way, then there would seem to be a certain kind of impotence to using just war theory to argue against any technology that has the potential to change conventions via military necessity. Not only does this position mean that we have to accept all new technologies and the new conventions that arise from them, but also that we cannot judge the morality of devising various sorts of weapons. The question is: If I can only defend myself with an indiscriminate and disproportionate weapon, because that is the only militarily effective weapon I have, then was I acting unjustly when I chose to arm myself with that weapon rather than another weapon which could be discriminate and proportionate? Do I have a moral duty to invest in weapons that will not tend to put me in positions where I may be motivated to act unjustly (indiscriminately and disproportionately) in the future? If so, could robot soldiers be such a technology?

This failure in Walzer's formulation stems from its loose foundational considerations. While Walzer is willing to assert individual rights as the basis for prohibitions against killing civilians, he mistakenly asserts that soldiers forgo their rights not to be killed by merely taking up arms. Further, he seems to believe that the restrictions on the use of weapons against soldiers, and the rights of soldiers to surrender, rescue, medical aid, *etc.*, are a matter of convention between states who see these conventions as being in their mutual interests. Thus, there is no firm moral foundation to prevent states from abandoning these conventions when they are deemed not to be in their mutual interest. A convention depends only upon both sides assenting to it, as in Walzer's analysis of the Doenitz decision which rests upon the fact that both sides of the conflict observed the same convention.

Apart from convention, Walzer might appeal to moral sentiments in determining the morality of certain military strategies and technologies. To the extent that it derives its principles from moral sentiments, just war theory is an attempt to describe sentiments that occur *after* an event. In the case of many new technologies, we do not really know how that technology will function in the complex socio-technical system of war. Submarines, radar and airplanes armed with torpedoes had never been used together in warfare before WWII, so nobody really knew how they would be used. Indeed, the German admiralty only abandoned the sea rescue convention for submarines in 1942, well into the war. Thus it seems that if we cannot predict military necessity very well, just war theory as it stands cannot tell us much about which technologies might be best left undeveloped.

The more critical issue that just war theory faces is that the conventionalist and sentimentalist interpretations both fail to secure a moral foundation for restrictions on actions against combatants *in bello*. Most generally, if we accept that the combatants on a just side of a war have not waived their rights not to be killed [2], then no conventional agreement between states can waive or trump that right. Similarly, if sailors have a moral right to be rescued after their ship is sunk, then neither the demands of military necessity, nor the technological limitations of submarines, nor the conventional agreements between belligerent navies can waive that right, even if it becomes impractical to respect it. The practicality issue comes into play only when we come to consider the legal restrictions on combat, not its fundamental morality. Thus, we might accept a certain degree of immorality in our laws because of the impracticality of judging and enforcing morally justified laws [2].

The real question then becomes one of what moral rights individuals have against the use of specific technologies, and of the moral duties of states in the development of arms that might be used in hypothetical future wars. Again there is the distinction between fundamental morality and practical law, but it seems possible in principle to develop a moral foundation for arms control and limitations on the design and use of various technologies. While it is well beyond the scope of this essay, it will remain a topic for further research.

4.1 Distinguishing Civilians & Combatants

On Walzer's interpretation of just war theory, the most fundamental distinction made by just war theory is that between combatants and civilians. While this distinction fails, like military necessity, to find solid moral grounding, it proves quite useful in establishing practical laws for regulating war. This distinction makes it legally permissible, at least sometimes, for combatants to kill enemy combatants. It also makes it possible to say that it is almost never legally justified for combatants to kill innocent civilians. There are, of course, shades of grey. Even combatants retain certain rights, like the right to surrender, and not to be killed unnecessarily. There are also cases in which it is legally permissible to kill civilians—but these cases must meet a very strict and limiting set of conditions, and even those are contentious. Further problems arise in guerrilla and insurgent warfare, in which combatants pose as civilians.

In this section I want to consider several different aspects of the problem of distinguishing civilians and combatants as it relates to autonomous systems. First, the practical ability of autonomous technologies to draw this distinction correctly is crucial. On the one hand, it has been argued that this ability makes the use of such systems *morally required* if they are available. What is more surprising is that it is human rights groups, such as Human Rights Watch [5] in demanding the use of only "smart" bombs in civilian areas, who have made this argument. On the other hand, it is the fear of indiscriminate violence, perhaps mixed with impoverished cultural and social intelligence, that makes robotic soldiers seem particularly dangerous and morally undesirable.

The relevance of the civilian-combatant distinction to robotic soldiers is that if they are to be autonomous in choosing their targets, they will have to be able to reliably distinguish enemy combatants from civilians. It seems that this capability will remain the most difficult theoretical and practical problem facing the development of such robots. While there are technologies for picking out humans based on computer vision, motion and heat patterns, it is extremely difficult to identify particular people, or even types of people, much less to categorize them reliably into groups such as "friend" or "foe," the boundaries of which are often poorly defined and heavily value-laden.

In keeping with the Human Rights Watch argument, there is a line of reasoning which asserts that advanced technologies have the potential to be superior to human capabilities. Arkin [4] argues that if we can achieve the proper discriminatory capabilities in robots, they may very well be *morally superior* to human soldiers. The argument maintains that if a machine is better able to discriminate civilians from combatants, then it will make fewer mistakes than humans. Moreover, because it is a machine, it will not feel the psychological stress of warfare and emotions like fear and revenge that a human experiences, and thus will not be as likely to commit war crimes or atrocities as humans. As such, there is not only a moral obligation to use such systems when they are available, but also to build them (insofar as war is taken as an unavoidable feature of human civilization). This all depends, of course, on the actual abilities of the technology, and the abilities of combatants to fool such systems into misidentification.

4.2 "Push-Button" Wars

Walzer notes that a radical transformation in our understanding of the war convention occurred with the rise of the modern nation-state. Before this, warfare was largely conducted by individuals who freely chose to participate in a given war, and a given battle. With the rise of the modern nation-state came the power to recruit and conscript individuals into standing armies. Because of this, nearly all individual soldiers lost their freedom to choose which wars and which battles they would fight in, even if they had the choice of whether to volunteer for military service. The consequences for moral estimations of conduct in war were thus reshaped by our knowledge that many of the actual combatants in war are not there freely, and thus deserve a certain degree of moral respect from their own commanders as well as from enemy commanders. While it is permissible to kill them, they still have the right to surrender and sit-out the rest of the war as a prisoner. It is also morally required that commanders seek out ways of winning battles that minimize killing on both sides. That is, the lives of the enemy still have moral weight, even if they weigh less than the civilians and combatants on one's own side. And the lives of one's own soldiers also count in a new way. Whereas it might be moral to lead a group of soldiers on a suicidal charge if they all volunteer for that charge, ordering conscripted soldiers into such a charge is usually immoral. In the same way, it is deemed highly honorable to throw oneself on a grenade to save one's comrades, but not to throw one's comrade onto the grenade—the autonomy of the individual soldier to choose his or her fate has moral implications.

The use of autonomous systems may similarly change our conception of the role of soldiers in war, by fully realizing a "push button" war in which the enemy is killed at a distance, without any immediate risk to oneself. This approach to war could be deemed unjust by traditional conventions of war because those doing the killing are not themselves willing to die. This principle is fundamental because it powerfully influences our sense of fairness in battle, and concerns the nature of war as a social convention for the settling of disputes. Insofar as it can serve this purpose, both sides must essentially agree to settle the dispute through violence and, by the norms of the convention, the violence is to be targeted only at those who have agreed to fight, *i.e.* the combatants. Thus it is immoral to kill civilians, who have not agreed to fight. This convention is only abandoned in a "total war" in which no actions are considered unjust because the stakes of losing are so high. By fighting a war through pressing a button, one does not fully become a combatant because one has not conformed to the norms of war in which both sides agree to risk death in settling the dispute. The limitations of such a conventionalist notion of just war have been noted above, however, and there would seem to be no deeper moral obligation for a just combatant to risk their own lives in defense of their state.

We could imagine a war in which both sides sent only robots to do the fighting. This might be rather like an extremely violent sporting contest in which the robots destroy each other. For this to actually count as a war, and not merely a sport, however, political decisions would have to be made as a result of this competition, such as ceding territory. While it might seem unlikely that a nation would simply give up its territory or autonomy once its robots were destroyed, this is not an unreasonable or impossible outcome. It might also be deemed moral to fight to the last robot, whereas it is generally not deemed moral to fight to the last human. While many nations have surrendered after the crushing defeat of their armies but before the actual conquest of their lands, it would seem likely that a state might continue fighting with humans after its robots have been destroyed, rather than simply capitulate at that point. In general, I think it is fair to say that an exclusively robotic war might even be a highly preferable way of fighting to what now exists. In its most extreme form, we could even imagine a decisive war fought without a single human casualty.

Such a war would not be completely without its costs and risks, however. First, such a war would have to take place somewhere, and it seems likely that the destruction of natural resources and civilian property would be highly likely in most locations. As the most common military objectives are to hold cities and towns, there is both the risk of harming civilians in the course of fighting, and the problems of holding towns, and thus controlling and policing civilian populations with robots. There would also be the cost in terms of the time, money and resources devoted to building up these robot armies.

At the other extreme lies the completely asymmetric "push-button" war. Thanks to science fiction and the Cold War, it is not hard to imagine an autonomous military system in which the commander needs only to specify the military action, and press a button, the rest being taken care of by a vast automated war machine. We could even imagine a civilian government that has completely replaced its military with a fully automated system, perhaps designed and staffed by civilian technicians, but one that did not require any uniformed soldiers to operate. Such a system would, I believe, seriously challenge the conventional concept of war.

In a completely asymmetric war, in which one side offers no legitimate uniformed combatants in battle, but only robots, our moral sentiments could be profoundly upset. If one nation fights a war in which its soldiers never appear on the battlefield, offering no opportunity for them to be killed, then the combatants are all machines and the humans are all civilians. As in a guerrilla war, one side presents no legitimate human targets to be killed. A legitimate army would not have any opportunity to reciprocally kill the soldiers of their opponents in such a situation (and could only inflict economic damage on their robots). This could thereby be interpreted as a fundamental violation of the war convention itself, like showing up for a duel in armor or sending a proxy, and thereby as a nullification of the associated conventions. Seen another way, such a situation might also be presented as an argument in favor of terrorism against the civilians who sit behind their robotic army. It could be argued that those who build, equip, maintain, or direct the robot army are in fact combatants, despite any claims otherwise. This would make them similar to partisans, guerillas or other irregular and non-uniformed combatants, and liable to being legitimately killed despite not wearing uniforms or carrying arms. It could also be argued that because such an army is the product of a rich and elaborate economy, the members of that economy are the next-best legitimate targets. This possibility should alert us to the unsuitability of conventions and moral sentiments, rather than individual rights, as a basis for just war theory, since we would not want a theory of just war which legitimizes terrorism against civilians.

If we instead see the foundations of just war as deriving from individual rights, it would be unreasonable to insist that a nation fighting for a just cause is obliged to let an unjust aggressor kill its citizens even though it has the technological means of preventing this. Indeed, outside of Walzer's interpretation of the moral equality of soldiers, we do not expect a technologically superior nation to refrain from using its available technologies simply because they give too great of an advantage, nor do we expect a larger army to use special restraint in fighting a smaller army out of a moral sense of fairness. Similarly, as long as the robot army is no more likely to cause unjust harms than a human army, it would seem to offer a superior military advantage in limiting the risks to one's own citizens.

There is a compelling rationale for a nation desiring to defend itself without risking human lives. That is, a nation could quite reasonably decide that it does not want its children to be trained as soldiers or sent to war, and so develops a technological solution to the problem of national defense that does not require human soldiers, namely a robot army. In such a case it would not seem to be immoral to develop and use that technology, and we might go even further and say it is morally required for that nation to protect its children from becoming soldiers if it is within their technological capacity to do so. If an aggressor invaded this nation, I do not think many people would raise a moral objection to their using robot soldiers to defend themselves.

Of course, the push-button war is already available in a certain sense, namely for those countries with superior air forces and a willingness to bomb their enemies, or with long-range missiles. The practical consequence of such wars is the asymmetry in which one side is so obviously technologically powerful that it does not make much sense for the opposition to face it in the traditional manner. The result is often guerrilla warfare, and sometimes terrorism. The advent of robot armies may further exacerbate such situations, but would not seem to be fundamentally different. Their development and employment should, however, take into consideration that these are likely responses to the use of robot armies, even if they are not morally just responses.

5. CONCLUSIONS

Ultimately, just war theory concludes that the use of autonomous technologies is neither completely morally acceptable, nor is it completely morally unacceptable under Walzer's [1] interpretation of just war theory. In part this is because the technology, like all military force, could be just or unjust, depending on the situation. This is also, in part, because what is and is not acceptable in war, under this interpretation, is ultimately a *convention*, and while we can extrapolate from existing conventions in an attempt to deal with new technologies, like autonomous killing machines, this process can only be speculative. It is up to the international community to establish a new set of conventions to regulate the use of these technologies, and to embody these in international laws and treaties. Such a process can be informed by Walzer's theory, but his approach is to appeal to conventional practices as the ultimate arbiter of military necessity when it comes to technological choices. In light of this, we may wish to extend or revise the theory of just war to deal more explicitly with the development and use of new military technologies. In particular, we might seek to clarify the moral foundations for technological arms control, perhaps upon individual rights or another solid moral ground. Such a theory might also begin to influence the practical control of autonomous weapons systems through international laws and treaties. I believe that this would be a promising approach for further work.

NOTES

1. Walzer's book was a standard text at the West Point Military Academy for many years, though it was recently removed from the required reading list.

2. The military of South Korea already has plans to deploy autonomous robots armed with machine guns and live ammunition along the border with North Korea. The system is designed by Samsung Techwin, and will detect and could shoot at any human attempting to cross the DMZ.

REFERENCES

[1] M. Walzer, *Just and Unjust Wars: A Moral Argument with Historical Illustrations*, Basic Books, NY, 1977.

[2] J. McMahan, The Sources and Status of Just War Principles, *Journal of Military Ethics*, 6(2), 91–106, 2007.

[3] J. S. Canning, A Concept of Operations for Armed Autonomous Systems: The difference between "Winning the War" and "Winning the Peace," presentation at the Pentagon, 2007.

[4] R. C. Arkin, Governing Lethal Behavior: Embedding Ethics in a Hybrid Deliberative/Reactive Robot Architecture, Georgia Institute of Technology, Technical Report GIT-GVU-07-11, 2007.

[5] Human Rights Watch, International Humanitarian Law Issues in the Possible US Invasion of Iraq, *Lancet*, Feb. 20, 2003.

*Peter M. Asaro is an assistant professor at The New School For Public Engagement, School of Media Studies and Film in New York City.

Reprinted from Peter M. Asaro, "How Just Could a Robot War Be?," *Current Issues in Computing and Philosophy*, edited by Adam Briggle, Katrinka Waelbers, and Philip A. E. Brey (Amsterdam: IOS Press, 2008), 50-64, with permission from IOS Press.

Part 5: Absolute Prohibitions: Terrorism and Torture

In previous parts we have considered whether absolute prohibitions could ever be violated in a "supreme emergency" situation in war. The resurgence of transnational terrorism and the constant threat posed to civilian populations have, in some people's minds, created a recurring "supreme emergency" that requires a rebalancing of ethical and legal constraints. Might the use of terrorism or torture as war tactics be justified by changes in 21st century conflict dynamics? Is there something singular about terrorism or torture that distinguishes these practices or tactics from other types of killing, harm, or destruction in warfare?

TERRORISM

Despite efforts to define and outlaw terrorism that stretch back to the 1930s, the international community does not agree on the definition of terrorism.[1] The 2004 United Nations Security Council Resolution 1566 defined terrorist acts as

> criminal acts, including against civilians, committed with the intent to cause death or serious bodily injury, or taking of hostages, with the purpose to provoke a state of terror in the general public or in a group of persons or particular persons, intimidate a population or compel a government or an international organization to do or to abstain from doing any act. . . .[2]

The UN resolution continues by codifying the widely held view that terrorism is "under no circumstances justifiable."[3]

Although terrorism today inspires images of bloody carnage—defenseless civilians killed or mutilated while going about their daily lives—the image of terrorism has historically had more mixed, if still not entirely positive, connotations. As the old adage goes, "One man's terrorist is another man's freedom fighter."[4] Terrorist tactics were used in many anticolonialist independence movements in the 20th century, including by nationalists against the French in Algeria (1954–1962), by Israeli settlers seeking independence from British domination in the 1930s, and by those resisting British colonialism in Kenya in the 1950s, among others. Terrorist tactics were also used by anti-Apartheid activists in South Africa. While few applaud the violence inherent in these struggles, many at least understand the rationale behind the use of violence.

In the first selection, "Terrorism and War," Virginia Held points out that the use of terror is not exclusive to terrorist networks or individuals. States have used terror as a tool against domestic political rivals, or have supported foreign terrorist groups or tactics as an extension of their foreign policy. Some acts within war also might be considered terrorism. Allied forces during World War II carpet-bombed cities such as Dresden, Germany, and Tokyo, Japan, with the aim of terrorizing civilians and undermining their morale.

While we would likely find such acts equally unjustifiable (and unlawful), the point of Held's comparison is that terrorism might not be any more or less morally wrong than other types of state violence or armed conflict. State violence is judged by the degree to which it complies with international law, or its perceived ethical position, while terrorism tends to be rejected categorically. In contrast, Held argues that "*if* war can be justified, so can some terrorism be."[5] Many definitions of terrorism presume that terrorists target innocent civilians, but Held points out that not all civilians are "innocent," and that terrorism frequently attacks military targets, for example, the Al Qaeda attack on the *USS Cole* in 2000. Even if terrorist attacks were to bring about civilian deaths, armed conflicts result in innocent civilian deaths but are considered morally justifiable. We simply accept that in some cases the ends (of war) may justify the means (of killing in war). Why should terrorism be any different?

In "Is Terrorism Morally Distinctive?" Samuel Scheffler takes the contrary position, arguing that terrorism is morally distinct and categorically wrong in all cases. While some types of violence or killing might be rationalized (as many acts of war are in the just war tradition), certain acts, including torture or genocide, are categorically wrong regardless of the end result or rationale. Using terror as a tool is another such categorical "no." The "corrosive power of fear" inhibits normal social and economic activity in a society, argues Scheffler. This has far more serious consequences than the immediate harm caused by other types of attack in warfare, because it threatens to unravel basic social stability.

Additionally, terrorism is morally distinctive from other types of warfare because it uses individuals as a means to an end, Scheffler argues. As noted in the general introduction, absolutists believe that using an individual as a means to achieve an end violates basic humanity. Terrorism, says Scheffler, does just that. Terrorists kill, harm, and otherwise threaten individuals to cause fear in others, in order to achieve a particular political end.

Torture

Debates over torture in many ways represent the same type of arguments as those over terrorism: Can even the most unspeakable, amoral acts ever be justified in the name of higher ends? Or are such acts illegitimate, even in the most extreme emergencies?

Torture is arguably the most vilified practice in global public opinion. It is banned in numerous human rights treaties and broadly under most countries' domestic constitutions. Torture has been so widely condemned that it is a so-called "peremptory norm" of international law—one that can never be derogated from under any circumstances.[6] Absolutists argue that torture is always wrong, and that no ends can justify it because it is the intentional infliction of bodily harm and suffering. In addition, similar to Samuel Scheffler's objections to terrorism, one might object to the practice of torture because individuals are treated as a means to an end. Torture uses an individual's suffering and pain as a means to extract information against his or her will. Since torture interferes with an individual's will in addition to causing physical harm, some consider it even worse than murder.

Yet despite the strength of this prohibition in past thinking, it has been called into question more frequently in the wake of renewed global concern over terrorism in the last decade.[7] Some voice the realist position that prohibitions on torture are useless because states ultimately will commit torture in order to counter these threats anyway. Others argue that given the nature of terrorism, and terrorists themselves, torture might be necessary to save lives in "emergency" situations.

The most frequently used thought experiment to explore whether torture might ever be justifiable is the so-called "ticking time bomb" scenario. Imagine that a time-activated bomb is set to go off in an undisclosed location. The person who planted the bomb, or has sufficient knowledge of it is in custody and being questioned by state authorities, but will only disclose its location if tortured. Otherwise, the bomb will not be found in time and will explode, killing an untold number of innocents. In such a case, is torture justified?

Writing in 2002, shortly after the September 11 attacks, attorney Alan M. Dershowitz, in "The Case for Torture Warrants," argues that the ticking time bomb scenario has become all too real and likely in the context of modern terrorism. Torturing suspects, he argues, "may sound brutal, but it does not compare in brutality with the prospect of thousands of preventable deaths at the hands of fellow terrorists."[8] He maintains that in an actual ticking time bomb scenario, states (or their subordinate state actors) would use torture anyway. Given this, it would be better if society exercised some controls on when torture can be used by having "torture warrants" authorized by an independent magistrate, similar to search warrants for law enforcement officers. Regulating—and thus limiting the duration or extent—of such practices might reduce the risk of permanent harm. A more open system would increase accountability for torture, and thus be more consistent with democratic values. Dershowitz argues this would also give the individual who is about to be tortured an alternative to torture (namely, confessing freely) since he would be made aware of the warrant and its purpose in advance. Giving the would-be torture victim a means to choose torture or not would obviate arguments that torture is ethically questionable because it undermines an individual's free will.

Critics of the "ticking time bomb" scenario argue it is not only morally wrong, but also unrealistic. In practice, state authorities would never be in a position to know the details that make the ticking time bomb hypothetical so compelling. For example, they might not know with certainty that a bomb existed, that it could not be found through other means in time, that the person in question was actually involved and/or possessed the necessary information, or that she would not provide the information any other way. Others argue that torture simply does not work because victims will say anything to make the torture stop, leading to more false than accurate information.

Writing nine years after Dershowitz's article, human rights activist Aryeh Neier revisits the "torture debates" that were so heated shortly after the September 11 attacks. In subsequent years, revulsion over exposed torture and coercive interrogations at U.S. detention facilities overseas, including at the Abu Ghraib detention center in Iraq, U.S. military bases in Afghanistan, and other undisclosed intelligence "black sites," undercut the type of consequentialist or realist arguments Dershowitz raised. Yet following the killing of Al Qaeda mastermind Osama bin Laden by a covert U.S. Navy SEAL team in Abbottabad, Pakistan, in May 2011, former Bush administration officials suggested that coercive interrogations provided the information that led to his discovery and ultimate killing.[9] This sparked some renewed debate over whether torture works, and if it does, might it be ethically justified in extreme cases?

In "'Enhanced' to the Point of Torture," Neier rebukes pragmatists in both pro- and anti-torture camps. There will never be a way to empirically evaluate claims that (on the pro-side) torture, or merely the threat of torture, results in greater information sharing from terrorists, or (in the con-camp) that torture elicits unreliable information and creates additional costs in terms of lost international reputation and increased terrorist recruiting. Both sides may have points, Neier admits, but ultimately whether or not torture is permissible is a question of principle: "It is a debate between advocates of cruelty or torture that suffices to overcome resistance, regardless of its costs, and opponents of cruelty or torture, regardless of its advantages."[10] Neier adopts an absolutist position, asserting that torture is wrong on principle and is illegal.

Engaging in ethical balancing on both torture and terrorism can be extremely difficult, given the visceral reactions both tend to produce. While one might argue that they are abominable practices, in the relative amorality of wartime, what sets terrorism or torture apart? Consider the following discussion points:

- One might argue that many tactics and impacts of war may terrorize a population. If so, what distinguishes acts of terrorism from other wartime tactics?
- Virginia Held points out that terrorist tactics often kill far fewer innocents than other tactics of war. If you had to choose between an act of terrorism that killed only two people but had the same strategic impact as a traditional means of combat (in a declared war) that killed 60 and destroyed several hundred homes, which would you choose? How would you defend your choice on ethical grounds?
- Acts of terrorism are sometimes criticized where they take advantage of the other party's attempts to act ethically, by sparing or protecting civilians. In doing so, we might posit, they erode all parties' belief in and willingness to follow ethical constraints. Should such overall concerns matter in evaluating individual acts of terrorism? Why or why not?
- Do you find realist arguments, like Alan Dershowitz's claim that state agents will use torture anyway in extreme circumstances salient? Why?
- Do you think torture is a distinctly unethical practice, fundamentally different from other killing or harm in warfare? If so, what distinguishes it?
- Ethical and policy debates over the use of terrorism gained renewed interest after the September 11 attacks on the United States and the perceived greater threat of global terrorism. Do you think this factual situation has changed the ethical calculus over the use of torture? Why or why not?

Notes

1. The earliest attempt to craft an internationally accepted definition of terrorism and to outlaw it was the drafting of the 1937 League of Nations Convention. See League of Nations Convention, Article 1.1.

2. U.N. Security Council, 5053rd meeting, "United Nations Security Council Resolution 1566," 8 October 2004, http://www.state.gov/j/ct/rls/other/un/66959.htm (accessed June 4, 2012).

3. Ibid.

4. This adage first appeared in Gerald Seymour, *Harry's Game* (New York: Overlook Press, 1975).

5. Virginia Held, "Terrorism and War," *Journal of Ethics* 8 (2004): 65.

6. As opposed to many other norms of international law—those protecting civil or political rights or prohibiting the use of force by states—there are no exceptional circumstances that can justify breaking peremptory norms. The peremptory norms of international law are the prohibitions on torture, genocide, slavery, acts/wars of aggression, and piracy.

7. For a concise exploration of renewed arguments for using torture against terrorists, see Bruce Hoffman, "A Nasty Business," *Atlantic Monthly*, Jan. 2002, 49–52, http://www.theatlantic.com/past/docs/issues/2002/01/hoffman.htm.

8. Alan M. Dershowitz, "The Case for Torture Warrants," (2002), http://www.alandershowitz.com/publications/docs/torturewarrants.html (accessed Nov. 12, 2011).

9. Aryeh Neier, "Enhanced to the Point of Torture," *Washington Post*, May 13, 2011, http://www.washingtonpost.com/national/rumsfeld-enhanced-interrogation-aided-in-finding-bin-laden/2011/05/08/AFZ3VqRG_video.html (accessed Nov. 12, 2011).

10. Ibid.

Terrorism and War

by Virginia Held*

ABSTRACT. *There are different kinds of terrorism as there are of war. It is unpersuasive to make the deliberate targeting of civilians a defining feature of terrorism, and states as well as non-state groups can engage in terrorism. In a democracy, voters responsible for a government's unjustifiable policies are not necessarily innocent, while conscripts are legitimate targets. Rather than being uniquely atrocious, terrorism most resembles small war. It is not always or necessarily more morally unjustifiable than war. All war should be avoided, but some war is more unjustifiable than other war. Comparable judgments should be made about terrorism. It is appropriate to compare civilians killed by those seeking political change and those using violence to prevent such change. Sometimes the debate should focus on the justifiability or lack of it of the aims sought. While violence should always be used as little as possible, those in power are responsible for making other means than violence effective in achieving justifiable political change. When considering the likely causes of violence, one that has received inadequate attention is humiliation. Humiliation is not the same as shame. Causing humiliation can and should be avoided.*

There are different kinds of war: world wars, small wars, civil wars, revolutions, wars of liberation. A serious mistake to be avoided, in current discussions of terrorism, is to suppose that all terrorism is alike. There are different kinds of terrorism as there are of war.

The United States Right is currently asserting that to hold anything else than that all terrorism is the same is to undermine the "moral clarity" needed to pursue the war on terrorism. U.S. neo-conservatives, Christian fundamentalists, and the Israeli Right are especially intent on arguing that the terrorism carried out by Palestinians is the same as the terrorism carried out by Osama bin Laden and the Al Qaeda network,[1] agreeing with Israeli prime minister Ariel Sharon that "terrorism is terrorism is terrorism anywhere in the world."[2] Sharon has asserted that Israel is battling the same enemy as the U.S., saying that "the cultured world is under a cruel attack by radical Islam. It is an enemy composed of lunatic individuals, lunatic regimes and lunatic countries."[3]

Those holding that all terrorism is the same argue that the same countermeasures, such as military obliteration and preventive attack, should be used against all terrorists, and the same principles, such as "never negotiate with terrorists or with those who support them" should be applied. To U.S. vice president Dick Cheney, with terrorists "no policy of containment or deterrence will prove effective. The only way to deal with this threat is to destroy it, completely and utterly."[4] Those who share these views are intent on rejecting any comparisons between deaths caused by terrorists and deaths caused by their opponents, on the grounds that there is "no moral equivalence" between terrorism and fighting against terrorism.

It is not only the Right, however, that seeks a simple, all-purpose moral condemnation of all terrorism. *The New York Times* correspondent Nicholas Kristof, while acknowledging the difficulties in seeking "moral clarity," nevertheless advocates it with respect to terrorism.[5] He suggests that a moral revulsion against killing civilians could develop akin to the moral revulsion that developed after World War I delegitimizing the use of poison gas. But this assumes we can clearly distinguish "civilians" from "legitimate targets," and this is among the issues that can be contested. It is voting publics that often put in power the governmental leaders, and support the policies, that terrorists oppose. *If* other means have failed and *if* violence against the members of a state's armed services is justified, it is unclear why those who bring about that state's policies and give its armed services their orders should be exempt. At least such an argument could muddy the moral clarity of the moral revulsion against terrorism the proponents of such revulsion seek.

Furthermore, the occasions for moral revulsion are unlikely to be limited in the way suggested. Ted Honderich, for instance, shares the moral revulsion of so many others at the carnage of 11 September 2001.[6] But he is also greatly outraged by the many millions of lives cut short and made miserable in the poor countries of the world by the global economic forces promoted by the U.S. He sees enough of a connection between such misery and the appeal of terrorism to its potential recruits that he finds the U.S. partly responsible for the terrorism practiced against it. Moral revulsion can thus be so appropriately multiplied that the uniqueness of terrorism is undermined, and with this goes the sought-for moral clarity. We seem to be left, then, with needing to make complex and disputable moral judgments, here as everywhere else. This is not at all to suggest that persuasive judgments are impossible, but they are unlikely to plausibly focus as exclusively on terrorism as the proponents of moral clarity about it in particular wish.

Persuasive judgments should, for instance, consider how the actions of states opposing terrorist groups have frequently killed far more civilians than have terrorists. The Reagan administration's "War on Terror" in Central America in the 1980's killed approximately 200,000 people and produced over a million refugees.[7] A frequently used argument of states engaged in what they call "countering terrorism," but which the recipients of their violence often consider terrorism, is that they do not "target" civilians; if civilians are killed it is by accident, even though foreseeable. But such states' possession of weapons of precision capable of attacking, when they choose to, targeted persons intentionally and civilians only unintentionally is just another way in which their superior power allows them to be dominant. It may be that such domination is what a group engaging in terrorism is resisting. It will in any case be unpersuasive to hold that such a group ought to use means of which it is incapable. If such groups had the means to challenge the armed forces of the states whose domination they oppose they might well do so, but their lack of power is often the reason why terrorism is their weapon in the first place. As any number of commentators have noted, terrorism is the weapon of the weak.[8] Moreover, as war is increasingly "riskless" for armed forces with overwhelming power who, understandably, try to minimize their own casualties as much as possible, there may be less and less possibility for opposing groups to attack the actual combatants of powerful countries.[9] For an argument that terrorism should never be used to be persuasive, it would have to be assumed that the weapons used against it and against those who support it are always used for morally justifiable goals and in morally justifiable ways, and moral clarity about such an assumption is impossible for any reasonable person.

Those of us who are engaged year after year in slogging through arguments seeking moral clarity can reject the U.S. and Israeli Right's versions of it with respect to terrorism. But we are far from agreeing on what terrorism is and how to understand it, let alone on how to respond to it and what to do about it.

My judgments in this paper will be comparative. I will not argue that terrorism can be justified or that war can be justified, but that terrorism is not necessarily worse than war. The direction of a great deal of recent discussion of terrorism is that terrorism is so morally unacceptable as a means that we do not need even to consider the political objectives of those who engage in terrorism. War, on the other hand, is seen as quite possibly justified. My intent will be to compare war and terrorism, and to show how war can be morally worse.

Defining "Terrorism"

Understanding how "terrorism" should be defined is notoriously difficult. It is one of the *most* contested concepts and obviously difficult to be clear about.

Governments characteristically define "terrorism" as something only their opponents can commit, as something only those who seek to change policies, or to attack a given political system or status quo can engage in.[10] The definition used by the U.S. State Department, for instance, includes the claim that it is carried out by "subnational groups or clandestine agents."[11] And international law seems to concur.[12] This is obviously unsatisfactory. When the military rulers of Argentina caused thousands of their suspected opponents to "disappear" in order to spread fear among other potential dissidents, this was state terrorism. And as the Israeli and U.S. political scientists Neve Gordon and George Lopez say, "Israel's practice of state-sanctioned torture also qualifies as political terrorism. It is well known that torture is not only used to extract information or to control the victim; it is also used to control the population as a whole."[13] They conclude, and I agree, "that states can terrorize and can use soldiers, airplanes, and tanks to do so . . . terror should not be reduced to the difference between nonstate and state action."[14]

There can also be state sponsored terrorism as when the government of one state funds and supports terrorism carried out by members of groups or states not under its control. The U.S. routinely lists a number of countries such as Iran and Syria which, it claims, support terrorist groups elsewhere. And U.S. support in the 1980's for the Contras in Nicaragua who spread fear of what would happen to people if they joined or supported the Sandinista rebels would fall also into this category. This is a kind of terrorism most states recognize when engaged in by their adversaries, if not when they themselves aid such terrorists.

Terrorism is certainly violence, and it is political violence. One can doubt that Al Qaeda has a *political* objective in the sense in which most of us understand politics, but since it aims at the religious domination of the political, its violence is itself political, though perhaps not open to the usual responses to political aims through dialogue and compromise. War is also political violence, on a larger scale, though if the most alarming plans of current terrorist groups would be successful, they would often amount to war as currently understood. And political violence can also be more limited than most terrorism, as in the assassination of a particular political leader. Terrorism usually seeks to terrorize, to spread fear among a wider group than those directly harmed or killed.

An important definitional question to which I would like to devote some attention is whether the targeting of civilians must be part of the definition of "terrorism," and whether such targeting turns other political violence into terrorism. Many of those writing on terrorism build the targeting of civilians into their definitions, among them Michael Walzer,[15] C. A. J. Coady,[16] and in recent work Carol Gould and Alison Jaggar.[17] It should be pointed out that this is the meaning of "terrorism" that may be emerging in international law. Since the development of international law is something to which progressives must attach great importance, we should certainly hesitate to challenge its positions. But international law is itself evolving, and has serious limitations. As currently formulated, it is highly biased in favor of existing states and against non-state groups. This may be a bias we should accept in a dangerous world, but considering the moral issues involved is surely appropriate.

I think there are serious problems with a definition of "terrorism" that sees "the deliberate killing of innocent people" as Walzer puts it, to be its defining characteristic, or what distinguishes it from other kinds of political violence and war, and makes it automatically morally unjustifiable in the same way that murder is.

First, consider some of the descriptive implications. If targeting civilians must be part of terrorism, then blowing up the U.S. Marine barracks in Lebanon in 1983 and killing hundreds of marines, and blowing a hole in the U.S. destroyer USS Cole and killing 17 sailors in Yemen in October of 2000, would not be instances of terrorism, and yet they are routinely described as examples of terrorism. Although we might say that such descriptions are simply wrong, I am inclined to think they are not.

Even more awkward for the proposed definition that killing civilians is the defining characteristic of terrorism is that we would have to make a very sharp distinction between the September 11th attack on the World Trade Center, which was certainly terrorism, and the attack that same day and with entirely similar means, on the U.S. Pentagon building, which on this definition would not be (although some civilians work at the Pentagon, it is certainly primarily a military target).[18] And this seems very peculiar.

If one tries with this definition to include rather than exclude these cases as instances of terrorism, and thinks that instead of those who are technically "civilians" one simply means those who are not now shooting at one, like the Marines when they were asleep or the colonels in the Pentagon at their desks, and suggests that only those actually presently engaged in combat are legitimate targets, one will make it illegitimate for the opponents of terrorism to target terrorists when they are not actually engaged in bombings and the like. And distinguishing when members of the armed forces are actual present threats that may be targeted, as distinct from only potential threats because now resting, has not been part of the distinctions worked out asserting that noncombatants should not be targeted. As Robert Fullinwider writes, "combatants are first of all those in a warring country's military service. They are . . . fair targets of lethal response . . . even when they are in areas to the rear of active fighting and even when they are sleeping."[19] What counts is whether they are members of the armed forces or fighting group, or not.

An even more serious problem with a proposal to tie the definition of "terrorism" to the targeting of civilians (but to include the attack on the Pentagon among instances of terrorism because members of the armed forces working at the Pentagon should be thought of as if they were civilians) is that it puts the burden of being a "legitimate target" on the lowest levels of the military hierarchy, the ordinary soldiers and sailors and pilots and support personnel, and exempts the persons who give them their orders, send them into combat, and make them instruments of violence.

Furthermore, if attacking civilians *is* the defining characteristic of terrorism, a great many actions that are standardly *not* called terrorism would have to be considered to be: the bombings of Hiroshima, Nagasaki, Dresden, London, and all those other bombings of places where people live and where civilians become targets, and where the aim to spread fear and demoralization among wider groups was surely present. U.S. bombings in the war in Vietnam would be prime examples. Perhaps we should just get used to calling all these "acts of terrorism." But perhaps we should find a definition of "terrorism" that does not ask us to.

What a lot of discussions of terrorism try of course to do is to come up with a definition such that what *they* do is terrorism and is *unjustified*, whereas what *we* and our friends do is not terrorism but a justified response to it, or is justified self-defense. Building the targeting of civilians into the definition of "terrorism" is often used to accomplish this, since "intentionally killing innocent people" seems by definition wrong and unjustified. However, the net then catches not only the usual miscreants of terrorism, but also much bombing carried out by, for instance, the U.S. and its allies, bombing that proponents are very reluctant to consider unjustified. And they end up with the kind of double standard that moral discussion ought to avoid. Walzer, for instance, has argued that terrorism is never justified, even in a just cause, because it deliberately kills innocents, but that at least some allied bombing of German cities in World War II was justified even though many innocent civilians were deliberately killed.[20]

Of course, there has been a great deal of discussion of what "deliberately" amounts to. The claim is often made that terrorism intentionally targets civilians, while the violence of governments seeking to suppress it only accidentally causes comparable loss of life among civilians, and that this makes all the moral difference. I find this a dubious claim. Only governments with highly sophisticated weaponry can afford to be highly selective in their targets—the Allies in World War II, for instance, could not afford to be—and we know that even "smart bombs" often make mistakes. So the relevant comparison with respect to civilians seems to me to be: in the pursuit of their political goals, which side is causing the greater loss of civilian life. And if the deaths caused by both sides of a political conflict in which terrorism is used by at least one side are roughly equivalent, the argument may appropriately focus especially on the justice, or lack of it, of the political goals involved.

It is not a popular point to make in the wake of September 11th, but we might keep in mind that the actual loss of life caused by terrorism in comparison with conventional warfare remains relatively modest. It is the fear that is large rather than the actual numbers killed. Of course this may change if nuclear weapons come to be used by terrorists; but the *comparative* figures may easily not change if the Pentagon has its way and nuclear weapons become a much more standard and routine part of the arsenal of "defense."

Another difficulty with building the killing of civilians, or noncombatants, or "the innocent," into the definition of "terrorism" is that, as previously mentioned, it is not at all clear who the "innocent" are as distinct from the "legitimate" targets. Let us explore this issue somewhat further.

We can agree, perhaps, that small children are innocent, but beyond this, there is little moral clarity. First of all, many members of the armed forces are conscripts who have no choice but to be combatants. Many conscripts in the Israeli army, for instance, may disapprove of their government's policies. Many others of those who participate in armed conflict, in the U.S. armed forces for instance, have been pressed into service by economic necessity and social oppression. Many other combatants around the world are themselves children, pulled into combat at age 12, 13, or 14, for instance. Studies by international inquiries put the numbers of children in combat in the hundreds of thousands.

More complicatedly, many civilians, the so-called "innocents," may have demanded of their governments the very policies that opponents are resisting, sometimes using terrorism to do so. A political analyst for an Israeli newspaper, for instance, said that even more than Sharon's inclinations, it was the Israeli public's demands that caused the recent violent reoccupation of Palestinian territories and massive destruction there,[21] though Sharon may not have needed much help in deciding on these actions. In January of 2003, the Israeli public had the chance to accept or reject the policies of the Sharon government: voters returned Sharon and his Likud party to power with double the number of seats in parliament they had before.[22] Unfortunately, terrorism that kills civilians to oppose a government's policies does not distinguish between those who support and those who oppose that government.[23] But neither does counter-terrorism that kills civilians distinguish between those who support and those who do not support terrorist groups.

Especially in the case of a democracy, where citizens elect their leaders and are ultimately responsible for their government's policies, it is not clear that citizens should be exempt from the violence those policies may lead to while the members of their armed services are legitimate targets. *If* a government's poli-cies are *unjustifiable*, and *if* political violence to resist them is *justifiable* (these are very large "ifs," but not at all unimaginable) then it is not clear why the political violence should not be directed at those responsible for these policies. As one lawyer and political scientist asks, "In the history of modern democracy, a history that includes racial and colonial terrorism, was the use of terrorism by others *never* justified?"[24]

We are so accustomed to associate suicide bombings with Palestinians and with Al Qaeda members that it may come as a surprise to learn that suicide bombings were used extensively in the 1980's by the Liberation Tigers struggling for a homeland in Sri Lanka for their Tamil ethnic minority. Prior to Septem-ber 11th they had carried out about 220 suicide attacks, killing a Sri Lankan president, a former Indian prime minister, various government ministers, and mayors. Hundreds, perhaps thousands, of civilians were killed in these attacks "though civilians were never their explicit target."[25] According to the Tigers' political leader, S. Thamilchelvam, suicide bombings were used to make up for the Tamils' numerical disadvantage; the goal was "to ensure maximum damage done with minimum loss of life."[26]

I do not mean to suggest that no distinction at all can be made between combatants and civilians, or that the restraints on the conduct of war demand-ing that civilians be spared to the extent possible be abandoned. Rather, I am suggesting that the distinction cannot do nearly as much moral work as its advo-cates assign it. I reject the view that terrorism is inevitably and necessarily mor-ally worse than war, which many assert because they declare that, by definition, terrorism targets civilians.

In sum, then, I decline to make targeting civilians a defining feature of ter-rorism. Terrorism is political violence that usually spreads fear beyond those attacked, as others recognize themselves as potential targets. This is also true of much war. The "Shock and Awe" phase of the U.S.'s war against Iraq in March of 2003 was a clear example. Terrorism's political objectives distinguish it from ordinary crime. Perhaps more than anything else, terrorism resembles small-scale war. It can consist of single events such as (in the U.S.) the Oklahoma City bombing, whereas war is composed of a series of violent events. And there are many kinds of terrorism, as there are many kinds of war.

TERRORISM AND JUSTIFICATION

Governments try hard to portray groups that use terrorism as those who cause violence that would otherwise not exist, and to portray their own efforts to suppress that violence, however violently they do so, as a justified response to provocation. But if the governments would agree to what the groups seek—independence for Chechnya for instance—the violence of the terrorists would not take place. So the violence used to suppress terrorism is the price paid to maintain the status quo, as the violence used by the dissatisfied group is the price paid to pursue its goal. From a moral point of view, it is entirely appropriate to compare these levels of violence. The status quo is not in itself morally superior; it may include grievous violations of rights or denials of legitimate aims. Whether the goals of a dissatisfied group are morally defensible or not needs to be examined, as does whether a government's refusal to accede to these goals is morally defensible. Using violence to bring about change is not inherently worse from a moral point of view than using violence to prevent such change. No doubt stability has value, but its costs need to be assessed.

A more promising argument against terrorism is that it does not achieve what its advocates seek, that other means are not only more justifiable but more successful. But then the burden of making them more successful is on governments and those with power. When nonviolent protest is met with violence and fails consistently to change the policies protested against even when such policies are unjustifiable, it will be hard to argue that nonviolence works where terrorism does not. The terrorist Leila Khaled said about Palestinian hijackings in the 1970's that they "were used as a kind of struggle to put the question—who are the Palestinians—before the world. Before we were dealt with as refugees. We yelled and screamed, but the whole world answered with more tents and did nothing."[27] Terrorists often believe, whether mistakenly or not, that violence is the only course of action open to them that can advance their political objectives. It is the responsibility of those who are able to do so to make this assessment untrue.

As many have noted, one of the most effective ways to reduce the appeal of terrorism to the disaffected is to enable them to participate in the political processes that affect them. Democracy is more effective than counter-terrorism. As Benjamin Barber writes,

Violence is not the instrument of choice even under tyrannical governments because confrontations based on force usually favor the powerful... But it can become the choice of those so disempowered by a political order (or a political disorder) that they have no other options. . . . To create a just and inclusive world in which all citizens are stakeholders is the first objective of a rational strategy against terrorism . . . [28]

Lloyd Dumas examines the ineffectiveness of violent counter-terrorism, noting that "for decades, Israel has doggedly followed a policy of responding to any act of terrorism with violent military retaliation."[29] The result has been that "there exists today more terrorism directed against Israel than ever before . . . Israelis live in fear and Palestinians live in misery."[30] He concludes that "in the long run, encouraging economic and political development is the single most effective counter-terrorist approach."[31]

Claiming that all terrorism is the same and necessarily evil and that the so-called "war on terrorism" must *end* terrorism, or must stamp it out once and for all, or claiming that all responses to terrorism should be the same, is worse than unrealistic and misleading. It invites those who set up the eradication of terrorism as a goal to be humiliated when it is not achieved, and to be thus provoked into even more unjustified violence.

Of course there is no good terrorism. All terrorism is awful, just as all war is awful, and it is outrageous that human beings have not yet managed to avoid, head off, control, and put an end to war (and to terrorism).

But this said, we can recognize that some war is worse than other war, that moral judgments are possible of its purposes and of the way it is carried out. We are accustomed to making such judgments with respect to war; we should become accustomed to making them with respect to terrorism.

One may have grave doubts whether the criteria for a just war offered by just war theory can *ever* be satisfied, especially in the case of wars fought with contemporary weaponry. But one can still agree that some wars carried out by some states or groups and fought in some ways for some purposes are *more unjustifiable* than others. And *if* war can be justified, so can some terrorism be. As Andrew Valls argues, "if just war theory can justify violence committed by states, then terrorism committed by nonstate actors can also, under certain circumstances, be justified by it as well."[32]

The United Nations, and most states, are intent on holding that to be legitimate, violence must be carried out by states, not non-state groups. But the UN also recognizes a fundamental right to self-determination which includes rights to resist "colonial, foreign and alien domination." As Fullinwider notes, "since the United States is a country founded on violent rebellion against lawful authority, we can hardly endorse a blanket disavowal of the right by others violently to rebel against their own oppressors."[33] What is so disturbing about terrorists, he concludes, is that they appeal to morality directly without appealing to law; they rely on "private judgment." But private judgment is not only a menace when exercised by non-state groups. When states put private judgment ahead of international law, as the U.S. has been doing increasingly under the George W. Bush presidency, the chances of escaping Hobbesian chaos are undermined.

It is very important to be able to make some relevant distinctions about terrorism. If its purpose is to impose a religious tyranny on unwilling citizens, it is worse than if it seeks a legitimate purpose. If its success would bring about the end of democratic discourse and the violation of its subjects' human rights, it is more unjustifiable than if its success would create acceptable political outcomes. Judgments of the purposes aimed at are of great, though of course not conclusive importance, as they are in judging war. Judgments of the kinds of violence used to try to achieve or to prevent political purposes are also of great importance. Terrorism that kills large numbers of children and relatively non-responsible persons is obviously worse than terrorism that largely targets property, or that kills only small numbers of persons responsible for an unjustifiable policy. Terrorism that kills many civilians is worse than that which does not, as is war that does so.

No form of violence can be justified unless other means of achieving a legitimate political objective have failed. But this is *also* a moral requirement on the governments that oppose change and that seek to suppress terrorism. And those with greater power have a greater obligation to avoid violence and to pursue other means of obtaining political objectives.

It is not only potential terrorists who should find non-violent means to press their demands; those resisting these demands should find non-violent means to oppose terrorism—to give a voice to opponents, and not just an empty voice, but to respond to legitimate demands to, for instance, end an occupation, cease a colonization, and stop imperialistic impositions. Governments that use violence—military and police forces—to suppress their opponents are often as guilty of using unjustified violence as are those struggling for a hearing for their legitimate grievances. And sometimes they are more at fault because alternative courses of action were more open to them.

Understanding and judging terrorists as distinct from terrorism involves attention to their motives. In 1986, Benjamin Netanyahu, a former prime minister of Israel, described the terrorist as "a new breed of man which takes humanity back to prehistoric times, to the times when morality was not yet born."[34] In 2002, he repeated nearly the same words, calling terrorists "an enemy that knows no boundaries," and saying "we are at the beginning of a war of worlds"— Israel and other democracies against "a world of fanatic murder[ers] trying to throw on us inhuman terror, to take us back to the worst days of history."[35]

On this view there is absolutely no justification for considering the arguments of terrorists; they are not within the same realm of discourse or circle of humanity. In contrast, those who actually talk with and study many terrorists are often amazed at how "normal" they seem, how articulate and rational.[36] They may be misguided but they are not necessarily more morally depraved than many members of the armed forces of established states who speak in terms of the costs of weaponry and personnel and of the military gains they can achieve with them. On both sides, there may be a gross lack of feeling for the victims of their violence, or, if there is feeling it is overridden by the calculations of necessity. So, in preventing terrorism, we might often achieve much more by engaging in moral argument with its potential recruits than by declaring that terrorists and their supporters are, *a priori*, beyond the moral pale.

There are many, not only in the current U.S. administration and on the U.S. Right, but even among liberals, who equate trying to understand terrorism with excusing it. Perhaps philosophers can resist such mistakes; especially if we are ethical non-naturalists we can persuasively distinguish between causal explanations and normative evaluations. We are all in need of both sorts of inquiries. We need to understand terrorism in a way that includes understanding how terrorists think and feel and the arguments they find persuasive. This is not to excuse terrorism. But it may well involve also not excusing those who willfully fail to understand it.

THE CAUSES OF TERRORISM

Suppose we look for causes more immediate than the despair that may be best addressed in the long run by democracy and development. I would like to take up very briefly the question of the causes of terrorism.

There is some agreement that it is not poverty, *per se*, that causes terrorism.[37] By this claim the point is not that individual terrorists themselves are not usually from impoverished families, since it is well known that the leaders of revolutions and political movements are usually from the middle class. But if such leaders represent (and struggle in behalf of) others who are impoverished and with whom they identify, one could say that poverty was the cause of the movement. In the case of terrorism, however, we often do not seem to be able to say exactly this. Many places in the world suffer more severe poverty than those from which many terrorists arise. So other causes can be looked to. Religious zealotry has become primary among them. This is the main direction of Walter Laqueur's latest dissection of terrorism.[38] He recognizes that some terrorists have had good reasons for their violent acts: Russian revolutionaries in the 19th century and Irish Patriots in the early 20th century are his examples. But he comes close to denying this in anyone who is Muslim. What is new about terrorism, he thinks, is that it is largely motivated by Islamic fanaticism added to psychological predisposition.

Many terrorists are not religious zealots, however, so religious fervor is at most a partial explanation. Certainly the factors of gender play a causal role. That masculinity is constructed in terms of the willingness to use violence, and that he who does so can thereby become a hero, enter fundamentally into the causal story.[39] But these factors affect men who do and men who do not become terrorists, and more is needed to ignite them. Some time ago, on the basis of what I had read, I ventured the suggestion that the most salient factor in causing terrorism seemed to me to be *humiliation*. Since then I have been on the lookout for supporting evidence or counter-evidence, and I find much to support this view, though no single-cause explanation is likely to be helpful here or elsewhere in human affairs.

Support for paying special attention to humiliation comes from an inquiry by Laura Blumenfeld, who went to Israel seeking revenge for the wounding of her father in a terrorist attack by a Palestinian.[40] Her goal was to make her father's attacker see him as a human person, and she succeeded. In an interview, she says that "humiliation drives revenge more than anything else . . . I think for the Palestinians, they feel honor and pride are very important in their culture, and they feel utterly humiliated . . . I found that feelings of humiliation and shame fuel revenge more than anything else."[41] Nasra Hasson, a UN relief worker, interviewed nearly 250 Palestinian militants and their associates, and found that there is an ample supply of willing suicide bombers. "Over and over," he reports, he "heard them say, 'The Israelis humiliate us. They occupy our land, and deny our history.' "[42]

It is not hard to understand the humiliation felt by Palestinians: The continued and expanded settlement activity that eats up their land, the constant checkpoints, the confinement of Arafat, the destruction of one symbol after another of Palestinian self-rule, and lately the destruction of not just the symbols but the reality of the Palestinian Authority.[43] And one can understand the humiliation of Israelis, whose overwhelming military superiority is so unable to stop the suicide bombings, and whose government engages in its own kind of terrorism as in the scores of assassinations of suspected Palestinian militants, several of which have occurred *after* periods in which Palestinians refrained from violence as Israel had demanded.

But why so much of the rest of the Islamic world feels humiliation, if it does, is much less clear. In addition to sympathy with the Palestinians it seems in part the result of the economic disadvantage affecting much of the region. With its quite glorious intellectual and artistic past and substantial resources, the region's current economic weakness may well be somewhat galling. And as many have pointed out, the lack of openings for political expression engenders frustration. But what seems to be the most serious source of felt humiliation is cultural. The inability of traditional Islamic patterns of life to withstand the onslaught of capitalist culture and Western images may well be experienced as humiliating. Barber considers "the aggressively secular and shamelessly materialistic tendencies of modernity's global markets and its pervasive, privatizing attachment to consumerism."[44] Though fundamentalism is an invention of the West, he notes—"the Crusaders were the first great Jihadic warriors"—it should not be a surprise that "a handful of the children of Islam imagine that the new global disorder [brought about by the global market] spells the death of their children, their values, and their religion."[45]

What is humiliation? It has not received adequate philosophical attention.[46] Avishai Margalit is one of the few philosophers who has written about humiliation. He sees it as "any sort of behavior or condition that constitutes a sound reason for a person to consider his or her self-respect injured."[47] He sees the decent society as one "whose institutions do not humiliate people."[48] This is a normative sense of humiliation rather than an account of how it is experienced, but he later describes it as "a loss of human dignity"[49] and makes the interesting claim that when we remember being humiliated we relive the emotion. I am skeptical that this is more true of humiliation than of some other strongly felt emotions, but the claim merits investigation.

I will here only suggest that I think humiliation is not the same as shame. One feels shame because of some felt deficiency in oneself. One feels humiliation because of what someone else has done to diminish one or to show disrespect. Certainly shame and humiliation are related; if one did not have the deficiency one is ashamed of, the other would perhaps not be able to humiliate one. But one could have the deficiency and still not be humiliated by that other if that other was considerate, sensitive, and respectful. If, on the other hand, one *is* humiliated, and especially if one is intentionally humiliated, the result is often anger, as well as and perhaps even more than shame. And the response may quite easily be violent.

Some humiliation is caused intentionally. It is hard to believe that many of Sharon's policies and actions toward the Palestinians are not intentionally humiliating. But the kind of humiliation that the U.S. may be causing in the Islamic world seems often unintentional, more like the blustering of the huckster who cannot imagine that anyone does not want his touted new product or promoted new service. But if the U.S. cultural onslaught does produce humiliation, whether intentional or not, it behooves us all to develop more sensitivity and to be more considerate and respectful.

Feminist approaches to morality can certainly contribute here. Feminists may be especially helpful in understanding humiliation and how to deal with it in ways that do not lead to self-defeating spasms of violence. There seems to be a connection in men between adopting a macho posture, and feeling humiliation when it is challenged or shaken. Women have had much and rich experience with humiliation, but seldom respond with violence (or terrorism).[50] Understanding why could be highly relevant.

Acknowledgments

I would like to thank the organizers of and participants in the Conference on Moral and Political Aspects of Terrorism, University of Arizona, 7–9 March 2003, and the Conference on Value Inquiry, University of North Dakota, 1–12 April 2003. I received many helpful comments on earlier versions of this paper when they were presented at these conferences.

NOTES

1. Alison Mitchell, "Israel Winning Broad Support from U.S. Right," *The New York Times* (21 April 2002), pp. A1, 13.

2. *The New York Times* (19 March 2002), p. A12.

3. James Bennet, "Israelis Storm a Gaza Camp; 11 Palestinians Are Killed," *The New York Times* (7 March 2003), p. A10.

4. Sam Dillon, "Reflections on War, Peace, and How to Live Vitally and Act Globally," *The New York Times* (1 June 2003), p. A28. A response to this way of thinking is offered by Benjamin R. Barber: "Do we think we can bomb into submission the millions who resent, fear and

sometimes detest what they think America means?" [Benjamin R. Barber, "Beyond Jihad vs. McWorld," *The Nation* (21 January 2002), p. 12].

5. Nicholas D. Kristof, "A Toast to Moral Clarity," *The New York Times* (27 December 2002), Op-ed page.

6. Ted Honderich, *After The Terror* (Edinburgh: Edinburgh University Press, 2002).

7. Noam Chomsky, *Power and Terror* (New York: Seven Stories Press, 2003), p. 49.

8. See Walter Laqueur, *No End to War: Terrorism in the Twenty-First Century* (New York: Continuum, 2003), p. 113.

9. See Paul W. Kahn, "The Paradox of Riskless Warfare," in Verna V. Gehring (ed.), *War After September 11* (Lanham: Rowman & Littlefield Publishers, 2003).

10. See, "Terrorism, Rights, and Political Goals," in R. G. Frey and Christopher W. Morris (eds.), *Violence, Terrorism, and Justice* (Cambridge: Cambridge University Press, 1991), pp. 59–85.

11. US Department of State, *Patterns of Global Terrorism 1997*, Department of State Publications, 10321 (Washington, DC: United States Department of State, 1998), p. vi.

12. "Under international law, terrorism cannot be committed by states qua states. State sponsored terrorism, however, is another matter . . . ," John Alan Cohan, "Formulation of a State's Response to Terrorism and State-Sponsored Terrorism," *Pace International Law Review* XIV (2001), pp. 77–119, 88–89.

13. Neve Gordon and George A. Lopez, "Terrorism in the Arab-Israeli Conflict," in Andrew Valls (ed.), *Ethics in International Affairs* (Lanham: Rowman & Littlefield Publishers, 2000), p. 110.

14. Gordon and Lopez, "Terrorism in the Arab-Israeli Conflict," p. 110.

15. Michael Walzer, "Five Questions about Terrorism," *Dissent* 49 (2002), pp. 5–10.

16. C. A. J. Coady, "Terrorism and Innocence," in this issue of *The Journal of Ethics*.

17. Carol C. Gould at the "Gender and Terrorism" panel discussion, American Philosophical Association (Pacific Division), Seattle, Washington, 30 March 2002; Alison M. Jaggar, "Responding to the Evil of Terrorism," *Hypatia* 18 (2003), pp. 175–182.

18. C. A. J. Coady has suggested in discussion that what makes the attack on the U.S. Pentagon an attack on civilians and thus terrorism is that a plane with civilians on board was hijacked and civilians killed in attacking the Pentagon. But if we pursue this line of argument, we would need to separate the two events of hijacking the plane and then crashing it into the Pentagon rather than some other target, and it would be the latter that I would point to as causing a problem for the definition in question.

19. Robert Fullinwider, "Terrorism, Innocence, and War," in Verna V. Gehring (ed.), *War After September 11* (Lanham: Rowman & Littlefield Publishers, 2003), p. 22.

20. Michael Walzer, *Just and Unjust Wars*, 3rd edition (New York: Basic Books, 2003), Chapter 16.

21. Serge Schmemann, "Not Quite an Arab-Israeli War, But a Long Descent into Hatred," *The New York Times* (22 April 2002), pp. A1, A11.

22. James Bennet, "Israeli Voters Hand Sharon Strong Victory," *The New York Times* (29 January 2003), pp. A1, A8.

23. This point was made by Sigal Benporath.

24. Angelia Means, "The Idea of the Enemy," typescript, p. 4. Quoted with permission.

25. Amy Waldman, "Masters of Suicide Bombing: Tamil Guerrillas of Sri Lanka," *The New York Times* (14 January 2003), pp. A1, A6.

26. Waldman, "Masters of Suicide Bombing: Tamil Guerrillas of Sri Lanka," pp. A1, A6.

27. Kamel B. Nasr, *Arab and Israeli Terrorism* (Jefferson: McFarland & Co., 1997), p. 57.

28. Benjamin R. Barber, "The War of All against All," in Verna V. Gehring (ed.), *War After September 11* (Lanham: Rowman & Littlefield Publishers, 2003), pp. 77, 88.

29. Lloyd J. Dumas, "Is Development an Effective Way to Fight Terrorism," in Verna V. Gehring (ed.), *War after September 11* (Lanham: Rowman & Littlefield Publishers, 2003), p. 73.

30. Dumas, "Is Development an Effective Way to Fight Terrorism," p. 73.

31. Dumas, "Is Development an Effective Way to Fight Terrorism," p. 73.

32. Andrew Valls, "Can Terrorism Be Justified?" in Andrew Valls (ed.), *Ethics in International Affairs* (Lanham: Rowman & Littlefield Publishers, 2000), p. 66.

33. Fullinwider, "Terrorism, Innocence, and War," p. 24.

34. Benjamin Netanyahu (ed.), *Terrorism: How the West Can Win* (New York: Farrar, Straus & Giroux, 1986), pp. 29–30.

35. Michael Wines, "Mourners at Israeli Boys' Funeral Lament a Conflict with No Bounds," *The New York Times* (2 December 2002).

36. Bruce Hoffman, *Inside Terrorism* (New York: Columbia University Press, 1998), "Preface."

37. See, e.g., Alan B. Krueger and Jitka Maleckova, "Seeking the Roots of Terrorism," *The Chronicle of Higher Education* (6 June 2003), B10–11.

38. Laqueur, *No End to War*.

39. See, e.g., Robin Morgan, *The Demon Lover: The Roots of Terrorism* (New York: Washington Square Press, 2001); and Virginia Held, *Feminist Morality: Transforming Culture, Society, and Politics* (Chicago: University of Chicago Press, 1993), Chapter 7.

40. Laura Blumenfeld, *Revenge: A Story of Hope* (New York: Simon and Schuster, 2002).

41. "Q&A," *The New York Times* (6 April 2002), Section B, p. 9.

42. Krueger and Maleckova, "Seeking the Roots of Terrorism," B11.

43. See, e.g., Richard Falk, "Ending the Death Dance," *The Nation* (29 April 2002), pp. 11–13.

44. Benjamin Barber, "The War of All against All," p. 78.

45. Benjamin Barber, "The War of All against All," pp. 79–80.

46. *The Philosopher's Index* for the entire period 1940–2002 lists only six articles or reviews that deal substantially with humiliation, and none for which it is the major topic.

47. Avishai Margalit, *The Decent Society* (Cambridge: Harvard University Press, 1996), p. 9.

48. Margalit, *The Decent Society*, p.1.

49. Avishai Margalit, *The Ethics of Memory* (Cambridge: Harvard University Press, 2002), p. 118.

50. Of course, a few suicide bombers have been women, as a few rulers of states have been women, but the numbers are comparatively small.

*Virginia Held is distinguished professor of the Graduate Center at City University of New York. She is the author of *The Ethics of Care: Personal, Political, and Global*; *The Public Interest and Individual Interests*; *Rights and Goods: Justifying Social Action*; and *Feminist Morality: Transforming Culture, Society, and Politics*.

With kind permission from Springer Science+Business Media: *Journal of Ethics*, "Terrorism and War," 8, 2004, 59–72, Virginia Held. © 2004 Kluwer Academic Publishers.

Is Terrorism Morally Distinctive?

*by Samuel Scheffler**

The term "terrorism" may by now have become too ideologically freighted to have any analytic value. If the term is to be an aid to understanding, two opposed but complementary ways of employing it will have to be resisted. On the one hand, there is the tendency, among the representatives and defenders of governments facing violent threats from non-state groups and organizations, to use the term to refer to all forms of political violence perpetrated by non-state actors. On the other hand, there is the tendency, among the representatives and defenders of non-state actors engaged in political violence, to insist that "the real terrorists" are the officials or the military forces of those states with which they are locked in conflict. Under the combined influence of these two tendencies, the word "terrorism" is in danger of becoming little more than a pejorative term used to refer to the tactics of one's enemies.

In this paper, I will proceed on the assumption that the concept of terrorism retains more content than that, and that we recognize a use of the term in which it refers to a special kind of phenomenon or class of phenomena. My primary aim will not be to produce a definition of the term but rather to consider whether there is anything morally distinctive about the type of phenomenon to which it refers. Clearly, it will be impossible to do this without making some attempt to characterize the phenomenon. Still, my aim is not to produce a definition of the term "terrorism" or to identify necessary and sufficient conditions for its application.[1] What I will do instead is to describe a certain familiar pattern to which terrorist actions often conform, and to argue that instances of terrorism which fit this pattern do indeed have a morally distinctive character. There is no doubt that the term "terrorism" is frequently applied to conduct that does not fit this pattern. I will not insist that this is always inappropriate. I believe that the term is misapplied in some of these cases, but I do not mean to deny that there are cases in which its use is appropriate despite the absence of the morally distinctive features to which I will call attention.

Two other caveats are in order. First, I will assume that terrorism is a *prima facie* evil, and that the use of terrorist tactics is presumptively unjustified, but I will remain agnostic on the question of whether there can ever be circumstances in which such tactics may nevertheless be justified, all things considered. Second, I take it to be obvious that, although terrorism is a *prima facie* evil and its use is presumptively unjustified, it may sometimes be a response to policies that are also unjustified and which may be as objectionable as the terrorist response itself. Furthermore, the fact that terrorism is unjustified does not mean that all of the measures used to oppose it are themselves justified. In short, I assume that terrorism is a *prima facie* evil and my concern is with the kind of evil it is. Terrorism may sometimes be a response to great wrongs, and great wrongs may be committed in opposing it. But I will not be concerned here with the nature of those other kinds of wrongs nor will I address the question of whether the presumption against engaging in terrorism can ever be defeated.

Some other recent writers have taken a different approach to this subject. Their primary focus, understandably enough, has been on questions about the justification of terrorism, and they have sought to arrive at a definition of the term that would cohere with their justificatory conclusions. This has led many of them to endorse a broad definition according to which terrorism is simply politically or ideologically motivated violence that is directed against civilians or noncombatants. In fact, this broad definition has become sufficiently widespread that Jeff McMahan refers to it as the "orthodox definition."[2] Its popularity may reflect a concern about some of the apparent implications of relying on a more narrowly circumscribed definition. Since any narrower definition will presumably fail to classify certain types of political violence against civilians as forms of terrorism, any such definition may seem to imply that the types of violence it excludes deserve less severe condemnation. This implication is bound to seem troubling, especially if it is assumed that a narrow definition would single out forms of violence characteristically engaged in by non-state actors and exclude forms of violence characteristically engaged in by states. Given this assumption, it may seem that reliance on a narrow definition would unwittingly import an uncritical pro-state bias.

Although I understand this concern, I think it is a mistake to begin an inquiry into the morality of terrorism by endorsing a broad definition. Such a starting point may lead us to overlook relevant distinctions and to give an oversimplified description of the moral terrain. I prefer to begin, not by trying to settle on a definition, but rather by thinking about certain familiar forms of violence that most people would not hesitate, prior to analysis, to classify as instances of terrorism. I want to ask whether there is anything morally distinctive about these specific patterns of activity. As I hope will emerge from my discussion, this relatively narrow focus will serve to highlight some morally salient features and distinctions that might otherwise be easier to overlook. And, as I will try to make clear, such a focus need not import an uncritical pro-state bias, both because state activity can fall within the narrower sphere of activity on which

I will concentrate and because many forms of violence that do not fall within that sphere nevertheless deserve severe condemnation, whether or not they are classified, in the end, as instances of terrorism.

Although terrorism is a political phenomenon, the resources of contemporary political philosophy are of limited assistance in trying to understand it. In recent years, a valuable new philosophical literature on terrorism has begun to emerge, and philosophical interest in the subject has, of course, intensified since the September, 2001 attacks on the World Trade Center and the Pentagon.[3] But, with one or two exceptions, the major political philosophies of the past several decades have been little concerned with the political uses of terror or with political violence more generally. On the whole, they have been philosophies of prosperity, preoccupied with the development of norms for regulating stable and affluent societies. To a great extent, for example, they have concerned themselves with issues of distributive justice, and they have implicitly addressed this topic from the perspective of a secure and well-established society with significant wealth to distribute among its citizens. Even when philosophers have looked beyond the boundaries of their own societies and have addressed issues of global justice, as they have increasingly begun to do, they have generally done so from the perspective of affluent, western societies whose responsibilities to the rest of the world are in question precisely because their own power and prosperity are so great. Contemporary political philosophers have not in general needed to concern themselves with threats to the survival or stability of their societies or with the conditions necessary for sustaining a viable social order at all. None of this is intended as criticism. It is entirely appropriate that political philosophers should address themselves to the questions that actually vex the societies in which they live. But it does suggest that the recent political philosophy of the affluent, liberal west may not afford the most useful point of entry for an investigation into problems of terror and terrorism.

A number of contemporary writers on terrorism have found it natural to situate their discussions in relation to the traditional theory of the just war.[4] For my purposes, it will be helpful to begin instead with the pre-eminent philosopher of fear in our tradition, Thomas Hobbes. It is striking that, in his famous catalogue of the "incommodities" of the state of nature, Hobbes describes fear as the worst incommodity of all. The state of nature, he says, is characterized by a war of "every man against every man," and such a war comprises not merely actual battles but an extended "tract of time" in which "the will to contend by battle is sufficiently known."[5] This means that, in the war of every man against every man, a condition of general insecurity prevails for an extended period. "In such condition," he says, "there is no place for industry, because the fruit thereof is uncertain; and consequently no culture of the earth; no navigation, nor use of the commodities that may be imported by sea; no commodious building; no instruments of moving and removing such things as require much force; no knowledge of the face of the earth; no account of time; no arts; no letters; no society; *and which is worst of all, continual fear, and danger of violent death*. And the life of man, solitary, poor, nasty, brutish, and short" (Ch. 13, para. 9, pp. 95–6, emphasis added).

Hobbes makes at least three points in this passage and the surrounding text that are relevant to our topic. First, there is his insistence on how bad a thing fear is. Continual fear—not momentary anxiety but the grinding, unrelenting fear of imminent violent death—is unspeakably awful. It is, he suggests, worse than ignorance. It is worse than the absence of arts, letters and social life. It is worse than being materially or culturally or intellectually impoverished. Fear dominates and reduces a person. A life of continual fear is scarcely a life at all. Someone who is in the grip of chronic terror is in a state of constant distress; he "hath his heart all the day long gnawed on by fear of death, poverty, or other calamity and has no repose, nor pause of his anxiety, but in sleep" (Ch. 12, para. 5, p. 82).

The second point is that fear is incompatible with social life. On the one hand, sustained fear undermines social relations, so that in addition to being worse than various forms of poverty and deprivation it also contributes to them, by destroying the conditions that make wealth and "commodious living" possible. Fearful people lead "solitary" lives. Alone with their fears, trusting no one, they cannot sustain rewarding forms of interpersonal exchange. On the other hand, the establishment of society offers relief from fear and, in Hobbes' view, it is to escape from fear that people form societies. The fear of death, he says, is the first of "the passions that incline men to peace" (Ch. 13, para. 14, p. 97). Indeed, and this is the third point, it is *only* within a stable political society that the miserable condition of unremitting fear can be kept at bay. In addition to being incompatible with social life, sustained fear is the inevitable fate of pre-social human beings.

Terrorists take these Hobbesian insights to heart. In a familiar range of cases, at least, they engage in violence against some people in order to induce fear or terror in others, with the aim of destabilizing or degrading (or threatening to destabilize or degrade) an existing social order. Without meaning to beg the very questions of definition that I said I would not be addressing, I will call these "the standard cases." I do so in part on the boringly etymological ground that these cases preserve the link between the idea of terrorism and the root concept of terror. But I will also go on to argue—indeed, it is my primary thesis—that the etymology points us to something morally interesting which might otherwise be easier to overlook.

In "the standard cases," terrorists undertake to kill or injure a more or less random group of civilians or noncombatants;[6] in so doing, they aim to produce fear within some much larger group of people, and they hope that this fear will in turn erode or threaten to erode the quality or stability of an existing social order. I do not mean that they aim to reduce the social order to a Hobbesian state of nature, but only that they seek to degrade or destabilize it, or to provide a credible threat of its degradation or destabilization, by using fear to compromise the institutional structures and disrupt the patterns of social activity that help to constitute and sustain that order. The fear that terrorism produces may, for example, erode confidence in the government, depress the economy, distort the political process, reduce associational activity and provoke destructive changes in the legal system. Its ability to achieve these effects derives in part from the fact that, in addition to being intrinsically unpleasant to experience, the fear that terrorism produces may inhibit individuals' participation in a wide range of mundane activities on which a polity's social and economic health depends. In some cases people may become mistrustful of the other participants in the activity (one of the other passengers may be a hijacker or suicide bomber), while in other cases they may fear that the activity will be targeted by terrorists who are not participants (someone may toss a hand grenade into the night club or movie theater). In the various ways I have mentioned and others that I will describe, the fear that is generated by terrorism can lead to significant changes in the character of society and the quality of daily life, and at the extremes these changes can destabilize a government or even the social order as a whole. In the standard cases, then, terrorists use violence against some people to create fear in others, with the aim of degrading the social order and reducing its capacity to support a flourishing social life—or at least with the aim of credibly threatening to produce these effects.[7]

Terrorist violence may, of course, have many other aims as well, even in the standard cases.[8] The terrorists may hope that their violent acts will attract publicity for their cause, or promote their personal ambitions, or provoke a response that will widen the conflict, or enhance their prestige among those they claim to represent, or undermine their political rivals, or help them to achieve a kind of psychological or metaphysical liberation. Nor need they conceive of their actions exclusively in instrumental terms. They may also be seeking to express their rage. Or they may believe that their victims are not in the relevant sense innocent, despite being civilians or noncombatants, and they may think of themselves as administering forms of deserved punishment or retribution.

There are many other respects in which what I am calling standard cases of terrorism can differ from one another. But they all have the following minimum features: 1) the use of violence against civilians or noncombatants, 2) the intention that this use of violence should create fear in others, including other civilians and noncombatants, and 3) the further intention that this fear should destabilize or degrade an existing social order, or at any rate that it should raise the specter of such destabilization or degradation. The destabilization or degradation of the social order may itself have many different aims. Among other things, it may be intended a) as a prelude to the imposition of a different social order or the reconstitution of the existing order on different terms, b) as a way of effecting some change in the policy of an existing state or society, c) as a form of deserved punishment, and hence as an end in itself, or d) as some combination of these.

What makes terrorism of the standard kind possible is the corrosive power of fear. As Hobbes suggests, sustained or continual fear is a regressive force both individually and socially. It can induce the unraveling of an individual's personality and, as we have already seen, its cumulative effects on large numbers of people can degrade the social order and diminish the quality of social life. Its capacity to achieve these effects is enhanced by the infectiousness of fear, the fact that it can so easily be transmitted from one person to another, even when the second person is unaware of the reasons for the first person's fear. The latter case is the one that Hobbes called "panic terror," and which he described as "fear without the apprehension of why or what." In such cases, he added, "there is always in him that so feareth, first, some apprehension of the cause, though the rest run away by example, every one supposing his fellow to know why. And therefore this passion happens to none but in a throng, or multitude of people" (Ch. 6, para. 37, p. 45). The fear induced by terrorism does not ordinarily fit the description of panic terror, since those who are subject to it normally know the reasons for their fear. But terrorism still benefits from the infectiousness of fear, because the fact that something has frightened one person may itself frighten another person, and the fearful attitudes of different people can exert mutually reinforcing and intensifying effects. In this age of instant communication, moreover, the capacity of terrorist acts to cause fear, and to exploit the phenomena of mutual reinforcement and intensification, is greatly increased. The news media can be counted on to provide graphic coverage of each terrorist outrage, so that a bomb blast anywhere can generate fear and insecurity everywhere. These attitudes in turn become newsworthy and are dutifully reported by the media, thus contributing to the syndrome of mutual reinforcement.

I said earlier that, in the standard cases, terrorist violence is usually directed against a "more or less random" group of civilians or noncombatants. It is difficult to be more precise. Sometimes virtually any civilians will do. At other times, terrorists will select a particular population group, defined by occupation or ethnicity or religion or social class, and will target people indiscriminately within that group. Or they will select a symbolic target (the World Trade Center), and those who are killed or injured will be those who happen to be in the chosen location at the wrong time. Even when the target class is maximally wide, the victimization is random in the sense that it is indiscriminate within that class but not in the sense that it is pointless or irrational. And even when the target class is relatively narrow, there is an advantage in preserving some degree of indiscriminateness within that class. In both cases, the randomness or indiscriminateness has the same point. It is to maximize (within the relevant parameters) the numbers of people who identify with the victims, thus subverting the defensive ingenuity with which people seize on any feature that distinguishes them from the victims of misfortune to preserve their own sense of invulnerability. In this way, the appearance of randomness is used to exploit the psychic economy of identification in such a way as to maximize the spread of fear.

This is not to say that it is always easy to achieve one's aims using terrorist tactics. In fact, it is usually difficult for terrorist acts to destabilize an otherwise stable social order. This is not merely because such acts can backfire, and reduce support for the terrorists' goals. Nor is it merely because of the large armies, police forces and intelligence services that stable societies normally have available to fight those who employ terrorism. Just as important is the fact that stable societies, and individuals raised in such societies, have substantial social and psychological resources with which to resist the destructive effects of fear. People can be remarkably tenacious in their determination to preserve the lives they have made for themselves in society, and if fear can be infectious so too can courage and the determination to persevere in the face of great danger. These too have mutually reinforcing and intensifying effects.

But terrorism does not need to destabilize a social order altogether in order to transform and degrade it and, as we have seen, often such transformation and degradation will suffice to enable those who employ terrorist tactics to achieve some or all of their aims. The problem is that living with fear can have corrosive effects even for those who are courageous and determined to persevere. One might put the point provocatively and say that courage itself—or the need to sustain it over long periods of time—can be corrosive. Living each day with the vivid awareness that one's children may be killed whenever they leave home, or that a decision to meet one's friends at a restaurant or café may result in violent death, or that an ordinary bus ride on a sunny day may end with lumps of flesh raining down on a previously peaceful neighborhood, exacts a cost. Nor is this true only if one yields to one's fears and keeps one's children at home, gives up socializing and avoids public transportation. It is also true if one grits one's teeth and resolves to carry on as normal. People often say, in explaining their determination to maintain a normal routine in the face of terrorist activities or threats, that to do otherwise would be to "give the terrorists what they want." This is not wrong, but it understates the problem. Maintaining one's normal routine does not suffice to preserve normalcy. Terrorism undermines normalcy almost by definition. One cannot, simply through an act of will, immunize one-self against the effects of continual fear and danger on one's state of mind or on the quality of one's life. These effects are distressingly easy for groups that use terrorist tactics to achieve and distressingly difficult for the members of targeted populations to avoid.

This is one reason why terrorism is so popular, even if it is not always ulti-mately successful. Apologists for terror often claim that it is the weapon of the weak, who have no other tools available for fighting back against their oppres-sors. This may be true in some circumstances. As far as I can see, however, those who engage in terrorism rarely invest much time in exploring the availability of other tools. All too often terrorism is the tool of choice simply because the perceived advantages it offers are so great. It costs relatively little in money and manpower. It has immediate effects and generates extensive and highly sensa-tionalized publicity for one's cause. It affords an emotionally satisfying outlet for feelings of rage and the desire for vengeance. It induces an acute sense of vulnerability in all those who identify with its immediate victims. And insofar as those victims are chosen randomly from among some very large group, the class of people who identify with them is maximized, so that an extraordinary number of people are given a vivid sense of the potential costs of resisting one's demands. Figuratively and often literally, terrorism offers the biggest bang for one's buck.

If what I have said to this point is on the right track, then it does seem that terrorism is morally distinctive, at least insofar as it conforms to the pattern of what I have been calling "the standard cases." In these cases, at least, it differs from other kinds of violence directed against civilians and noncombatants. By this I do not mean that it is worse, but rather that it has a different moral anatomy. By analogy: humiliation is morally distinctive, and so too are torture, slavery, political oppression and genocide. One can investigate the moral anatomy of any of these evils without taking a position on where it stands in an overall ranking of evils. Many people are pluralists about the good. We can be pluralists about the bad as well.

In the "standard cases," some people are killed or injured (the primary victims), in order to create fear in a larger number of people (the secondary victims), with the aim of destabilizing or degrading the existing social order for everyone. The initial act of violence sets off a kind of moral cascade: death or injury to some, anxiety and fear for many more, the degradation or destabilization of the social order for all. Nor is this simply a cascade of harms. It is, instead, a chain of intentional abuse, for those who employ terrorist tactics do not merely produce these harms, they intentionally aim to produce them. The primary victims are used—their deaths and injuries are used—to terrify others, and those others are used—their fear and terror are used—to degrade and destabilize the social order.

The fact that the secondary victims' fear and terror are used in this way is one thing that distinguishes the standard cases from other cases in which civilians are deliberately harmed in order to achieve some military or political objective. In other cases of deliberate, politically-motivated violence against civilians, the perpetrators display a callous disregard not only for the lives of their victims but also for the misery and suffering of the people who care about or identify with them. Since those who commit such acts are willing to kill or injure their victims, it is hardly surprising that they should be indifferent to the intensely painful human reactions—fear, horror and grief—that their acts are liable to produce in others. In the "standard cases," however, the primary victims are killed or injured *precisely in order* to elicit such reactions—precisely in order to elicit fear, horror and grief—so that those reactions can in turn be exploited to promote the perpetrators' ultimate, destabilizing objectives. Using Kantian terminology, we might say that the primary victims are treated not just as means to an end but as means to a means: that is, they are treated as means to the end of treating the secondary victims as means to an end. Those who engage in this kind of terrorism do not merely display callous indifference to the grief, fear and misery of the secondary victims; instead, they deliberately use violence to cultivate and prey on these reactions. This helps to explain why there is something distinctively repellent about terrorism, both morally and humanly.[9]

As I have said, not all instances of terrorism fit the description of the "standard cases." Sometimes, for example, terrorist tactics may be employed not to destabilize or degrade an entire social order but rather to make the place of a particular social group or class within that order insecure, as in cases where the ambition is to drive the members of the targeted group into another country or territory ("ethnic cleansing"). In cases like this, the description of the "moral cascade" will differ somewhat, but the moral anatomy of these cases will still bear a clear and recognizable relation to that of the standard cases. Other instances in which the term "terrorism" is likely to be employed may differ more substantially from the standard cases. An example might be a situation in which violence is directed against civilians solely for the purpose of provoking a response and thereby producing an escalation in the level of a conflict; the fact that the violence also generates fear, although predictable and not unwelcome, is no part of the perpetrators' aim. In a similar vein, insurgents might take civilian hostages simply as a way of pressuring a government to release some of their imprisoned comrades, and not for the purpose of spreading fear, although fear may be one predictable effect of their actions. Still other examples, meanwhile, may seem sufficiently different from the standard cases that the propriety of the term "terrorism" becomes doubtful, even if it is often applied to them. This may be true, for example, of targeted political assassinations or acts of sabotage.

In general, we should be sensitive to the wide variety of actual cases we are likely to encounter, and we should avoid theory-driven oversimplifications of the phenomena. My own aim, as I have already said, is not to produce a definition of the term "terrorism" or to provide a set of necessary and sufficient conditions for its application. Accordingly, I will take no position on the question of how far an act can depart from the standard cases while remaining an instance of terrorism. In any event, the fact that some form of conduct is not best thought of as amounting to terrorism does not mean that there is no objection to it. As the doctrine of the pluralism of the bad reminds us, there are many different kinds of atrocities and many different forms of horrific behavior, and we learn more by attending to the differences among them than by assimilating them all to a single category. One of the many unsettling features of the Bush administration's post-9/11 moral discourse, with its frequent references to "evildoers" and "bad guys," is that it uses moral categories to inhibit rather than to promote moral understanding. It relies on simplifying dichotomies that appeal to psychologically primitive sources of moral motivation and, in so doing, it encourages a dangerously reductive conception of the moral domain.

As I noted at the outset, the term "terrorism" is sometimes used, by representatives and defenders of governments facing violent threats from non-state groups and organizations, to refer to all forms of political violence perpetrated by non-state actors. This makes it impossible by definition for states to engage in terrorism. Although I have not endorsed this—or any other—definition, my narrow focus on the standard cases and my emphasis on terrorism's destabilizing aims may seem to imply that it can only be the tactic of insurgents or other non-state actors. But this is not in fact a consequence of my view. States can certainly employ terrorist tactics in the manner I have described as a way of destabilizing other societies. They can do this in wartime, through the use of such tactics as "terror bombing," or in peacetime, through covert operations targeting another country's civilian population. And domestically, a government might use such tactics in order to create a limited degree of instability, with the aim of discrediting its opponents or generating increased support for repressive policies. Of course, it is crucial in such cases that the government should not appear to be the perpetrator of the terrorist acts, since its aim is precisely to ascribe those acts to others. Still, the fact remains that governments can engage in terrorism both against other societies and, with the qualification just mentioned, domestically as well.

Governments may also use terror as an instrument of policy without this amounting to terrorism of the "standard" type. Indeed, here I am prepared to engage in at least partial, stipulative definition, and to say that governments may use terror as an instrument of policy without this amounting to terrorism at all. This will be true, in my view, when a government uses terror internally—and is willing to be seen as doing so—in order to stifle dissent and opposition, to maintain its grip on power and to preserve the established order. I will use the term "state terror" to describe this phenomenon, and in the usage I have stipulated there is an important contrast between state terror and terrorism, even terrorism that is perpetrated by states. The point of the stipulation is not to suggest that one of these phenomena is better or worse than the other, but rather to highlight what I take to be a significant distinction between two different political uses to which terror may be put. Terrorism, as I understand it, standardly involves the use of violence to generate fear with the aim of destabilizing or degrading an existing social order. State terror, as I understand it, standardly involves the use or threat of violence to generate fear with the aim of stabilizing or preserving an existing social order. Of course, other people may use the terms "terrorism" and "state terror" in different ways, but the point is not merely terminological, and anyone whose use of the relevant terminology differs from mine needs to find some other way of expressing the contrast I have described.

It is an interesting fact that fear and terror can be used either to undermine an existing social order or to preserve one. They can be made to serve not only revolutionary but also conservative purposes. How is this possible? How, in particular, is it possible that fear and terror can be used to preserve a social order if, as I said earlier, they undermine social life? Hobbes, who certainly understood the second of these points, also emphasized the first. He wrote: "Of all passions, that which inclineth men least to break the laws is fear. Nay, excepting some generous natures, it is the only thing (when there is appearance of profit or pleasure by breaking the laws) that makes men keep them" (Ch. 27, para. 19, p. 222). For Hobbes, fear can be used to preserve order because it is a passion "that relate[s] to power" (Ch. 31, para. 9, p. 269). In the state of nature—in the war of all against all—each person has sufficient power to pose a threat to every other person. Hence each person has reason to fear every other person, and this undermines the conditions of social life. But the concentration of power in a sovereign produces a redistribution of the capacity to inspire fear, and this makes social life possible. On the one hand, people's attitudes toward one another need no longer be dominated by fear and mistrust, and so the development of social relations is no longer inhibited. On the other hand, everyone has reason to fear the sovereign's power, and hence to obey the sovereign's laws, and so the social order is stabilized.

But this suggests that fear does not, after all, undermine social life, at least not in all cases. It undermines social life only when, in the absence of a common authority, fear is radically decentralized, and each person has reason to fear every other person. There is something to this, but as stated it overlooks the differences between ordinary political authority and a regime of state terror. In a decent society that is governed by the rule of law, crimes are punished and the fear of punishment can be said to provide individuals with a reason for obeying the laws. Here the phrase "fear of punishment" functions as a way of characterizing a certain kind of reason for action; people's presumed desire to avoid punishment is a consideration that counts in favor of obedience. But this does not mean that people are actually afraid or that they lead lives full of fear.[10] On the contrary, one of the primary advantages of the rule of law, and of a predictable, publicly promulgated and impartially administered system of punishments and sanctions, is that it enables people to avoid fear. By structuring their lives in accordance with what the law allows, they can predictably avoid the punishments and sanctions attached to violations. Of course, people who break the law, or are accused or suspected of doing so, may find themselves genuinely fearing punishment. But, leaving aside false accusations and unwarranted suspicions, law-abiding citizens need not actually experience any fear of the state, even if we can truly say that the fear of punishment gives them a reason to obey. In a well-functioning state, the "fear of punishment" is not normally a condition of fear at all. For this reason, it provides no obstacle to the development of rich social relations, and indeed helps to facilitate them. For the very same reason, however, it also provides no counterexample to the thesis that a state of continual fear undermines social life.

Things are very different under a regime of state terror. Here the state deliberately keeps people afraid as a way of maintaining its grip on power and preserving the established system. In order to do this, it deliberately eliminates the features of impartiality and predictability associated with the rule of law. Power is exercised and laws are administered arbitrarily. Although there may be forms of conduct that can reliably be expected to result in arrest and punishment, there are few if any reliable ways of avoiding such outcomes. Networks of secret agents and informers may denounce people for any reason or none, and there is no independent judiciary or regime of rights to protect those who are accused. People may be imprisoned, or lose their jobs, or have their property confiscated, or be tortured or killed, without ever knowing why. Since citizens have no basis for confidence in their ability to avoid such calamities, they are kept perpetually fearful, uncertain, anxious. And since they have no way of knowing who may be an informer or an agent of the state, they are kept perpetually wary and mistrustful of one another. The point of inducing this Hobbesian condition of ongoing mutual mistrust is precisely to restrict the development of social relations and to inhibit the cooperative and solidaristic attitudes that accompany them. A regime that rules by terror recognizes these relations and attitudes as potential threats. By using fear to constrict and impoverish social life, it confirms both that fear undermines social relations and that a free social life is the antidote to fear. Thus, the fact that genuine terror can be used to preserve an established order does not falsify the observation that fear undermines social life, for social relations are indeed inhibited under a regime of terror. Notwithstanding the existence of centralized rule and a set of rigidly constrained social and economic institutions, such a regime has as much in common with the Hobbesian state of nature as it does with a political society that is subject to the rule of law.[11]

I have drawn the contrast between a regime of terror and the rule of law starkly, but I do not mean to deny that there can be intermediate cases. On the one hand, even the most brutal totalitarian states may need to provide selective relief from terror for certain groups of people in order to achieve their aims.[12] On the other hand, even relatively decent governments may find it irresistible at times to use fear as a way of deflecting criticism or deflating political opposition. A judiciously administered dose of alarm can do wonders in inducing a compliant frame of mind and encouraging people to rally round their leaders. Ironically, the fear of terrorism—which is in part to say the fear of fear—seems to be a particularly effective tool for this purpose. This is one reason why governments are so eager to label their enemies as terrorists; in addition to discrediting them, the very use of the label may help to induce a state of timid docility in an otherwise restive population. But none of this undermines the argument I have been developing.

The upshot of that argument is that there are two different ways in which fear might be said to be capable of contributing to the preservation of order. Although Hobbes, to the detriment of his political theory, did not distinguish between them, neither of them falsifies the claim that fear undermines social life. It is true that, when the rule of law prevails, the fear of punishment gives people a reason to obey, yet social life is not inhibited. But since the "fear of punishment" is not, in these circumstances, a condition of actual fear, the idea that fear undermines social life remains intact. Under a regime of terror, by contrast, genuine fear is indeed used to preserve order, but since social relations are severely restricted under such a regime, the tendency of fear to compromise social life is confirmed rather than disconfirmed.

This argument may seem to prove too much for my purposes, however. If, as I have insisted, a regime of state terror does indeed undermine social life, then it may seem that such a regime cannot, after all, be said to aim at stabilizing or preserving the existing social order. Surely undermining social life is incompatible with preserving the social order. What my analysis really shows, it may be suggested, is that both terrorism and state terror use fear to destabilize or degrade the social order. The difference between them is just that terrorism hopes thereby to destabilize the existing *political* configuration, whereas state terror hopes to reinforce or consolidate that configuration. I resist this interpretation because I believe that state terror typically aims to stabilize more than just the existing political configuration. It also seeks to preserve a set of tightly controlled social and economic institutions, and in this sense it aims to stabilize an entire social order—albeit a severely constrained one—and not merely a government. Despite the fact that it uses fear to inhibit certain kinds of social relations and thus to restrict social life, in other words, it does nevertheless seek to preserve a rigidly constrained social order, in the sense just specified. To be sure, the fact that social life is so severely compromised under such a regime means that the social order that is preserved is bound to be a grim and dystopian one. Still, I think it would be a mistake to deny that it is a social order at all or to ignore the fact that the regime aims to stabilize and preserve it.[13]

If this is correct, then it is possible to reaffirm and to expand upon my earlier observations about the relationship between terrorism and state terror. In the standard cases, I have said, terrorism involves the use or threat of violence to generate fear, with the aim of degrading or destabilizing an existing social order. State terror, on the other hand, standardly involves the use or threat of violence to generate fear, with the aim of stabilizing or preserving an existing social order—albeit a grim and tightly controlled one. There is, accordingly, a significant difference between terrorism—even terrorism perpetrated by a state—and state terror. They represent different ways of using terror for political purposes. But they exploit a common mechanism: the capacity of fear to undermine social life. As I have argued, terrorism of the standard kind uses this mechanism to degrade the institutional structures and patterns of activity that help to constitute and sustain an existing social order. State terror, by contrast, uses the same mechanism to subvert or prevent the emergence of cooperative social relationships that might pose a threat to the power of the state or to the character of the prevailing social and economic arrangements. People are kept chronically fearful and mistrustful of one another so that, even if they have the resources and opportunities to do so, they will be unwilling or unable to form the kinds of groups, associations and social networks that might become independent centers of influence, facilitate the emergence of critical voices and perspectives, or in other ways challenge the status quo. Under a regime of state terror, fear is used by the state to keep social relations impoverished so that a rigidly constrained social and economic order can be preserved and protected from challenge.

I think that this contrast helps to explain why terrorist violence is so often calculated to attract maximum publicity, whereas so much of the violence associated with state terror is carried out in secret. Terrorists aim to promote chaos and disarray as a way of subverting the social fabric. They want people running for cover. The perpetrators of state terror want to promote order and regimentation. They want people marching in step. Spectacular acts of public violence are designed to produce disruption and panic. The shadowy operations of secret police and paramilitary groups are designed to produce silence, conformity and the desire to make oneself inconspicuous, to attract no notice.[14]

One additional complication should be noted. I have been distinguishing between terrorism and state terror: between the use of fear to degrade or destabilize an existing order and the use of fear to stabilize or preserve an existing order. But I have emphasized that states can engage in both forms of activity. It is natural to wonder whether the reverse is also true. Can non-state groups use fear to stabilize an existing order? Although the label "state terror" is obviously not appropriate to such cases, I believe that the answer is yes. For example, non-state groups may use violence to terrorize an oppressed or subordinated population, with the aim of reinforcing an established system of caste or hierarchy or defeating attempts to dismantle such a system. (Think, for example, of the Ku

Klux Klan.) We can think of these as cases of "sub-state terror," in which fear is used to police the boundaries of a social hierarchy, to block the development of new social movements, or to inhibit social change. The use of fear to stabilize an existing order is no more the exclusive province of the state than the use of fear to destabilize such an order is the exclusive province of non-state actors. The reason for distinguishing between terrorism, on the one hand, and state or sub-state terror, on the other, is to highlight the distinction between these two different uses of fear, and not to suggest a distinction between two different categories of agents.

Conclusion

The title of this paper poses a question. The answer that has emerged from my discussion is as follows. Terrorism is morally distinctive insofar as it seeks to exploit the nexus of violence and fear in such a way as to degrade or destabilize an existing social order. Terrorist acts may have many functions other than the degradation of the social order, and the degradation of the social order may itself be intended to serve different purposes. But insofar as it conforms to the "standard" pattern I have described, terrorism has a morally distinctive character, whatever other functions and purposes individual instances of it may also serve. If, as is often the case, the term is applied more widely, then one consequence may be that terrorism so understood is not always morally distinctive. For example, we saw earlier that many philosophers now believe the term should be taken to refer to any politically motivated violence that is directed against civilians or noncombatants. If we accept this usage, then some acts of terrorism may turn out not to differ much in their moral character from murders and assaults that do not qualify for the "terrorist" label. David Rodin, who advocates a definition of this sort, concludes that terrorism is just "the political or ideological species of common violent crime."[15] This usage makes the distinctive character of the "standard cases" easier to overlook. And the distinctiveness of those cases will certainly be easier to overlook if terrorism is defined instead as political violence that is perpetrated by non-state actors. If we rely on this kind of definition, then some of what I have been calling "the standard cases" will turn out to be instances of terrorism while others will not.

I do not take these considerations as reasons for insisting on a definition of terrorism that limits it to the standard cases. But I do think that the word "terrorism" is morally suggestive precisely because "terror" is its linguistic root, and that if we define the term in a way that effaces or even breaks the connection between terrorism and terror, as the definitions just mentioned do, then we are liable to miss some of the moral saliences toward which the word "terrorism" gestures.[16] The currency of that particular word, which adds to the already rich vocabulary we have for describing violence of various kinds, testifies to the power of fear and to the peculiar moral reactions evoked by its deliberate use for political ends. It is perfectly possible that, under the pressure of ideology or confusion or convenience, our usage of the term may evolve in such a way that it applies in some cases where fear plays no role and does not apply in some of what I have been calling the standard cases. Indeed, this may already have happened. But then we will need to find other ways of reminding ourselves of how bad a thing fear is, of the diabolical ways in which it can be provoked and exploited for political purposes, and of the specific character of our moral reactions when that happens.[17]

NOTES

1. Many different definitions have been proposed. For discussion, see C. A. J. Coady, "Terrorism and Innocence," *Journal of Ethics*, 8 (2004), 37–58, and Jenny Teichman, "How to Define Terrorism," *Philosophy*, 64 (1989), 505–517.

2. See Jeff McMahan, "The Ethics of Killing in War," *Ethics*, 114 (2004), 693–733, at p. 729. Variants of the broad definition have been defended, for example, by C. A. J. Coady and David Rodin. See Coady, "The Morality of Terrorism," *Philosophy*, 60 (1984), 47–69; Coady, "Terrorism and Innocence;" Coady, "Terrorism, Morality, and Supreme Emergency," *Ethics*, 114 (2004), 772–789; Rodin, "Terrorism without Intention," *Ethics*, 114 (2004), 752–571.

3. Two valuable early anthologies are R. G. Frey and C. W. Morris eds., *Violence, Terrorism, and Justice* (New York: Cambridge University Press, 1991), and M. Warner and R. Crisp eds., *Terrorism, Protest, and Power* (Aldershot: Edward Elgar, 1990). Two significant post-9/11 anthologies are V. Gehring ed., *War after September 11* (Lanham, MD: Rowman and Littlefield, 2003), and I. Primoratz ed., *Terrorism: The Philosophical Issues* (London: Palgrave Macmillan, 2004). See also the symposia on terrorism published in special issues of *Ethics* (Volume 114, Number 4) and *The Journal of Ethics* (Volume 8, Number 1) in 2004.

4. See, for example, the writings by Coady and Rodin cited above. See also F. M. Kamm, "Failures of Just War Theory: Terror, Harm, and Justice," *Ethics*, 114 (2004), 650–92, and Noam Zohar, "Innocence and Complex Threats: Upholding the War Ethic and the Condemnation of Terrorism," *Ethics*, 114 (2004), 734–51. The pioneering contemporary revival of just war theory is, of course, Michael Walzer's *Just and Unjust Wars* (New York: Basic Books, 1977). Walzer devotes one chapter of that book to terrorism, and he also discusses terrorism in several of the essays included in *Arguing about War* (New Haven, CT: Yale University Press, 2004). The application of just war theory to terrorism is vigorously criticized by Robert Goodin in *What's Wrong with Terrorism?* (Cambridge: Polity Press, forthcoming).

5. Thomas Hobbes, *Leviathan*, chapter 13, paragraph 8. Quotation taken from the edition edited by A. P. Martinich (Peterborough, Ont.: Broadview Press, 2002), p. 95. Subsequent references, including chapter, paragraph, and page number in the Martinich edition, will be given parenthetically in the text.

6. The relevance of civilian or noncombatant status to the definition of terrorism is contested, but since I am setting aside questions of definition I will not address the issue. For pertinent discussion, see Coady, "The Morality of Terrorism" and "Terrorism and Innocence;" Robert Fullinwider, "Terrorism, Innocence, and War," in Gehring ed., *War After September 11*; Virginia Held, "Terrorism, Rights, and Political Goals," in Frey and Morris eds., *Violence, Terrorism, and Justice*, pp. 59–85; Virginia Held, "Terrorism and War," *Journal of Ethics*, 8 (2004), 59–75; Igor Primoratz, "The Morality of Terrorism," *Journal of Applied Philosophy*, 14 (1997), 221–233; Noam Zohar, "Innocence and Complex Threats." There is, of course, a large literature on the principle of noncombatant immunity in wartime.

7. For a related discussion, see Jeremy Waldron, "Terrorism and the Uses of Terror," *Journal of Ethics*, 8 (2004), 5–35, at pp. 22–23.

8. Waldron has a good discussion of many of these aims in "Terrorism and the Uses of Terror," Section 6.

9. There are three misunderstandings to be avoided. First, in saying that there is "something distinctively repellent" about terrorism, I am not saying that it is *more* repellent than any other type of atrocity. I am saying only that some of the reasons why it is repellent are distinctive. Second, I am not saying that *all* of the reasons why terrorism is repellent are distinctive; obviously, it is also repellent for some of the same reasons that other types of unjustified violence are. Finally, I am not claiming that what is distinctively repellent about terrorism is also what is *morally worst* about it. What is distinctively repellent about terrorism is, roughly, that it treats the primary victims as means to a means, but what is morally worst about it may simply be that it involves (for example) the unjustified killing of the innocent.

10. This is related to Jeremy Waldron's distinction between "Jack Benny-style coercion" and "Arendtian terrorization." See Waldron, "Terrorism and the Uses of Terror," pp. 15–16.

11. My discussion in this paragraph is indebted to Waldron, "Terrorism and the Uses of Terror," pp. 18–20.

12. Indeed, just as terrorist tactics are sometimes used, not to destabilize the entire social order but rather to make the place of a particular group within that order insecure, so too the apparatus of state terror is sometimes used against a subset of the population rather than against the population as a whole. Of course, such limitations tend to be unstable. Once terror is put to political use, it is hard to keep it within bounds.

13. I am grateful to Jay Wallace and to an anonymous referee for prompting me to clarify these points.

14. Of course, show trials and public executions can also help to produce these effects, and they too are familiar devices of state terror. But silence and conformity are not normally achieved by setting off bombs in public places or by using other standard terrorist tactics.

15. See David Rodin, "Terrorism without Intention," p. 757.

16. Many other writers have insisted on the importance of fear for an understanding of the morality of terrorism. See, for example, Robert Goodin, *What's Wrong with Terrorism?*, Jeremy Waldron, "Terrorism and the Uses of Terror," and Carl Wellman, "On Terrorism Itself," *Journal of Value Inquiry*, 13 (1979), 250–258.

17. This paper was originally written for a conference on terrorism organized by Joseph Raz at the Columbia Law School in December, 2004. A later version was presented as a lecture at the Mershon Center at Ohio State University in May, 2005. I am indebted to both audiences for valuable discussion. I also received helpful written comments from Julie Tannenbaum, Jay Wallace, Robert Goodin and three anonymous referees for this journal.

*Samuel Scheffler is university professor of philosophy and law at New York University.

Samuel Scheffler, *Journal of Political Philosophy*, "Is Terrorism Morally Distinctive?" 14, no. 1
(2006): 1–17 © 2006 The Author. Journal compilation © 2006 Blackwell Publishing Ltd.,
9600 Garsington Road, Oxford OX4 3DQ, UK and 350 Main Street, Malden, MA 02148,
USA.

The Case for Torture Warrants

*by Alan M. Dershowitz**

Now that it has been disclosed that our government had information of "un-determined reliability", from an agent whose code name is Dragonfire, that New York City may have been targeted for a 10 kiloton nuclear weapon, the argu-ments for empowering law enforcement officials to do everything necessary to prevent a catastrophic terrorist attack are becoming more compelling. In the immediate aftermath of the September 11th attacks, FBI officials leaked a story about their inability to obtain information from suspected terrorists by conven-tional means, such as buying the information by offers of cash or leniency, or compelling the information by grants of immunity and threats of imprisonment for contempt of court. Those who leaked the story suggested that there may come a time when law enforcement officials might have to resort to unconven-tional means, including non-lethal torture. Thus began one of the most un-usual debates in American legal and political history: should law enforcement be authorized to torture suspects who are thought to have information about a ticking bomb?

This ticking bomb scenario had long been a staple of legal and political phi-losophers who love to debate hypothetical cases that test the limit of absolute principles, such as the universal prohibition against the use of torture which has long been codified by international treaties. The ticking bomb case has also been debated, though not as a hypothetical case, in Israel, whose security services long claimed the authority to employ "moderate physical pressure" in order to secure real time intelligence from captured terrorists believed to know about impending terrorist acts. The moderate physical pressure employed by Israel was tougher than it sounds, but not nearly as tough as the brutal methods used by the French in interrogating suspected terrorists during the Algerian uprisings. The Israeli security service would take a suspected terrorist, tie him to a chair in an uncomfortable position for long periods of time with loud music blaring in the background, and then place a smelly sack over his head and shake him violently. Many tongues were loosened by this process and several terrorist acts prevented, without any suspects being seriously injured.

Torture, it turns out, can sometimes produce truthful information. The Israeli experience suggested that information obtained as a result of torture should never be believed, unless it can be independently confirmed, but such information can sometimes be self-proving, as when the subject leads law enforcement to the actual location of the bomb.

Nonetheless, the Israeli Supreme Court outlawed all use of even moderate, non-lethal physical pressure. It responded to the ticking bomb scenario by saying that if a security agent thought it was necessary to use physical pressure in order to prevent many deaths, he could take his chances, be prosecuted, and try to raise a defense of "necessity". In my book *Shouting Fire*, I wrote critically of this decision on the ground that it places security officials in an impossible dilemma. It would be better if any such official could seek an advanced ruling from a judge, as to whether physical pressure is warranted under the specific circumstances, in order to avoid being subject to an after the fact risk of imprisonment. Thus was born the proposal for a torture warrant.

Actually it was a rebirth, because half a millennium ago torture warrants were part of the law of Great Britain. They could be sought only in cases involving grave threats to the Crown or the Empire and were granted in about one case a year. Judges even in those times, were extremely reluctant to authorize the thumb screw.

Why then should we even think about returning to an old practice that was abolished in England many years ago. The reason is because if we ever did have a ticking bomb case—especially a ticking nuclear bomb case—law enforcement officials would in fact resort to physical force, even torture, as a last resort. In speaking to numerous audiences since September 11th—audiences reflecting the entire breadth of the political and ideological spectrum—I have asked for a show of hands as to how many would favor the use of non-lethal torture in an actual ticking bomb case. The vast majority of audience members responded in the affirmative. So have law enforcement officials to whom I have spoken. If it is true that torture would in fact be used in such a case, then the important question becomes: is it better to have such torture done under the table, off the books and below the radar screen—or in full view, with accountability and as part of our legal system? This is a very difficult question with powerful arguments on both sides. On the one hand, we have had experience with off the book policies such as President Nixon's "plumbers" and Oliver North's "foreign policy initiatives". In a democracy, accountability and visibility must be given high priorities. On the other hand, to legitimate torture and make it part of our legal system, even in extreme cases, risks reversion to a bad old time when torture was routine.

One key question is whether the availability of a torture warrant would, in fact, increase or decrease the actual amount of torture employed by law enforcement officials. I believe, though I cannot prove, that a formal requirement of a judicial warrant as a prerequisite to non-lethal torture would decrease the amount of physical violence directed against suspects. Judges would require compelling evidence before they would authorize so extraordinary a departure from our constitutional norms, and law enforcement officials would be reluctant to seek a warrant unless they had compelling evidence that the suspect had information needed to prevent an imminent terrorist attack. Moreover the rights of the suspect would be better protected with a warrant requirement. He would be granted immunity, told that he was now compelled to testify, threatened with imprisonment if he refuses to do so and given the option of providing the requested information. Only if he refused to do what he was legally compelled to do—provide necessary information which could not incriminate him because of the immunity—would he be threatened with torture. Knowing that such a threat was authorized by the law, he might well provide the information. If he still refused to, he would be subjected to judicially monitored physical measures designed to cause excruciating pain without leaving any lasting damage. A sterilized needle underneath the nail might be one such approved method. This may sound brutal, but it does not compare in brutality with the prospect of thousands of preventable deaths at the hands of fellow terrorists.

Let me cite two examples to demonstrate why I think there would be less torture with a warrant requirement than without one. Recall the case of the alleged national security wiretap being placed on the phones of Martin Luther King by the Kennedy administration in the early 1960's. This was in the days when the Attorney General could authorize a national security wiretap without a warrant. Today no judge would issue a warrant in a case as flimsy as that one. When Zaccarias Moussaui was detained after trying to learn how to fly an airplane, without wanting to know much about landing it, the government did not even seek a national security wiretap because its lawyers believed that a judge would not have granted one. If Moussaui's computer could have been searched without a warrant, it almost certainly would have been.

It is a great tragedy that we have to be discussing the horrors of torture. Some even believe that any discussion of this issue is beyond the pale of acceptable discourse in 21st century America. But it is far better to discuss in advance the kinds of tragic choices we may encounter if we ever confront an actual ticking bomb terrorist case, than to wait until the case arises and let somebody make the decision in the heat of the moment.

An analogy to the shooting down of a passenger-filled hijacked airliner heading toward a crowded office building will be instructive. Prior to September 11th it might have been a debatable issue whether the plane should be shot down. Today that is no longer debatable. But would anyone suggest that the decision should be made by a low ranking police officer? Of course not. We all agree that this should be a decision made at the highest level possible—by the President or the Secretary of Defense, if there is time to have such a dreadful decision made by accountable public figures. The use of torture in the ticking bomb case, like the shooting down of the hijacked airplane, involves a horrible choice of evils. In my view this choice should be made with visibility and accountability, either by a judicial officer or by the President of the United States. It should not be made by nameless and unaccountable law enforcement officials, risking imprisonment if they guess wrong.

*Alan M. Dershowitz is an American lawyer, jurist, and political commentator. He is Felix Frankfurter Professor of Law at Harvard Law School.

Alan M. Dershowitz, "The Case for Torture Warrants," 2002, http://www.alandershowitz.com/publications/docs/torturewarrants.html

Used by permission.

'Enhanced' to the Point of Torture

by Aryeh Neier*

We ought to put to rest the debate about whether "enhanced interrogation," the euphemism for torture or cruel, inhuman or degrading treatment promoted by Dick Cheney and some other officials of the Bush administration, contributed to the death of Osama bin Laden more than two years after the end of that administration and several years after it reportedly abandoned such practices. Almost certainly, the main arguments put forward by both sides in this debate are valid some of the time and not valid at other times. Ultimately, however, this is a debate that leads nowhere.

Proponents of torture claim that it enables interrogators to obtain information they could not otherwise obtain, helping in such instances as locating a fugitive such as bin Laden or foiling another terrorist attack. However much one loathes the idea of torture, it is impossible to say that it never yields such a result.

Yet opponents of torture point out that it also elicits unreliable information that misleads interrogators and that may delay or impede their investigations. Again, this probably happens in some cases. More important, opponents argue that a reputation for engaging in torture discredits the governments that use such practices and, thereby, serves the purposes of their enemies. It may help terrorist organizations to enlist recruits. Here, too, it is impossible to refute such arguments. This happens in at least some cases, perhaps all the time.

As it is evident that torture sometimes provides advantages in an investigation and sometimes, possibly all the time, also has disadvantages, is there a way to determine whether the arguments on one side outweigh those on the other side? Probably not. By its nature, torture is a secretive practice. Its practitioners do not subject their activities to public scrutiny. There is no way to conduct a scientific study. One can take note of the self-serving claims of practitioners, but one cannot reliably measure their supposed achievements. Assessing how significant the practice is in arousing antagonism against governments that employ torture is also beyond measure.

And if there is no way to settle the argument about whether torture confers practical advantages that outweigh its disadvantages, it is fruitless to pursue it. The only way to resolve the debate is on the basis of principle. Do we want our government to engage in torture? Those who believe the United States should practice torture should not attempt to refute the claims of those who point out its costs. Similarly, those who argue that the United States should never engage in torture should not attempt to refute all assertions that it can confer advantages. Both sides in that debate may have points, but they should acknowledge that the other side probably also has its points.

I am against torture as a matter of principle. Torture and cruel, inhuman and degrading treatment are prohibited by customary international law; by a host of international treaties, including some to which the United States is a party; and by the Eighth Amendment. I am against practices that are clearly condemned by U.S. law and by international laws that the United States has committed to respecting.

It seems noteworthy that many of those who disagree are unwilling to state flatly that, as a matter of principle, they favor torture. Instead, they hide behind the euphemism of enhanced interrogation. Yet the advantages they claim are possible only if the enhancement on which they rely is sufficient to make those detainees who are members of a terrorist network disclose information they would otherwise withhold. The methods they use have to cause enough pain or distress in individuals who have probably been trained to resist to overcome such resistance. If enhanced interrogation is to produce the advantages that its proponents claim, it is only because what is done to detainees is enhanced to the point where it constitutes cruel, inhuman and degrading treatment or torture.

So the real debate is not between those who claim that enhanced interrogation works and those who say it is counterproductive. Nor is it between those who oppose torture on principle and those who espouse the use of the moderately discomforting methods that a term such as "enhanced interrogation" is intended to evoke. It is a debate between advocates of cruelty or torture that suffices to overcome resistance, regardless of its costs, and opponents of cruelty or torture, regardless of its advantages.

Which side are you on?

***Aryeh Neier** is president emeritus of the Open Society Foundations.

Aryeh Neier, "'Enhanced' to the Point of Torture," *Washington Post*, May 13, 2011, http://www. washingtonpost.com/opinions/enhanced-to-the-point-of-torture/2011/05/13/AFQhDz2G_ story.html.